Stricklin
Psych

PUBLIC
SPEAKING

An
Audience-Centered
Approach

W9-BBX-960

Speech 101

PUBLIC SPEAKING

An
Audience-Centered
Approach

Steven A. Beebe
Southwest Texas State University

Susan J. Beebe
Southwest Texas State University

PRENTICE HALL, Englewood Cliffs, NJ 07632

Library of Congress Cataloging-in-Publication Data

Beebe, Steven A.
    Public speaking : an audience centered approach / Steven A. Beebe,
Susan J. Beebe.

    p. cm.
    ISBN 0-13-738956-6
    1. Public speaking. 2. Oral communication. I. Beebe, Susan J.
II. Title.
PN4121.B385 1991
808.5'1—dc20
                                  90–6950
                                       CIP

Editorial/production supervision: *Kathleen Schiaparelli*
Interior design: *Lorraine Mullaney*
Manufacturing buyers: *Ed O'Dougherty/Debbie Kesar/Marianne Gloriande*
Cover design: *Lorraine Mullaney*
Cover art: "The Candidate" 90″ x 120″ 1988–89 (detail), *Patrick Webb. Courtesy of the artist. Photo by West Co.*

Printed in the United States of America
10 9 8 7 6 5 4 3 2

ISBN 0-13-738956-6

Prentice-Hall International (UK) Limited, *London*
Prentice-Hall of Australia Pty. Limited, *Sydney*
Prentice-Hall Canada Inc., *Toronto*
Prentice-Hall Hispanoamericana, S.A., *Mexico*
Prentice-Hall of India Private Limited, *New Delhi*
Prentice-Hall of Japan, Inc., *Tokyo*
Simon & Schuster Asia Pte. Ltd., *Singapore*
Editora Prentice-Hall do Brasil, Ltda., *Rio de Janeiro*

Dedicated to our parents,
Russell and Muriel Beebe
Herb and Jane Dye
and to our sons,
Mark and Matthew Beebe

Contents

3   43

Listening to Others

8 157

Organizing Your Speech

9 181

Outlining Your Speech

13   267

Using Words Well: Speaker Language and Style

14   291

Speaking to Inform

15   311

Principles of Persuasive Speaking

Preface

Public Speaking: *An Audience-Centered Approach* was written to serve as the primary text for a college-level public speaking course. Its key goal is to serve as a teaching tool to help students become skilled public speakers.

We realize, however, that students do not learn how to become skilled public speakers just by reading a book. Students need more than information alone. They need an opportunity to practice their skills and feedback about their ability to master the skills. Any book needs the gifts and talents of a dedicated teacher to help students learn.

Our approach in teaching public speaking is based upon a *tell-show-do-feedback* approach. First, we *tell* students how to prepare and deliver a speech. Our key emphasis throughout the book is to encourage students to be audience-centered. Second, we present numerous examples and excerpts from sample speeches—both from successful students and noted orators—to *show* students how to implement an audience-centered approach to public speaking. Students need to have the skills modeled for them to help them visualize becoming a successful speaker. Third, students need to practice or *do* the skill. To that end we offer numerous suggested activities and exercises at the end of each chapter. It is also assumed that students will be given many opportunities to prepare and present speeches to their classmates. Finally, students need *feedback* to help them clinch the mastery of their skill. Textbooks have an inherently limited ability to offer feedback to students about their skill attainment; the instructor and the student's colleagues play instrumental roles in offering constructive comments to help the novice speaker improve. Our text, based upon our many years of teaching the course, is designed to facilitate the *tell-show-do-feedback* approach to teaching public speaking skill development.

AN AUDIENCE-CENTERED APPROACH

Our book is based upon the centrality and importance of the audience in the speech-crafting and delivery process. Consequently, our audience-centered model of the steps involved in public speaking, introduced in Chapter 2, becomes a unifying organizational theme throughout the text. The model is reintroduced each time a new speech preparation task is presented to show the relationship between task and the audience.

Preparing and delivering a speech is both a process and a sequential series of steps. Our audience-centered model captures both the step-by-step sequence of speech preparation and the process nature of focusing on the speech goal: communicating well with your audience. Even though we organize the chapters around the audience-centered model, each chapter is self-contained and may be used in the course whenever the instructor wishes. We offer a suggested plan but leave the final decision about chapter assignments up to the instructor.

SPECIAL FEATURES

In our efforts to help students become both better speakers and consumers of public speaking, we have incorporated many special teaching elements throughout the book.

Numerous Examples

As we noted earlier, students learn best if they are given examples to help them focus on the goal. Students need good models. Our text uses numerous examples from both excellent student speeches and some of the noted orators of the past two centuries. The Appendix also includes several speeches for discussion and analysis, both classic and contemporary, that illustrate the use of skillful speaking ability.

Colorful, Lively Design

Just as we teach our students the value of speech delivery in communicating a message, we model that principle throughout the book with an open, colorful, and appealing book design. The liberal use of color is not just superfluous window dressing but is an integral part of the text's teaching mission.

Effective Pedagogy

Chapter objectives, summaries, discussion questions, and suggested activities are used throughout the book. Color-highlighted recap boxes, which provide internal summaries of key principles, are sprinkled throughout the text. In addition, key terms are clearly defined in the margin when they are introduced in each chapter. These pedagogical features help students remember the key principles and suggestions of the speech-making process. The book is written and designed to help students learn.

Useful Supportive Resources

In addition to the text itself, the public speaking teacher has a wealth of additional resources to help teach students the art and science of public speaking. Specifically:

An **Annotated Instructor's Edition** of the book is available from the publisher. This unique and valuable resource is a complete reprinting of the student text, with teaching tips, lecture and discussion ideas, and classroom activities printed in the margin.

In addition to the annotated instructor's edition, there is a comprehensive **Instructor's Resource Manual** that includes additional teaching suggestions, course syllabi suggestions, speech evaluation and audience analysis forms as well as guidelines for using the videos and other important parts of the teaching package.

An extensive **computerized Test Item File** is available from the publisher.

A **Public Speaking Instructional Video** not only illustrates how to prepare and present a speech but also includes useful suggestions for helping the instructor teach and evaluate speeches.

Color overhead transparencies of key charts, diagrams and models are available to add zest to class lectures and discussions.

The **ABC NEWS/PH VIDEO LIBRARY FOR PUBLIC SPEAKING** provides videotapes of three famous speeches reprinted in Appendix C—by Martin Luther King, Jr., Barbara Jordan, and John F. Kennedy. Drawn from the Archives of ABC NEWS, The Martin Luther King, Jr., Foundation, and Richard Kaplan Productions, the speeches are available on two videocassettes and illustrate visually the full dimension of the speech texts printed in the appendix.

THE NEW YORK TIMES and PRENTICE HALL are sponsoring **A CONTEMPORARY VIEW:** a program designed to enhance student access to current information of relevance in the classroom.

Through this program, the core subject matter provided in the text is supplemented by a collection of time-sensitive articles from one of the world's most distinguished newspapers, **THE NEW YORK TIMES.** These articles demonstrate the vital, ongoing connection between what is learned in the classroom and what is happening in the world around us.

To enjoy the wealth of information of **THE NEW YORK TIMES** daily, a reduced subscription rate is available. For information, call toll-free: 1-800-631-1222.

PRENTICE HALL and **THE NEW YORK TIMES** are proud to co-sponsor **A CONTEMPORARY VIEW.** We hope it will make the reading of both textbooks and newspapers a more dynamic, involving process.

ACKNOWLEDGMENTS

Even though our names appear on the cover of the book as the authors, there have been literally hundreds of people who have helped to produce this volume. We are grateful to all of the authors and speakers we have quoted or referenced; their work and wisdom have added to our experience. While we have made an effort to footnote known sources, we have also drawn upon information from the public domain for examples and illustrations. We regret any error if we have failed to document information from others.

Our editors at Prentice Hall have done an outstanding job of offering just the right amount of information, motivation, support, and attention to detail to help us keep on schedule. We thank Steve Dalphin for his support from the inception of this project. Ray Mullaney offered excellent suggestions for refining our ideas. We particularly want to thank our developmental editor, Sid Zimmerman, for his invaluable skill in helping us shape our prose; his knowledge and word-for-word attention to detail shines through every chapter.

Many reviewers took the time and energy to respond to drafts of the manuscript. We thank the following people for their insightful comments and suggestions:

Nancy Arnett,
Brevard Community College

David E. Axon
Johnson County Community College

John Bee
University of Akron

Jaima L. Bennett
Golden West College

Donald S. Birns
SUNY-Albany

Barry Brummett
University of Wisconsin, Milwaukee

John Buckley
University of Tennessee

Thomas R. Burkholder
Southwest Texas State University

Marilyn J. Cristiano
Paradise Valley Community College

Dan B. Curtis
Central Missouri State University

Ann L. Darling
University of Illinois/Urbana-Champaign

Phyllis Heberling
Tidewater Community College

Wayne E. Hensley
Virginia Polytechnic Institute and State University

Judith S. Hoeffler
The Ohio State University

Robert S. Littlefield
North Dakota State University

Jim Mancuso
Mesa Community College

Carol L. Radetsky
Metropolitan State College

Val Safron
Washington University

Aileen Sundstrom
Henry Ford Community College

Beth M. Waggenspack
Virginia Polytechnic Institute and State University

Lynn Wells
Saddleback College

Tom Burkholder from Southwest Texas State University served as both reviewer and author of Appendix A. Russ Wittrup also from Southwest Texas State University wrote and produced the video tape that accompanies this book. We also want to thank Nancy Arnett from Brevard Community College, for her useful suggestions and her excellent work on the Annotated Instructor's Edition, Instructor's Resource Manual, and Test Item File.

We appreciate the support and ideas we have received from our colleagues at

Southwest Texas State University. Tom Willett at William Jewel College, Dan Curtis at Central Missouri State University, and John Masterson and Thompson Biggers at the University of Miami are long-time friends and exemplary teachers who have influenced our work. Laurie and Dennis Romig, from Performance Resources, Inc. Austin, Texas, offered encouragement and invaluable advice. We also thank Julie Webb, our manuscript typist and proofreader, who helped keep the production of the book on schedule with her skill.

Both of us have been blessed with gifted teachers who have helped us develop as educators. Mary Harper, former speech and drama teacher at Grain Valley High School, Grain Valley, Missouri, and Margaret Dent, retired speech teacher at Hannibal High School, Hannibal, Missouri, provided initial instruction in public speaking that remains with us today. We appreciate the patience and encouragement we received from Robert Brewer, our first debate coach at Central Missouri State University. We both served as student teachers under the unforgettable guidance of Louis Banker at Fort Osage High School. We have also both benefited from the skilled instruction of Mary Jeanett Smythe from the University of Missouri-Columbia. Loren Reid, also from the University of Missouri-Columbia, is another educator whom we wish to acknowledge; to us he is the quintessential speech teacher.

Finally, we appreciate the support, patience, endurance, and love of our sons, Mark and Matthew Beebe. They sacrificed time away from Mom and Dad so this book could be written.

Steve Beebe
Sue Beebe
San Marcos, Texas

PUBLIC SPEAKING

An
Audience-Centered
Approach

1

Introduction to Public Speaking

OBJECTIVES

After studying this chapter, you should be able to

1. Explain how public speaking differs from casual conversation

2. List six ways in which public speaking benefits society

3. List five ways in which public speaking benefits the individual speaker

4. Draw and explain a simple process model of communication

5. Draw and explain the factors involved in a components model of communication

A journey of a thousand miles begins with a single step. (Oskar Schlemmer, Bauhaus Stairway, 1932. Oil on canvas, 63⅞ × 45". Collection, The Museum of Modern Art, New York. Gift of Philip Johnson.)

OLD CHINESE PROVERB

You were glad to get the invitation. After all, if anyone knows about antique toys, you do. Your grandfather gave you his old tin soldiers while you were still in elementary school. At first you just set them on a shelf without much thought. Then you found five more in a dusty little shop. Since then, you've scoured flea markets, garage sales, and antique shops to increase your collection. In addition, you've read just about all the guidebooks published on the subject. So why does giving this talk loom as such a dark blot on your future? Your mind is a blank—and you shudder to imagine yourself up in front of all those people. Your brother was no help, either; he only laughed and said that since you talk constantly anyway, speaking publicly should be a breeze!

You may have a great deal of knowledge and you may be a fast talker, but if the scene we just described seems all too familiar, you are probably not an experienced public speaker.

Human communication begins at birth. Babies' first cries signal their distress at being thrust from the dark comfort of the womb out into a cold, hard, bright world. Their communication continues as they learn that their own smiles will bring smiles from their parents. And it leaps to a higher plane as they come to understand that certain sounds will make Dad scurry to bring juice or a beloved teddy.

The pervasiveness of communication is well expressed by the saying that humans cannot *not* communicate. Every action or sound that you make communicates *something*. Even falling asleep while you are in class says something of your excitement about the material you are studying or the way it is presented. So why do you need to study something as natural as communication, something that you've done so often and for so long? Simply because hit-or-miss experimentation—which is basically how you learn to communicate as a child—works to a certain point but does not necessarily lead to effective communication. Furthermore, as you reexamine your feelings about giving that lecture on antique toys, you realize that speaking in public is different from chatting with friends over dinner. Because public speaking is indeed a unique form of communication, few people learn to do it well without study and practice.

SPEAKING IN PUBLIC: A UNIQUE COMMUNICATION FORMAT

▼
intrapersonal communication
Communication that occurs within yourself; talking to yourself.

How does public speaking differ from casual conversation with a friend or an animated discussion among members of your speech class? What are its distinctive characteristics? These questions can best be answered by examining and comparing the four levels of communication: *intrapersonal, interpersonal, group,* and *public.*

Intrapersonal communication is communication within yourself, which in very simple terms means talking to yourself. But this level also includes subconscious comprehension, interpretation, analysis, and evaluation of stimuli. Often, intrapersonal communication comes unbidden into the mind. You have undoubtedly had thoughts and ideas occur to you "out of the clear blue sky." Such an experience is a form of intrapersonal communication.

Interpersonal communication occurs between two people. Though often informal, it is more intentional than intrapersonal communication. It requires you to make conscious decisions about what to say and how to respond to someone.

Group communication occurs when three or more people meet to exchange ideas, reach a common goal, or perform a mutual task. Because it involves more people, it is more complex than either intrapersonal or interpersonal communication. At this level, people will usually spend more time listening and less time speaking than at the interpersonal level. Chapter 18 will focus on the group level of communication.

Finally, **public speaking** is a sustained presentation made by one speaker to an audience. Usually the result of forethought and planning rather than a spontaneous event, it is more intentional than any of the other three levels. Whereas persons communicating interpersonally or in small groups may alternately talk and listen, perhaps even interrupting one another, in public speaking, the roles of speaker and listener are clearly defined and remain stable. Rarely do audience members interrupt or even talk to speakers. Even when speakers field questions, they finish their planned remarks first. Successful speakers, however, must be audience-centered, considering the needs, expectations, and responses of their audiences as they prepare and deliver their speeches.

Public speaking is also more formal than the other levels of communication. The slang or casual language often used at the interpersonal or group level is not appropriate in a public speaking setting. "This old redcoat is really sharp," you tell your friend as you take down a favorite toy soldier. Holding up the same soldier as you deliver your speech, you say instead, "This British soldier from the American Revolutionary War period is an example of a nineteenth-century lead soldier in excellent condition."

Not only is the language of public speakers relatively formal, but so is their nonverbal communication. When people communicate interpersonally or in small groups, they often sit or stand close together, gesture spontaneously and sometimes excessively, and move about restlessly. By contrast, the physical distance between public speakers and their audiences is usually greater than the distance between people communicating interpersonally or in small groups. Public speakers also use gestures and movements that are carefully orchestrated to add meaning or emphasis to their spoken messages.

interpersonal communication
Face-to-face communication between two people.

group communication
Communication between three or more people who meet to exchange ideas, reach a common goal, or perform a mutual task.

public speaking
A sustained presentation made by a speaker to an audience.

Having examined how public speaking differs from conversation, you may now understand what public speaking is. But you may still not be convinced that it is something you particularly want or need to study. Just what will you have gained once you have achieved some skill in public speaking? Of what value is your newly developed ability? A logical way to answer this question is to examine next what public speaking does and whom it benefits.

**THE ROLES AND VALUES
OF PUBLIC SPEAKING**

Public Speaking and the Individual

Probably uppermost in your mind as you begin a course in public speaking is the question, "What's in it for *me*?" As well as enabling you to participate in a historically significant activity, the study of public speaking provides many other direct and indirect benefits to the individual.

Analyzing and Adapting to an Audience   When one of the authors of this book taught for several semesters in the Bahamas, he had to change the way he had previously taught public speaking. Audiences in the United States have come to expect their speakers to use a fairly informal, extemporaneous (not read or memorized) speaking style. Therefore, public speaking classes in this country have for several decades focused on an informal speaking style. During the first class in the Bahamas, students were aghast at the suggestion that they try to achieve a conversational, informal manner. Bahamian audiences, the author quickly discovered, expect formal oratory from their speakers, very much as American audiences in the nineteenth century preferred the grandiloquence of Stephen A. Douglas to the quieter, homespun style of Abraham Lincoln. Not only did the author have to teach his students to adapt to the more informal expectation, but he himself had to adapt to his Bahamian class in the way he taught them.

Not just delivery but all aspects of public speaking should be adapted to an audience's expectations. Public speaking is by nature an audience-centered activity. Topic, pattern of organization, and even the dress of the speaker should vary according to who the listeners are, what subject or subjects they are interested in, where and for how long the speaker will be speaking, and other aspects of the speaking situation. Public speakers who learn to analyze their audiences and adapt to the audiences' expectations will find these skills useful in numerous settings. The job interview, the business presentation, the city council campaign—even the marriage proposal—will call on the skills of analysis and adaptation you learn as a student of public speaking. As the title suggests, this book will focus on public speaking as an audience-centered activity.

Organizing Ideas   Another of the important skills a public speaker develops is the ability to organize ideas into a logical pattern that can be followed and understood by others. The focus of this text is public speaking as an audience-centered activity. If a speaker rambles or is obscure, chances are that the audience will at best remember only a few disjointed ideas. At worst, they may tune the speaker out early, in despair at getting anything worthwhile from someone who can't even organize his or her own thoughts. If the speaker is an advertising salesperson making a presentation to potential clients, the penalty for an unorganized presentation will be not only failure to communicate but also loss of revenue.

When writers organize ideas, they have one important advantage over public speakers. Writers know that even if readers do miss a point or idea the first time, they can always go back and reread. Speakers have to work harder to make sure that audience members understand and remember their ideas, because if listeners miss a point once, they cannot reclaim the idea without the speaker's help. Candidates for seats in the state legislature cannot rely on their audiences to remember the planks of their campaign platforms if they list these planks only once. Not only do public speakers study and learn to apply various patterns of organization (chronological, topical, cause-effect, problem-solution), but they also learn about previewing and summarizing—methods of oral organization that ensure repetition of their main ideas.

Gathering Information   You can probably think of a topic or two about which you consider yourself an expert. Chances are that if you gave a short speech about a hobby that you practiced for years or about a recent experience that you had, you would not need to gather much additional information. But you would probably exhaust such topics very quickly. Sooner or later, you will need to gather information about a topic in order to speak on it intelligently to an audience. As you study public speaking, you will learn and practice the skill of researching a topic. If your college classes up to this point have required only a brief foray into the imposing stacks of the library, that experience is about to change shortly. By the time you have given several speeches in this course, you will have learned to use at least several of the following sources: the card catalog, the *Social Sciences Index*, the *Directory of American Scholars*, government document holdings, and the reference section. In addition, you will learn how to gather information through interviews and how and to whom to write for information on various topics.

The student who has taken a public speaking class usually finds any future project that requires research to be much less formidable. Both the master's thesis and the state-of-the-company report that you may do years from now will prove easier because of the research skills you learn as you study public speaking.

Presenting Ideas Effectively   "He knows his stuff, but his lectures will put you to sleep!" No doubt you have heard fellow students criticize some professor in this way. At times you may grit your teeth and determine to pick the man's brain anyway; other times, you may simply avoid the class or sign up to take it under another instructor. Sadly, many people who are brilliant authorities in their chosen fields are unable to communicate their knowledge and ideas in an interesting and effective manner. They are information-centered rather than audience-centered. By enrolling in a public speaking class, you are taking an important step toward ensuring that this predicament never applies to you! As you study public speaking, you will learn what factors make up "good delivery." You will learn how to capture and maintain the attention of your audience through the use of vocal variation, physical movement, humor, narration, and other techniques. You will also learn to control your nervousness so that it actually *helps* you speak. You may well debate the old question, "Which is more important, content or delivery?" But whatever side you choose to defend, you will come to recognize the importance of effective delivery to successful public speaking—and more important, to practice it!

Listening Critically   How many spoken messages do you hear daily? Consider the lectures you hear in class, the conversations you have with friends, the auditory bombardment of radio, television, tapes, and records, and your calculation quickly reaches triple digits. You learn to avoid "auditory overload" by simply *hearing* but not really *listening* to many of these messages. In fact, your ability *not* to listen becomes almost automatic, much like blinking an eye to protect it from an approaching object or jerking a hand back from a hot surface. The problem is that when your ability to "tune out" becomes automatic, it is no longer selective. Not only do you tune out unimportant messages, but you also lose much of your acuity in listening to important ones. A course in public speaking can help you to sharpen your dulled listening skills in two ways.

First, during your study of public speaking, you will also study listening. In fact, the next section of this chapter will show that communication cannot exist without both speaker and listener. Chapter 3 is devoted to helping you understand what happens when you listen and to suggesting specific ways in which you can improve your listening skills. Finally, many of the skills you learn and practice as a speaker will also improve your ability to listen critically. As you learn to analyze your audience, select and develop appropriate topics, generate and support ideas, and organize and deliver speeches, you will also become more aware of the way other speakers use these same skills. You will be better able to recognize such faults as an unsupported conclusion and a questionable source of evidence, whether they occur in a classmate's presentation, in a colleague's strategy for increasing company productivity, or in the speech of a politician seeking local, state, or national office.

Your public speaking course will provide not only the means to improve listening skills but also many opportunities to apply them. You will spend more time listening to speeches than you will spend giving them. Most public speaking classes include at least some time for oral critique of speeches, and as the semester progresses, your instructor may even ask you to provide written analyses of classmates' speeches. The opportunity to sharpen your critical listening ability will occur frequently.

LEARNING ABOUT PUBLIC SPEAKING HELPS YOU . . .

Organize your ideas
Analyze and adapt to an audience
Develop information-gathering skills
Present ideas to others
Listen critically to the ideas of others

Public Speaking and Society

Widespread literacy is fairly recent in the annals of human history. But long before people could read, they listened to public speakers. They listened to the politicians and poets of ancient Greece and Rome and to the clergy of medieval Europe. They gathered eagerly to hear Martin Luther expound his fourteen Articles of Faith. They listened to the town criers and impassioned patriots of colonial America. Vast audiences heard such nineteenth-century speakers as Henry Clay and Daniel Webster debate the issue of slavery and Lucretia Mott argue for women's suffrage. In the twentieth century, radio made it possible for people around the world to hear King Edward VIII of England abdicate to marry an American divorcee. And they listened as President Franklin D. Roosevelt proclaimed December 7, 1941, "a day that will live in infamy." The impact of public speaking on human history is indisputable. To understand why, let's examine some of the specific functions of public speaking in society.

People gather in town meetings to listen to public speakers.
(*Dick Hanley/Photo Researchers, Inc.*)

Providing Information   One important function of public speaking is to provide information to groups of people. Professor Collins, lecturing to her American History 101 class, for example, is primarily interested in providing the information her students need to pass the next test, pass her course, and become people who have a reasonable amount of knowledge about American history. Connie Chung, delivering the evening news, is mainly interested in providing information about the news of the day. Your goal in speaking publicly about your antique soldiers is to give your audience information about that subject. Rarely do you go through a day without hearing a public speaker deliver information. It is unlikely that you would be enrolled in a college or university now if you did not expect to gain at least some new information from the spoken, as well as the written, word. Public speaking is a major source of new information for people of all times and places.

Influencing Thought   Some experts believe that the desire to influence thought underlies all speech, whether that objective is acknowledged or not. In the 1960s, Dr. Martin Luther King, Jr., used his skill in public speaking to convince the nation that racial discrimination is unjust. The political candidate who delivers a vehement attack on an opponent's record is attempting to change your opinion about that opponent's suitability for office—or, if you already agree that the opponent is unqualified, to reinforce that opinion. Your arguments in front of the university president's special advisory board, urging them to change their ban on freshmen cars in dormitory lots, is an obvious effort to get them to reconsider their current position. Whether world leader or university student, a public speaker can effect lasting changes in the thoughts and opinions of his or her audience.

Stimulating Action   Very often speakers who try to influence thought go one step further and also urge their audiences to take some related action. Politicians campaigning for office do not usually end their speeches with a summary of the issues but with a ringing call to vote for them in the upcoming election. Student activists arguing against apartheid in South Africa may urge their audiences to sign antiapartheid petitions or to write letters to university presidents in protest of university holdings in South African companies. The Red Cross representative who speaks to your fraternity on the facts about blood donation will almost certainly ask you to donate blood. These speakers know that one of the best ways to ensure lasting commitment to a cause is to get the audience to *do* something—vote, write a letter, give blood, donate to the United Way, volunteer at the local nursing home, or whatever the message may require.

Providing Inspiration   Just as people rely on public speakers for information and incentive, so too do they often seek inspiration from the spoken word. The citizens of a torn and bitter nation found new cause for courage and optimism in Abraham Lincoln's second inaugural address. A century later another president inspired his listeners by admonishing them, "Ask not what your country can do for you, ask what you can do for your country." Martin Luther King, Jr., not only provided logical arguments against racial discrimination, but he also provided the watchwords of the movement by proclaiming, "I have a dream!"

These examples come from different historical periods, deal with different subjects, and have different purposes. But they have this in common: As people struggle in any endeavor, they grow weary. And as they tire, they seek inspiration to continue their ventures. That inspiration often comes from public speakers.

Paying Tribute   "Fourscore and seven years ago our forefathers brought forth on this continent a new nation, conceived in liberty and dedicated to the proposition that all men are created equal." Abraham Lincoln agonized over these words during the train ride from Washington, D.C., to Gettysburg, Pennsylvania, where he was to take part in consecrating one of the great battlefields of the Civil War. He scratched, crossed out, and rewrote his brief remarks on the back of an envelope. Unsatisfied with the final result, he considered the speech a failure. Yet the Gettysburg Address has become one of the most enduring examples of a speech of tribute. Many of you will, at one time or another, be asked to speak in tribute to a person or group of persons. Whether the occasion is a dinner honoring a highly valued person, an award ceremony, or a memorial, this type of speech is frequently in demand.

Entertaining   "And now, heeeeere's Johnny!" A whole generation of Americans have grown up anticipating the famous monologue that follows these words each weekday evening. Johnny Carson's opening speech is not meant to provide information, influence, inspire, or pay tribute—its objective is to entertain. So too are many of the sketches and monologues of such comedians as Bill Cosby, Joan Rivers, Jay Leno, and Roseanne Barr. Many after-dinner speakers also speak primarily to entertain.

Even though the six functions of public speaking are varied, they are not mutually exclusive. An entertainer such as political comedian Mark Russell may, for example, influence thought through his comedy. Winston Churchill was renowned for his wit, even as he gave thought-provoking and inspiring speeches during the dark hours of World War II.

Speech Ethics: Balancing Individual Freedom and Social Responsibility

Affirming the value of public speaking both to individuals and to a free society, the First Amendment to the United States Constitution guarantees that "Congress shall make no law . . . abridging the freedom of speech." Since 1791, Congress and the federal courts have sought to define free speech in a number of ways. Only a few years after the adoption of the Bill of Rights, Congress passed the Sedition Act, providing punishment for those who spoke out against the government. Jefferson and Madison decried the act as unconstitutional, and it was allowed to lapse in 1801. In the twentieth century, free speech was again restricted, particularly during times when the nation found itself threatened by war. In 1919 the Supreme Court restricted speech that presented "a clear and present danger" to the nation; in 1940 Congress declared it illegal to urge the violent overthrow of the federal government. More recently, approaching the bicentennial of the Bill of Rights, the Supreme Court expanded the parameters of free speech. In a controversial 1989 decision, they defended the burning of the U.S. flag in political protest as a "speech act" protected by the First Amendment.

Even though the *legal* boundaries of free speech will continue to be debated in the legislatures and courts of this country, practitioners and teachers of public speaking have long agreed that public speakers must assume *ethical* responsibility for their words and actions. The morals and values of speakers and their ideas were of concern even to the ancient rhetoricians. In the fourth century B.C., Aristotle warned, "Let men be on their guard against those who flatter and mislead the multitude. . . ." Four hundred years later, Quintilian urged that an orator be a good person, speaking well.

Although there is no definitive standard of ethics for the public speaker, Quintilian's admonition provides a convenient basis for a discussion of your ethical responsibilities as a speaker. Let's examine his mandate more closely.

"A Good Person"   What is meant by saying that a speaker be "a good person"? In short, an audience has a right to expect that a speaker be honest. Speakers have a responsibility to study and research their topics until they know and understand the information thoroughly. They must then relay the truth as they know it. Offering false or misleading information to an audience is a violation of this ethical responsibility. When former Reagan White House spokesman Larry Speakes admitted inventing presidential quotes during several highly publicized occasions, his confession sparked a national scandal and widespread censure. Reagan wryly observed that as president "you get to quote yourself shamelessly and, if you don't, Larry Speakes will."[1] We will discuss the ethical uses of supporting materials in more detail in Chapter 6.

Speakers also have an ethical responsibility to give credit for ideas and information not their own. In August 1987, U.S. Senator and Democratic presidential candidate

Joseph Biden plagiarized British Labor Party Leader Neil Kennock in a speech in Des Moines, Iowa. When the plagiarism was exposed, along with evidence of previous plagiarism from Robert Kennedy, Biden was forced to withdraw from the presidential race. He had violated the ethical responsibility of honesty.

An interesting ethical question regarding attribution of remarks is the increasing use of ghost writers by speakers in such diverse fields as politics, business, and sports. It is openly acknowledged, for example, that ghostwriter Peggy Noonan has written some of the most memorable and successful speeches of Presidents Ronald Reagan and George Bush. To her credit are such speeches as Reagan's 1986 eulogy to the Challenger astronauts and Bush's 1988 speech accepting the Republican nomination for president. Is the use of such ghostwriters a violation of speech ethics? Reliance on professional writers, as long as the speech is being written expressly for you, is not generally considered dishonest, although the practice certainly lacks the drama of Abraham Lincoln's scratching the Gettysburg Address on the back of an envelope. Ghostwriting is an ethical question you may wish to explore and discuss in more detail.

"Speaking Well"   The second part of Quintilian's definition focuses not on the speaker, but on the speech itself. A speech should have an ethical goal. Law and ethics merge on this point. As we have pointed out, Congress and the Supreme Court have legally limited speech that incites sedition, violence, and riot. History condemns Adolf Hitler's attempts to persuade the German people to hatred and genocide. More recently, Chinese leader Deng Xiaoping urged Chinese citizens to reveal the whereabouts of leaders of the unsuccessful student uprising of 1989— disclosure that would lead to almost certain execution. Again, those who uphold free speech denounce the goal as unethical.

A speaker must also use ethical methods of persuasion rather than coercion. Coercion involves the use of force, either physical or psychological. The brainwashing and physical torture experienced by American POWs during the Vietnam War is one example of unethical coercion. Ethical persuasion relies on the use of evidence and reasoning. We will discuss ethical persuasion in detail in Chapter 16.

In short, ethics reconcile the individual and social roles and values of public speaking.

THE SPEECH COMMUNICATION PROCESS

The next time you have a chance to visit an elementary school classroom, look around at the number of mock-ups and models on display. In the typical second-grade classroom, you will probably see a large cardboard or plastic clock face, often with gears exposed so that the students get some idea of how the hands synchronize. Hanging on the wall may be a large thermometer, marked off in both Celsius and Fahrenheit. On a shelf or table you may find an "invisible man," a plastic human figure whose internal organs and bones are visible under his clear plastic "skin." And you may also see a chart that pictures one whole apple cut into four pieces.

The use of such learning aids is not, of course, limited to the second grade. Many of the facts, scientific principles, and processes that we continue to learn throughout life are introduced and explained to us by models and diagrams. The process of public speaking is no exception. To understand better just what it is we are going to study and practice throughout this course, let's look at some models that illustrate what is involved when we speak in public or sit in an audience and listen to a public speaker.

Public Speaking as a Process

One interesting model makes little attempt to break public speaking down into individual components; rather, it focuses on its inherent vital nature. Unlike the static invisible man in the second-grade classroom, public speaking is a *process*—an ongoing series with no discernible beginning or end. Figure 1.1 illustrates the process of communication as a helical spiral, infinite at both ends. It represents the continuous nature of the communication process, influenced by the past and linked to the future.

For example, the American history professor, even as he lectures, is affected by his childhood experiences, his own education, and the discussion he had just before class with his department chairman. His students, too, are listening as individuals affected by their pasts. The impact of the communication moment on the future can only be imagined. Even the seemingly ordinary lecture is, in fact, a complex process.

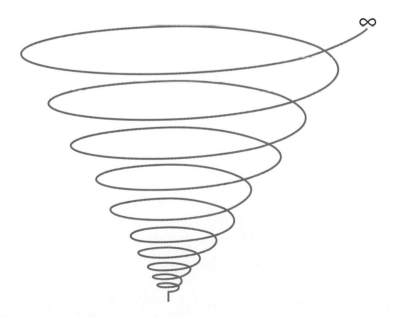

FIGURE 1.1

A helical model of communication.
(*Copyright © F. E. X. Dance in* Human Communication Theory. *Holt, Rinehart, and Winston, 1967, p. 294. Reprinted with permission.*)

source
The origin of a communication message.

encode
The process through which messages are translated into signals.

receiver
The individual or group of individuals (audience) toward whom communications are intentionally or unintentionally directed.

The interpretive process of assigning meaning to a message.

codes
Verbal or nonverbal symbols which can be interpreted by another.

message
Verbal or nonverbal symbols to which a receiver assigns meaning; the content of the speech.

The Elements of the Process

Other, more traditional models of communication focus on separating the various elements of the process. Although these models may differ from textbook to textbook, they usually look something like Figure 1.2 and include the following factors.

Source   A public speaker is a **source** of information and ideas to an audience. The job of the source or speaker is to **encode** or translate the ideas and images in his or her mind into a system of signals that will be recognized by an audience. The speaker may encode into words (for example, "The fabric should be two inches square") or into gestures (showing the size with hands).

Receiver   The **receiver** of the speaker's information or ideas is the individual audience member. The receiver's task is to **decode** the sender's verbal and nonverbal messages, translating the speaker's verbal and nonverbal symbols (or **codes**) back into mental ideas and images. Unfortunately, the decoded message will never be exactly the thought or idea the speaker intended to convey. The receiver's perception of the message is dependent on his or her own unique blend of past experiences, attitudes, beliefs, and values. As we have already emphasized, an effective public speaker should be receiver or audience-centered.

Message   The **message** in public speaking is the speech itself—both what is said and how it is said. As just noted, the speaker's intended message may differ from the meaning the audience decodes. A speaker may have trouble finding words to

FIGURE 1.2

The basic components of communication.

(*From* Invitation to Effective Speech Communication *by John T. Masterson, Steven A. Beebe, and Norman H. Watson. Copyright © 1989 by Scott, Foresman and Company. Reprinted by permission of Harper Collins, Publisher.*)

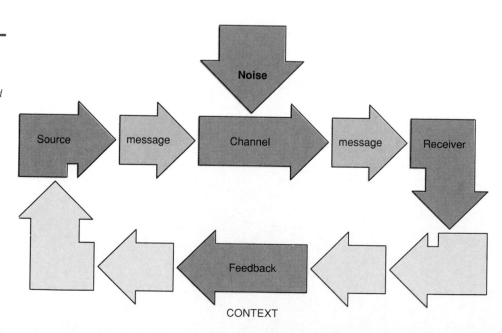

convey his or her ideas. Right away the message suffers. A flat monotone and lack of eye contact may belie any real interest in the subject, contradicting and confusing the verbal message. And because the listeners' frame of reference may be very different from that of the speaker, they may interpret what they hear and see in a manner that was not at all what the speaker intended. Again, the potential for message distortion exists.

Ideally, an intended message will differ little from the actual message perceived by an audience. The less distortion of the message between sender and receiver, the more accurate and successful the communication.

Channel   A message is usually transmitted from sender to receiver via two **channels:** visual and auditory. The audience sees the speaker and decodes his or her nonverbal messages—eye contact (or lack of it), facial expressions, posture, gestures, and dress. If the speaker uses any visual aids, such as graphs or models, these too are transmitted along the visual channel. The auditory channel opens as the speaker speaks. Then the audience hears his or her words and such vocal cues as inflection, rate, and voice quality.

channels
The pathway through which messages and symbols pass between a source and a receiver.

Feedback   As we noted earlier, one way in which public speaking differs from casual conversation is that the public speaker does most or all of the talking. But public speaking is still an interactional process. Remembering the old question of whether a falling tree can make noise if no one is around to hear, we may well ask whether one can engage in public speaking without an audience to hear and provide **feedback.**

The answer is no. Skillful public speakers are audience-centered. They depend on the nods, facial expressions, and murmurings of the audience to adjust their rate of speaking, volume, vocabulary, type and amount of supporting material, and other variables in order to maximize the success of their communication. Remember, people cannot *not* communicate—and feedback is communication.

feedback
A response to a message.

Context   The **context** of a public speaking experience includes such elements as the time, the place where the speech occurs, and the physical and psychological factors affecting both speaker and listener. To paraphrase John Donne, "No speech is an island." No speech occurs in a vacuum. Rather, each speech is a unique blend of circumstances that can never occur in exactly the same conjunction again.

The person whose job it is to deliver an identical message to a number of different audiences at different times and in different places can attest to the uniqueness of each speaking experience. If the room is hot, crowded, or poorly lighted, these conditions affect both speaker and audience. The audience who hears a speaker at 10:00 in the morning is likely to be fresher and more receptive than the audience who hears the speaker at 4:30 in the afternoon—that is, of course, unless the audience who comes later has had the day off in breathless anticipation of the speech. If the speaker is coming down with a cold, this malaise is likely to affect his or her performance. If the speaker fought rush-hour traffic for ninety minutes to arrive at his or her destination, exhaustion and frustration may make it difficult

context
The communication environment; the external physical and psychological factors that affect a message.

Noise *refers to any distractions that interfere with a speaker's ability to speak.*
(*Bob Daemmrich/Stock, Boston*)

to muster much enthusiasm. All these factors make up the element of the public speaking process that we call context.

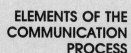

noise
Anything that interferes with the accurate communication of a message.

Noise   When variables interfere with the communication of a message, we call them **noise.** Noise may be literal, or *external*. If your 8:00 A.M. public speaking class is frequently interrupted by the roar of a lawn mower running back and forth under your window, it may be difficult to hear a speaker. A noisy air conditioner, a crying baby, or incessant coughing may also make it difficult for audience members to hear or concentrate on a speech.

Noise may also be *internal*, a term that refers to some of the other factors we have discussed. Internal noise may directly affect either the source or the receiver. A speaker's bad cold may cloud his or her memory or subdue a usually enthusiastic delivery. An audience member who is worried about an exam later in the day is unlikely to remember much of what a speaker says. Just before lunch, an audience's hunger may interfere with their ability to concentrate; just after lunch they may be too sleepy to pay much attention. All these factors interfere with the transmission of a message from sender to receiver.

RECAP

ELEMENTS OF THE COMMUNICATION PROCESS	Source	Encodes ideas and images into symbols
	Receiver	Decodes or translates symbols into ideas and images
	Message	The content of the speech
	Channel	The means by which the message is carried to the receiver through visual and auditory cues
	Feedback	Response to the message
	Context	The external and internal physical and psychological factors that affect the speech
	Noise	Variables that interfere with the accurate communication of a message

Public speaking is a unique form of communication that is more highly structured and more formal than casual conversation. Public speaking benefits individual speakers by helping them learn to analyze and adapt to an audience, organize ideas, gather information, present ideas effectively, and listen critically. It benefits society by providing information, influencing thought, stimulating action, providing inspiration, paying tribute, and entertaining people. These various roles of public speaking must all be tempered by speakers' ethical responsibility for their words and actions.

   In defining public speaking, this chapter presented both a process model and a components model of communication. The process model illustrates the ongoing nature of the public speaking process. The components model emphasizes the various elements of the process, which include sender, receiver, message, channel, feedback, context, and noise. Finally, the chapter emphasized that a successful speaker must be audience-centered, a concept that will guide the remainder of this text.

SUMMARY

1. What are the differences between a public speech and an interpersonal conversation?
2. Provide examples of how a speech you heard influenced your thinking about an issue or stimulated you to action.
3. How will a course in public speaking help you with your career goals?
4. What are the elements of the communication process?
5. Provide examples of noise in a public speaking situation.

QUESTIONS FOR DISCUSSION AND REVIEW

1. Provide an example from your own experiences of how a public speech has (a) provided you with information, (b) influenced your thought, (c) stimulated you to action, (d) inspired you, (e) paid tribute to someone, and (f) entertained you.
2. Several values of public speaking to the individual were discussed in this chapter. Rank these abilities, indicating which one you feel you need to learn first, second, third, fourth, and fifth.
   _____ Organizing ideas
   _____ Analyzing and adapting to an audience
   _____ Gathering information
   _____ Presenting ideas effectively
   _____ Listening critically
3. Listen to an entire public speech, either on TV or in person. Write a brief analysis of the speech, identifying each of the elements of the communication process discussed in this chapter: sender, receiver, message, channel, feedback, content, and noise.
4. Write an essay in which you identify the value of learning how to become an effective public speaker. How will public speaking help you in school? In your career? In your personal life?

SUGGESTED ACTIVITIES

2
Overview of the Speechmaking Process

If all my talents and powers were to be taken from me by some inscrutable Providence, and I had my choice of keeping but one, I would unhesitatingly ask to be allowed to keep the Power of Speaking, for through it, I would quickly recover all the rest. (*Oscar de Mejo*, Framing the Constitution, *1983. Aberbach Fine Art, New York.*)

DANIEL WEBSTER

Unless you have some prior experience in higher mathematics, you may not have the foggiest notion of what calculus is when you first take a class in that subject. But when you tell people that you are taking a public speaking class, most at least have some idea what a public speaker does. A public speaker talks while others listen. You hear speeches almost every day. Each evening, when you turn on the news, you get a "sound bite" of some politician delivering a speech. Each day when you attend class, an instructor lectures. But even after hearing countless speeches, you may still have questions about how a speaker prepares and presents a speech.

In Chapter 1, we identified several functions of public speaking and reviewed the process and elements of human communication. In this chapter, we will look closely at the preparation and presentation skills needed in public speaking. We will first examine several characteristics of an effective speaker, and then we will present a comprehensive view of the public speaking process. Our examination is designed to help you with early speaking assignments by giving you a look at the entire process. Because most beginning speakers feel nervous about giving speeches, we will end this chapter by providing several suggestions for managing speech anxiety.

CHARACTERISTICS OF EFFECTIVE SPEAKERS

It looks so simple. All you have to do is stand in front of a group of people and start talking. An effective public speaker makes it look easy. But what skills make this possible? The ancient Greeks and Romans identified several traits a speaker had to have to be effective. These traits or qualities are still relevant today. An effective speaker

Has good ideas
Organizes ideas
Chooses the right words
Delivers the message well
Possesses excellent research skills
Is ethical

Effective Speakers Have Good Ideas

"A good many people can make a speech," said H. V. Prochnow, "but saying something is more difficult." Effective speakers are good thinkers; they say something. They know how to play with words and thoughts. The Romans called this skill **invention**—the ability to develop or discover ideas that result in new insights or new approaches to old problems. Cicero called this aspect of speaking the process of "finding out what [a speaker] should say."

One of the things effective speakers do well is think; ideas may come to them late at night or early in the morning. Some of the best ideas may come during a morning walk. When speakers know they have a speech coming up, they do not wait until they sit down at a desk or get to the library before pondering their task. They know it takes time to develop good ideas.

▼
invention
The ability to develop or discover ideas and new insights.

Effective Speakers Organize Their Ideas

Ideas, information, examples, illustrations, stories, and statistics need to be presented in a logical order. Classical rhetoricians, early students of speech, called this process **disposition.** Speakers need to know how to develop an orderly sequence of ideas and illustrations. Therefore, one of the key skills taught in most public speaking courses is the technique of logically arranging ideas.

disposition
The organization and arrangement of ideas.

Effective Speakers Choose the Right Words to Express Their Ideas

"Style," said Jonathan Swift, "is proper words in proper places." The words you choose and your arrangement of those words make up the style of your speech. Your style can be very simple or highly poetic. To be a good speaker, you must become familiar with language and know how to select the right word or phrase to communicate an idea. Work to develop an ear for how words will sound to an audience.

Effective Speakers Deliver the Message Well

One of your chief responsibilities as a speaker is to present your message with appropriate posture, gestures, eye contact, and voice. Many listeners will base their judgment of your success on how well you deliver the message, regardless of what you actually say. If you are excited and interested in your message, your attitude will be reflected by your delivery.

Effective Speakers Develop Good Research Skills

Woodrow Wilson once admitted, "I use not only all the brains I have, but all that I can borrow." Though it is important to have good ideas, it is equally important to know how to build on existing knowledge. To be an effective speaker, you must know how to use a library. You must also know to be constantly on the lookout as you read, watch TV, and listen to the radio for ideas, examples, illustrations, and quotations that could be used in a speech.

Effective Speakers Are Ethical

An ethical speaker is a truthful speaker. Ethical speakers give credit where credit is due. It is unethical to **plagiarize,** that is, to claim that the words and ideas of others are your own.

plagiarize
To claim the words and ideas of others as your own.

An ethical speaker is also one who uses evidence accurately. Do not make up evidence just to prove a point. Do not suppress evidence that you know is contrary

*A good speaker is a good
person speaking well.*
(*Architect of the Capital*)

to the ideas you are supporting. As we noted in Chapter 1, a good speaker is a good person, speaking well.

RECAP

EFFECTIVE SPEAKERS . . .	Have good ideas	Deliver their messages well
	Organize their ideas	Possess excellent research skills
	Choose the right words	Are ethical

PREPARING YOUR FIRST SPEECH: A LOOK AT THE SPEECHMAKING PROCESS

You have been speaking since before you were 2. Speaking has seemed such a natural part of your life that you never really stopped to analyze the process. But now you are sitting at your desk, thinking about your assignment to deliver your first speech. The assignment may be to introduce yourself to the class. Or your first speech may be a brief informative talk in which you are to describe something to your audience. Regardless of the specific assignment, your bewilderment is the same: "What do I do first?"

It would be useful to read *Public Speaking: An Audience-Centered Approach* from cover to cover before tackling your first speech. Many related principles and skills are needed to design and deliver an effective speech. Yet there is no better way to learn how to deliver a speech than to start speaking publicly. To help you prepare your first speech, we will provide a short preview of the major steps that will be discussed in more detail later in this book. This overview will help you with your early speaking assignments and will also give you a scaffolding on which to build your skill in public speaking.

The model in Figure 2.1 shows the various public speaking tasks and emphasizes the audience as central to any speech. We'll refer to this audience-centered model of public speaking throughout the text as we study speech preparation and delivery.

Audience Analysis: Central to the Speechmaking Process

Why should the central focus of public speaking be the audience? Why is it not topic selection, outlining, or research? The simple truth is, your audience influences the topic you choose and every later step of the public speaking process. We place

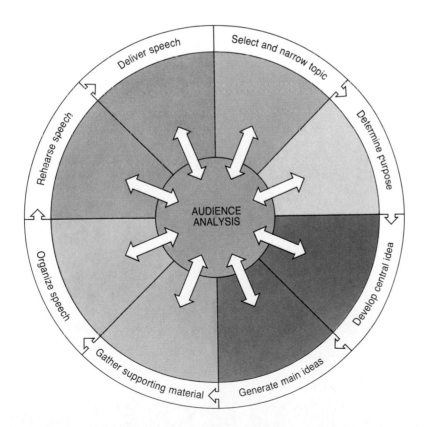

FIGURE 2.1

Model of the audience-centered public speaking process.

audience analysis in the center because it is an activity that touches every phase of the speech preparation and delivery process.

The reason to analyze your audience is to learn how your listeners will respond to you and your message. The more you learn about your audience, the greater your chances of making choices that will help achieve your goals. Your selection of topic, purpose, and even major ideas should be based on a thorough understanding of your listeners. In a very real sense, your audience "writes" the speech.

As Figure 2.2 shows, audience analysis is not something you do only once before beginning the other speech preparation tasks. The analysis is an ongoing activity. After you select your topic, you need to consider how the audience will respond to your examples, your organization, and your delivery. As suggested by the model, audience-centered public speaking means that at any point during the process, you may need to revise tasks you have already performed. If, for example, you decide to change the central idea of your speech, you may also need to reconsider your topic or the purpose of your speech. The needs, attitudes, beliefs, values, and other characteristics of your audience play a leading role in helping you prepare and present your message. Chapter 4 contains a comprehensive discussion of the principles and strategies involved in the analysis of your audience.

FIGURE 2.2

At each step of the speech preparation process, focus on how your listeners will respond to you and your message.

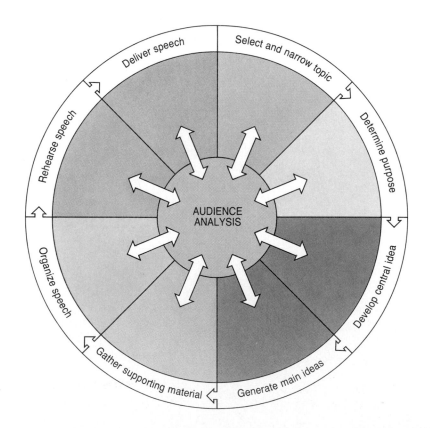

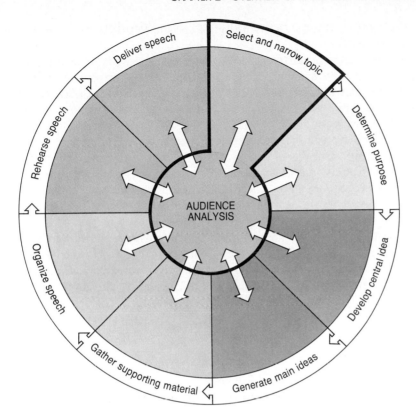

FIGURE 2.3
Selecting and narrowing the speech topic is an early task of public speakers.

Select and Narrow Your Topic

If your first speech is to introduce yourself to the class, the topic of your speech has been selected for you—*you* are the topic. It is not uncommon to be asked to speak on a specific subject. But there will be many times when you will be asked to speak and not given a topic. As Figure 2.3 illustrates, the task of selecting and narrowing a topic will be yours. Choosing or finding a topic on which to speak can be frustrating. "What should I talk about?" can become a haunting question with no easy answer.

One reason selecting a topic may be difficult is that your desire to find the ideal topic may make you overly critical of your creative processes. But if you have begun to think about your audience, you have already started the topic selection process. You also need to consider your own interests and experiences. The best topics usually come from your own experiences. What issues do you feel strongly about? Reflect on jobs you've held, news stories that catch your interest, your major or minor, your career goals, or interesting people that you have met. Another place to find ideas for a speech is the calendar—what anniversary of a famous person's birth or death occurs close to the time you are to speak? For your first speech, you will be most comfortable if you speak on a topic you already know something

The key to an effective entertaining speech lies in the speaker's choice of stories, examples, and illustrations, as well as in his or her delivery.
(*AP/World Wide Photos*)

about. Chapter 5 contains a discussion of specific strategies for finding topics on which to speak.

Once you have chosen your topic, you must narrow it to fit the time set for your talk. Let's say that you recently went on vacation in Europe and that after considering your interests and those of your audience, you decide to talk about your European holiday. Your trip took three weeks, but you have only ten minutes in which to give your speech.

To start whittling your topic down to size, think of the variety of topics you could talk about: your day in Paris, your trip to several castles in Germany, or your tour of historic buildings in London. There would be enough information on each of these to fill an hour lecture. Clearly, you need to narrow your topic further. You might talk about the Louvre Museum in Paris—that's more specific, but still too broad for the ten minutes that you have. After further thought, you decide on the following topic: "Two famous paintings in Paris's Louvre Museum." This topic focuses your speech much more sharply than a general topic, such as "European vacation spots," would. Chapter 5 also explains how to narrow your topic. As our model suggests, your audience should also be considered when you need to narrow your topic.

Determine Your Purpose

You might think that once you have your topic, you are ready to start the research process. Before you do that, however, you need to decide on both a general and a specific purpose, as shown in Figure 2.4.

Chapter 5 describes three types of general purposes for giving a speech: to *inform*, to *persuade*, and to *entertain*. Even though we usually discuss each purpose separately, they often overlap to some extent. For example, you may decide on a speech purpose that calls for both informing and entertaining your audience while suggesting creative ways to avoid long lines during registration. In speech classes, your main general purpose will most often be set by your instructor.

Speaking to inform is the primary objective of class lectures, seminars, and workshops. When you inform, you teach, define, illustrate, clarify, or elaborate on a topic. We have devoted Chapter 14 to informative speaking.

Persuading listeners is a second type of general purpose in speaking publicly. Ads on TV and radio, sermons, political speeches, and sales presentations are examples of persuasion. Persuasive speaking is the process of changing or reinforcing attitudes, beliefs, values, or behavior. To be persuasive, you need to be sensitive to your audience's attitudes toward you and your topic. Chapters 15 and 16 will discuss the principles and methods of persuasion.

To entertain an audience is the third general purpose for giving a speech. After-dinner speeches and comic monologues are mainly intended for entertainment. Skill in using humor is essential to an entertaining speech. Often the key to an effective entertaining speech lies in your choice of stories, examples, and illustrations, as well as in your delivery.

After making sure you understand your general purpose, you need to zero in

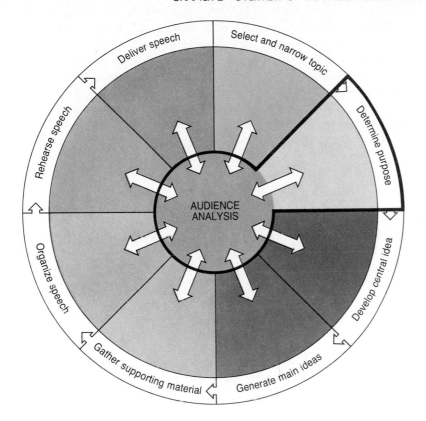

FIGURE 2.4
After selecting and narrowing your topic, you need to determine your speech purpose.

on a specific purpose. **A specific-purpose sentence** is a concise statement indicating what you want your listeners to be able to do when you finish your speech.

Perhaps you have had the experience of listening to a speaker and wondering, "What's the point? I know he's talking about education, but I'm not sure where he's going with this subject." You may have understood the speaker's general purpose, but the specific one wasn't clear. If you can't figure out what the specific purpose is, it is probably because the speaker does not know either.

Deciding on a specific purpose is not difficult once you have narrowed your topic. Let's say that when you decided to tell your class about two famous paintings in the Louvre Museum in Paris, you chose as your general purpose "to inform the class about what makes the Louvre an interesting place to visit." You chose two paintings at the museum as your main examples of what makes the place interesting. You then wrote as your specific purpose: "At the end of my speech, the class will be able to describe the excitement I felt at seeing the originals of two great paintings I had long admired in reproduction."

Notice that the purpose is phrased in terms of what you would like the audience to know, do, or feel at the end of the speech—specifically, to understand your excitement at seeing two famous paintings in the museum. Your specific purpose should be a fine-tuned, audience-centered goal. For an informative speech, you

specific-purpose sentence
A concise statement indicating what you want your listeners to be able to do when you finish your speech.

may simply want your audience to restate an idea, define new words, or identify, describe, or illustrate something. In a persuasive speech, you may try to rouse your listeners to take a class, buy something, or vote for someone.

Once you have formulated your specific purpose, write it down on a piece of paper or note card and keep it before you as you read and gather ideas for your talk. Your specific purpose should guide your research and help you choose the most relevant and interesting materials. As you continue to work on your speech, you may even decide to modify your purpose. The important point to remember is that you should have an objective in mind at all times as you move through the preparation stage.

RECAP

DETERMINE YOUR PURPOSE

Decide on your general purpose:

To inform:	To share information by defining, describing, or explaining
To persuade:	To change or reinforce an attitude, belief, value, or behavior
To entertain:	To amuse through humor, stories, or other illustrations

Decide on your specific purpose:

What do you want your audience to be able to do when you finish your speech?

General Purpose	Specific Purpose
To inform:	At the end of my speech, the audience will be able to describe my excitement at seeing the originals of two famous paintings in Paris's Louvre Museum.
To persuade:	At the end of my speech, the audience will schedule a visit to the Louvre Museum on any future European vacation itinerary.
To entertain:	At the end of my speech, the audience will be able to relate my three mishaps at the Louvre Museum.

Develop Your Central Idea

As Figure 2.5 illustrates, you should now be able to write the central idea of your speech. Whereas your statement of a specific purpose indicates what you want your audience to do when you have finished your speech, your central idea identifies the essence of your message. Think of it as a one-sentence summary of your speech. Here are two examples.

Topic: Compact disks
General Purpose: To inform

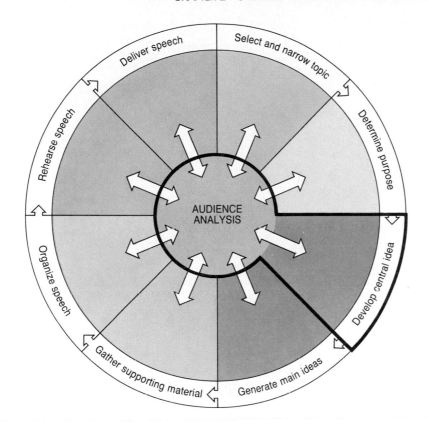

FIGURE 2.5

Your central idea is a one-sentence summary of your speech.

Specific Purpose: At the end of my speech, the audience will be able to identify the key reason compact disks have greater sound fidelity.

Central Idea: Compact disks have greater sound quality because they "read" the music information digitally, rather than analogically.

Topic: Optical illusions

General Purpose: To inform

Specific Purpose: At the end of my speech, the audience will be able to discuss three reasons why optical illusions occur.

Central Idea: Optical illusions occur because the brain tries to provide closure, seeks order, and attempts to organize information based on past experience.

Generate Main Ideas

With a narrowed topic, a specific purpose, and a well-worded central idea on paper, the next task is to identify the major divisions of your speech, as shown in Figure 2.6. The major divisions of your speech are the key points that you wish to develop.

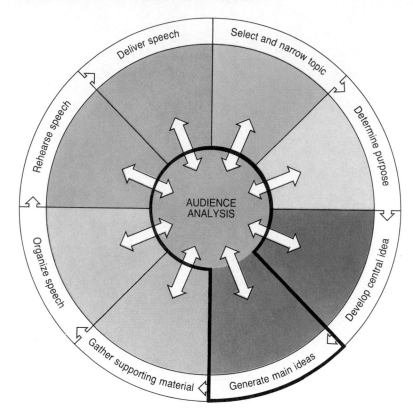

FIGURE 2.6

To generate main ideas, consider subdividing your central idea around logical divisions, reasons why the central idea is valid, or steps.

To determine how to subdivide your central idea, we recommend that you ask three questions about it:

1. Does the central idea have logical *divisions*?
2. Can you think of several *reasons* why the central idea is true?
3. Can you support the central idea with a series of *steps*?

Let's look at each of these questions and note some examples of their application.

1. *Does the central idea have logical divisions?* If the central idea is "There are three ways to interpret the stock market page of your local newspaper," your speech could be organized around the three ways to interpret the financial page. You will simply identify the key suggestions you want to make and use each suggestion as a major point of your presentation. In this case, the central idea has logical divisions that become the main ideas of your speech. A speech about the art of applying theatrical makeup could be organized according to the natural divisions of eye makeup, face makeup, and hair makeup. Look for natural divisions in your speech topic as one way to determine the major ideas you wish to communicate.

2. *Can you think of several reasons why the central idea is true?* If your central idea is "Medicare should be expanded to include additional coverage for individuals of

all ages," each major point of your speech could be a reason you think Medicare should be extended. For example, Medicare should be expanded because (1) not enough people are being served by the present system, (2) the people currently being served receive inadequate medical attention, and (3) the elderly cannot afford to pay what Medicare does not now cover. If your central idea is a statement that suggests that whatever you are talking about is good or bad, you should focus on the reasons your central idea is true. Use these reasons as the main ideas of the speech.

3. *Can you support the central idea with a series of steps?* Suppose that your central idea is "Running for a campus office is easy to do." Your speech could be developed around a series of steps, telling your listeners what to do first, second, and third to get elected. Speeches describing a personal experience or explaining how to build or make something can usually be organized in a step-by-step progression.

Your time limit and topic will determine how many major ideas will be in your speech. It is possible that a three- to five-minute speech may have only one major idea. Don't spend time trying to divide a topic that does not need dividing. For example, a speech topic about optical illusions may just have one major idea: Optical illusions occur because your brain can be easily fooled.

Gather Supporting Material

With your main ideas in mind, your next job, shown in Figure 2.7, is to gather material to support them. Even though you may have been thinking about possible sources of information since you first began working on your speech, you can now gather information for a specific purpose.

Supporting material consists of facts, examples, definitions, and quotations from others that illustrate, amplify, clarify, and provide evidence for your major ideas. A speech is not just a statement of your major ideas. If they were, most speeches would be very short indeed! The bulk of what you say in a speech consists of supporting material.

The examples, facts, definitions, and other support you choose will affect your ability to keep your audience interested. Here, as elsewhere in preparing your speech, the importance of being an audience-centered speaker cannot be overemphasized. An old saying has it that an ounce of illustration is worth a ton of talk. If a speech is boring, it is usually because the speaker has not chosen supporting material that is relevant or interesting to the audience.

What makes supporting material interesting? It should be personal and concrete, and it should appeal to your listeners' senses. Personal stories or examples hold interest. Information that relates to your listeners' lives will also hold their attention. If your first speech is to introduce yourself to the class, your supporting material will undoubtedly consist mainly of personal examples.

Concreteness is a second characteristic of supporting material that will hold the attention of your audience. Concrete supporting material is more interesting to most people than abstract ideas. Vivid descriptions of things that are tangible allow your audience to visualize what you are talking about. In addition, stories or illustrations that can be visualized or seen in the mind's eye help hold interest.

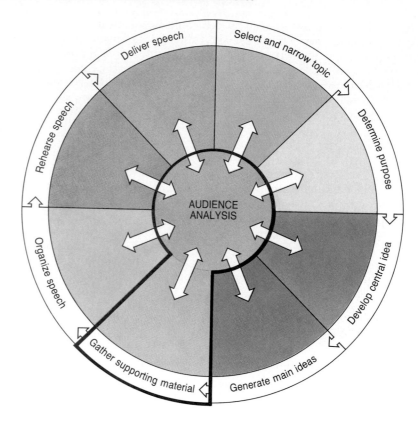

FIGURE 2.7

Like other aspects of preparing and presenting a speech, supporting material should be selected with the audience in mind.

Supporting material can appeal to other senses besides sight, including touch, hearing, smell, and taste. The more senses you can trigger with words, the more interesting your talk will be. In a speech about yourself, you may want to describe an interesting job that you held or a unique place that you visited. Describe the job or place with words that appeal to your listeners' senses. If they had your experience, what would they have seen, heard, touched, tasted, or smelled? Personal, concrete illustrations with "sense appeal" will usually capture an audience's interest and hold its attention. Descriptions such as "rough, splintery surface of weather-beaten wood" or "the sweet, cool, refreshing flavor of cherry jello" evoke sensory images. We will examine the various types of supporting material in Chapter 11.

Organize Your Speech

As a wise person once said, "If effort is organized, accomplishment follows." While generating your ideas for the speech, you actually began the task of organizing your message. After additional research, you need to give a final shape to your organization: As Figure 2.8 suggests, you need to develop an outline of your talk.

A clearly and logically structured speech helps your audience remember what you say. A well-organized message provides another bonus; it helps you feel more in control of your speech, and greater control will help you feel more comfortable while delivering your message.

Every speech has three major divisions: the introduction, the body, and the conclusion. The introduction helps capture attention, serves as an overview of the speech, and provides your audience with a reason to listen to you. The body presents the main content of your speech. The conclusion summarizes your key ideas. You may have heard this advice on how to organize your speech: tell them what you're going to tell them (the introduction), tell them (the body of the speech), and tell them what you told them (the conclusion).

Since your introduction previews your speech and your conclusion summarizes it, most speech teachers recommend that you prepare your introduction and conclusion after you have carefully organized the body of your talk. If you have already generated your major ideas by divisions, reasons, or steps, you are well on your way to developing an outline. Your major ideas should be indicated by Roman numerals. Use capital letters for your supporting points. Use Arabic numerals if you need to subdivide your ideas further. You should *not* write your speech word for word. If you do, your speech will sound silted and unnatural. It may be useful, however, for you to use brief notes—written cues on note cards—instead of a complete manuscript.

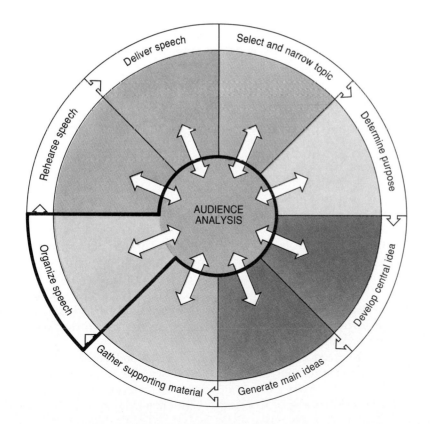

FIGURE 2.8

Every speech includes three main parts: introduction, body, and conclusion.

You may want to look in Chapters 8 and 9 for sample outlines and approaches to organizing a message. Chapter 10 provides more detailed suggestions for beginning and ending your speech. For your first speech, you may want to adapt the following outline format to your talk.

Topic: Could be assigned by your instructor, or you may need to select your own topic

General Purpose: To inform, persuade, or entertain—your instructor will probably assign your general purpose

Specific Purpose: A clear statement indicating what your audience should be able to do after hearing your speech

Central Idea Sentence: A one-sentence summary of your talk

Introduction: Attention-catching opening line:

Preview of major ideas:

Tell your audience why they should listen to you:

Body:

  I. Major Idea:

      A. Supporting idea:

      B. Supporting idea:

 II. Major Idea:

      A. Supporting idea:

      B. Supporting idea:

III. Major Idea:

      A. Supporting idea:

      B. Supporting idea:

Conclusion: Summarize major ideas

Once you are comfortable with the structure of your talk, you are ready to rehearse.

Rehearse Your Speech

Remember the joke in which one man asks another, "How do you get to Carnegie Hall?" The answer: "Practice, man, practice." The joke may be older than Carnegie Hall itself, but it is still good advice to all beginners, including novice speakers. A speech is a performance. As with any stage presentation, be it music, dance, or theater, you need to rehearse. A sage once said, "The best rule for talking is the one carpenters use: Measure twice, saw once." Rehearsing your speech, the step highlighted in Figure 2.9, is a way to measure your message so that you get it right when you present it to your audience.

The best way to practice is to rehearse your speech aloud, standing just as you will when you deliver it to your audience. As you rehearse, try to be comfortable with the way you phrase your ideas, but don't try to memorize your talk. In fact, if you have rehearsed your speech so many times that you are using exactly the

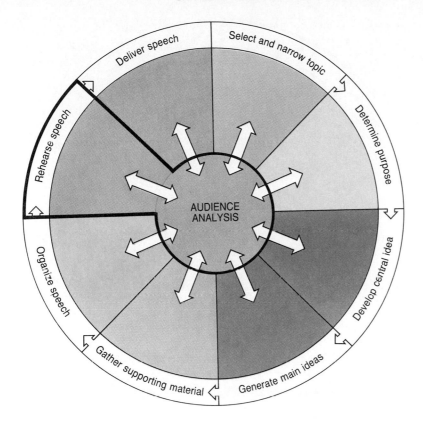

FIGURE 2.9

Visualize your audience when you rehearse your speech.

same words every time, you have rehearsed long enough. Rehearse just enough so that you can discuss your ideas and supporting material without leaving out major parts of your speech. It is all right to use notes, but most speech instructors will limit the number of notes you may use.

As you practice, seek as much eye contact with your audience as you can. Also be certain to speak loudly enough for all in the room to hear. If you are not sure what to do with your hands when you rehearse, just keep them at your side. Focus on your message, rather than worrying about how to gesture. Avoid jingling change with your hand in your pocket or using other gestures that could distract your audience. If you practice your speech as if you were actually delivering it, you will be a more effective speaker when you talk to the audience.

Deliver Your Speech

The time has come, and you're ready to present your speech to your audience. As Figure 2.10 illustrates, delivery is the final step in the preparation process. When you are introduced, walk calmly and confidently to the front of the room, establish eye contact with your audience, smile naturally, and deliver your opening sentence.

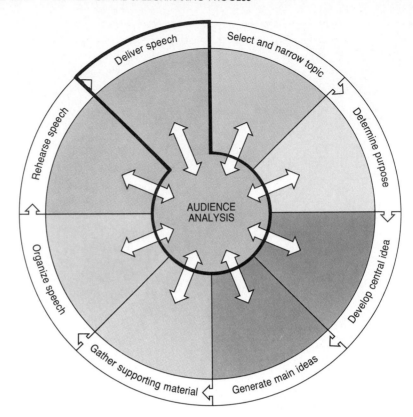

FIGURE 2.10

An effective public speaker monitors the audience during the delivery of the speech; remain audience-centered from start to finish.

Refer to your notes as you need to, and concentrate on your message and your audience. Your goal should be to deliver your speech in a conversational style in which you establish rapport with your listeners. This final delivery should not be the first time you have heard the speech. You should have mastered your speech sufficiently to know you can speak within the time limits. Deliver your speech just as you rehearsed it before your imaginary audience: Establish eye contact early and often, speak loudly enough to be heard, use some natural variation in pitch, and don't be overly concerned about gestures. And finally, remember the advice of columnist Ann Landers: "Be sincere, be brief, and be seated."

MANAGING SPEECH ANXIETY

One of the most anxiety-producing sentences in the English language is, "And it gives me great pleasure to introduce our speaker for this afternoon," followed by your name.

The nervousness that you may feel before delivering a speech is shared by most people. A recent survey found that fear of speaking publicly ranks as the number one fear of most people.[1] Forty-one percent reported public speaking as their most significant fear; fear of death ranked only sixth!

Though almost everyone worries about communication to some degree, studies suggest that about 20 percent of college students are highly apprehensive about communicating with others.[2] If you feel that you are more nervous than most people, some principles can help. Even if your anxiety is not acute, you can benefit by some positive approaches that will allow your nervousness to work *for* you. First, we'll help you manage your anxiety by helping you understand it. Knowledge is power. Second, we will make specific suggestions that will help you speak with greater comfort and less anxiety.

Understanding Speech Anxiety

What causes you to feel nervous about speaking in public? Why do your hands shake and your knees quiver? Why does your voice go up an octave? Why are there butterflies in your stomach? When you are nervous, you may notice that your breathing rate changes, and you may perspire more. What is happening to you? Believe it or not, your brain is signaling your body to help you with a difficult task.

Your view of the speaking assignment, your self-image, and your self-esteem interact to create anxiety. You want to do well, but you are not sure you can or will. Presented with this conflict, your body responds by increasing your breathing rate, pumping more adrenalin, and causing more blood to rush through your veins. In short, you have more energy to deal with the conflict you are facing. To put it more technically, you are experiencing physiological changes because of your psychological state. Increased energy and other physical changes explain why you may have a more rapid heartbeat, shaking knees and hands, a quivering voice, and increased perspiration. You may experience butterflies in your stomach because of changes in your digestive system. Due to your discomfort, you may also make less eye contact with your audience, use more vocalized pauses ("Um," "Ah," "You know"), and speak too rapidly. Though you see these occurences as hindrances, your body is simply trying to help you with the task at hand. To help you further understand and channel the fear you experience, consider the following observations.

1. *You are going to feel more nervous than you look.* When he finished his speech, Daryl sank into his seat and muttered, "Ugh, was I shaky up there! Did you see how nervous I was?"

"Nervous? You were nervous?" asked Larry, surprised. "You looked pretty calm to me."

You should realize that you are not going to seem as nervous as you feel. If you worry that you are going to appear nervous to others, you may, in fact, increase your anxiety. Your body will exhibit more physical changes to deal with your self-induced state of anxiety.

2. *Almost every speaker experiences some degree of nervousness.* President Kennedy was noted for his superb public speaking skills. When he spoke, he seemed perfectly at ease. Former Prime Minister Winston Churchill was also hailed as one of this century's great orators. Amazingly, both Kennedy and Churchill were extremely

fearful of speaking in public. Almost everyone experiences some anxiety when speaking. It is unrealistic to try to eliminate speech anxiety. Instead, your goal should be to manage your nervousness so that it does not create so much internal noise that it keeps you from speaking effectively.

3. *Anxiety can be useful.* Extra adrenalin, increased blood flow, and other physical changes caused by anxiety improve your energy level, and this enables you to function better than you might otherwise. Your heightened state of readiness can help you speak better. Speech anxiety rarely keeps a speaker from delivering a speech. Don't let your initial fear convince you that you cannot possibly give a speech.

Suggestions for Managing Speech Anxiety

"What can I do to help me feel less nervous?" thought Joan, as she sat at her desk worrying about her first speech assignment. Although understanding the causes of your anxiety may give you some insight, you may want more specific advice to help you cope. Here are some suggestions.

Know Your Audience   A key theme throughout this text is to know to whom you are speaking and to learn as much about your audience as you can. The more you can anticipate the kind of reaction your listeners will have to your speech, the more comfortable you will be in shaping your message. Chapter 4 will provide a detailed approach to analyzing and adapting to your audience. Be audience-centered.

Be Prepared   The following formula will apply to most speaking situations you experience: The better prepared you are for the speech, the less anxiety you will experience. The more prepared you are, the more comfortable you will feel when you actually deliver your speech. Being prepared means that you have researched your topic, you have organized your material, and you have practiced your speech several times before you deliver it.

Select an Appropriate Topic   In the chapters ahead, we will offer more detailed guidance about how to select a topic. You will feel less nervous if you talk about something with which you are familiar or have some personal experience. Your comfort with the subject of your speech will be reflected in your delivery.

Re-create the Speech Environment When You Rehearse   When you rehearse your speech, try to imagine that you are giving the speech to the audience you will actually address. Stand up. Imagine what the room looks like. What will you be wearing? Practice rising from your seat, walking to the front of the room, and beginning your speech. Practice aloud, rather than just saying the speech to yourself. A realistic rehearsal will increase your confidence when your moment to speak arrives.

Know Your Introduction and Your Conclusion   You are likely to feel the most anxious during the opening moments of your speech. Therefore, it is a good idea to have a clear idea of how you will start your speech. We aren't suggesting a word-for-word memorization of your introduction, but you should have it well in mind. Being familiar with your introduction will help you feel more comfortable about the entire speech.

If you know how you will end your speech, you will have safe harbor in case you lose your place. If you need to end your speech prematurely, a well-delivered conclusion can permit you to make a graceful exit.

Visualize Your Success Studies suggest that one of the best ways to control your anxiety is to imagine a scene in which you exhibit skill and comfort as a public speaker.[3] As you imagine giving your speech, picture yourself walking confidently to the front and delivering your well-prepared opening remarks. Visualize yourself giving the entire speech as a controlled, confident speaker. Imagine yourself calm and in command.

Be Organized You will be more comfortable delivering a speech that is logically coherent than one that is disorganized and difficult to follow. Transitional phrases and summaries help you present a well-structured, easy-to-understand message.

Use Deep Breathing Techniques One of the symptoms of your nervousness is a change in your breathing and heart rates. Nervous speakers tend to take short, shallow breaths. To help break the anxiety-induced breathing pattern, consider taking a few slow deep breaths before you rise to speak. No one will be able to detect that you are taking deep breaths if you just slowly inhale and exhale from your seat before your speech begins. Besides breathing deeply, try to relax your entire body. Use unobtrusive, deep, slow breathing, coupled with the visualization just mentioned, to help you relax.

Act Calm to Feel Calm Evidence suggests that you can bring on certain emotions by behaving as if you were feeling those emotions. If you wish to feel greater calmness, behave in a calm way. Give yourself extra time to arrive at your speaking destination so you won't have to rush around hurriedly to find the right building or room. As you are waiting to be introduced, try not to fidget. Walk to the front of your audience as though you were calm and collected. Before you present your opening sentence, take a moment to look at your audience. Look for a calm, supportive, friendly face. Think calm and act calm to feel calm.

Focus on Your Message Rather than Your Fear The more you think that you are anxious about speaking, the more you will increase your level of anxiety. Think about what you are going to say instead. In the few minutes before you address your listeners, mentally review your major ideas, your introduction, and your conclusion. Focus on your ideas rather than on your fear.

Seek Speaking Opportunities The more experience you gain as a public speaker, the less nervous you will feel. As you develop a track record of successfully delivering speeches, you will have more confidence. Success breeds confidence. A course in public speaking is designed to give you opportunities to enhance both your confidence and your skill by frequent practice.

RECAP

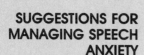

SUGGESTIONS FOR MANAGING SPEECH ANXIETY

Things to Do	Things Not to Do
Prepare	Just try to "wing it"
Select a topic you are interested in or know something about	Talk about something unfamiliar
Learn as much as possible about your audience; be audience-centered	Make little effort to learn who the audience is
Rehearse aloud	Spend little time rehearsing
Be familiar with how you begin and end the speech	Be unfamiliar with your introduction and uncertain how your speech will end
Visualize being successful	Imagine that you will fail
Be organized	Have a poorly organized message
Take deep breaths to relax	Make no attempt to relax
Behave calmly before the speech begins	Arrive late, frantic and frenzied
Focus on the message	Focus on your fear
Seek other speaking opportunities to gain experience and confidence	Avoid all speaking opportunities

SUMMARY   In this chapter, we presented an overview of the entire process of delivering a speech. In the following chapters, we will discuss each phase of speechmaking in greater detail than here. But each step will make more sense now that you have had an overall look at the process.

As part of that overview, we pointed out that effective speakers have several characteristics. Effective speakers

Have good ideas	Deliver the message well
Organize their ideas	Research the speech in search of supporting material
Choose the right words	Are ethical

To help you prepare for an early speaking assignment, we introduced the steps involved in presenting a speech. As our model of public speaking proposes, an effective speaker keeps the audience as the central focus at each stage of the speech preparation and delivery process.

One of the major concerns of most beginning public speakers is the nervousness that they feel, sometimes when just thinking about giving a speech. Don't be surprised if you feel more nervous than you look to others. Realize that almost every speaker experiences some nervousness and that some anxiety can actually be useful. We offered several specific suggestions to help you manage your apprehension:

Know your audience.	Re-create in your imagination the speech
Be prepared.	environment when you rehearse.
Select an appropriate topic.	Know your introduction and your conclusion.

Visualize your success.   Act calm to feel calm.
Be organized.   Focus on your message rather than your fear.
Use deep breathing techniques.   Seek speaking opportunities.

QUESTIONS FOR
DISCUSSION AND
REVIEW

1. What are the characteristics of an effective public speaker?
2. What are the most annoying characteristics of an ineffective public speaker?
3. Why is audience analysis at the center of the public speaking model presented in this chapter?
4. What are the tasks involved in preparing and presenting a speech?
5. Why do people become nervous before they speak?
6. How can a person manage speech anxiety?

SUGGESTED ACTIVITIES

1. Interview someone who gives public presentations as part of his or her job (minister, politician, lawyer, business person, etc.). Ask what steps the person follows in preparing a speech.
2. Whom would you nominate as one of the outstanding public speakers in the country? Write a brief paper noting how your nominee exemplifies the six characteristics of an effective speaker discussed in this chapter.
3. Write one informative and one persuasive specific speech purpose for each of the following topics:

   Nuclear power plants   Caffeine   Public speaking
   Political parties   Your school

4. For the following central idea sentences, identify possible major divisions in the speech according to one of these questions:

   Does the central idea have logical *divisions*?
   Can you think of several *reasons* why the central idea is true?
   Can you support the central idea with a series of *steps*?

   The conflict in the Persian Gulf had a long history.
   The method of choosing a president in the United States is flawed.
   Any of several diets could help you lose weight.
   The 65-mile-per-hour speed limit is a bad idea.
   Our national parks need more resources to maintain their beauty.
   Cable TV has an interesting history.
   IQ can be measured in several ways.
   There are several ways of following a stress-free lifestyle.

5. Deliver a three- to five-minute speech introducing yourself to the class. Use the model presented in this chapter to help you prepare your talk.
6. Identify at least three suggestions for helping you manage your speech anxiety. Write a brief paragraph stating why you think those techniques will be helpful to you. Implement the techniques.

3
Listening to Others

OBJECTIVES

After studying this chapter, you should be able to

1. Identify the stages in the listening process
2. Describe the four types of listening
3. List and describe six barriers to effective listening
4. Discuss strategies to become a better listener
5. Identify suggestions for improving your note-taking skill

It takes two to speak the truth—one to speak and another to hear.
(Missouri State Capitol, Jefferson City, Missouri.)

HENRY DAVID THOREAU

You are sitting in your geography class on a Friday afternoon. It's a beautiful day. You slump into your seat, open your notebook, and prepare to take notes on the lecture. As the professor talks about an upcoming assignment, you begin to think about how you are going to spend your Saturday. One thought leads to another as you mentally plan your weekend. Suddenly you hear your professor say, "You will be expected to know the principles I've just reviewed on Monday's test." What principles? What test? Since you were present in class, you heard the professor's lecture, but you're not sure what was said.

You hear over one billion words each year. Words surround you. Yet how much information do you retain? In this chapter, we are going to focus on improving your listening skill. If you apply the principles and suggestions we offer, we believe that you will be not only a better listener but also a better public speaker. You will understand what often causes a person to stop listening to a speaker.

Improving your listening skill has other virtues besides just increasing your ability to understand and deliver speeches. In a democratic society, you make decisions about political leaders and the important issues of the day based on your ability to listen accurately to others. Improved listening skills can also enhance your one-on-one interpersonal listening. In this chapter, we will discuss how you listen, types of listening, and the barriers and pitfalls that keep you and your audience from listening well. Finally, we will make some suggestions for improving your listening and note-taking skills.

STAGES IN LISTENING

Listening is not the same as hearing. Hearing is a physiological process. You hear sounds when sound waves strike the eardrums and cause them to vibrate. These vibrations cause the hammer, anvil, and stirrup of the middle ear to vibrate too,

Hearing the professor's lecture is not the same as listening. (*Junebug Clark/Photo Researchers, Inc.*)

thereby producing sound. Eventually the vibrations reach the auditory nerve, which turns the vibrations into electrical energy. This energy ultimately reaches your brain.

You *heard* your geography professor. Sound waves became electrical energy that passed to your brain. However, you cannot recall a thing your professor said because you weren't *listening*. You didn't decode the message.

When we listen, we hear the words and try to make sense out of what we hear. Listening involves the processes of *selecting*, *attending*, *understanding*, and *remembering*. Let us look at each of these four stages of the listening process in greater detail.

Selecting

Sounds constantly surround you. Stop reading this book for a moment and take note of the sounds you hear. Do you hear the whir of an air conditioner or furnace, the wind, a ticking clock, voices, a car, train, or plane? You have the ability to **select** what you will listen to. Instead of listening to the noises about you, you can read this book and concentrate on the ideas in it, or you can focus on your own thoughts. As you deliver your speech to an audience, keep in mind that your potential listeners have the same choice. Your job as a speaker is to motivate them to select *your* message.

Attending

Attention is the sequel to selecting. When you select a sound you attend to it; you focus on it. Even though you may pay attention to a sound for only a fraction of a second, your mind must be focused on it for listening to occur. One of your key challenges as a public speaker will be to capture and hold the attention of your audience. What helps you or your audience listen to a message? The following factors will make an audience pay attention: (1) *activity* or *movement*, whether physical movement by you or movement you describe in a story or illustration; (2) something that is *real* and *concrete*, as opposed to something that is vague and abstract; (3) something *close* to the audience that they can identify with; (4) something *familiar* to the audience; (5) something *new* or *different* that audience members have not seen or heard before; (6) a *story* or an illustration that creates *suspense* because the outcome is not known; (7) *conflict*; (8) *humor*; and (9) something *vital* to the audience's wellbeing.[1]

▼
attention
Focusing on something.

Understanding

As you select and attend to a sound, you try to make sense out of what you hear. **Understanding** is the process of assigning meaning to the stimuli we attend to.

Though there is no single theory that explains how we are able to make sense of our world, we do know that we understand what we hear by relating it to

▼
understanding
Assigning meaning to stimuli to which we attend.

One of the key challenges of a public speaker is to capture and hold the attention of the audience.
(*Spencer Grant/Stock, Boston*)

something we have already seen or heard. If you are talking about oxymorons (a combination of contradictory words in the same phrase) and your audience does not know what an oxymoron is, they probably won't understand you. Your job as a speaker is to make sure that your audience has the knowledge to understand what you are saying.

Remembering

How do you know whether someone listened to you or not? Most listening experts believe that you can find out if someone has listened to you only by testing whether they can **remember** what they heard. Your geography professor determines how well you understand geography by testing you on the content of his or her lecture. But intentionally or not, the professor is also testing your listening skill as well as your knowledge of geography.

You have both a *short-term memory* and a *long-term memory*. You use short-term memory for most of the information you come across. But you won't remember it long. For example, what were you doing August 8, 1985? You probably could have answered on August 9, one day later, but unless something important happened on August 8 or you linked the date with some other experience, it is unlikely that you could retrieve the information now. Long-term memory is facilitated by events and information that are important to us. It is also the result of repeated exposure to information. To help people remember your message, you will need to build in redundancy. When learning the basics of written composition, you were undoubtedly taught to avoid repeating yourself. Oral communication, however, needs to be more redundant. An introductory statement announcing your major ideas, a clear presentation of your major points, and a summary of your key thoughts are ways of building redundancy into your message to help your audience remember it. Also, audience members will be more likely to remember your message if you can relate it to their interests.

RECAP

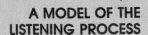

| **A MODEL OF THE LISTENING PROCESS** | **Selecting** from internal and external sources
Attending to a specific message
Understanding the message; making sense out of what you hear
Remembering the message |

TYPES OF LISTENING

If you are a typical student, you spend over 80 percent of your day involved in activities related to communication. Of that time, you spend about 11 percent writing, 15 percent reading, 32 percent speaking, and at least 42 percent listening.[2] These statistics suggest the importance of developing good listening skills. You spend a lot of time listening.

But why do you listen? We will discuss four distinct reasons: (1) *listening for pleasure*, (2) *listening to evaluate*, (3) *listening to empathize*, and (4) *listening to gain information*. Understanding the various purposes for listening can help you improve your skills in different situations.

Listening for Pleasure

Did you tune in your car radio, watch a talk show on TV, go to a movie, or listen to your stereo today? In each of these situations, your chief purpose is to listen for pleasure or entertainment. You will not be tested on "I Love Lucy" reruns. Nor will you be asked to remember each song you heard on the radio this afternoon. Probably, you were not concerned to remember or evaluate what you heard in any of these situations. You just wanted to relax and enjoy yourself.

One reason we spend so much of our time listening is that we want to enjoy ourselves. Information presented mainly for your listening pleasure incorporates many of the attention-grabbing factors we identified a little earlier. If you analyze the presentations of those that give you pleasure when you listen, you will learn how to improve your own presentations. How do they capture and hold your attention? What do they do? Why do you find the presentation of their material enjoyable? We are not suggesting that your speeches should be delivered the same way as Joan Rivers or Jay Leno delivers a comedy routine. You can, however, observe how their use of novelty, familiar references, and other attention-getting devices keep you interested in their messages.

When you hear a politician speak, you evaluate whether the information is reliable, true, or useful.
(Owen Franken/Stock, Boston)

Listening to Evaluate

When you evaluate a message, you are making a judgment about its content. You are interested in whether the information is reliable, true, or useful. For example, when you hear a national politician proclaim that his approach to solving the federal deficit will result in no new taxes, you wince. You don't believe him, and you are critical of his plan.

When evaluating a speech, you may become so critical of the message that you can miss a key point the speaker is making. In such instances, you must be able to juggle two very difficult tasks; you must be able to make judgments as well as understand and recall the information you are hearing. Our point is this: When you are listening to a message and also evaluating it, you have to work harder than at other times to understand the speaker's message. Your biases and judgments act as noise, sometimes causing you to misunderstand the intended meaning of the message.

Remember that when you are speaking, your audience will be judging *you* and *your message*. Therefore, you should make sure you have enough evidence to support your ideas and sound logic to support your conclusions.

Listening to Empathize

It was one of those days. You were late for your first class because you overslept and then couldn't find a parking place. Your English professor returned your term paper and gave you a D because you didn't type it; you didn't even realize it had to be typed. When you got home this evening, you realized you needed another book from the library to complete your history assignment. After a hassle-filled day, you certainly didn't feel like driving the 5 miles back to campus just for one book. Finally, your roommate came home and you began telling him about your troubles. After a ten-minute recitation of all of your woes, you felt slightly better; your roommate is a good listener. You didn't need any advice, wisdom, or information, just someone who would understand the kind of day you had. Your roommate performed an important service; he just listened and tried to understand your feelings of frustration.

Listening to empathize with another takes place mainly in interpersonal contexts. When you listen to empathize, you listen in an effort to understand the feelings of another. Empathizing with someone serves an important therapeutic function. You are not listening to judge that person's behavior or even to recall at a later time all that was said. Rather, you listen because the process of sharing is a soothing one for the person who is speaking. Telling others about hassles can often restore a sense of balance and perspective to problems.

Listening to Gain Information

Since elementary school, you have been in listening situations in which someone wanted you to learn something. As soon as you entered kindergarten, adults began bombarding you with bits of information to help you become "educated."

Now that you are an adult, you too may want to transmit information to others. In that case, one of your jobs as a public speaker is to help your listeners gain information. You can do that by identifying, organizing, and delivering it to them. If you understand the principles of good listening, we think you can also be a better public speaker. You can anticipate and help audience members avoid some of the pitfalls of poor listeners.

RECAP

TYPES OF LISTENING	Listening Type	Description	Example
	Listening for pleasure	Seeking enjoyment	Listening to music or TV
	Listening to evaluate	Judging the content of a message	Listening critically to a political speech
	Listening to empathize	Trying to understand the feelings and emotions of another person	Listening to a family member describe a hassle-filled day
	Listening to gain information	Trying to comprehend the content of a message	Listening to a class lecture

BARRIERS TO EFFECTIVE LISTENING

Are you a good listener? Considerable evidence suggests that your listening skills could be improved. Within twenty-four hours after listening to a lecture or speech, you will only recall about 50 percent of the message. Forty-eight hours later, you are above average if you remember more than 25 percent of the message. (And in a recent survey of adult listeners, only 15 percent reported that they were above-average listeners!)

A psychology professor tested listening habits in his classroom with his students.[3] The professor dedicated his life to teaching and had worked hard to prepare interesting lectures, yet he found his students sitting through his talks with glassy-eyed expressions. Wanting to learn what was wrong, he conducted an experiment to gauge how well his students were listening. He also wanted to know what was on their minds if they were not focusing on psychology. In the middle of a lecture, he would, without warning, fire a blank from a gun and ask his students to record their thoughts at the instant they heard the shot. The professor's findings provide valuable insights into the listening habits of his college students. Here is what he found:

20 percent were pursuing erotic thoughts or sexual fantasies.

20 percent were reminiscing about something (they weren't sure what they were thinking about).

20 percent were worrying about something or thinking about lunch.

8 percent reported they were pursuing religious thoughts.

20 percent said they were listening.

12 percent were able to recall what the professor was talking about when the gun fired.

Why don't we always listen efficiently? As we examine some of the specific barriers to effective listening, you will learn how to manage listening problems, as well as discover the ways a speaker can overcome the barriers.

Prematurely Rejecting a Topic

Have you ever been told to listen to a speech that you really didn't want to? If you went to the speech grudgingly, certain that there was nothing the speaker could say that would interest you, you probably didn't listen well. Most of us have not given our full attention to a speech because we decided beforehand that it was going to bore us.

As a public speaker, you have to get your listeners to believe that your speech will be valuable to them. Skilled public speakers use their opening statements to grab the audience's attention. As a listener, you should extend to a public speaker the same courtesy you would grant any person talking to you. You would pay attention to what is said. Second, you should try to keep an open mind. Almost every speech will tell you something new that may prove valuable some day.

Suffering From Information Overload

As we mentioned earlier, you spend a large part of each day listening. That's good news and bad news. The good news is that because you listen a lot, you have the potential of becoming a very effective listener. The bad news is that most of us don't do that. Instead, we get tired of listening because we hear so much information that we "tune out."

As a public speaker, you need to deliver a message that is clear and easy to understand. As we observed earlier, you will have to build redundancy into your message so that if listeners miss an idea the first time you present it, perhaps they will catch it during your concluding remarks.

As a listener, you need to realize that listening is hard work. Effective listening requires concentration and discrimination. You have to be able to decide on what is important in a speech and focus on that. For example, in a talk advocating gun control, you will want to focus on the reasons for having controls and the objections to those controls.

Thinking About Personal Concerns

Your own thoughts are among the biggest competitors for your attention when you are a member of an audience. Most of us would rather listen to our own inner speech than to the message of a public speaker. As the psychology professor with the gun found, sex, lunch, worries, and just daydreaming are major distractions for the majority of listeners.

Your first task as a listener is to recognize when your own agenda is keeping you from listening to someone. You then need to focus on the speaker's message. Later in this chapter, we will offer some suggestions for improving your listening skill when you find your attention flagging. As an audience-centered public speaker, you need to ensure that your message is attention-maintaining so that your listeners don't tune you out.

Succumbing to Outside Distractions

While sitting in class, you notice a flickering fluorescent light toward the front of the room. Two of your classmates behind you are swapping stories about their favorite soap opera plots. Out the window you see a varsity hero struggling to break into his car to retrieve the keys he left in the ignition. As your history professor drones on about the Bay of Pigs invasion, you find it difficult to focus attention on his lecture. Most of us don't listen well when there are physical distractions that compete with the speaker's lecture.

As a speaker, try to control the physical arrangements of the speaking situation before you begin your speech. Do the best you can to reduce or eliminate distractions (close windows and window shades to limit sight and sound to the room in which you are speaking; turn off blinking fluorescent lights if you can; try to discourage whispering in the audience). Try to empathize with your listeners. Check out the room ahead of time, sit where your audience will be seated, and look for possible distractions. Do your best, given the resources and time available, to minimize the distractions.

As a listener, you too will need to do your best to control the listening situation. If you have to, move to another seat. If the speaker has failed to monitor the listening environment, you may need to close the blinds, turn up the heat, turn off the lights, close the door, or do whatever is necessary to enhance your listening potential.

Judging Too Quickly

Your buddy is a staunch Democrat. He rarely credits a Republican with any useful ideas. So it's not surprising that when the Republican governor from your state makes a major televised speech outlining suggestions for improving the state's sagging economy, your friend finds the presentation ludicrous. As the speech is broadcast, your buddy constantly argues against each suggestion, mumbling something about Republicans, Iran, and crooks. The next day he is surprised to see editorials in the press praising the governor's speech. "Did they hear the same speech I did?" your friend wonders. Yes, they heard the same speech, but they listened differently. When you prejudge a message, your ability to understand it decreases.

Similarly, you need to guard against too readily accepting something someone says just because you like the way the person looks, sounds, or dresses. For example, Tex believes that anyone with a Texas drawl must be an honest person. Such positive prejudices can also inhibit your ability to listen accurately to a message.

As a listener, you need to guard against becoming so critical of the message that you don't listen to it or so impressed that you decide *too quickly* that the speaker is trustworthy.

When addressing an audience that may be critical or hostile toward your message, use arguments and evidence that your listeners will find credible. Strong emotional appeals will be less successful than careful language, sound reasoning, and convincing evidence.

Wasting Speech Rate and Thought Rate Differences

Ralph Nichols, a pioneer in listening research and training, has identified a listening problem that centers on the way you process the words you hear.[4] Generally, most people talk at a rate of 125 words a minute. However, you have the ability to listen to up to 700 words a minute. Some studies suggest that you may even be able to listen to 1200 words a minute. Regardless of exact numbers, you have the ability to process words much faster than you generally need to. The problem is that the difference between hearing words at about 125 words a minute and processing them at over 700 words a minute gives you time to ignore a speaker periodically. Eventually, you stop listening. Your "extra" time allows you to daydream and drift from the message.

Nichols suggests that the different rates of speech and thought need not be a listening liability. Instead of drifting away from the speech, you can enhance your listening effectiveness by mentally summarizing what the speaker is saying from time to time.

As a speaker, you need to be aware of your listeners' tendency to stop paying attention. If they can process your message much faster than you can say it, you need to build in message redundancy, be well organized, and make your major ideas clear. We will make several suggestions for developing a clear message when we discuss approaches to informative speaking in Chapter 14.

RECAP

BARRIERS TO EFFECTIVE LISTENING	**Barrier:**	**As a listener, you should:**	**As a speaker, you should:**
	1. Prematurely rejecting a topic	Listen for information that meets your needs.	State early in your speech why your listeners should pay attention to what you have to say.
	2. Suffering from information overload	Concentrate harder on the message; identify the most important parts of the message.	Develop a message that is clear and easy to understand. Build in redundancy.
	3. Thinking about personal concerns	Focus on the speaker's message rather than on your own self-talk.	Present a speech that is adapted to the interests of your audience. Speak to their needs so that they won't turn to their own thoughts.
	4. Succumbing to outside distractions	Aggressively attempt to control the listening environment.	Monitor the physical arrangements before you begin your speech. Take action by doing such things as closing the shades if there are distractions outside or turning up the air conditioner if it's too warm.
	5. Judging too quickly	Focus on the message, not the messenger.	Use credible evidence to support your conclusions.
	6. Wasting speech rate and thought rate differences	Mentally summarize the speaker's message while you listen.	Be aware that your audience has a tendency to lose contact with your message. Build in redundancy. Present a well-organized message. Maintain your audience's attention throughout your speech.

HOW TO LISTEN EFFECTIVELY

Fortunately, the barriers to good listening can be overcome. We have already provided a few clues for effective listening; we will now offer some more specific suggestions for improving your listening skills.

Adapt to the Speaker

Adapt to the Speaker's Delivery   Good listeners focus on a speaker's message, not his or her style. Thus, to be a good listener, you will have to adapt to the particular idiosyncrasies some speakers have. You will have to ignore or overlook a speaker's tendency to mumble, speak in a monotone, or fail to make eye contact. Perhaps more difficult still, you may even have to forgive a speaker's lack of clarity or coherence. Rather than mentally criticizing an unpolished speaker, you may need to be sympathetic and try harder to concentrate on the message. Good listeners focus on the message, not the messenger.

But poor speakers are not the only challenge to good listening. You also need to guard against glib, well-polished speakers. Just because a speaker may have an attractive style of delivery does not necessarily mean that a speaker's message is credible. Delivery can distract from the message. Don't let a smooth-talking salesperson convince you to buy something only because of the polish of the presentation. Respond to the message content rather than the speaker's style.

Listen with Your Eyes as Well as Your Ears   Even though we have cautioned you against letting a speaker's style of delivery distract you, don't totally ignore a speaker's body language. Nonverbal clues play a major role in communicating a speaker's message. One expert has estimated that as much as 93 percent of the emotional content of a speech is conveyed by nonverbal clues. For example, facial expressions help identify the emotions being communicated; a speaker's posture and gestures can reinforce the intensity of his or her emotion.[5] The face may express anger, while gestures and other bodily movements communicate intense rage. If you have trouble understanding a speaker, either because he or she speaks too softly or in an unfamiliar dialect, get close enough so that you can see the speaker's mouth. A good view of a speaker can increase your level of attention and improve your understanding.

Avoid Overreacting Emotionally to a Message   Heightened emotions can affect your ability to understand a message. If you become angered at a word or phrase a speaker uses, your listening comprehension decreases. Because of our differing cultural backgrounds, religious convictions, and political views, we may become emotionally aroused by certain words. Words that connote negative opinions about a person's ethnic origin, nationality, or religious views can trigger strong emotions. Cursing and obscene language are red flags for some listeners.

Ralph Nichols tells the story of how a particular word affects his own listening ability.[6] When he was on the debating team in college, one of his opponents spoke disparagingly about "niggers" immigrating to the United States. Nichols's debating partner was a black student who was outraged by the racial slur. In response, he delivered a brilliant, but irrelevant, speech denouncing the bigoted remark. Nichols reports that to this day, all someone has to do is use the word *nigger* in a conversation and he becomes highly emotional and unable to listen effectively.

When someone uses a word or phrase that you find offensive, you need to overcome your repugnance and continue to listen. You should not allow the speaker's language to close down your mind. Someday you may find yourself in opposition to the offending ideas and to combat them effectively, you will need to know what they consist of.

As a speaker, you need to monitor your language so that you do not interfere with your communication objective. Careful analysis of your audience will help you avoid alienating your listeners with red-flag words or phrases.

Adapt to the Message

Avoid Reaching the Wrong Conclusion   "Not another speech about religion," you groan to yourself as your classmate, Frank Fuller, a divinity student, gets up to speak. "He's always preaching to us rather than simply giving an informative speech." As Fuller begins his slide lecture, you slump down in your seat, prepared to be bored and bothered. Sure enough, his opening line is "The Bible: It's not what you think!" It's about halfway through the speech before you start listening to Fuller and realize that he is presenting some fascinating historical evidence connected with Noah's Ark. He's not trying to convert you; he's just describing some of the archaeological evidence related to the Bible. At the end of the speech, your classmates give him a hearty round of applause. It's one of the best talks presented during the semester. Now you're sorry you missed the first part of the speech.

Don't jump prematurely to conclusions. Give a speaker time to develop and support his or her main point before you decide whether you agree or disagree or think the message has any value. As we've already noted, if you mentally criticize a speaker's style or message, your listening efficiency will decline. You may miss some useful and interesting ideas.

Be a Selfish Listener   Although it may sound crass to suggest that you be a selfish listener, it can help you maintain your powers of concentration. If you find your attention waning, ask yourself questions like "What's in it for me?" and "How can I use information from this talk?" Granted, you will find more useful information in some presentations than others, but you should nonetheless be alert to the possibility in all speeches. Find ways to benefit from the information in the speech you are listening to. We learn by connecting what we hear with our own experiences and needs.

Listen for Major Ideas   In a classic study, Nichols asked both good and poor listeners what their listening strategies were.[7] The poor listeners indicated that they listened for facts, such information as names and dates. The good listeners reported that they listened for major ideas and principles. Facts are useful only when you can connect them to a principle or a concept. In speeches, facts as well as examples are used primarily to support major ideas. You should try to summarize mentally the major idea that the specific facts support.

If you had been present on that brisk March morning in 1933 to hear Franklin Delano Roosevelt deliver his first inaugural address, you would have heard one key idea stressed in his message. His major idea was introduced in the fourth sentence of the speech: "This great Nation will endure as it has endured, will revive and will prosper. So, first of all, let me assert my firm belief that the only thing we have to fear is fear itself." Good listeners try to focus on the major ideas.

How can you tell what the major ideas in a speech are? A speaker who is well organized or familiar with good speaking technique will offer a preview of the major ideas early in the speech. If no preview is provided, listen for the speaker to enumerate major points, as in "My first point is to talk about the history of Jackson County." Transitional phrases and a speaker's internal summaries are other clues that can help you identify the major points. If your speaker provides few overt indicators of major points, you may be on your own to try to discover them. In that event, mentally summarize the ideas that are most useful to you. As we suggested earlier, be a selfish listener. Treat a disorganized speech as a gold mine to be scoured. Take your mental mining pan and search for the nuggets of thought you discover. Use your capacity of mental summary to help you remember the ideas you glean.

Mentally Summarize Key Ideas   Although we suggested earlier that you summarize the major ideas as you listen to the speech, we want to make sure that you understand this suggestion's power to increase your listening skill. Since the speed with which you think is far greater than the slow pace of a speaker's delivery, you can mentally summarize several minutes' content in just a few seconds. This mental activity can help keep you alert and following the speaker's flow of ideas. Even if the speaker is unorganized, you can attempt to organize the ideas you hear.

Spoken communication should be more redundant than written communication. Repetition helps learning. As we will discuss later, good speakers build in redundancy with internal summaries and clear transitions.

Practice Listening

Since we've noted that you spend over 42 percent of your time listening each day, you may wonder why we suggest that you practice listening. Improving your listening skill does not automatically happen as you hear speeches. Skill can be acquired only by study, in speech as in other activities. You learn to swim by swimming with proper instruction; you don't develop your aquatic skills by just jumping in the water and flailing around. Similarly, you learn to listen by practicing the methods we recommend. Researchers believe that poor listeners are inexperienced listeners. They tend to listen to and watch TV situation comedies rather than more challenging documentaries or other informative programs. Good listening habits result from practicing your listening skills while listening to demanding content.

RECAP

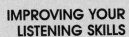

IMPROVING YOUR LISTENING SKILLS	The Good Listener	The Bad Listener
	Adapts to the speaker's delivery	Is easily distracted by the delivery of the speech
	Looks for nonverbal clues to aid understanding	Focuses only on the words
	Controls emotions	Emotionally erupts when listening
	Listens before a judgment is made about the value of the content	Reaches the wrong conclusions about the value of the message
	Mentally asks, "What's in it for me?"	Does not attempt to relate to the information personally
	Listens for major ideas	Listens for isolated facts
	Mentally summarizes key ideas	Does not mentally summarize
	Adapts to the speaking environment	Does not manage the environment and assumes no responsibility for it
	Seeks opportunities to practice listening skills	Avoids listening to difficult information

IMPROVING YOUR NOTE-TAKING SKILL

"What's everyone taking notes for?" wondered Carolyne. "Can't they remember the key points without trying to scribble them in their notebooks?" At the end of the lecture, however, Carolyne found the speaker's talk so informative that she tried to borrow the notes of one of her fellow listeners.

Throughout this chapter, we have suggested ways to improve your listening skill. But we also recognized that you will not remember everything you listen to. It is usually difficult to recall the details of a lengthy speech unless you have taken notes. Coupling improved listening skill with increased skill in taking notes can greatly enhance your ability to retrieve information.

Read the following suggestions for improving your note-taking skill.

1. *Prepare.* Come prepared to take notes, even if you're not sure you need to. Bring a pencil or pen and paper to the listening situation.

2. *Determine whether you need to take notes.* After the presentation has started, decide whether you need to take notes. If you receive a handout that summarizes the content of the message, it may be best to pay attention, concentrate on the message, and take very few if any notes.

3. *Make a decision about the type of notes you need to take.* If notes seem to be needed, decide whether you need to outline the speech, identify facts and principles, jot down key words, or just record major ideas. Some speakers do not follow organized outline patterns, in which case it will be tricky to outline the message. If you are going to take an objective test on the material, you may need to note

only facts and principles. Noting key words may be enough to help you recall what was said if you are going to prepare a report for someone else to read. Or you may just want to write down major ideas. The type of notes you take will depend on how you intend to use the information you get from the speech.

4. *Beware of taking too many notes.* Many note takers spend so much of their energy trying to transcribe an entire speech that they miss its major points. Decide how important the information is to you and why you should remember what is being said. Then take the kind of notes best suited to your needs. Also, if you are going to summarize the information to someone else on the same day, you generally do not need to write down everything that is said.

RECAP

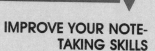

IMPROVE YOUR NOTE-TAKING SKILLS

1. Prepare.
2. Determine whether you need to take notes.
3. Make a decision about the type of notes you need to take.
4. Beware of taking too many notes.

NOTE-TAKING TECHNIQUES

Key Word Outline

Appendix C includes a speech by T. Richard Cheatham titled "Developing Your Capacities." The following illustrates different approaches for taking notes from that speech.

We must develop our capacity to:

Love
Learn
Labor
Laugh
Leave

Facts versus Principles

Facts	Principles
Four types of love: eros, storge, phileo, agape	Develop a capacity to love.
A person does not have enough intellectual capital coming out of graduate school to sustain a 35- to 40-year career.	Develop a capacity to learn.

Facts versus Principles

Facts	Principles
Babe Ruth struck out 1330 times during his career of 714 home runs.	Develop a capacity to labor.
A good laugh helps the digestive system.	Develop a capacity to laugh.
We all have failed relationships and shattered dreams.	Develop a capacity to leave.

Traditional Outline Notes

I.   Develop a capacity to love.
    A. Ancient Greeks knew the importance of love.
        1. Eros
        2. Storge
        3. Phileo
        4. Agape
    B. Social support can enhance wellness.

II. Develop a capacity to learn.

III. Develop a capacity to labor.
    A. Success takes work.
    B. Leaders need to take risks.

IV. Develop a capacity to laugh.
    A. Laugh and the world laughs with you; weep and you weep alone.
    B. Studies suggest medical benefits associated with a good laugh.

V.   Develop a capacity to leave.

SUMMARY

Learning to be a better listener is a challenging task. Evidence indicates that most people could improve their listening skill. In this chapter, we described the listening process, identified some barriers to good listening, and suggested some methods of improving our listening habits.

Listening is a process that involves selecting, attending, understanding, and remembering. Some of the barriers that keep us from listening at peak efficiency include deciding that a topic is not interesting, suffering from too much information, focusing on personal concerns and outside distractions, jumping to conclusions, and wasting the difference between speech rate and thought rate. We offered several suggestions to overcome these barriers and improve your listening skill. Our recommendations include these:

Adapt to the speaker
  Adapt to the speaker's delivery
  Listen with your eyes as well as your ears
  Avoid emotionally overreacting to a message
Adapt to the message
  Avoid reaching the wrong conclusion
  Be a selfish listener
  Listen for major ideas
  Mentally summarize key ideas
Practice listening

We concluded the chapter with suggestions for taking effective notes.

QUESTIONS FOR DISCUSSION AND REVIEW

1. What are the stages in the listening process?
2. Describe four different types of listening.
3. What are the barriers that keep you from listening at peak efficiency?
4. What can a speaker do to overcome listening barriers?
5. Identify methods for helping adapt to the speaker, the message, and the environment when you listen.

SUGGESTED ACTIVITIES

1. Identify examples of the following types of listening from your own listening experiences in the past twenty-four hours: (a) listening for pleasure, (b) listening to evaluate, (c) listening to empathize, and (d) listening to gain information.
2. Rank from most significant to least significant the "barriers to effective listening" discussed in this chapter as they apply to your own listening habits.
   _____ Prematurely rejecting a topic.
   _____ Suffering from information overload.
   _____ Thinking about personal concerns.
   _____ Succumbing to outside distractions.
   _____ Judging too quickly.
   _____ Wasting speech rate and thought rate differences.
   Describe your plan to help manage your three most troublesome listening barriers.
3. After listening to a speech by one of your classmates, see how well you can outline it. Compare your notes with the outline your classmate prepared. If your outline is markedly different from your classmate's, try to analyze why.
4. Watch a documentary on TV. Every four or five minutes, mentally summarize key ideas presented in the program. When the program is over, write down the

key ideas and summarize as much of the information as you can. The next day, repeat the process of writing down a summary of the program content. Note differences between your immediate recall and your twenty-four-hour recall. Two weeks after viewing the program, repeat the process of summarizing the program; note further differences between your immediate response, your twenty-four-hour recall, and your two-week memory.

4

Analyzing the Audience

OBJECTIVES

After studying this chapter, you should be able to

1. Describe informal and formal methods of analyzing your audience
2. Discuss the importance of audience analysis
3. Explain how to gather demographic, attitudinal, and environmental information about your audience and the speaking occasion
4. Identify methods of assessing your audience's reactions to your speech while it is in progress
5. Identify methods of assessing audience reactions after you have concluded your speech

For of the three elements in speechmaking—speaker, subject, and person addressed—it is the last one, the hearer, that determines the speech's end and object. (*George Caleb Bingham,* Stump Speaking. *Boatmen's National Bank, St. Louis, Missouri.*)

ARISTOTLE

It seemed harmless enough. Charles Williams was asked to speak to the Cub Scout pack about his experience as a young cowboy in Texas. The boys were learning to tie knots, and Williams, a retired rancher, could tell them how to make a lariat and how to make and use other knots.

His speech started out well. He seemed to be adapting to his young audience. However, for some reason, Williams thought the boys might also enjoy learning how to exterminate the screw worm, a pesky parasite of cattle. In the middle of his talk about roping cattle, he launched into a presentation about the techniques for sterilizing male screw worms. The parents in the audience fidgeted in their seats. The 7- and 8-year-olds didn't have the foggiest idea what a screw worm was, what sterilization was, or how male and female screw worms mate.

It got worse; his audience analysis skills deteriorated even more. Williams next talked about castrating cattle. Twenty-five minutes later he finally finished the screw worm-castration speech. The parents were relieved. Fortunately, the boys hadn't understood it.

Williams's downfall resulted from his failure to analyze his audience. He may have had a clear objective in mind, but he hadn't considered the background or knowledge of his listeners. Audience analysis is essential for any successful speech.

BECOMING AN AUDIENCE-CENTERED SPEAKER

Chapter 1 identified the key elements in communication: sender, channel, message, receiver. All four elements are important, but perhaps the most important is the receiver. In public speaking, the receiver is the audience and the audience is the reason for a speech event.

In Chapter 2, we presented a model that provides an overview of the entire process of speech preparation and delivery (see Figure 4.1). We stressed there and reemphasize here the concept of public speaking as an audience-centered activity. At each stage in crafting your speech, you need to be mindful of your audience. The audience analysis skills and techniques that we present in this chapter will help you throughout the public speaking process. Consciousness of your audience will be important as you select a topic, determine your speech purpose, develop your central idea, write a preliminary outline, choose supporting material, firm up your organization, rehearse, and deliver your speech.

When you think of your audience, don't think of some undifferentiated mass of people waiting to hear your message. Instead, think of individuals. Public speaking is the process of speaking to a group of individuals, each with a unique point of view. Your challenge as an audience-centered public speaker is to find out as much as you can about these individuals. From your knowledge of the individuals, you can then develop a general profile of your listeners.

WHAT IS AUDIENCE ANALYSIS?

Audience analysis is the process of examining information about the expected listeners to a speech. That analysis helps you adapt your message so that your listeners will respond as you wish. You analyze audiences every day as you speak to others or join in group conversations. Most of us do not deliberately make

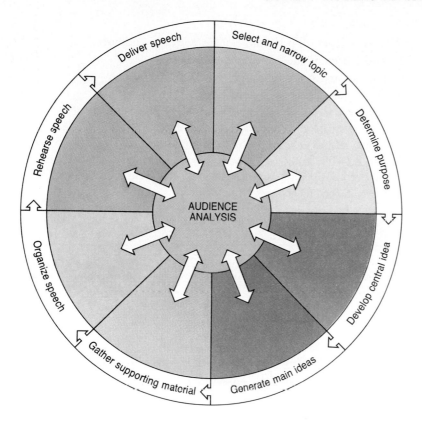

FIGURE 4.1
Audience analysis is central
to the speechmaking
process.

audience analysis
The process of examining information about the expected listeners to a speech.

offensive comments to our family and friends. Rather, we adapt our message to the individuals with whom we are speaking.

For example, Mike spent a glorious spring break at Daytona Beach. With three close friends, he piled in a car and headed for a week of adventure. When he returned from the beach, sunburned and fatigued from merrymaking, people asked how his holiday went. He described his escapades to his best friend, his mother, and his communication professor.

To his best friend, he bragged: "We partied all night and slept on the beach all day. It was great!" He informed his mother, "It was good to relax after the hectic pace of college." And he told his professor, "It was mentally invigorating to have time to think things out." It was the same vacation—but how different the messages were! Mike adapted his message to the people he addressed; he had analyzed his audiences.

When speaking in public, the same process should occur. The principle is simple, yet powerful: An effective public speaker is audience-centered. Several key questions can help formulate the approach to your audience.

To whom am I speaking?

What does my audience expect from me?

What topic would be most suitable to my audience?

What is my objective?

What kind of information should I share with my audience?

How should I present the information to them?

How can I gain and hold their attention?

What kind of examples would work best?

What method of organizing information will be most effective?

In this chapter, you will learn both formal and informal strategies for gathering information about your audience. You will examine how to analyze and adapt to your audience before, during, and after your speech. You will also learn to use the information you gather to achieve your purpose.

ANALYZING YOUR AUDIENCE BEFORE YOU SPEAK

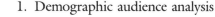

▼
demographics
Information about the age, race, gender, educational level, and religious views of an audience.

Information about the age, race, sex, educational level, and religious views of your audience can help you better understand them.
(Bob Daemmrich/Stock, Boston)

Because knowledge of your audience can help you choose a topic, a purpose, an outline, and other components of your speech, it is important to analyze your audience before doing anything else. There are three basic approaches you can use for prespeech analysis:

1. Demographic audience analysis
2. Attitudinal audience analysis
3. Environmental audience analysis

Demographic Analysis

A basic approach to analyzing an audience is to identify its demographic makeup. **Demographics** involves population data, including such characteristics as age, race, gender, educational level, and religious views. Let's consider how demographic information can help you better understand your audience.

Age   Knowing the age of your audience can be very helpful in choosing your topic and your approach. Although you must use caution in generalizing from only one factor such as age, that information can suggest the kinds of examples, humor, illustrations, and other types of supporting material to use in your speech.

For example, many of the students in your public speaking class will probably be in their late teens or early twenties. However, older students may also be present. The younger students may know the latest rap performers or musicians, for example, but the older ones may not be familiar with D. J. Jazzy Jeff and the Fresh Prince or Bobby Brown. If you are going to give a talk on rap music, you will have to explain who the performers are and describe or demonstrate their style if you wish to have all the members of your class understand what you are talking about.

Gender   Another key question to ask when considering your audience is "What is the ratio of males to females?" As in other instances, you should avoid making sweeping judgments based on stereotypes of gender. However, current research does suggest some differences in the way males and females respond to messages.

Some researchers have found that men and women have different listening styles.[1] Male listening styles, on the one hand, have been described as continually shaping, forming, observing, inquiring, and directing energy toward a chosen goal. Men have also been described as more emotionally controlled than women. A man tends to view a message from the perspective of his goals. Women, on the other hand, are more likely to seek relationships in a pattern and to rely on intuition. As a public speaker, you need to organize your message so that it can be heard by every audience member, regardless of gender-based listening styles.

Cultural, Ethnic, and Racial Background   The cultural, ethnic, and racial background of your audience will influence the way your message is received. If you are speaking to an audience with international students or to one whose members have a distinctive ethnic or cultural background, you will have to take this factor into account, just like age and sex. During your prespeech analysis, determine what cultural expectations your audience holds, and adjust your approach accordingly.

One study suggests that members of some cultures prefer formal oratory rather than a conversational speech style.[2] Bahamian audiences, for example, expect a public speaker to address an audience with formal phrases, such as, "Mr. Chairman, honored guests, ladies and gentlemen . . ." They also expect speakers to use formal gestures and intonation, even when speaking to a class.

Religion   Marsha is a follower of Scientology, and she believes that *Dianetics* is as important as the Bible. Planning to speak before a Bible-belt college audience, many of whose members view Scientology as a cult, Marsha would be wise to consider how her listeners will respond to her message. This is not to suggest that she should refuse the speaking invitation. She should, however, be aware of her audience's religious beliefs as she prepares and presents her speech.

When touching on religious beliefs or audience values, you must use great care in what you say and how you say it. Few beliefs are held with the same intensity as religious ones. You have to be careful not to offend your listeners and must therefore plan and deliver your speech with much thought and sensitivity.

Educational Level   If your audience consists of your classmates, it is easy to identify its educational level. But outside the class, this can sometimes be difficult. You can, however, make certain inferences from the speaking situation. If, for example, you are going to talk to a PTA meeting in a poor, inner-city neighborhood, you may suspect that the many of your listeners will have had little more than a high school education. By contrast, if you are going to address the parents at a prep school, you may be sure that most of them will have completed college and some will have advanced degrees. In other words, social and economic status can give you clues to your audience's educational level. Knowing the educational background of your audience can help you make decisions about your choice of vocabulary, language style, and your use of examples and illustrations.

Identifying Demographic Information about Your Audience

We have just examined some of the demographic characteristics of audiences. But how do you get the information on which to base an analysis of an audience? There are two approaches you can take, informal and formal. Let's look at these two approaches in greater detail.

Informal Demographic Audience Analysis   To analyze your audience informally, you simply observe them and ask questions about them. For example, you can observe how many members of your audience are male or female, and you can also make some inferences from their appearance about their educational level, ethnic or cultural traits, and approximate age.

You should also talk with people who know something about the audience members you will be addressing. If you are invited to speak to a group you have not seen before, ask the person who invited you some general questions about the audience. What is the average age of the audience? What are the political affiliations of the audience members? What religious beliefs do they hold? At what income level are most of them? As best you can, try to get as much information about your audience as you can before you give your speech.

Formal Demographic Audience Analysis   There may be times when you cannot determine the traits of your audience from observation or informal discussions. In these instances, formal sources of information are needed. The best formal source of demographic information on your audience is a brief questionnaire. Although administering a formal questionnaire is not always possible, you should have some familiarity with surveys of audience demographics. Here is a sample questionnaire.

DEMOGRAPHIC AUDIENCE ANALYSIS QUESTIONNAIRE

1. Name (optional):_____

2. Sex: Male □   Female □

3. Occupation:_____

4. Religious affiliation:_____

5. Marital status: Married □   Single □   Divorced □

6. Major in school:_____

7. Years of schooling beyond high school:_____

8. Annual income:_____

9. Age:_____

10. Hometown and state:_____

11. Political affiliations: Republican ☐   Democrat ☐   Other ☐   None ☐

12. Membership in professional or fraternal organizations:_____

_____

You can modify this questionnaire according to your audience and topic. If your topic concerns the best approach to finding a rental apartment and you are speaking in a suburban area, find out how many members of your audience own their home and how many are presently living in an apartment. You should also ask how they found their current apartment, how many are now searching for an apartment, and how many anticipate searching for one. Answers to these questions can give you useful information about your audience and may also provide examples to use in your presentation.

Although we have emphasized the importance of learning as much as possible about the makeup of your audience, we must caution that inferences based on generalized information may lead to faulty conclusions. For example, it might seem reasonable to infer that an audience of 18- to 22-year-olds would not be deeply interested in retirement programs. But unless you have talked to them specifically about pensions and retirement, your inference may be in error. To learn more about your audience's attitudes, you need to undertake a second type of analysis: attitudinal analysis.

Attitudinal Analysis

Demographic information allows you to make some useful inferences about your audience and its likely response. Learning how the members of your audience feel about your topic and purpose may provide specific clues to their possible reaction. Attitudinal or psychographic audience analysis explores an audience's attitudes toward a topic, purpose, and speaker, while at the same time probing the underlying beliefs and values that might affect these attitudes.

Attitudes, Beliefs, and Values   It is important for a speaker to distinguish among *attitudes*, *beliefs*, and *values*. The attitudes, beliefs, and values of an audience may greatly influence a speaker's selection of a topic and specific purpose, as well as various other aspects of speech preparation and delivery.

An **attitude** reflects likes or dislikes. Do you like health food? Are you for or against capital punishment? Do you think that it is important to learn cardiopulmonary resuscitation (CPR)? Should movies be censored? What are your views of nuclear energy? Your answers to these widely varied questions will express your attitudes.

A **belief** is what you hold to be true or false. Beliefs underlie attitudes. Why do you like health food? You may *believe* that natural products are better for your

attitude
An individual's likes or dislikes.

belief
The way an individual structures reality to determine what is true or false.

health. That belief explains your positive attitude. Why are you against capital punishment? You may *believe* that it is wrong to kill people for any reason. Again, your belief explains your attitude. It is useful for a speaker to probe audience beliefs. If the speaker can understand why audience members feel the way they do about a topic, he or she may be able to address that underlying belief, whether trying to change an attitude or reinforce one.

Values are enduring concepts of good and bad, right and wrong. More deeply ingrained than either attitudes or beliefs, they are therefore more resistant to change. Values support both attitudes and beliefs. For example, you like health food because you believe that natural products are more healthful. And you *value* good health. You are against capital punishment because you believe that it is wrong to kill people. You *value* human life. As with beliefs, a speaker who has some understanding of an audience's values will be better able to adapt a speech to them.

Audience and Topic   The topic of a speech provides one focus for an audience's attitudes, beliefs, and values. It is useful to know how the members of an audience feel about your topic. Are they interested or apathetic? How much do they already know about the topic? If the topic is controversial, are they for it or against it? Knowing the answers to these questions from the outset allows you to adjust your message accordingly. For example, if you plan to talk about increasing taxes to improve education in your state, you may want to know how your listeners feel about taxes and education.

If audience members are interested and supportive, your job is relatively easy. If they are indifferent or bored, you have to employ techniques to gain and hold their attention. If they are against your topic, you will have to use convincing supporting materials, while being sensitive to the audience's underlying beliefs and values. At any rate, knowing how an audience feels about a topic helps you plan and deliver your message.

Audience and Specific Purpose   Just as an audience may be interested or disinterested, knowledgeable or ignorant, supportive or hostile toward a topic in general, so too may they express these attitudes toward a specific purpose. Because a specific purpose reveals a speaker's exact position on a topic, an audience is even more likely to agree or disagree with a specific purpose than a general topic.

What about a topic or a specific purpose that challenges or contradicts audience attitudes, beliefs, or values? The speaker may be able to change a casual attitude. For example, Matt discovered that although his audience is interested in his topic, the military draft, they disagree with his specific purpose: "At the end of my speech, the audience will support mandatory registration of all 18- to 21-year-olds for military service." Further investigation showed that the audience's attitude is not based on any firm antiwar belief. Rather, because most of the audience consists of 18- to 21-year-olds, they see their future careers threatened by military service. Armed with this knowledge, Matt feels he can successfully change the audience's attitude by presenting strong evidence that mandatory registration does not necessarily lead to military service and that military service itself can help advance some careers.

value
Enduring concepts of good and bad, right and wrong.

Whereas Matt may succeed in changing his audience's attitude, Jennie may face a more difficult challenge. She plans to speak in favor of capital punishment. Most of her listeners are opposed because they believe that killing is wrong and that human life has the highest value. Jennie knows that beliefs and values are not likely to change. Rather than alienate her audience, she decides to change her specific purpose and try to show that her ideas are in keeping with the audience's beliefs and values. From "The audience will be able to list three arguments in support of capital punishment," Jennie changed her purpose to "The audience will be able to explain how capital punishment actually protects human life." Her new statement of purpose indicates that she understands her audience's beliefs and values and that she can show how capital punishment supports rather than negates them.

Additional tactics for dealing with favorable, neutral, and unfavorable audiences can be found in Chapter 13.

Audience and Speaker   The audience's attitude toward a speaker is a third factor that can influence reaction to a speech. Regardless of how they feel about a topic or purpose, if members of an audience regard a speaker as credible, they are much more likely to be interested in and supportive of what he or she has to say.

When a high school health teacher asks a former drug addict to speak to a class about the dangers of cocaine addiction, he recognizes that the speaker's experiences make his message far more convincing than if the teacher himself lectured on the perils of cocaine use.

An audience's positive attitude toward you as a speaker can overcome negative or apathetic attitudes they may have toward your topic or purpose. If your analysis reveals that your audience does not recognize you as an authority on your subject, you will need to build your credibility into the speech. For example, Doug had received a police citation for driving while intoxicated. Because Doug had directly experienced the harsh penalties of drunk driving, his talk was much more effective than a carefully researched objective speech on the topic would have been. If you have had personal experience with your topic, be sure to let the audience know. You will gain credibility instantly.

While preparing a speech for your speech class, you may want to talk to a few of your classmates to determine what their attitudes are about you and your topic.
(Laima Druskis)

Identifying Attitudinal Information about Your Audience

Informal Attitudinal Analysis   You can gather attitudinal information about your audience informally by simply asking people who are familiar with your audience to tell you something about its attitudes, beliefs, and values. The person who invited you to speak is again probably your best first source of attitudinal information. While preparing a speech for your speech class, you may want to talk to a few of your classmates to determine what their attitudes are about you and your topic. Such informal questioning can reveal a great deal of useful information about your audience's attitudes.

Formal Attitudinal Analysis   Rather than just relying on inferences drawn from conversations with a few audience members, you may want to conduct a more formal survey of your listeners' attitudes, beliefs, and values if time and resources permit. A formal survey can bring to light more of your audience's attitudes, beliefs, and values than casual conversation can.

How do you go about developing a formal attitudinal survey? Your first task is to decide what you want to know about your audience that you don't already know. Once you have made that decision, you should next plan the questions that will give you this information. There are two basic types of questions. **Open-ended questions** allow for unrestricted answers, without limiting answers to choices or alternatives. Use open-ended questions when you want more detailed information from your audience. Essay questions, for example, are open-ended. **Closed-ended questions** offer several alternatives from which to choose. Multiple-choice, true-false, and agree-disagree questions are examples of closed-ended questions.

After you develop the questions, it is wise to test them on a small group of people to make sure that they are clear and will bring forth meaningful answers.

Suppose that you plan to address an audience about school-based health clinics that dispense birth control pills in high schools. The following sample questions illustrate various open and closed formats.

open-ended questions
Questions which allow for unrestricted answers, without limiting answers to choices or alternatives.

closed-ended questions
Questions which offer an alternative for an answer, such as true-false, agree-disagree, or multiple-choice questions.

SAMPLE QUESTIONS

Open-ended questions

1. What are your feelings about having health clinics in high schools that dispense birth control pills?
2. What are your reactions to the current rate of teenage pregnancy?
3. What would you do if you discovered your daughter was receiving birth control pills from your high school health clinic?

Closed-ended questions

1. Are you in favor of dispensing birth control pills to high school girls in school-based health clinics?

   Yes □   No □
2. Birth control pills should be given to high school students who ask for them in school-based health clinics. (Circle the statement that best describes your feeling.)

   Agree strongly   Agree   Undecided   Disagree   Disagree strongly
3. Check the statement that most closely reflects your feelings about school-based health clinics and birth control pills.

   ___ Students should receive birth control pills in school-based health clinics whenever they want them, without their parents' knowledge.
   ___ Students should receive birth control pills in school-based health clinics whenever they want them, as long as they have their parents' permission.
   ___ I am not certain whether students should receive birth control pills in school-based health clinics.
   ___ Students should not receive birth control pills in school-based health clinics.

4. Rank the following statements about school-based health clinics and birth control pills, from most desirable (1) to least desirable (5).

___ Birth control pills should be available to all high school students in school-based health clinics, whenever students want them, and even if their parents are not aware that they are taking the pills.
___ Birth control pills should be available to all high school students in school-based health clinics, but only if their parents have given their permission.
___ Birth control pills should be available to high school students without their parents' knowledge, but not in school-based health clinics.
___ Birth control pills should be available to high school students, but not in school-based health clinics, and only with their parents' permission.
___ Birth control pills should not be available to high school students.

What are some of the pitfalls of developing an attitudinal questionnaire? According to experts, some of the common problems in designing effective surveys are (1) developing clear and unbiased questions, (2) selecting a large enough sample to be representative of the entire audience if you are speaking to a large group, (3) writing questions that are both clear to the reader and easy for you to interpret, and (4) making sure that the questions will give you the information you need.[3] Simply being aware of these problems may help you avoid them as you plan your formal attitudinal analysis.

Environmental Analysis

Analyzing demographics and attitudes are ways to find out about your audience. But in addition to learning about your audience, it is useful to find out as much as you can about the environment in which you will be speaking. In your speech class, you have the advantage of knowing what the room looks like, but in a new speaking situation, you will not have that advantage. You therefore need to visit the place in which you will speak to examine the physical setting and find out, for example, how far the audience will be from the lectern. Physical conditions can have an impact on your performance, the audience's response, and the overall success of the speech.

Studies suggest that the room arrangement and decor can affect how people behave.[4] A classic study by Maslow and Mintz examined whether room decor has an effect on the occupants of the room. These researchers decorated three rooms. One was furnished as an "ugly room." It resembled a drab, cluttered janitor's storeroom and was rated as "horrible" and "repulsive" by observers assigned to examine it. The second room was made to look like an "average room," described as "similar to a professor's office." The third room, decorated with carpeting, drapes, tasteful furniture, and attractive objects, was labeled a "beautiful room." Subjects were assigned to one or another of the three rooms and were given the task of rating several facial photographs. The results indicated that the environment had a significant effect on how the subjects rated the faces. Facial photographs were

Room arrangement and decor can affect how people behave.
(*Steven Marks/Stock, Boston*)

rated as more pleasant in the beautiful room than in the ugly room. Subjects in the ugly room also reported that the task was more unpleasant and monotonous than subjects who were assigned to the beautiful room. Finally, subjects assigned to the ugly room attempted to leave sooner than subjects assigned to the beautiful room.

The relevance of this study to public speaking is that room arrangement and decor may affect the way an audience responds. You should be aware of the arrangement and appearance of the room in which you will speak. If your speaking environment is less than ideal, you may need to work especially hard to hold your audience's attention. Although it is unlikely that you would be able to make major changes in the speaking environment, it is ultimately up to you to obtain the best speaking environment you can. The arrangement of chairs, the placement of audiovisual materials, and the opening or closing of drapes should all be within your control.

In preparing for a speaking assignment, keep the following environmental questions in mind:

1. What are the physical arrangements for the speaking situation?
2. How will the audience seating be arranged?
3. How many people are expected to attend the speech?
4. Will I be expected to use a microphone?
5. Will I speak from a lectern?
6. Where will I appear on the program?
7. What is the room lighting like? Will the audience seating area be darkened beyond a lighted stage?
8. Will I be on a stage or raised platform?
9. How close will I be to the audience?
10. Will I have adequate equipment for my visual aids?

Try to avoid last-minute surprises about the speaking environment and the physical arrangements for your speech. A well-prepared speaker adapts his or her message not only to the audience but also to the speaking environment.

ELEMENTS OF AUDIENCE ANALYSIS

Demographic Characteristics
Age
Gender
Cultural, ethnic, or racial background
Religion
Education

Attitudinal Characteristics
Attitudes
Beliefs
Values

Environmental Characteristics	Microphone availability
Furniture arrangement	Number of people present
Seating arrangement	Room lighting and decor

So far, you have focused on discovering as much as possible about an audience before the speaking event. Prespeech analyses help with each step of the public speaking process: selecting a topic, formulating a specific purpose sentence, gathering supporting material, identifying major ideas, organizing the speech, and planning its delivery. Each of these components of your speech is dependent on understanding your audience. But audience analysis and adaptation do not end when you have crafted your speech. To the contrary, audience analysis continues as you deliver your speech.

Generally, a public speaker does not have an exchange with the audience unless the event is set in a question-and-answer or discussion format. Once the speech is in progress, the speaker must rely on nonverbal clues from the audience to judge how it is responding to the message. Let's look at some types of audience behavior that may yield clues to your listeners' responses as you are giving your speech.

ADAPTING TO YOUR AUDIENCE AS YOU SPEAK

Identifying Nonverbal Audience Clues

Eye Contact   Perhaps the best way to determine whether your listeners are maintaining interest in your speech is to note the amount of eye contact they have with you. The more contact they have, the more likely it is that they are listening to your message. If you find them looking down at the program (or, worse yet, closing their eyes), you can reasonably guess that they have lost interest in what you're talking about.

Facial Expression   Another clue as to whether an audience is "with you" is facial expression. An attentive audience not only makes direct eye contact but also wears an attentive facial expression. Beware of a frozen, unresponsive face. This sort of expression we call the "in-a-stupor" look. The classic in-a-stupor expression consists of a slightly tilted head, a faint, frozen smile, and often a hand holding up the chin. This expression may have the appearance of interest, but it more often means that the person is daydreaming or thinking of something other than your topic.

Restless Movement   An attentive audience doesn't move much. An early sign of inattentiveness is fidgeting fingers, which may escalate to pencil wagging, leg jiggling, and arm wiggling. Seat squirming, feet shuffling, and general body movement often indicate that members of the audience have lost interest in your message.

Nonverbal Responsiveness   An interested audience is one in which members verbally and nonverbally respond when encouraged or invited by the speaker. When you ask for a show of hands and audience members sheepishly look at one another and eventually raise a finger or two, you can reasonably infer lack of interest and enthusiasm. Frequent applause and head nods of agreement with your message are indicators of interest and support.

Verbal Responsiveness   Not only will some audiences indicate agreement non-verbally, but some will also indicate their interests verbally. Audience members may shout out a response or more quietly express agreement or disagreement to people seated next to them. A sensitive public speaker is constantly listening for verbal reinforcement or disagreement.

Responding to Nonverbal Clues

The value in recognizing nonverbal clues from your listeners is that you can respond to them appropriately. If your audience seems interested, is supportive, and appears attentive, your prespeech analysis clearly guided you to make proper choices in preparing and delivering your speech.

Audience inattentiveness should alert you to the need to make some changes even while delivering your message. If you find your audience drifting off, you may want to make impromptu changes in your presentation. Spontaneity may revive the flagging interest of your audience. You may also wish to call on one or another of the following suggestions:

Use more examples.
Use illustrations that appeal to the senses of your listeners.
Use personal examples.
Pause for dramatic effect.
Change your speaking rate.
Remind your listeners why they should pay attention.
Clarify the overall organization of your message to your listeners.

Later chapters on supporting material, speech organization, and speech delivery will discuss other techniques for adjusting your style while delivering your message.

RECAP ▼

ADAPT TO YOUR AUDIENCE AS YOU SPEAK

Observe audience eye contact.
  Are they looking back at you?
Monitor audience facial expression.
  Are they responsive to your message?
Monitor audience movement.
  Are they restless?
  Is there lots of movement of fingers and feet?

Assess whether the audience is responsive to you.
　　Do they respond to your requests?
　　Do they laugh and applaud when appropriate?
Assess audience verbal response.
　　Do they respond verbally when appropriate?

After you have given your speech, you should indulge in a little Monday-morning quarterbacking. It is important to evaluate your audience's response. Why? Because it can help you prepare your next speech. Postspeech analysis helps you polish your speaking skill, regardless of whether you will face the same audience again. From that analysis you can learn whether your examples were clear and your message was accepted by your listeners. Your future success as a public speaker can be enhanced if you learn from your previous speaking experiences. Let's look at some specific methods of assessing your audience's response to your speech.

ANALYZING YOUR AUDIENCE AFTER YOU SPEAK

Nonverbal Responses

The most obvious nonverbal response is applause. Is the audience simply clapping politely, or is the applause robust and enthusiastic, indicating audience pleasure and acceptance?

Besides noting the kind of applause, a speaker should monitor other nonverbal clues. Responsive facial expressions, smiles, and nods are other nonverbal signs that the speech was well received.

Nonverbal responses at the end of the speech may provide some measure of the general feeling of the audience, but they are not much help in identifying which strategies were the most effective. You should also consider what the members of the audience say, both to you and to others, after your speech.

Verbal Responses

What might members of the audience say to you about your speech? General comments, such as "I enjoyed your talk" or "Great speech," are good for the ego— which is important—but are not of much analytic help. Specific comments can indicate where you succeeded and where you failed. If you have the chance, try to ask audience members how they responded to the speech in general and to specific points in which you have a particular interest.

Survey Responses

You are already aware of the value of conducting audience surveys before speaking publicly. You may also want to survey your audience after you speak. You can then assess how well you accomplished your objective. The same survey techniques that were discussed earlier can be used. Develop survey questions that will help you determine the general reactions to you and your speech, as well as specific responses to your ideas and supporting materials. This is often done where public speaking counts. For example, a significant portion of political campaign budgets is spent to evaluate how a candidate is received by his or her constituents. Politicians want to know what portions of their messages are acceptable to their audiences so that they can use this information in the future. Postspeech surveys are especially useful when trying to persuade an audience. Comparing prespeech and postspeech attitudes can give you a clear idea of your effectiveness.

If your speech objective has been to teach your audience about some new idea, you may decide that a posttest would be a useful assessment of whether you expressed your ideas clearly. One probably too familiar type of posttest is the classroom exam. Not only do exams assess your study skills and reading comprehension, but they also help determine whether the information presented was clear and easily understood.

Behavioral Responses

If the purpose of your speech was to persuade your listeners to do something, you will want to learn whether they ultimately behave as you intended. If you wanted them to vote in an upcoming election, you might survey your listeners to find out how many did vote. If you want to win support for a particular cause or organization, you might ask them to sign a petition after your speech. The number of signatures would be a clear measure of your speech's success. Some religious speakers judge the success of their ministry by the amount of contributions they receive. Your listeners' actions are the best indicators of your speaking success.

SUMMARY   This chapter has emphasized the importance of being an audience-centered speaker. To be an effective speaker, it is essential to learn as much as you can about your listeners. There are three major steps in gaining knowledge about your audience: prespeech analysis, analysis during the speech, and postspeech analysis.

Part of preparing your speech involves analyzing your audience. There are three methods of doing so: demographic, attitudinal, and environmental analyses. You can use informal and formal approaches to gather information about your listeners for your analyses.

While speaking, it is important to look for feedback from your listeners. Audience eye contact, facial expression, movement, and general verbal and nonverbal responsiveness provide clues as to how well you are doing.

Finally, you should evaluate audience reaction after your speech. Again, nonverbal clues as well as verbal ones will help you judge your speaking skill. The best indicator of your speaking success is whether your audience is actually able or willing to follow your advice or remembers what you have told them.

1. What is an audience-centered speaker?
2. What are the key demographic characteristics that a speaker should know in order to understand an audience?
3. Describe the differences between an informal and a formal approach to audience analysis.
4. What are the attitudinal factors of audience analysis?
5. What are some questions you should ask to learn about the speaking environment?
6. What can you do to adapt to your audience while you are delivering your speech?
7. How can you find out if your speech was successful?

1. Conduct a demographic analysis of your speech class. Identify as much information as you can by observing (informal method). Then, using a formal method, construct a survey to assess other demographic characteristics of your audience. Compare the formal and informal methods of gathering information for accuracy and completeness.
2. Conduct a formal attitudinal analysis of your speech class, assessing their attitudes about one of the following topics:
   The federal budget deficit
   The arms race
   Children of divorce
   Open adoption
   Abortion and birth control
   Preventing minority student dropouts
   Financing a college education
   Student politics
   Criteria for choosing a career
   Opening student credit accounts
   Nursing home care
3. Design a survey to evaluate attitudes about the quality of education on your campus. Include both open-ended questions and closed-ended questions in your survey.
4. Conduct an environmental analysis of your speech classroom. What positive and negative features of your classroom make it appropriate or inappropriate as a lecture hall? What changes would you make in the speaking environment to enhance speaking success?
5. Each class member should be given a white card, a red card, and a green card. While a student is rehearsing a speech, the class members should hold up the green card if they agree with what the speaker is saying, the red card if they disagree, and the white card if they are neutral or indifferent about the speech content. The speaker should attempt to adapt to the audience feedback.
6. Make a list of the nonverbal clues that let you know that your audience is enjoying your speech or agreeing with your message. Make a second list identifying the nonverbal clues that communicate audience disagreement or boredom.

5
Developing Your Speech

OBJECTIVES

After studying this chapter, you should be able to

1. Select a topic for a class-room speech that is appro-priate to the audience, the occasion, and yourself

2. Narrow a topic so that it can be thoroughly dis-cussed within the time limits allotted for a specific as-signment

3. Write a behavioral purpose statement for an assigned topic

4. Explain the three ways of generating a skeleton out-line from a central idea

5. Apply to a speaking as-signment the four steps for getting from a blank sheet of paper to a preliminary outline for the speech

In all matters, before beginning, a diligent preparation should be made.
(*Diego Rivera,* Young Man with Stylograph—Portrait of Best Maugard, *1914. Oil on canvas, 31³/₄ × 25⁵/₈". Collection, Señora Dolores Olmedo, Phoenix Art Museum.*)

Cicero

Mike Richards has arranged the books and papers on his desk into neat, even piles. He has sharpened his pencils and laid them out parallel to one another. He has even dusted his desktop and cleaned the computer monitor screen. Mike can think of no other task to delay writing his speech. He loads his word processing program, carefully centers the words *Informative Speech*, and then slouches in his chair, staring glumly at the blank expanse that threatens his well-being. Finally, he types the words *College Football* under the *Informative Speech* heading. Another long pause. Hesitantly, he begins his first sentence: "Today I want to talk to you about college football." Rereading his first ten words, Mike decides that they sound moronic. He deletes the sentence and tries again. This time the screen looks even blanker than before. He writes-deletes-writes-deletes. Half an hour later, Mike is exhausted and still mocked by a blank screen. And he is frantic—this speech *has* to be ready by 9:00 tomorrow morning.

Getting from a blank screen or sheet of paper to a speech outline is often the biggest hurdle you will face as a public speaker. Fortunately, however, it is one that you can learn to clear. If your earlier efforts at speech writing have been like Mike Richards', take heart. Just as you learned to read, do long division, drive a car, and get through college registration, so too can you learn to prepare a speech.

The first steps in preparing a speech are as follows:

1. Select and narrow the topic.
2. Determine the purpose.
3. Develop the central idea.
4. Generate main ideas.

At the end of step 4, you will have a rough outline of the speech and will be ready to develop and polish your ideas further.

As we observed in Chapter 4, audience-centered speakers consider the needs, interests, and expectations of their audience during the entire speech preparation process. As you move from topic selection to outlining, remember that you are preparing a message for your listeners. Always keep the audience as your central focus.

STEP 1: SELECT AND NARROW THE TOPIC

Your first task, illustrated by Figure 5.1, is to choose a topic on which to speak. You will also need to narrow this topic to fit your time limits. Sometimes you can eliminate one or both of these steps; the topic has been chosen and properly defined for you. For example, because you visited England's Lake District on your tour of Great Britain last summer, your English literature teacher asks you to speak about the mountainous landscape of that region before your class studies the poetry of Wordsworth and Coleridge. Or imagine a future day in which the Noon Lion's Club asks you to speak at their weekly gathering about the goals of the local drug abuse task force, which you chair. In both cases, your topic and its scope have been decided for you.

In other instances, the choice of topic may be left entirely to you. In your public speaking class, your instructor may provide such guidelines as time limits and type

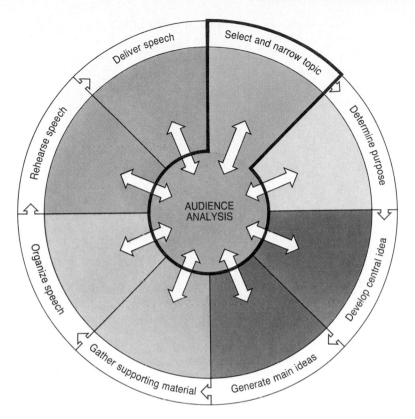

FIGURE 5.1

Selecting and narrowing the topic is an early speechmaking task.

of speech (informative, persuasive, or entertaining) but allow you to choose your topic freely. In this event, you should realize that the success of your speech may rest on this decision. But how do you go about choosing an appropriate, interesting topic?

Guidelines for Selecting a Topic

Consider the Audience   First, you must think of your audience. In Chapter 4, we discussed the reasons and methods for finding out about the traits of your audience. Knowing something about the average age, male-female ratio, political convictions, educational level, occupations, and socioeconomic level (demographic factors) of your listeners allows you to make important inferences about their interests, needs, expectations, and knowledge.

Suppose that Sally Rogers, a physical education major, has been asked by her grandmother to speak to a group of people living in the grandmother's retirement community. This elderly, mostly female audience may doze through Sally's most enthusiastic discussion of marathon training, but they will participate eagerly in her demonstration of stretching and relaxation exercises that they can do while seated. The second topic meets the *interests* and *needs* of this particular audience.

In addition to satisfying the interests and needs of her grandmother's friends, Sally must recognize and acknowledge their *expectations*. The women asked her to speak because they wanted to hear about some aspect of physical education. Similarly, a university president invited to speak to a civic organization is expected to talk about some facet of the university. A police officer speaking to an elementary school's PTA should address the audience's concern for the safety of their young children.

Not only should a speaker's choice of topic be relevant to the interests and expectations of his or her listeners, but it should also take into account the *knowledge* they already have about the subject. A student giving a visual aid speech several semesters ago forgot or ignored this requirement when she chose to speak on "how to pop popcorn." Although the listeners were interested in popcorn (and, in fact, eagerly awaited samples), they had trouble focusing on the speech because it bored them. Few college students do not know how to pop corn in an electric popper! The speech offered no new information. In addition, it was much shorter than required, simply because there was not enough to say about the subject. Your topic needs to provide intellectual stimulation.

"What interests and needs does this audience have in common?" "Why did they ask *me* to speak?" and "What do they already know about the subject I am considering?" are important questions to ask yourself as you mull over potential topics for a speech. The answers may yield an appropriate topic surprisingly quickly.

RECAP

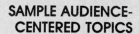

SAMPLE AUDIENCE-CENTERED TOPICS

Audience	Topic
Retirees	Preserving Social Security benefits
Military cadets	Honor, duty, obedience to the law
Civic organization	The Special Olympics needs you!
Church members	Starting a community food bank
First graders	What to do in case of a fire at home
Teachers	Building children's self-concepts
College fraternity	The designated-driver program

Consider the Occasion   Several years ago, the guest speaker at a graduate school commencement failed miserably in his assignment. The topic he chose—how a graduate degree prepares one for the challenges of life—showed that he had given a good deal of thought to the interests, needs, expectations, and knowledge of his audience. Still, his speech both stunned and angered the graduates, friends, and relatives gathered in that auditorium. For more than an hour, the speaker argued that there are no jobs for people with graduate degrees and that those degrees are not of much value in one's personal life.

Was this speaker's topic of *interest* to his listeners? Undoubtedly. Did they *expect* to hear someone talk about life after graduation? Yes. Could he *add to their knowledge* of the subject? Probably. Was his topic *appropriate to the occasion*? Definitely not! A commencement address calls for praise of hard-earned accomplishments and an optimistic sending forth of the graduates. The unrelenting pessimism of the speaker was *not* appropriate to this occasion. Neither was the length of this speech appropriate to a ceremony in which the focus should be on the graduates. Even though this speaker had thought of his audience, his speech showed that he had not considered the occasion. He therefore failed. To be successful, a topic must be appropriate to both audience *and* occasion.

Consider Yourself   What do you talk about with good friends? You probably discuss school, mutual friends, political or social issues, hobbies or leisure-time activities, or other topics of interest and important to you. As with most people, your liveliest, most animated conversations revolve around topics of personal concern and conviction.

The best public speaking topics are also ones that interest you especially or reflect your personal experience. The student speeches you will remember long after your public speaking class is over will be those in which the speaker was intensely interested and personally involved.

The authors of this text participated in competitive forensics during their undergraduate years. One speech that we vividly remember was given by a teammate whose brother was held prisoner by the North Vietnamese in the waning years of the Vietnam War. "Won't you please bring my brother home?"—the closing line of that speech—never failed to inspire tears and righteous outrage in the audience. It was a tragic topic, but appropriate to audiences of that time and one with which that speaker was passionately concerned.

"I'm in big trouble now," you're groaning as you finish reading what has just been said. "My life is *so* boring. I've never done anything interesting. I don't have any hobbies. And I'll *never* be able to come up with a decent topic."

Most beginning public speakers feel that way. There is some truth to the notion that choosing a topic becomes easier as you get older and have more life experiences on which to draw. However, by the time you are a freshman in college, you can draw on a wealth of experiences and interests for good speech topics. Where have you lived? Where have you traveled? Describe your family or your ancestors. Have you held any part-time jobs? Describe your first days at college. What are your favorite classes? What are your hobbies or interests? What is your favorite sport? What social issues concern you?

Here's one list of topics that was generated by such questions:

Music and art in Kansas City
"Yankee, go home": The American tourist in France
Growing up in a blended family
The impact on my family of my sister's marriage outside our faith
Parrots as pets
Behind the counter at McDonald's

My first day at college
Why Freshman Seminar should be required
Who are the homeless?
How I helped to elect the president: Getting involved in political campaigns
The impact of the Beatles on twentieth-century music

Of course, whatever topic you choose, you need to relate it to the interests of your audience. Remember, all good speakers are audience-centered.

RECAP ▼

GUIDELINES FOR SELECTING A TOPIC	Consider the audience.
	Consider the occasion.
	Consider yourself.

Techniques for Selecting a Topic

All successful topics reflect audience, occasion, and speaker. But just contemplating those guidelines does not automatically produce a good topic. Sooner or later, we all face a speech for which we cannot think of a good topic, whether it is the first speech of the semester, that all-important final speech, or a speaking engagement long after your school years are over. Nothing is so frustrating to a public speaker as floundering for something to talk about!

Fortunately, there are several techniques that can help generate speech topics. They are somewhat more artificial than thinking of audience, occasion, and self to produce a "natural" topic choice. Nevertheless, they can yield good topics.

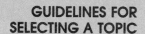

brainstorming
A creative problem-solving technique used to generate many ideas.

Brainstorming   **Brainstorming** is a problem-solving technique widely used in such diverse fields as business, advertising, writing, and science.[1] It can easily generate ideas for speech topics as well. To brainstorm a list of potential topics, get a sheet of paper and a pencil or pen. Set a minimum time limit of, say, three to five minutes. Write down the first topic that comes to mind. Do not allow yourself to evaluate it. Just write it down, as a simple word or a phrase, a vague idea or a well-focused one. Now jot down a second idea—again, anything that comes to mind. The first topic may remind you of a second possibility. Such "piggybacking" of ideas is perfectly OK. Continue without any restraints until your time is up. Your goal is quantity—as long a list as you can think up in the time you have.

The following list of twenty possible topics came from a brainstorming session of about three minutes:

Antiques
Where to find antiques
Decorating with antiques
Quilts
Quilt patterns and their history
Cats
Wild animals
The problem of keeping wild animals as pets
Zoos
Natural-habitat zoos
Breeding endangered species
Holidays
Children's birthday parties
Schools
School volunteer programs
Job hunting
Preparing an effective résumé
Teaching as a career
Plants
How to care for common houseplants
Poisonous plants native to this region
Wildlife native to this region

As you read the list, you will notice that certain ideas seem to form "clusters"—that is, to be related—which result from one topic's suggesting another. Notice too that some ideas are rather general while others are more specific; some are more sensible than others. At this stage, *anything goes*. The goal is just to get ideas on paper. When your brainstorming session is finished, go back over your list with a critical eye. You will quickly see that some ideas do not meet the guidelines we have discussed. But brainstorming sessions usually yield several ideas that have merit as speech topics. You can then refine those ideas or use them to stimulate your thinking of other, related topics, perhaps in a second brainstorming session. Just be sure that your final selection will suit your audience and occasion and is one in which you are interested, knowledgeable, or experienced.

If your brainstorming yields several good topics, so much the better! Set aside a page or two in your class notebook for topic ideas, and list the extra topics there. You can then consider them when you get your next assignment.

RECAP

HOW TO BRAINSTORM   1. Get a blank sheet of paper.
FOR A TOPIC   2. Set a time limit for brainstorming.

3. Begin writing as many possible topics for a speech as you can.
4. Do not stop to evaluate your topics; just write them down.
5. Let one idea lead to another—free-associate; piggyback off your own ideas.
6. Keep writing until your time is up.

Listening and Reading for Topic Ideas   Very often something you see, hear, or read triggers an idea for a speech. A current story on the evening TV news or in your local paper may suggest a topic. The following list of topics was brought to mind by recent headline stories in a large daily newspaper:

How to read and interpret stock market indicators

Prison overcrowding

Health codes and restaurants

The Nobel Prize

Neighborhood crime watch programs

How record prices for art and artifacts are affecting museum acquisitions

Television evangelism

A current news story may trigger an idea for a speech.
(*Laima Druskis*)

Deteriorating interstate highways
Mothers Against Drunk Driving

In addition to discovering topics in news stories, you might find them in an interesting segment of "60 Minutes," "20/20," or "Donahue." Chances are that a topic covered in one medium will have been covered in another as well, making extended research on the topic possible. For example, Oprah Winfrey's interview of a surrogate mother may be paralleled by *Newsweek*'s report on a much publicized court case concerning surrogacy.

You may also find speech topics in one of your other classes. A lecture in an economics or political science class may arouse your interest and provide a good topic for your next speech. The instructor of that class could probably suggest additional references on the subject you choose.

Sometimes even a subject that you discuss casually with friends can be developed into a good speech topic. You have probably talked with classmates about such campus issues as dormitory regulations, inadequate parking, or frustrations with registration and advisers. Campuswide concerns would be relevant to the student audience in your speech class, as would such matters as how to find a summer job or the pros and cons of living on campus or off campus. The college work-study program provided the topic for this recent student speech:

> One day not long ago, a freshman in this university entered the office of the Economics Department, hoping she was in the right place. There she stood, shaking in front of the secretary's desk, holding the assignment for her first job.
>
> Let me tell you that that girl was *me*! Currently I work for the Economics Department in the Business School as a member of the College Work-Study Program.
>
> The College Work-Study Program is a federal financial aid program that combines the benefits of financial assistance with valuable work experience. In the next few minutes I will talk about this program, outlining the requirements, responsibilities, and pay plan it involves.[2]

Just as you jotted down possible topics generated by brainstorming sessions, remember to write down topic ideas that you get from the media, class lectures, or informal conversations. What seems like a great topic today may be only a frustrating blank tomorrow if you rely on memory alone.

Scanning Lists and Indexes   By now, you probably have a list of topics from which to choose. But if all your efforts have failed to produce any ideas that satisfy you, try this technique. Turn to a reference work such as a dictionary, encyclopedia, or the *Reader's Guide to Periodical Literature* to stimulate your thinking. Open one of these books at random and look down the lists of words and phrases they contain. If you read them long enough, some idea will probably strike you as a possible speech topic.

The following topics were suggested by a portion of the *S* listings in a popular dictionary:

The Salvation Army
Saccharin and other artificial sweeteners

The role of sacrifice in religion
Seat belts
Saint Nicholas: the man and the legend
The Salk vaccine
Salt and blood pressure
Margaret Sanger and the modern birth control movement
Saturn
Theater scenery
Changing the traditional school year
Sects and cults

Of course, you still need to think of your audience, your occasion, and yourself when considering any topic as a possibility and continue to add to your list of potential topics.

A final word of caution before moving forward in the speech preparation process. For most brief classroom speeches (under ten minutes), you should allow at least one week from topic selection to speech delivery. A week gives you enough time to develop your ideas. Many habitual procrastinators (like Mike Richards, the speaker who opened this chapter) who reluctantly agree to begin their assignments a week in advance learn to their surprise that the whole process is far easier than when they delay work until the night before they are supposed to deliver their speech.

Narrowing the Topic

After brainstorming, reading the newspaper, watching TV, and talking to friends, you have come up with a topic. For some students the toughest part of the assignment is over at this point. But others soon experience additional frustration because their topic is so broad that they find themselves overwhelmed with information. How can you cover all aspects of a topic as large as "television" in three to five minutes? Even if you trained yourself to speak as rapidly as an auctioneer, it would take days to get it all in!

The solution is to narrow your topic so that it fits within the time limits set by your assignment. The challenge lies in *how* to do this. The following method works well for most students.

Draw a tabular form, such as the one shown here, on a blank sheet of paper.

At the top of the table, write your original topic idea.

Television		

Now divide your topic into two or three more specific categories. You may decide that different types of entertainment are logical subdivisions of television. So you write in the next spaces *Comedy*, *Drama*, and *Variety*.

Television		
Comedy	Drama	Variety

You are most interested in television comedy, so you choose to focus on that category. Now ask yourself, "Is the time I've got enough to give a speech on television comedy?" Your answer would be no, for you realize that the topic is still too broad. So you must subdivide further.

How can you logically divide the subject of television comedy? You could talk about famous comic actors. So you scrawl *Actors* under *Comedy*. You could also talk about the subjects of television comedies. You write *Subjects* beside *Actor*. Or you could talk about comic techniques. So you add *Techniques* to the other two components of television comedy.

Television				
Comedy			Drama	Variety
Actors	Subject	Techniques		

Again you consider the possibilities. Can one of these comic elements be turned into a topic for a good three- to five-minute speech? Success is certainly closer than it was when your topic was "television." You find the *subjects* of television comedies especially interesting but realize that the topic is still rather broad. Around what subjects do most television comedies center? Under *Subjects* you write *Family life*, *Friendship*, and *Work*.

Can you prepare a good three- to five-minute speech on how today's television comedies reflect modern family life? You remember reading an interview with Bill Cosby in which he discussed that very subject. You have some knowledge of the subject yourself, being a fan of "The Cosby Show," "Roseanne," and "Kate and Allie." Moreover, you know that most of your class will also have seen these programs, at least occasionally. And you feel confident that the subject can be covered fairly thoroughly in three to five minutes. Your original idea has been narrowed to a workable topic for the assignment.

You may find later that your topic is still a bit too broad. Too many family comedies reflect the wide diversity of family arrangements for a talk of no more than five minutes. So you choose one comedy, "Kate and Allie," let's say, and you decide to talk about how this treats the modern situation of blended families. It is also possible that you may find yourself in the very rare situation of having narrowed your topic so much that you cannot find enough information to talk for even three minutes. In that case, you go back a step. To stay with our example, you return to how family comedies reflect modern family life.

STEP 2: DETERMINE YOUR PURPOSE

As shown in Figure 5.2, now that you have selected and narrowed your topic, you need to decide on a purpose. If you do not know what you want your speech to achieve, chances are your audience won't either. Ask yourself, "What is really

FIGURE 5.2

Determine whether your speech purpose is to inform, persuade, or entertain, or some combination of these three speech purposes.

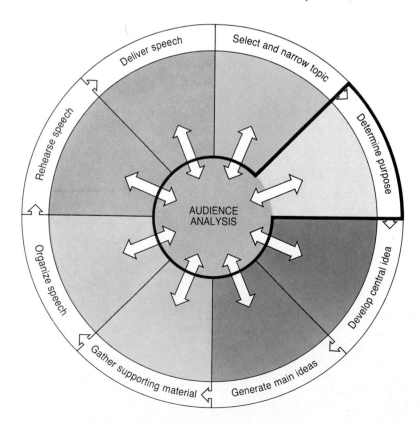

important for the audience to hear?" and "How do I want the audience to respond?" Clarifying your objectives at this stage will ensure a more interesting speech and a more successful outcome.

General Purpose

Virtually all speeches have one of three general purposes: to inform, persuade, or entertain. The speeches you give in class will generally be either informative or persuasive. It is important that you fully understand what constitutes each type of speech so that you do not confuse them and fail to fulfill an assignment. You certainly do not want to deliver a first-rate persuasive speech when an informative one was assigned! Although Chapters 14 through 17 will discuss the three general purposes at length, let's summarize them here so that you can understand the basic principles of each.

Speaking to Inform   An informative speaker is a teacher. Informative speakers give listeners information. They define, describe, or explain a thing, person, place, concept, process, or function. In this excerpt from a student's informative speech on anorexia nervosa, the student describes the disorder for her audience:

> Anorexia nervosa is an eating disorder that affects one out of every two hundred American women. It is a self-induced starvation that can waste its victims to the point that they resemble victims of Nazi concentration camps.

One of the President's objectives in his annual state of the union address is to inform.
(Carol T. Powers/The White House)

Who gets anorexia nervosa? 95% of its victims are females between the ages of twelve and eighteen. Men are only rarely afflicted with the disease. Anorexia nervosa patients are usually profiled as "good" or "model" children who have not caused their parents any undue concern or grief over other behavior problems. Anorexia nervosa is perhaps a desperate bid for attention by these young women.[3]

Most of the lectures you hear in college are informative. The university president's annual "state of the university" speech is informative, as is the Colonial Williamsburg tour guide's talk. Such speakers are all trying to increase the knowledge of their listeners. They may use an occasional bit of humor in their presentations, but their main objective is not to entertain but to inform. Chapter 14 provides specific suggestions for preparing an informative speech.

Speaking to Persuade   Persuasive speakers may also offer information, but in this case they use the information to try to change or reinforce an audience's convictions and often to urge some sort of action. One student used compelling examples and statistics to persuade her audience that ignorance of first-aid procedures causes unnecessary deaths:

Andrew Miller was eating dinner with his wife one night when suddenly a piece of meat lodged in his throat. He tried to cough it up but could not, and he passed out. His face became discolored. His wife panicked and called the neighbors, but no one knew the correct procedure. More neighbors were called. Finally, an ambulance was summoned.

Persuasive speakers try to change or reinforce an audience's convictions and often urge them to take some sort of action.
(*Robert Phillips*)

It was too late. Andrew Miller died in front of his wife and 13 of his friends and loved ones. Was the cause of death chicken-fried steak? No. It was ignorance.

Thousands of lives are saved each year because of simple application of first-aid techniques, but double that number of lives are lost because people simply don't know what to do. Ignorance kills.[4]

The representative from Mothers Against Drunk Driving (MADD) who spoke at your high school assembly urged you not to drink and drive and to help others realize the inherent dangers of the practice. The fraternity president talking to your group of rushees tried to convince you to join his fraternity. Appearing on television during the last election, the candidates for president of the United States asked for your vote. All three speakers gave you information, but they used that information to try to get you to believe or do something. Chapters 15 and 16 will focus in more detail on persuasive speaking.

Speaking to Entertain   The entertaining speaker tries to get the members of an audience to relax, smile, perhaps laugh, and generally enjoy themselves. Storyteller Garrison Keillor spins tales of the town and residents of Lake Wobegon, Minnesota, to amuse his listeners. Comedian Joan Rivers delivers a comic patter to make her audience laugh. Most after-dinner speakers talk to entertain their banquet guests. Like persuasive speakers, entertaining speakers may inform their listeners, but providing knowledge is not their main goal. Rather, their objective is to produce a smile at least and a belly laugh at best.

You need to decide at the beginning which of the three general purposes your speech is to have. This decision will keep you on track throughout the development of your speech. The way you organize, support, and deliver your speech will depend, in part, on your general purpose.

RECAP

GENERAL SPEECH PURPOSES		
	To inform	To share information by defining, describing, or explaining a thing, person, place, concept, process, or function
	To persuade	To change or reinforce a listener's attitude, belief, value, or behavior
	To entertain	To help an audience have a good time by getting listeners to relax, smile, and laugh

Specific Purpose

Now that you have a topic and you know generally whether your speech should inform, persuade, or entertain, it is time you decided on its specific purpose. Unlike the general purpose, which can be assigned by your instructor, the specific purpose of your speech must be decided by you alone, because it depends directly on the topic you choose.

To arrive at a specific purpose for your speech, you have to think in precise terms of what you want your audience to *do* at the end of your speech. This kind of goal or purpose is called a **behavioral objective** because you will specify the behavior you seek from the audience. For the speech on how television comedy represents the modern family, you might write, "At the end of my speech, the audience will be able to explain how comedy portrays American family life today." The purpose statement for a how-to speech using visual aids might read, "At the end of my speech, the audience will be able to use WordPerfect word processing software." For a persuasive speech on universal health care, your purpose statement could say, "At the end of my speech, the audience will be able to explain why the United States should adopt a plan of national health insurance." A speech to entertain will have a specific purpose, too. A stand-up comic may have a simple specific purpose: "At the end of my speech, the audience will laugh and applaud." An after-dinner speaker whose entertaining message has more informative value than that of the stand-up comic may say: "At the end of my speech, the audience will list four characteristics that distinguish journalists from the rest of the human race."

Wording the Purpose Statement   Note that all of our sample purpose statements begin with the same twelve words: "At the end of my speech, the audience will be able to . . ." The next word should call for an observable, measurable action that the audience should be able to take by the end of the speech. Use verbs such as *list*, *explain*, *describe*, or *write*. Do not use vague words like *know*, *understand*, or *believe*. You can discover what your listeners know, understand, or believe only by having them show their increased capability in some measurable way.

A statement of purpose does not say what you, the *speaker*, will do. The techniques of public speaking help you achieve your goals, but they are not themselves goals. To say "In my speech, I will talk about the benefits of studying classical dance" emphasizes your performance as a speaker. The goal of the speech is centered on you, rather than on the audience. Other than restating your topic, the statement of purpose provides little direction for the speech. But to say "At the end of my speech, the audience will be able to list three ways in which studying classical dance can benefit them" places the audience and its behavior at the center of your concern. This latter statement provides a tangible goal to guide your preparation and by which you can measure the success of your speech.

The following guidelines will help you prepare your statement of purpose.

1. *Use precise language in wording the specific purpose statement.*

Imprecise: "At the end of my speech, the audience will be able to explain some things about Hannibal, Missouri."
Precise: "At the end of my speech, the audience will be able to list five points of interest in the town of Hannibal, Missouri."

behavioral objective
The goal of your speech which describes what you want your audience to do after listening to your speech.

In the first example, the phrase "some things" is very general. It can refer to the town's economy, government, geography, tourist industry, school system, or any number of other facets of life in Hannibal. The second example offers a much more specific and limited goal for the speech.

2. *Limit the specific purpose statement to a single idea.* If your statement of purpose has more than one idea, you will have trouble covering the extra ideas in your speech. You will also run the risk of having your speech "come apart at the seams." Both unity of ideas and coherence of expression will suffer.

Two Ideas: "At the end of my speech, the audience will be able to make a picture frame and a planter."

One Idea: "At the end of my speech, the audience will be able to make a picture frame."

The enthusiastic carpenter who wrote the first statement would succeed only in exhausting himself and confusing his audience if he tried to achieve both goals in one speech. Choosing one project will result in a better speech.

3. *Be sure that your purpose statement meets the needs, interests, expectations, and level of knowledge of your audience.* Earlier in this chapter, we discussed the importance of considering the interests, needs, expectations, and knowledge of your audience when you select a speech topic. Consider these guidelines again as you word your purpose statement. They can help you ensure that you have not strayed from your topic.

Behavioral statements of purpose help remind you that the aim of public speaking is to win a response from the audience. In addition, using a purpose statement to guide the development of your speech will help you focus on the audience during the entire preparation process.

Using the Purpose Statement   Everything you do while preparing and delivering the speech should contribute to your specific purpose. The purpose statement can help in assessing the information you are gathering for your speech. For example, you may find that an interesting statistic, though related to your topic, will not help achieve your specific purpose. In that case, you can substitute material that will directly advance your purpose.

The specific purpose can also help you make decisions about the best use of visual aids. Let's say that your statement of purpose reads, "At the end of my speech, the audience will be able to recane old wicker chairs." In this instance, you will probably want a set of drawings to illustrate the process of recaning. The set, you may decide, will need at least two different kinds of drawings: one, rather realistic, to show the position of hands and tools when doing the lacing or interweaving, and a second that would diagrammatically illustrate the patterns of weaving for the various types of cane and wicker furniture. You will also have to decide whether to have reproductions of the drawings available for the audience after the lecture is over. As in all other aspects of preparing your speech, your specific purpose determines your decisions regarding visual aids.

As soon as you have decided on it, write the purpose statement on a 3-by-5 notecard. That way you can refer to it as often as necessary while developing your speech.

___

Having stated the specific purpose of your speech, you are ready to develop your central idea, the step shown in Figure 5.3. Closely related to the purpose statement, the central idea (sometimes called the *thesis*) is worded differently and functions differently during the speech writing process.

Central Idea Contrasted with Purpose Statement

Like a purpose statement, a central idea restates the speech topic. But whereas a purpose statement guides the speaker in preparing and delivering the speech, the central idea will eventually guide the audience in their understanding of the speech. Put another way, the purpose statement is what the speaker hopes to accomplish; the central idea is what he or she expects to say.

Purpose Statement: "At the end of my speech, the audience will be able to explain how censorship of school textbooks harms children."

FIGURE 5.3

Your central idea is a one sentence summary of your speech.

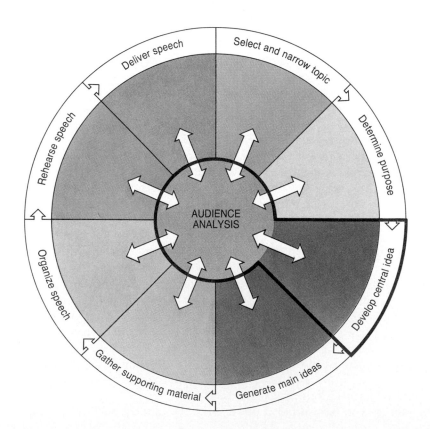

Central Idea: "Censorship of school textbooks threatens the rights of school-children.

Speakers rarely put their purpose statement into words for audiences. However, they usually state their central ideas at least twice: in the introduction and again in the conclusion of their speeches. If after a speech, an audience member is asked, "What was the speech about?" the answer is likely to be the speaker's central idea.

Wording the Central Idea

Unlike the purpose statement, which focuses on audience behavior, the central idea focuses on the content of the speech. The central idea is usually a one-sentence summary. From it the audience can tell what the speaker is going to discuss. The following guidelines will help put your central idea into words.

   1. *The central idea should not be a question; rather, it should be a declarative statement.*

Question: "Are caesarean births unnecessary?"
Declarative Statement: "Caesarean births are increasing at an alarming rate."

A central idea should not be phrased as a question. A question provides little direction for the speech and does not even suggest whether the speaker is going to support the affirmative or the negative answer. Imperative statements, or commands, are used as central ideas only rarely. One of the authors recently delivered a commencement address in which he used an imperative central idea, "Stop, look, and listen," for the sake of memorability. But such instances are rare. Similarly, a persuasive central idea might occasionally be worded as an exclamation if it is a surprising idea or a position the speaker holds strongly: "All abortion should be banned!" But in most cases, a declarative statement makes a speaker's position clear.
   2. *The central idea should be a complete sentence rather than a phrase or clause.*

Phrase: "car maintenance"
Complete Sentence: "Maintaining your car regularly can ensure that it provides reliable transportation."

The phrase "car maintenance" is really not a central idea but a topic. By the time you word your central idea, you should be ready to summarize your speech in a single sentence. The second example is a clear summary of the speech
   3. *The central idea should use specific language rather than vague generalities.*

Vague: "Responding to a hurricane warning involves lots of things."
Specific: "Responding to a hurricane warning requires that you secure your property and provide for your family's needs for at least one full week."

The specific wording provides not only the central idea of the speech but also a blueprint for the two main points of the speech: preparing property and providing for human needs before a hurricane strikes.

4. *The central idea should be a single idea.*

Two Ideas: "Water pollution and toxic waste dumping are major environmental problems in the United States today."

One Idea: "Toxic waste dumping is a major environmental problem in the United States today."

More than one central idea, like more than one idea in the purpose statement, will only lead to confusion and lack of cohesion in the speech.

5. *The central idea should reflect your consideration of the audience.* Just as you considered your audience when selecting and narrowing your topic and when composing your purpose statement, so should you consider your audience's needs, interests, expectations, and knowledge when stating your central idea. If you do not consider your listeners, you run the risk of losing their attention before you even begin developing the speech. If your audience consists mainly of college juniors and seniors, the second of the following central ideas would be better suited to your listeners than the first.

Inappropriate: "Whether or not you decide to go to college should be based on two important considerations: career goals and personal goals."

Appropriate: "Deciding whether to go to graduate school should be based on three factors: career goals, personal goals, and program availability."

Using the Central Idea

As mentioned earlier, central ideas are stated at least twice in most speeches. Speakers first present their central idea near the end of their introductions, when making a *preview statement* that includes the central idea and an outline of the main points of the speech. The following introduction, from a student's speech on sudden infant death syndrome, overtly states the thesis in its last sentence.

> Sudden infant death syndrome is known by many names. It is called crib death or SIDS. It is the leading cause of death in infants under a year old. SIDS is responsible for about 10,000 infants' lives per year. These infants usually range in age from two to four months. The reason SIDS is such a problem is because, after twenty years of research, SIDS still remains a mystery. *Today I would like to talk to you about the three major theories about sudden infant death syndrome.*[5]

In his conclusion, the speaker states his central idea again, this time naming the three theories.

> *In review, the three main theories of SIDS are the theory of maturation, the theory of dopamine, and the theory of asbestos in the lungs.* All SIDS deaths involve apnea. This is the stoppage of air flow to the lungs, either temporarily or permanently. The real answer to why apnea

occurs may be in one of the theories discussed today, or it could be something nobody has yet considered.

Although such overt repetition might be considered poor writing, it makes for good public speaking. Writers have an advantage over public speakers. Readers can reread a sentence or passage they missed the first time around. Listeners cannot do that. However, a listener who misses the central idea when it is stated in the introduction may be able to arrive at it from the main points in the speech. But if that is not possible for one reason or the other, surely the central idea will be made clear when the speaker repeats it in the speech's conclusion.

The central idea performs one other important function. You can use it to guide the division of your speech into main ideas. Such a preliminary outline can be constructed after you have written your central idea.

Next to choosing a topic, probably the most common stumbling block in developing speeches is the preliminary outline. Trying to decide how to subdivide your central idea into two, three, or four main points can make you chew your pencil, scratch your head, and end up as you began, with a blank sheet of paper. However, as shown in Figure 5.4, the task of generating the main points of your speech is essential. And it will be much easier if you use the following formula.

STEP 4: GENERATE MAIN IDEAS

FIGURE 5.4
Generate major ideas for your speech by looking for natural divisions, reasons, or steps to support your central idea.

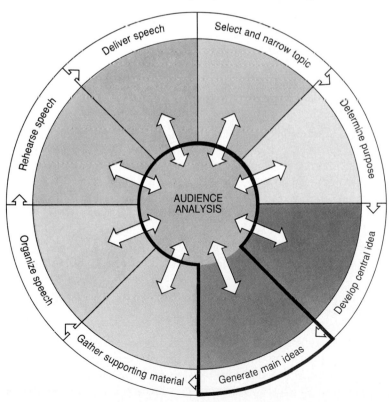

Write the central idea at the top of a clean sheet of paper. Then ask these three questions:

1. Does the central idea have *logical divisions*? (These may be indicated by such phrases as "three types" or "four means.")
2. Can you think of several *reasons* the central idea is true?
3. Can you support your central idea with a series of *steps* or a chronological progression?

You should be able to answer yes to one of these three questions. With your answer in mind, write down the divisions, reasons, or steps you thought of. Let's see this technique at work with several central idea statements.

Logical Divisions of the Central Idea

Suppose that your central idea is "A liberal arts education benefits the student in many ways." You now turn to the three questions. But for this example, you needn't go beyond the first one. Does the central idea have logical divisions? The phrase "many ways" indicates that it does. You can logically divide your speech into the many ways in which the student benefits. A brief brainstorming session then helps you come up with five main ways in which a liberal arts education benefits students:

1. Job opportunities
2. Appreciation of culture
3. Hobbies
4. Understanding history
5. Concern for humankind

At this stage, you needn't worry about Roman numerals, parallel form, or even the order in which the main ideas are listed. We will discuss these and the other features of outlining in Chapter 8. Your goal now is simply to generate ideas. Moreover, just because you write them down, don't think that the ideas you come up with now are engraved in stone. They can—and probably will—change. After all, this is a *preliminary* outline. It may undergo many revisions before you actually deliver your speech. In the case of our example, five points may well prove to be too many to develop in the brief time allowed for most classroom speeches. But since it is much easier to eliminate ideas than to invent them, list them all for now.

Reasons the Central Idea Is True

Suppose that your central idea is "Marriage is an endangered institution." Asking whether there are logical divisions of this idea will be no help at all. There are no key phrases indicating logical divisions—no "ways," "means," "types," or "methods" appear in the wording. The second question, however, is more profitable: You can think of *reasons* this central idea is true. Simply ask yourself, "Why?" after the statement "Marriage is an endangered institution." You can then list these three answers:

1. There are fewer marriages each year.
2. More men and women are living together outside of marriage.
3. More couples are getting divorced each year.

Notice that these main ideas are expressed in complete sentences, while the ones in the preceeding example were in phrases. At this stage, it doesn't matter. What does matter is getting your ideas down on paper. You can rewrite and reorganize them later.

Steps Supporting the Central Idea

"U.S. involvement in Latin American politics has increased tremendously since 1980." You stare glumly at the central idea you so carefully formulated yesterday. Now what? You know a lot about the subject; your political science professor has covered it thoroughly this semester. But how can you organize all the information you have? Again, you turn to the three-question method.

Are there logical divisions of the main idea? Hopefully, you scan the sentence, but you can find no key phrases suggesting logical divisions.

Can you think of several *reasons* the thesis is true? You read the central ideas again and add "Why?" to the end of it. Answering that question may lead you to talk about the *reasons* for U.S. involvement in Latin America. But your purpose statement reads, "At the end of my speech, the audience will be able to trace the evolution of United States involvement in Latin American politics since 1980." Giving *reasons* for that involvement would not directly contribute to your goal. So you turn to the third question.

Can you support your central idea with a series of steps? Almost any historical topic, or any topic requiring a chronological progression (for example, topics of how-to speeches), can be subdivided by answering the third question. You therefore decide that your main points will be the chronological sequence of events from 1980 to the present that led to increased U.S. involvement in Latin America. Jotting down the four or five most important events, you know that you can add, replace, or eliminate some ideas later. You have a start.

Notice that you consulted your purpose statement when you chose your main ideas in that last example. Although you needn't worry about form while constructing your tentative outline, you do need to refer to the purpose statement when deciding on your main points. If your outline will not help achieve your purpose, you need to rethink your speech. You may finally change either your purpose or your main ideas, but whichever you do, you need to synchronize them. Remember, it is much easier to make changes at this point than after you have done the research and produced a detailed outline.

It's much too long since we abandoned Mike Richards, the student in the opening paragraphs of this chapter who was struggling to write a speech on college football. Even though he has procrastinated, if he follows the steps we have discussed, he should be able to outline a successful informative speech.

Mike has already chosen his topic. His audience is likely to be interested in his subject. Since he is a varsity defensive tackle, they probably expect him to talk about college football. And he himself is passionately interested in and knowledgeable about the subject. It meets all the requirements of a successful topic.

But "college football" is too broad for a three- to five-minute talk. Mike needs to narrow his topic to a manageable size. He adjusts his monitor and begins.

College Football

What could he cover under *College Football*? Mike's school has recently been reprimanded by the NCAA for violating recruiting regulations. The audience might be interested in that subject. So he types *Recruiting* under *College Football*. Since he himself is a player, his audience might also like to hear about the game from a player's point of view. He adds *Playing* beside *Recruiting*.

College Football

Recruiting	Playing

The more he thinks about it, the more Mike feels he would like to talk about what happens on the playing field. But he realizes that his topic is still too broad. He decides to focus on either the *benefits* or the *disadvantages* of playing football. He types these terms under *Playing*.

College Football		
Recruiting	Playing	
	Benefits	Disadvantages

Mike knows that most of his classmates view football players as privileged, pampered students. To balance this view, he thinks that maybe he should talk about the disadvantages. In his three years on the team, Mike has encountered two major disadvantages: the demands made on a player's time and the threat and reality of physical injury.

College Football			
Recruiting	Playing		
	Benefits	Disadvantages	
		Time requirements	Injury

Mike himself has suffered several injuries and feels qualified to talk about this aspect of football. The topic "injuries in college football" should work.

Once he has worked out the topic, Mike needs a purpose statement. He decides that his audience may know something about how players are injured, but they probably do not know how these injuries are treated. He types, "The audience will be able to explain how the three most common injuries suffered by college football players are treated."

A few minutes later, Mike derives his central idea from his purpose: "Sports medicine specialists have developed specific courses of treatment for the three most common kinds of injuries suffered by college football players."

Deciding on a tentative outline is also fairly easy now. Since his central idea mentions three kinds of injuries, he can organize his speech according to those three ideas (logical divisions). Under the central idea Mike lists:

1. Bruises
2. Broken bones
3. Ligament and cartilage damage

Now Mike has a preliminary outline and is well on his way to developing a successful three- to five-minute informative speech.

SUMMARY   This chapter presented a logical way of getting from a blank piece of paper to a tentative speech outline. Four main steps are involved:

1. Selecting and narrowing the topic
2. Formulating both a general and a specific purpose
3. Determining the central idea
4. Generating main ideas

The difficulty of selecting a topic can vary greatly from speech to speech. Sometimes speakers are asked to address a specific topic. At other times they may be given only such broad guidelines as time limits and occasion. As speakers ponder their topic, they must consider the interests, needs, knowledge level, and expectations of their audiences. They must also consider the special demands of the occasion. Finally, all speakers must take into account their own interests, abilities, and experiences. Usually these "boundaries" will help them select appropriate topics. If they are still undecided, they may try such techniques as brainstorming, consulting the media, or scanning lists and indexes that might contain potential topics.

After having chosen a broad topic area, a speaker may need to narrow the topic. This chapter provided a method for narrowing a topic so that it fits within the time limits that have been set.

The next task a speaker faces is deciding on general and specific purposes. He or she must consider whether a speech is going to be informative, persuasive, or entertaining. With a general purpose in mind, the speaker can write a specific purpose statement. A purpose statement should be worded behaviorally, in terms of what the speaker wants the audience to be able to do at the end of the speech. The purpose statement serves as a yardstick by which the speaker can measure the relevance of ideas and supporting materials while developing the speech.

Purpose statements indicate what speakers hope to accomplish; central ideas, by contrast, summarize what will be said. The central idea should be worded as a simple declarative sentence. It is usually stated in both the introduction and the conclusion of a speech. From the central idea, the speaker can derive a preliminary outline.

One method for producing this outline is to determine whether the central idea has natural divisions, can be supported by a group of reasons, or can be achieved through a series of steps. These divisions, reasons, or steps will produce an outline from which the speaker can work while moving on to support and develop the speech.

QUESTIONS FOR DISCUSSION AND REVIEW

1. What are the guidelines to follow when you select a speech topic?
2. Identify three techniques for helping you select a speech topic.
3. Differentiate among speaking to inform, to persuade, and to entertain. Can the same speech have more than one general purpose?
4. Explain how to word a specific purpose statement. How does the speaker use this statement?
5. What is a central idea statement?
6. How do you find the main ideas for your speech?

1. Brainstorm a list of at least fifteen potential topics for an informative classroom speech. Applying the criteria discussed in this chapter, select the topics best suited to you, your audience, and the occasion. If you wish, use one of these topics for an assigned informative speech.

2. Browse through a current newspaper, newsmagazine, or *TV Guide*. See how many potential speech topics you can discover in the stories your source contains. Write them down. File or copy your list in your speech notebook.

3. Using a technique like the one described in this chapter, subdivide each of the following general categories into a workable topic for a three- to five-minute informative speech:

   The ocean
   Modern technology
   American politics

4. Write a behavioral purpose statement for each of the following informative speech topics:

   How to prepare a monthly budget
   The advantages and disadvantages of living in a college dormitory
   The need for an academic adviser
   There should be a national presidential primary

5. Select one of the topics for which you wrote a behavioral purpose statement in activity 4. Now write a central idea for that same speech. Decide whether your central idea can best be subdivided according to logical divisions, reasons, or steps, and write a preliminary speech outline.

SUGGESTED ACTIVITIES

6

Supporting Your Speech

OBJECTIVES

After studying this chapter, you should be able to

1. Explain the importance of supporting materials to a speech
2. List the six main types of supporting materials
3. Explain at least one guideline for using each of the six types of supporting materials
4. List and explain six criteria for determining which supporting materials to use in a speech
5. Explain and apply the four steps in integrating supporting materials into a speech

I use not only all the brains I have, but all I can borrow. (Jacob Lawrence, The Library. *National Museum of American Art, Smithsonian Institution. Gift of S.C. Johnson & Son, Inc.*)

WOODROW WILSON

A long-winded speaker was continuing to deliver his dry and lengthy address. He was running long over time. The master of ceremonies tried to get him to stop, but couldn't attract his attention. Finally, in desperation, he picked up the gavel, aimed and fired, but missed the speaker and hit a man in the first row. The man slumped down, then groaned, "Hit me again, I can still hear him."[1]

How many times have you, like that unfortunate man in the front row, been so bored listening to a long, dry speech that you would have welcomed unconsciousness? Perhaps you weren't granted relief by a flying gavel—you may have dozed off on your own, instead, to wake up startled but happy to find the speaker finished at last! Hardly an inspiring scenario, but one that occurs all too often—so often, in fact, that Mark Twain is said to have once advised a nervous speaker, "Just remember, they don't expect much."[2]

Why do many speakers so bore their listeners that most have come not to expect much? The problem may be due to failure at any stage of the speechmaking process. The failure may be because the best topic had not been chosen for the speaker's own interests and abilities, the audience's concerns, or the occasion. Or the topic may not have been narrowed enough to be covered adequately within the set time limits. Finally, the ideas may have been so poorly organized that the audience had difficulty following the speaker's train of thought. But the most likely explanation is that the speech lacks lively, relevant, and interesting examples, explanations, quotations, and other types of support. As Figure 6.1 illustrates, an essential step in the speech preparation process is gathering appropriate supporting material.

Supporting materials not only help a speaker capture and maintain an audience's attention, but they also serve as evidence to support what the speaker says. Without relevant examples and solid statistics, a speaker's ideas may be dismissed as only so much hot air. Clearly, a skilled public speaker must learn to choose and use supporting materials wisely. In this chapter, we will discuss the main types of supporting materials and present guidelines for their effective use.

TYPES OF SUPPORTING MATERIALS

Example and Illustration

The young woman walked to the front of the public speaking class and turned to face her classmates. She was about to deliver her final speech of the semester. Her audience prepared to listen politely, but without much enthusiasm, to yet another speech. In a low, soft voice, the speaker began:

> Four years ago a little girl was born in a hospital in this city. Her parents' excitement quickly turned to anguish as doctors quietly and sympathetically told them that their baby was suffering from several birth defects, the most severe a heart problem that would result in the baby's death if not repaired immediately. Less critical, but nevertheless disturbing, was a cleft lip and cleft palate that disfigured the baby's face and left her unable to suck normally.
>
> The parents' worry was multiplied by the fact that their medical insurance did not cover newborns. They despaired of being able to take care of their baby. Then an angel appeared—in the form of a representative from the March of Dimes. That organization, she explained, was prepared to help in emergencies just such as theirs. [Speaker holds

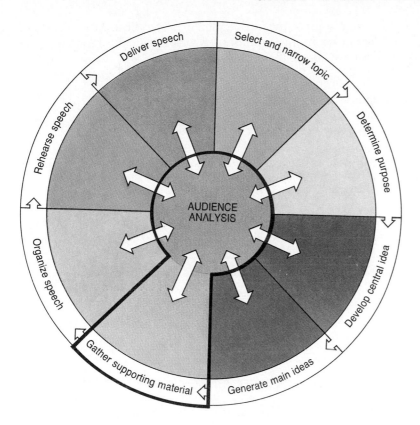

FIGURE 6.1

Supporting material clarifies your ideas and adds interest to your message.

up an 11-by-14 picture of a beautiful, smiling little 4-year-old girl.] Thanks to the efforts of the March of Dimes, here is that same little girl today. They truly made her life possible—I know, because she is my little sister.[a]

By this point in the speech, the room was silent. Eyes were tearing and attention was riveted on the speaker, who went on to talk about the work of the March of Dimes and to encourage support of that organization—and to earn an A on her final speech!

The reason for the success of that speech? The speaker had worked hard on many aspects of the assignment, but the primary reason for her success was her poignant personal illustration.

Political leaders, for whom storytelling is a means to an end, often become known as great speakers because of their ability to tell a pointed anecdote. Abraham Lincoln was a master storyteller. Winston Churchill use his narrative skills to great advantage. Lyndon Johnson was known for his "down home" humorous tales. Ronald Reagan often related folksy illustrations. *Everybody likes to hear a story*. If you remember nothing else from this chapter, remember that one principle! An illustration almost always ensures audience interest. Best of all, as in the March of Dimes speech, is the anecdote that comes from personal experience. Even usually mediocre speakers gain the advantages of conviction and enthusiasm when they talk about personal experiences.

Now that we recognize the importance of using illustrations, let's look more closely at different kinds of illustrations. As we examine the examples, we will also look at some tips for using them.

Brief Examples   Brief examples are short illustrations, often no longer than a sentence or two. A student talking about diploma fraud offered the following brief example of the problem:

> A 45-year-old man was able to impersonate a doctor and give anesthesia improperly during surgery to remove a bladder tumor. The patient lapsed into a coma and remains brain dead, according to the August 6, 1984, issue of *U.S. News and World Report*.[4]

Sometimes a series of brief examples can have more impact than either a single example or a detailed extended illustration. *Newsweek* opened an article on Lyme disease with the following string of examples:

> In the popular beach community of Fire Island, N.Y., it's the hot topic this season. In Appleton, Wis., parents wonder whether they should send their kids to camp or on nature hikes. And in Big Pine Key, Fla., Don Gerberich, 36, at last has a diagnosis for the baffling malady that has afflicted him for more than a year. "They don't ever expect me to recover 100 percent," he says, "but now at least I know it's a disease with a name."
>
> The name is Lyme disease, and the time to catch it is right now—possibly in your own backyard.[5]

The impact of those three examples is greater than that of any one by itself. A skeptical audience might dismiss a single example as atypical, but three instances indicate a trend about which people might need to be concerned.

Extended Illustrations   More detailed than the brief example is the extended illustration. The student who told about her baby sister used an extended illustration. It resembles a story: It is more vividly descriptive than the brief example, and it has a plot, which includes an opening, complications, a climax, and a resolution.

A student speaker opened her speech on the importance of burn education with this compelling extended illustration:

> For 10-year-old Dawn Lang, summer meant swimming, talking about boys and camping with her family in Michigan's Upper Peninsula. Like any typical camping trip, they loaded the family stationwagon, travelled for several long hours and envisioned "roughing it out" in the wilderness. As Dawn was sitting by the campfire, her father was pumping up the gas stove . . . when it exploded, catching Dawn's hair and clothing on fire. In a panic Dawn ran, just as any 10-year-old would. In a flash, the flames spread across her body. Her father managed to knock her down and her brother threw a rug on her to smother the flames. While this accident took less than 30 seconds, Dawn was burned over half of her body.[6]

To use an extended illustration takes more time than to cite a brief example, but longer stories can be more dramatic and emotionally compelling. Chapter 14 will discuss further the use of narration in public speaking.

Hypothetical Illustrations   Hypothetical illustrations may be either brief ex-amples or extended illustrations. They differ from the illustrations we have discussed so far in that they have not actually occurred. Rather, they are scenarios that *might* happen. The following hypothetical illustration might be used to introduce a speech on dormitory security:

> Imagine yourself returning to your dorm room at the end of a busy day of classes. As you reach the door, you find it slightly ajar. That seems strange, because you are always careful to close and lock it. Shrugging off what you assume was an isolated memory lapse, you swing open the door. The sight before you stops you in your tracks. Lamps are upset, dresser drawer contents are strewn everywhere, and your stereo and television unit is conspicuously empty. You have become a statistic in the rising count of dormitory burglaries.

Notice that the illustration begins with the word *imagine*. The purpose of a hypothetical illustration is not to trick your listeners into believing a bogus story. They should be aware from the beginning that the illustration is hypothetical. There is a very good reason for inventing a hypothetical illustration: The imagined example may serve your purpose better than any real examples by enabling you to get your audience to identify with someone in a particular situation. Of course, both the illustration and the situation must be plausible if you are to be convincing.

Using Illustrations Effectively   Illustrations are almost guaranteed attention get-ters, as well as a way to support your statements. But even this excellent form of support can be ineffective if not used to its best advantage. The following suggestions should help you use illustrations more effectively in your speeches.

1. *Be certain that your illustrations are directly relevant to the idea or point they are supposed to support.* As obvious as this principle seems, many student speakers, learning of the value of illustrations, go to great lengths to use as many of them as they can in their speeches. They are so eager, in fact, that some of their illustrations have little bearing on the specific point they are trying to make. Their listeners become confused. Never leave your audience in doubt as to why you used a certain illustration. Be sure that illustrations are obviously related to the idea they support.

2. *The illustrations you choose should represent a trend.* It is not fair to your audience to find one or two isolated illustrations and use them as though they were typical. If your illustrations are rare instances, you owe it to your listeners to tell them so.

3. *Make your illustrations lively and interesting.* You probably know people who cannot tell a joke. They just can't relate a story or deliver a punch line. Or they lack the sense of timing needed to make a joke funny. Unfortunately, some speakers bumble their best illustrations in a similar manner. Some years ago, a speech pro-fessor was fascinated to discover that one of his students had been on the last voyage of the Italian ship, the ill-fated *Andrea Doria*. Early in the semester, he urged the young man to relate his experience as part of an informative speech on how humans respond to danger. The professor expected a speech with great dramatic impact. Instead, much to his surprise, the student's narrative went something like this: "Well, there was a loud noise and then the sirens went off and we all got in lifeboats and the ship sank."[7] Hardly the stuff great drama is made of! If you have chosen to tell a poignant story, give it enough detail to make it come alive in the

minds of your listeners. Paint a mental picture of the people, places, and things involved.

4. *Search for illustrations with which your listeners can identify.* Just as you want to use illustrations that are typical, so too do you want to use illustrations with which the members of your audience can relate. If, upon hearing your illustration, your listeners mentally shrug and think, "That could never happen to me," the power of your story is considerably lessened. The best illustrations are the ones that your listeners can imagine happening to themselves. Other compelling stories, like the sinking of the *Andrea Doria*, can illustrate such great human drama that everyone listening will be immediately interested and attentive. If you cannot find a plausible example, you may want to invent a hypothetical one, which you can gear specifically to your audience. You can then be sure of its pertinence to your listeners.

5. *Remember that the best illustrations are personal ones.* A personal illustration—an experience that actually happened to you—will usually fascinate an audience. One student speaker, talking about hyperactive children, decided to tell about her own experiences as the sister of a hyperactive older brother. The extra attention and treatment needed by her brother had affected her entire family in both positive and negative ways. Because she had lived with this situation all her life, her illustration helped establish her credibility. And she told of her family's experiences with a fervor and intensity she probably could not have mustered for a third-person account. Of course, you will not have had personal experience with every topic on which you may speak. In a speech on the conflict between the legislative and executive branches of government, your best illustration might be that of Oliver North in the Iran-Contra affair. Nor could you offer personal experience if you were speaking on American military strategy during the Revolutionary War. Your best illustrations for that speech might come from the letters of George Washington. But if you *have* had personal experience with the subject on which you are speaking, be sure to describe that experience to the audience.

Explanation and Description

▼

explanation
A statement that makes clear how something is done or why it exists in its present or past form.

▼

description
Identifying facts, information, and details about something.

Probably the most commonly used forms of support are explanations and descriptions. An **explanation** is a statement that makes clear *how something is done* or *why it exists in its present or past form.* A **description** tells you *what something is like.* Descriptions provide the details that allow audience members to develop mental pictures of what their speakers are talking about.

Explaining How   Kathy had pet birds for many years. Her parents were part owners of an aviary, and the whole family was expert in the selection and care of various birds. For this reason, Kathy decided to give her first informative speech on parrots. She relied heavily on personal illustrations for much of the speech, but she also explained how to choose a pet parrot for those who might wish to buy one:

First, look for a healthy bird. Birds that are lethargic and uninterested in their surroundings or that have discharge from the eyes or nose are probably better left alone. Second, look for a tame bird. Unless you have had previous experience with parrots, you are better off to have an already tamed bird as your first pet. If the seller claims that the bird is tame, ask to handle it. A tame parrot should sit on your arm without biting, clawing, or trying to escape. Finally, if you are inexperienced in dealing with birds, your best insurance that you have a suitable candidate for a pet is to buy from a reliable aviary, rather than from a private owner or from a less-than-reputable dealer.[8]

Kathy's explanation of how to choose a healthy parrot came from her firsthand knowledge of the subject. Other explanations of how to do something or how something works may come from library research. Such is the case with this explanation of how ultraviolet light harms human skin:

Dermatologists point out that ultra-violet light breaks down the protein building blocks of skin, collagen for resilience and pliability and elastin for structure. When this happens, the skin becomes dryer, nobular and pebbly. All the characteristics associated with old age. So all the attempts at getting the body beautiful, or even unintentional exposure to the sun can actually result in unpliable, unresilient, and heavily lined skin.[9]

Speakers who discuss or demonstrate processes of any kind—whether selection of a parrot or effects of ultraviolet radiation—will rely at least in part on explanations of how those processes work.

Explaining Why   Explaining *why*—giving reasons for a policy, principle, or event—is perhaps even more common in speeches than explaining *how* something is accomplished. Even before Kathy explained *how* to choose a parrot, she discussed *why* her listeners should consider a parrot for a pet. Another speaker, discussing the battered wife syndrome, might begin with an explanation of why husbands become abusive. Once the causes are established, the speaker can then tailor the solutions to those specific causes. A student seeking to reverse a university policy against freshmen having cars on campus can first explain *why* that policy was adopted and then point out *why* it is no longer needed. In short, explaining *why* some condition or event exists provides an analysis that often leads to better solutions.

Describing   To describe is to produce **word pictures**—detailed sensory information that allows an audience mentally to see, hear, smell, touch, or taste the object of your description. The more senses you appeal to with your word pictures, the better. Good descriptions are vivid, accurate, and specific; they make people, places, and events come alive for the audience. More specific instructions for constructing word pictures are given in Chapter 14.

word picture
Detailed description that allows a listener to mentally see, hear, smell, touch, or taste the object of your description.

   Description may be used in a brief example, an extended illustration, a hypothetical instance, or by itself. In a speech on the Nicaraguan Contras, a student briefly, but effectively, describes the conflict: "A soldier slithers among the tall grass hoping to find someone who supports the current government: the enemy."[10] The serpentine term *slithers* vividly describes the tactics employed by the Contras.

Gestures and visual aids may help a speaker to describe something.
(Nancy J. Pierce/Photo Researchers, Inc.)

Using Explanations and Descriptions Effectively   Perhaps because they are the most commonly used forms of support, explanation and description are also among the most frequently abused. When large sections of a speech contain long, non-specific explanations, audience eyelids are apt to fall. The following suggestions will help you use explanation and description effectively in your speeches.

1. *Make your explanations and descriptions brief.* Length alone is often the reason for boredom with many explanations and descriptions. An explanation should supply only enough details for an audience to understand how or why something works or exists. Too many details may make your listeners say your speech was "everything I *never* wanted to know about the subject."

2. *Make the language of your explanations and descriptions as specific and concrete as possible.* Explanations tend to be general and thereby somewhat deadly. Vivid and specific language will bring your explanations alive. Liveliness will help you hold the audience's attention and paint in your listeners' minds the image that you are trying to communicate. Chapter 13 will provide more tips on making your language specific.

3. *Do not overuse explanation and description.* Even brief, specific explanations are boring if they are used alone, without other kinds of support. You will hold your audience's attention more effectively if you alternate explanations and descriptions with other types of supporting material, such as brief examples or statistics.

Definition

Steve thought and thought but couldn't come up with a good opening for his speech. In desperation, he turned to the dictionary. To introduce his speech on modern legal training in the United States, he decided to define *lawyer*. Much to Steve's disappointment, his introduction only succeeded in putting his 8:00 A.M. class soundly back to sleep. Steve's problem? He had misused a perfectly legitimate form of support. He did not need to define *lawyer* for a college class—or for any class beyond elementary school, for that matter. Steve had resorted to an unnecessary definition as a crutch, and it didn't hold up.

Definitions have two justifiable uses in speeches. First, a speaker should be sure to define any and all specialized, technical, or little-known terms in his or her speech. If Steve had discussed "tort reform," he would have needed to define that phrase early in his speech. Second, a speaker must define any term used in a unique or unusual interpretation if the meaning is not immediately clear from the context of the speech. A speaker must also clarify the intended meaning when a word has two or more meanings, if that is not obvious from the context. For example, a newspaper article on child abuse redefined that term in the following manner:

> When we hear of child abuse, we think of children physically battered. Yet there is a kind of abuse just as crippling, just as horrifying: emotional abuse. It leaves no scars on the body, but breaks a child's heart and spirit.[11]

A speaker may consult a dictionary for a definition of any specialized, technical, and little-known terms that appear in his or her speech.
(*Frank Siteman/Stock, Boston*)

The article's definition serves a useful purpose: It makes clear to the reader its somewhat unique view of child abuse.

If you need to define a term, you have two options. You may either take the definition from a dictionary or make up an original one.

Definition by Classification   If you have to explain the meaning of a term, you may use a standard dictionary definition from the *Oxford English Dictionary*, a desktop *Webster's*, or another reputable dictionary. Dictionaries define words by classification—that is, by first placing a term in the general class, group, or family to which it belongs and then differentiating it from all other members of that class. For example, if you look up the word *coypu*, you may find this definition: "a large beaverlike South American rodent, . . . valued for its fur."[12] The coypu *belongs* to the rodent family, but it *differs* from squirrels and rats in that it is native to South America, has a valuable pelt, and is aquatic.

A dictionary definition also has authority. This can be an important advantage, especially when you take a controversial stand. If you quote a reputable dictionary, the audience will usually accept without question the definition you provide.

Original Definition   Although it may be easier to rely on a dictionary for your definitions, there are times when you would do better not to use one. For example, the definition of *child abuse* that was quoted a little earlier did not come from a dictionary. A dictionary provides only a very general definition of the word *abuse* and may not have a separate entry for *child abuse*. Furthermore, the article's definition pinpointed exactly how the term was going to be used. Many words and phrases are best made clear by an original definition, as is any term that is applied in a unique or uncommon way.

Using Definitions Effectively   Three suggestions can help you use definitions more effectively in your speeches.

1. *Use definitions only when needed.* As we mentioned, novice speakers too often use definitions as an easy introduction or a time filler. Resist the temptation to provide a definition unless you are using a relatively obscure term or one with several definitions. Unnecessary definitions are boring and, more serious still, insulting to the audience's intelligence.

2. *Be certain that your definition is understandable.* You probably have had the frustrating experience of looking up a word in the dictionary, only to find that the full definition is as confusing as the word itself. The word *dogmatic*, for example, may be defined as "characterized by or given to the use of dogmatism." To find a more satisfactory definition, you have to look down the column until you find *dogmatism*. Your listeners do not have that capability, so make certain that you give them definitions that are immediately and easily understandable—or you will have wasted your time and perhaps even lost your audience.

3. *Be certain that your definition and your use of the term throughout a speech are synonymous.* If a dictionary does not define a term just as you intend to use it, create an original definition that is geared specifically to your intention. Even seemingly

simple words can create confusion if not defined and used consistently. For example, if you are giving a speech on the potential hazards of abusing nonprescription painkillers and you define *drugs* as nonprescription painkillers, use the term in that way throughout the speech. Referring at some point to "illegal drugs" or "prescription drugs" would confuse your audience.

Analogy

Analogy is related to definition but is used in different situations. Like a definition, an analogy gives you increased understanding; but unlike a definition, it deals with complex relations. An analogy increases understanding through comparison—the new to the old, the unknown to the known. Analogies can help your listeners understand unfamiliar ideas, things, and situations by showing how these matters are similar to something they already know.

analogy
A comparison.

There are two types of analogies. A *literal* analogy compares two things that are actually similar (two sports, two cities, two events). A *figurative* analogy may take the form of a literary simile or metaphor. It compares two things that at first seem to have little in common (the West Wind and revolution)[13] but share some vital feature (in this case, a fierce impetus for change).

Literal Analogy   The student whose description of the Nicaraguan Contras we looked at earlier went on to compare that struggle with the American Revolution:

> The Nicaraguan contras are following the pattern of that Revolutionary rebels. . . . Two details are important. Although the rebels are small in number, their numbers are increasing rapidly as they overcome their fears of the consequences of rebellion. As our Founding Fathers needed the military support of other countries, the contras' need for military support and knowledge is being felt. Recent reports indicate the rebels' supplies are limited. The United States, much like France in the late 1700's, has provided the contras with some needed military aid. While the Revolutionary rebels first used guerrilla warfare, this is the war tactic also used by the contras.[14]

Here the speaker points out a couple of ways in which the two rebellions are similar. He creates a literal analogy.

The literal analogy is often employed by people who wish to influence public policy. For example, proponents of trade restrictions argue that since Japan maintains its trade balance through stringent import controls, so should the United States. If Columbia, Missouri, solved both ecological and financial woes by successfully instituting an aluminum can tax, why not try the same approach in litter-plagued, budget-troubled Lawrence, Kansas? The more similarities a policymaker can show between the items being compared, the better his or her chances of being persuasive.

Figurative Analogy   On a warm July afternoon in 1848, feminist Elizabeth Cady Stanton delivered the keynote address to the first women's rights convention in Seneca Falls, New York. Near the end of her speech, she offered this impassioned analogy:

> Voices were the visitors and advisers of Joan of Arc. Do not "voices" come to us daily from the haunts of poverty, sorrow, degradation, and despair, already too long unheeded?

> Now is the time for the women of this country, if they would save our free institutions, to defend the right, to buckle on the armor that can best resist the keenest weapons of the enemy—contempt and ridicule.[15]

A literal analogy might have compared the status of women in medieval France to that of women in nineteenth-century America. But the figurative analogy Stanton employed compared the voices that moved Joan of Arc to the social causes motivating nineteenth-century women.

Because it does not rely on facts or statistics but rather on imaginative insights, the figurative analogy is not considered a form of "hard" evidence. But because it is creative, it is inherently interesting and may help grab an audience's attention. Speakers often employ figurative analogies in their introductions and conclusions.

Using Analogy Effectively   One suggestion for each type of analogy should help you to use both effectively.

1. *Be certain that the two things you compare in a literal analogy are very similar.* If you base your speech on a literal analogy, it is vital that the two things you compare be very much alike. In an informative speech, a literal analogy that doesn't quite work may hamper rather than help an audience's understanding of the thing or idea you are trying to explain. In a persuasive speech, few things give your adversaries as much joy as being able to point up a major dissimilarity in a literal analogy. For example, the two cities being compared are in actuality more different than alike, the opponent may argue. One is relatively poor; the other is wealthy. One has an elected mayor and a city council; the other has an elected board of commissioners and an appointed city manager. What worked in one will not work in the other. One reason socialized medicine has not been adopted in the United States is that critics of the idea have pointed out how dissimilar the United States is to most of the countries that have adopted such programs. What works in those nations would not work here, they argue. The more alike the two things being compared are, the more likely the analogy is to stand up under attack.

2. *The essential similarity between the two objects of a figurative analogy should be readily apparent.* When you use a figurative analogy, it is crucial to make clear the similarity on which it is based. If you do not, your audience will end up wondering what in the world you are talking about. And you will only confuse your listeners further if you try to draw on that same analogy later in your speech. It may be a good idea to try out a figurative analogy on an honest friend before using it during a speech. Then you can be certain that your point is clear.

Statistics

▼

statistics
Numerical data that summarize facts and examples.

Many of us live in awe of **statistics.** Perhaps nowhere is our respect for statistics so evident—and so exploited—as in advertising. If three out of four doctors surveyed recommend Pain Away aspirin, it must be the best. If Sudsy Soap is 99.9 percent pure (whatever that means), surely it will help our complexions. And if nine out of ten people like Sloppy Catsup in the taste test, we will certainly buy some for this weekend's barbecue. How can the statistics be wrong? Some people, however,

CHAPTER 6 SUPPORTING YOUR SPEECH

are suspicious of *all* statistics. They have witnessed too many erroneous weather forecasts and election predictions.

In reality, the truth about statistics lies somewhere between unconditional faith in numbers and the wry observation that "there are three kinds of lies: lies, damned lies, and statistics."[16]

Using Statistics as Support   To be effective, statistics must be understood and used with caution. Just as three or four brief examples may be more effective than just one, a statistic that represents hundreds or thousands of individuals may be more persuasive still.

Statistics can help a speaker express the magnitude or seriousness of a situation: "The National Center for Health Statistics estimates that by the end of this year 50,000 teenagers, in the U.S. alone, will attempt suicide; at least 5,000 will succeed."[17] Or statistics can express the relationship of a part to the whole: "Fully 80% of all completed suicides gave advance warnings of their intentions."[18]

Whatever their purpose, statistics are considered by most people to be the ultimate "hard" evidence—firm, convincing fact. The following discussion will help you analyze and use statistics effectively and correctly.

Using Statistics Effectively

1. *Evaluate your sources.* It has been said that figures don't lie, but liars figure! And indeed, statistics can be produced to support almost any conclusion desired. Your goal is to cite *reputable*, *authoritative*, and *unbiased* sources.

The most reputable sources of statistics are usually government agencies, independent survey organizations, and such statistical reference works as the *World Almanac* and the *Statistical Abstract of the United States*. Private businesses may also be reputable, but these must be viewed with a bit more caution. As we will discuss later, the data collection methods of these organizations may be questionable, or their data may be biased by special interests.

Statistical sources should also be authoritative. No source is an authority on everything and thus cannot be credible on all subjects. For example, we expect the U.S. surgeon general's office to gather and release statistics on smokers' risk of developing lung cancer. But we would look askance at statistics from that same office that deal with the numbers of long-range missiles presently deployed in Europe. The most authoritative sources are also original sources—the data collectors themselves. If you find an interesting statistic in a newspaper or magazine article, look closely to see if a source is cited. If it is, try to find that source and the original reporting of the statistic. Do not just assume that the secondhand account has reported the statistic accurately and fairly. As often as possible, go to the original source.

As well as being reputable and authoritative, sources should be as unbiased as possible. We usually extend to government research and various independent sources of statistics the courtesy of thinking them unbiased. Because they are, for the most part, supposed to be unaffiliated with any special interest, their statistics are presumed to be less biased than those coming from such organizations as the American Tobacco Institute, the AFL-CIO, or the Burger King Corporation. All three organizations have some special interest at stake and are more likely to reflect their biases when gathering and reporting data.

As you evaluate your sources, try to find out how the statistics were gathered.

For example, if a statistic relies on a sample, how was the sample taken? A Thursday afternoon telephone poll of twenty registered voters in Brooklyn is not an adequate sample of New York City voters. The sample is too small and too geographically limited. In addition, it excludes anyone without a telephone or anyone unlikely to be at home when the survey was conducted. Sample sizes and survey methods do vary widely, but most well-known polls involve samples of 500 to 2000 people, selected at random from a larger population. A valid and reliable statistical study may take weeks or months to complete. Of course, finding out about the statistical methodology may be more difficult than discovering the source of the statistic, but if you can find it, the information will help you to analyze the value of the statistic.

2. *Interpret statistics accurately.* People are often swayed by statistics that sound good but have in fact been misinterpreted. Urging medical schools to add courses in geriatrics (care of the elderly) to their curriculum, a student speaker pointed out such a misinterpretation. She noted:

> According to a *Report on Education and Training in Geriatrics and Gerontology* released in 1984, courses of this type [geriatrics] have more than doubled in the last five years. This looks very promising, but what the statistics don't say is that the majority of these courses are electives with shockingly low enrollments.[19]

As the student went on to explain, doubling the number of geriatric courses does not by itself mean that there is a corresponding increase in the numbers of doctors being trained in that specialized field.

Another student pointed out a misleading interpretation of data regarding research spending for Alzheimer's disease: "While federal research spending on Alzheimer's has increased almost tenfold since 1976, only $37.1 million was spent in 1984."[20] In this case, a tenfold increase in spending seems significant until one knows the meager total budget. One set of statistics often takes on meaning only in relation to other sets.

A misinterpretation of day care statistics was the focus of a third student's criticism:

> *Newsweek* estimates that two million children receive formalized day care in the United States today. Unfortunately, this still leaves out the 5½ million children left alone along with countless others under the care of unreliable relatives or neighbors. . . . And even if these children were in licensed day care, the facilities for most centers are wholly inadequate.[21]

The large number of children in formalized day care—two million—would seem to indicate that the problem of child care is under control. However, as the student speaker pointed out, that figure is not a measure of success at all. If anything, it is an indicator of the huge size of the problem.

All three speakers pointed out statistics that did not mean what they seemed to mean. In each of these cases, the speaker's skillful analysis helped listeners understand the true situation. Unfortunately, in other cases, the speaker may be the culprit in misinterpreting the statistics. Both as a user of statistics in your own speeches and as a consumer of statistics in articles, books, and speeches, you need to be constantly alert to what the statistics actually mean.

3. *Make your statistics understandable and memorable.* You can make your statistics easier to understand and more memorable in several ways. You can *compare* your

statistic with another that heightens its impact. Talking about telephone sales frauds, one student pointed out that such solicitations net over $50 million a year. To heighten the impact of that figure, he went on to say, "Comparatively speaking, this amounts to 15% of the overall cost of $373 million taken in all robberies in the United States in 1983."[22]

You might express a statistic in units that are more meaningful or easily understandable to your audience. For example, one student translated "300,000 man-hours of work" as "over 144 years of labor."[23]

Round off numbers whenever you can do so without distorting or falsifying the statistic. It is much easier to grasp and remember "two million" than 2,223,147. Percentages, too, are more easily remembered if they are rounded off. And most people seem to remember percentages even better if they are expressed as fractions. "About 30 percent" is a better way to express "31.69 percent," and "about one-third" is even easier to understand and remember.

Finally, use *visual aids* to present your statistics. Most audience members have difficulty remembering a barrage of numbers thrown at them during a speech. But if the numbers are placed on a chart or graph in front of your listeners, they can more easily grasp the statistics. You will still need to explain what the numbers mean, but you won't have to recite them. We will discuss visual aids in Chapter 12.

Opinion

Opinions are often used as supporting material in speeches. You might wish to quote another person's point of view on a topic for two important reasons. First, the person you quote may have "said it in a nutshell"—phrased an argument or observation clearly, succinctly, and memorably. Second, if the person you quote is a recognized authority in the area of your topic, citing his or her opinion may add credibility to your own arguments. Two types of opinions may be used in speeches, each with its specific purpose and advantages. When deciding to express an opinion, you may wish to quote either literary works or expert authorities. Let's look at each in turn.

opinion
Testimony or quotation that expresses the attitudes, beliefs, or values of someone else.

Literary Quotations   If you want to summarize your ideas or make a point in a memorable way, you may wish to include a literary quotation in your speech. A student speaking on the deterioration of the nation's library holdings quoted Joseph Addison on the significance of books: "Books are the legacies left to mankind, delivered down from generation to generation, as presents to the posterity of those yet unborn."[24] Addison's musings express the speaker's point in a poetic and memorable way. Note too that the quotation is short. Brief, pointed quotations usually have greater audience impact than larger, more rambling ones. As Shakespeare said, "Brevity is the soul of wit" (*Hamlet*, II:2).

Literary quotations have the additional advantage of being easily accessible. A number of quotation dictionaries exist in the reference sections of most libraries. Arranged alphabetically by subject, these compilations are easy to use.

Expert Authority   The opinions of expert authorities on your subject will be more persuasive than the views of famous writers. In a speech about adult illiteracy, the speaker quoted (and identified) Vyvyan Harding, the director of the Literacy Services of Wisconsin: "It seems like a futile battle against overwhelming odds. I have never seen so many nonreading adults in my life."[25] In this case, the words are not as poetic as Addison's thoughts on books, but the qualifications of the person quoted increase the credibility of the student speaker's opinion.

If your topic is controversial, the testimony of a recognized authority can add a great deal of weight to your own arguments. Or if your topic requires that you make predictions—thought processes that can be supported only in a marginal way by statistics or examples—the statements of expert authority may prove to be your most convincing support. You also have greater flexibility with expert opinion than with literary quotations. You can't change a famous writer's words. Experts may be either quoted directly or paraphrased, as long as you are careful not to alter the intent of the experts' remarks.

Using Opinion Effectively   Here are a few suggestions for using opinion effectively in your speeches.

1. *Be certain that your authority is an expert in the subject you are discussing.* Unless the authority you are calling on has expertise in the subject on which he or she is expressing an opinion, your quote will have little value. Quoting the opinions of an atomic scientist about works of art, for example, is to do little more than accept the opinions of the average person. Be sure, then, that the sources you quote are not merely recognized authorities but recognized in the particular subject area they are talking about. Advertisements, especially, ignore this rule when they use sports figures to endorse such items as flashlight batteries, breakfast cereals, and cars. Sports figures may indeed be experts on athletic shoes, tennis rackets, or stopwatches, but they lack any specific qualifications to talk about most of the products they endorse.

2. *Identify your sources.* Perhaps you chose an eminently qualified authority on your subject. Unless the audience too is aware of the qualifications of your authority, they may not grant him or her any credibility. If the student who quoted the director of the Literacy Services of Wisconsin had identified that person only as Vyvyan Harding, no one would have recognized the name, let alone acknowledged her authority.

3. *Cite unbiased sources.* Just as the most reliable sources of statistics are unbiased, so too are the most reliable sources of opinion. The chairman of General Motors may offer an expert opinion that the Chevrolet Celebrity is the best mid-sized car on the market today. His expertise is unquestionable, but his bias is obvious and makes him a less than trustworthy source of opinion on the subject. A better source would be the *Consumer Reports* analyses of the reliability and repair records of mid-sized cars.

4. *The opinion cited should be representative of prevailing opinion.* Perhaps you have found a bona fide expert who supports your conclusions. Unless his or her opinion is shared by most of the experts in the field, its value is limited. Citing such opinion only leaves your conclusions open to easy rebuttal.

5. *Quote your sources accurately.* If you quote or paraphrase someone, be certain that your quote or paraphrase is accurate and within the context in which the remarks were originally made. Major misunderstandings may result from someone's being quoted inaccurately. "Letters to the Editor" columns in major news

publications often include letters from irate readers who found themselves mis-quoted in recent articles. The gentleman who wrote the following letter, for example, was upset because a misquoted word implied heartlessness on his part:

> You quote me as "defending holiday layoffs at companies already rife with cutback rumors" by saying, "They're going to have a lousy Christmas anyway." . . . All I meant was that the disadvantages of pre- and postholiday cutbacks at the two companies under discussion tended to balance each other out, since the impending layoffs were a known fact and uncertainty regarding one's own job increases stress. I said, "They are going to have a lousy Christmas *either* way."[26]

6. *Use literary quotations sparingly.* Even though a relevant literary quote may be just right for a speech, use it with caution. Overuse of quotations often bores an audience and causes them to doubt your creativity and research ability and to view you as somewhat pretentious. It is sometimes better not to use any quotation than to use literary quotations out of desperation, just because you can't find anything better. Be sure that you have a valid reason for citing a literary quotation, and then use only one or two at the most in a speech.

RECAP

TYPES OF SUPPORTING MATERIALS FOR A SPEECH		
	Brief example	A short, relevant story
	Extended illustration	A more detailed story with an opening, complications, a climax, and a resolution
	Hypothetical illustration	An illustration that has not actually occurred but conceivably might happen.
	Explanation	A statement that makes clear how something is done or why it exists in its present or past form
	Description	An explication of what something is like
	Definition	A concise description of a word or concept
	Analogy	A comparison of one thing to another
	Statistics	Numbers that summarize data or examples
	Opinion	Testimony or a quotation from someone else

SELECTING THE BEST SUPPORTING MATERIALS

Particularly if you have found a wealth of information on your subject, you must make one final decision before integrating the supporting materials into your speech: what to use and what to eliminate. The following six suggestions should help you choose the most effective supporting materials.

1. *Proximity.* The more relevant to your listeners or "closer to home" the supporting material, the better. If an illustration describes an incident that could affect

the audience members themselves, that illustration is much preferable to another, more distant one. "This could happen to *you*" is a strong message.

2. *Significance*. Related to proximity, significance indicates the likelihood of a situation's happening. "Not only *might* this situation affect you, it will *probably* affect as many as one out of four of you," claims a speaker. One out of four is a "significant" number.

3. *Concreteness*. Abstract assertions and explanations by themselves run the risk of boring an audience. You may need to discuss principles and theories, but you should explain them with concrete examples and statistics. Otherwise, your audience will quickly tire of listening.

4. *Variety*. Even if your supporting material meets the first three requirements, if it is all of the same type, your audience may lose interest or question your research. A mix of illustrations, opinions, definitions and statistics is much more interesting and convincing than the exclusive use of any one type of supporting material.

5. *Humor*. A touch of humor in an example or opinion will probably be much liked by an audience. Only if your speech were *very* somber and serious would humor not be appropriate.

6. *Suitability*. Having considered the preceding suggestions, your final decision on whether or not to use a certain piece of supporting material will depend on its suitability to you, your particular speech, and the occasion. And, as we continue to stress throughout the book, you need to consider your audience. For example, you might well use many more statistics in a speech of a technical nature presented to a group of scientists than in an after-luncheon talk to the local Rotary Club.

INTEGRATING SUPPORTING MATERIALS INTO THE SPEECH

Your hard work has paid off. Now you have wonderful supporting material for your speech on the deteriorating interstate highway system. You have a dramatic extended illustration of a bridge collapse that recently sent twelve people plummeting to their deaths. Filled out with brief examples of washed-out roadways and untended potholes, your story of the collapsed bridge should really grab and hold your audience. You also have statistics on how many miles of interstate highways crisscross the country and what percentage of these are in need of major repair. And to clinch your argument, you have the testimony of expert authorities who feel that such repairs should be a high priority. On the other side of your desk sits the preliminary outline of your speech. That's great, but you're wondering, "How do I fit all this marvelous stuff into my outline?" You want to know how to integrate the supporting material you have gathered.

First, you have to decide where in the outline you are going to use each piece of supporting material. As will be discussed in Chapter 7, many people write the information they have gathered on 4-by-6 note cards so that they can physically shuffle and reorganize them as they work the material into the speech. As you decide where to use your material, pencil on the note card the number or letter of the point on the outline where you will use it. Some of your supporting material may be so interesting that you may even change your outline to accommodate it.

Or you may develop an entirely different approach to integrating the supporting material into your speech.

Word processors have made "cutting and pasting" much less troublesome. If you have access to such a device and can enter your outline and supporting materials into the word processor, you can organize and reorganize at will. However, you will still have to make the tough decisions about where in the speech you are going to use the examples, explanations, definitions, analogies, statistics, and opinions you have so carefully gathered.

You may find it useful at this point to revise your outline. We will cover outlining more fully in Chapter 8, but we will say here that you are now ready to begin work on a detailed full-content outline. Although you will stop short of writing your speech out word for word, this outline will contain main points and their subpoints, supporting materials, and various previews, transitions, and summaries. But for now, let's continue our discussion about pulling together your supporting materials.

Your goal is to incorporate the supporting material smoothly into your speech so as not to interrupt the flow of ideas. Notice how skillfully this goal is met by the speaker in the following example, who is talking about consumer abuse by utility companies:

> Phantom taxes is an example [of consumer abuse] that should profile the kinds of attitudes facing us as consumers. A 1983 issue of *Powerline* reported that in 1981 electric utilities billed rate payers 5.4 billion dollars in Federal income taxes, but they actually paid only 1.7 billion dollars to the IRS. This overcharge is what is known as phantom taxes.[27]

In this example, the speaker follows four steps in integrating the supporting material into the speech:

1. State the main idea.
2. Cite the source of the supporting material.
3. Present the supporting material.
4. Restate the main idea.

Let's examine briefly each of these steps.

1. *State the main idea.* First, you must state the main idea under discussion. This statement should be concise and clear so that the audience can grasp it immediately. It may be enumerated ("First, . . . Second, . . ."). In our example, the speaker's first sentence states the main idea. "Phantom taxes is an example that should profile the kinds of attitudes facing us as consumers."

2. *Cite the source of the supporting material.* You should provide as much detail as needed about your source. This does not mean that you need to give complete bibliographical information. It is unlikely that your listeners will either remember or copy down the volume number of a periodical. But quickly citing the name and date of a periodical or the name and brief qualifications of the expert whose opinion you are about to quote adds credibility to the supporting material and also provides a smooth transition into the material itself. The speaker in our example gives a brief but adequate source citation by mentioning "a 1983 issue of *Powerline*."

3. *Present the supporting material.* You now state the statistic, definition, illustration, or other form of supporting material you have chosen to substantiate your idea. In the example cited, the speaker points out, "In 1981 electric utilities billed

rate payers 5.4 billion dollars in Federal income taxes, but they actually paid only 1.7 billion dollars to the IRS."

4. *Restate the main idea.* You should finally explain how the supporting material you just cited does indeed support your main idea. Our example concludes with "This overcharge is what is known as phantom taxes." Your listeners will not remember too many specific facts and statistics after a speech, but they should remember the main points. This repetition makes it more likely that they will.

Your main idea may be a generalization based on more than one item of supporting material. If you use several items to support an idea, repeat steps 2 and 3 for each item before moving on to step 4. In this case, as you restate your idea, you may wish to summarize briefly the several items you used to support it. The following excerpt from a speech advocating more stringent federal trucking regulations integrates statistics from two sources.

Unprofessional drivers often engage in unsafe trucking practices, ranging from the use of controlled substances to driving while physically exhausted.	1. State the main idea
The Ralph Nader group conducted a study of substance abuse among truckers in the early 1970's, and discovered that 80% of the 1,300 polled believed amphetamine use was widespread in their ranks. Another 80% admitted to having dozed at the wheel despite the so-called pep pills.	2. Cite the source of the supporting material. 3. Present the supporting material
These figures assume even greater significance in light of a 1976 *Department of Transportation* study, which revealed that physical exhaustion on the part of the trucker played a major role in 32% of all serious trucking accidents [from 1973 to 1976].	*Transition* 2. Cite the source of the supporting material 3. Present the supporting material.
Drained by sleep deprivation, yet bolstered by the false bravado of controlled substances, it is little wonder that these drivers begin to commit disastrous errors.[28]	*Summary of supporting materials* 4. Restate the main idea.

SUMMARY   Interesting, convincing supporting materials are essential to a successful speech. You may choose from various types of supporting materials, including examples and illustrations, explanations and descriptions, definitions, analogies, statistics, and opinions.

Once you find material that may support your ideas, you should follow the guidelines presented in this chapter to be sure of the validity and reliability of your evidence. Further, if you find that you have an abundance of supporting materials, you may wish to consider the six additional factors of proximity, significance, concreteness, variety, humor, and suitability. These can help you choose the most effective support for your speech.

Finally, you must begin to integrate the supporting materials into your outline. Following the basic pattern of (1) stating the idea, (2) citing the source of the support, (3) presenting the support, and (4) restating the main idea will help you integrate your supporting materials smoothly and effectively.

1. Identify six different types of supporting materials.
2. Explain how to use effectively in a speech the six different types of supporting material discussed in this chapter.
3. What are criteria for selecting the best supporting material?
4. How do you integrate supporting materials into your speech?

QUESTIONS FOR DISCUSSION AND REVIEW

1. The following excerpts from student speeches contain various types of supporting material discussed in this chapter. Read each excerpt and then identify the type of supporting material it contains. (Some may contain more than one type. In that case, identify the *primary* type of supporting material contained in the excerpt.)
   a. _____ It was another beautiful day at the amusement park. Warm sunshine, the smell of cotton candy, the kids, and the rides. The roller coaster's whooshing 60 miles per hour speed was accompanied by the familiar screams of delight from kids of all ages. Another ride, the comet, was flying gracefully through the heavens when suddenly a chain broke, flinging one of the gondolas 75 feet into the air before it crashed, killing a man and seriously injuring his son.[29]
   b. _____ In 1983 the Consumer Product Safety Commission reported nearly 10,000 hospital emergency rooms treated injuries from amusement rides.[30]
   c. _____ "The bottom line," says former CPSC Chairperson Nancy Steorts, "is that the American consumer has no way of knowing the level of safety on a particular ride at a particular location. In effect, we are forcing the consumer to play amusement ride roulette with his or her family's safety."[31]
   d. _____ Maryland has one of the best safety records in the country, and it is essential that all states adopt and consistently enforce the same thorough regulations.[32]
   e. _____ Do you remember what the weather was like a few months ago? Recall when it was cold; when you would shiver getting out of bed, getting out of the shower, walking outside, when it was most wise to stay inside, wrap yourself in a warm blanket and turn up the heat.[33]
   f. _____ Imagine you are poor, according to a wide variety of government standards. It is nearly impossible for you to pay your heating bills. So you would be eligible for a portion of the . . . [money] allocated for this program for fiscal year 1985.[34]
   g. _____ . . . leptophos, a chemical pesticide which is not registered with the EPA . . .[35]
2. Read an investigative story in a newspaper or a national newsmagazine. See how many different types of supporting materials you can identify in the story.

SUGGESTED ACTIVITIES

7

Sources of Supporting Materials

OBJECTIVES

After studying this chapter, you should be able to

1. List four potential sources of supporting material for a speech

2. List and briefly describe the five types of library resources

3. Explain how to use the *Reader's Guide to Periodical Literature* and other similarly organized indexes to periodicals and newspapers

4. List at least five types of reference materials commonly used by researchers

5. List the three items a researcher should put on a note card

Learn, compare, collect the facts! . . . Always have the courage to say to yourself—I am ignorant. (Picasso, La Suze. *Washington University Gallery of Art, St. Louis. University purchase, Kende Sale Fund, 1946.*)

IVAR PETROVICH PAVLOV

Apple pie is your specialty. Your family and friends relish your flaky crust, spicy filling, and crunchy crumb topping. Fortunately, not only do you have a never-fail recipe and technique, but you also know where to go for the best ingredients. Fette's Orchard has the tangiest pie apples in town. For your crust, you use only Premier shortening, which you buy at Meyer's Specialty Market. And your crumb topping requires both stone-ground whole-wheat flour and fresh creamery butter, available on Tuesdays at the farmer's market on the courthouse square.

Just as your apple pie requires knowledge both of the ingredients you need and where to find them, so does the successful speech require a knowledge both of the supporting material you need and where to locate them. Chapter 6 emphasized choosing relevant, interesting, and varied supporting materials. Chapter 7 will tell you where to look for these materials: in your own personal knowledge and experience, in notes gathered during personal interviews, in mail-order publications, and in the library.

PERSONAL KNOWLEDGE AND EXPERIENCE

After Dorothy had spent a good deal of time and energy trying to get back to Kansas from the Land of Oz, the heroine of L. Frank Baum's classic *Wizard of Oz* learned from Glenda, the Good Witch of the North, that she had to look into her own heart for the solution to her problem. Like Dorothy, some speakers struggle to find supporting materials, only to realize eventually that they can rely at least in part on their own knowledge and experience.

Because you will probably give speeches on topics in which you have a special interest, you may find that *you* are your own best source. Your speech may be on a skill or hobby in which you are expert, such as tropical fish, stenciling, or stamp collecting. Or you may talk on a subject with which you have had some personal experience, such as buying a new car, deciding whether to join a club, or seeking nursing home care for an elderly relative. Don't automatically run to the library to try to find every piece of supporting material for every topic on which you speak. It is true that most well-researched speeches will include some objective material gathered from outside sources. But you may also be able to provide an effective illustration, explanation, definition, or other type of support from your own knowledge and experience. And using such personal support often has the additional advantage of heightening your credibility in the minds of your listeners. They will accord you more respect as an authority when they realize that you have firsthand knowledge of a topic.

INTERVIEWS

If you don't know the answers to some of the important questions raised by your topic, but you can think of someone who might, you should consider seeking an interview as a means of gaining material for your speech. For example, if you are preparing a speech on the quality of food in the school cafeteria, who better to ask about the subject than the director of Food Services? If you want to discuss the pros and cons of building a new prison in an urban area, you might interview

You might consider seeking an interview as a means of gaining material for your speech.
(*Laima Druskis*)

an official of the correctional services, a representative of the city administration, and a resident of the area. Or if you want to explain why we have retained the electoral college, you might consult your professor of political science or American history. A topic of local concern can almost always be supported by information from individuals who are involved directly. And often college or university faculty members can provide expert testimony on a wide variety of social, economic, and political topics.

A word of caution, however, before you decide that an interview is necessary: Be sure that your questions cannot easily be answered by available print materials. If you can find the answers to your questions in a newspaper article or in a book, turn to those sources, rather than take someone's valuable time. In other words, do some preliminary reading on your subject before you decide to interview someone about it. Once you decide that only an interview can give you the material you need, you can begin to prepare for the interview itself.

Determining the Purpose of the Interview

The first step in preparing for an interview is to establish a purpose or objective for it. Specifically, what do you need to find out? Do you need hard facts that cannot be gotten from other sources? Do you need the interviewee's expert testimony on your subject? Does the person you are going to interview have a particularly significant personal experience that you wish to hear described firsthand? Or do you need an explanation of some of the information you found in print sources? Before you even begin preparing for the interview, decide just what it is you want to have or know when the interview is over.

Setting Up the Interview

Once you have a specific purpose for the interview, decide with whom you are going to talk, and arrange a meeting. It is unwise to arrive unannounced at the office of a business person, public official, educator, or other professional and expect an on-the-spot interview. Even Mike Wallace has been refused under such circumstances! Instead, several days in advance telephone the office of the person you hope to interview, explain briefly who you are and why you are calling, and ask for a meeting. It is reasonable to request a certain date and time for the interview, but realize that it will have to be scheduled at the convenience of the person granting the interview. Try to be flexible. Most people are flattered to have their authority and knowledge recognized and will willingly grant interviews to serious students if schedules permit.

If there is any possibility that you may want to record or videotape the interview, ask for the interviewee's OK during this initial contact. If permission is refused, you will need to be prepared to gather your information without electronic assistance.

Planning the Interview

Now that you know what you need to find out, whom you will see, and when the meeting will take place, your next step is to prepare for the interview itself. Do not try to "wing it" and let the interviewee ramble at will. As a rule, this approach will not get the information you need. If you don't ask specific questions, you may end up with only a few minutes of awkward silence, or the interviewee may stray far from your topic. Even if the person you are interviewing does stay on track and talk freely about your topic, chances are that he or she won't provide exactly the information you need. To ensure the results you want, you need to plan a set of questions. A few suggestions can help you do so.

Gather Background Information   First, do your homework. Experienced interviewers are successful largely because they prepare so thoroughly for their interviews. Likewise, before you interview someone, find out as much as you can about your subject, the person, and the field of knowledge. Prepare questions that take full advantage of the interviewee's specific knowledge of your subject. You can do this only if *you* already know a good deal about your subject. Build your line of questioning on facts, statements the interviewee has made, or positions he or she has taken publicly.

Plan Specific Questions   In addition to learning something about your subject and the person you are going to interview, it is also helpful to learn the two basic types of interview questions: closed and open.

Closed questions are those which call for a yes or no answer or some brief statement of fact. "How many years have you served in the job?" and "Do you think that next month's tax referendum will pass?" are examples of closed questions.

If you ask only closed questions, you will limit and possibly frustrate your interviewee. You may also frustrate yourself. Open questions allow the interviewee to express a personal point of view more fully. They may also give you more of the kind of information you probably want: expert testimony and personal experience. "Why do you think grade inflation is a serious problem?" and "What, in your opinion, is the biggest challenge facing American public education today?" are examples of open questions. Open questions often follow closed questions. If the person you are interviewing answers a closed question simply yes or no, you may wish to follow up on the answer by asking, "Why?"

Plan a Sequence of Questions   Once you have designed your questions to yield the answers you want, you need to consider the order in which your questions will be asked. Questions may be organized according to subject categories, with three or four questions on one subject followed by three or four on another. They may also be arranged according to complexity of information, with the easiest questions first, partly to ensure that you accurately understand the subject. Or they may be put in the order of content sensitivity. Questions about your interviewee's participation in some covert or suspicious activity or about an unpopular stand on an issue should probably come last. Your organization of questions should be designed to build some rapport with your interviewee and to ensure that you get at least some information, should he or she decline to answer the more sensitive or difficult questions.

Plan a Recording Strategy   If the person you will see agrees to be electronically recorded, you will need to decide whether or not to tape the interview. Recording devices have both advantages and disadvantages. The obvious advantage is that a recorder can free you from having to take copious notes. You can concentrate instead on processing and analyzing the ideas and information being presented. Another advantage is that your record of the interview is complete. You will not have to decipher hastily scribbled notes a day or two after the interview.

The main disadvantage of using a recording device is that it makes some people more self-conscious and nervous than if you were scribbling notes. You want the person being interviewed to concentrate on your questions and not on physical appearance or vocal inflection. If you use an electronic recorder, be prepared to turn it off and switch to manual note taking if you sense at any time that the interviewee is distracted by the device.

When taping an interview, there are a number of questions that you should ask yourself. What kind of recording device should you use? Would a simple tape recorder with a built-in mike be less intimidating than a complex machine with a tabletop mike facing the interviewee? Although the person you are interviewing is aware that you are taping the interview, would he or she be more comfortable if the device were out of sight? Ask the interviewee. You might also want to ask some light questions before turning on the recorder so that both of you can ease into the interview proper.

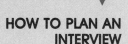

RECAP

HOW TO PLAN AN INTERVIEW

1. Obtain background information about the person you wish to interview.
2. Design the questions you will ask.
3. Plan a questioning sequence—what you will ask first, second, and so on.
4. Determine how you will record the responses of the person you interview: Will you use a tape recorder or video camera, or will you take notes?

Conducting the Interview

On Your Mark . . .   Dress for the interview. For most interviews conservative, businesslike clothes show that you are serious about the interview and that you respect the norms of your interviewee's world.

Take a pad and pen or pencil for note taking, as well as any electronic recording device you may have decided on. You may want to turn off the recorder at some point during the interview. Or Murphy's Law may snarl your tape or break your recorder. Being able to switch to manual note taking will ensure that the interview can continue, in spite of such mishaps.

Get Set . . .   Arrive for the interview a few minutes ahead of the scheduled hour. Be prepared, however, to wait patiently, if necessary. While the interview may be a high priority for you, the person you will interview has granted it as a courtesy and may need to complete some urgent business before speaking with you.

Once you are settled with the person you will interview, remind him or her of your purpose. If you are familiar with and admire the work the interviewee has done or published, don't hesitate to say so. Sincere flattery can help set a positive tone for the exchange. If you have decided to use a recorder, set it up. You may keep it out of sight once the interviewee has seen the recorder, but never try to hide it at the outset—such a ploy is unethical. If you are going to take written notes, get out your paper and pen. Now you are ready to begin asking your prepared questions.

Go!   As you conduct the interview, use the questions you have prepared as a guide but not a rigid schedule. If the person you are interviewing mentions an interesting angle you had not thought of, don't be afraid to pursue the point. Listen carefully to the person's answers, and ask for clarification of any ideas you don't understand. Again, be sensitive to your interviewee's reaction to any electronic recording device; turn it off if he or she seems overly aware of it or hesitant to talk freely because of it.

Do not prolong the interview beyond the time limits of your appointment. The person you are interviewing is probably very busy and has been courteous enough to fit you into a tight schedule. Ending the interview on time is simply to return the courtesy. Thank your interviewee for his or her contribution, and leave.

Following Up the Interview

As soon as possible after the interview, read through your notes carefully and copy over any portion that may be illegible. If you recorded the interview, label the tape with the date and the interviewee's name. You will soon want to transfer any significant facts, opinions, or anecdotes from either notes or tape to 4-by-6 index cards. You will find a format for transcribing information to note cards later in this chapter (see Figure 7–6).

MAIL-ORDER MATERIALS

Mail-order information is a fertile source of supporting materials. The federal government, businesses or industrial groups, nonprofit organizations, and professional societies produce pamphlets, books, fact sheets, or other information about an extraordinarily wide variety of subjects. This information is usually available at little or no cost.

How do you find out about these materials? One well-known listing is the U.S. Government Printing Office's *Monthly Catalog of U.S. Government Publications*. Since the government publishes information about almost every subject imaginable, the *Monthly Catalog* can lead to a number of excellent sources.

The reference section of your library will probably have the *Encyclopedia of Associations* and the *Directory of Nonprofit Organizations*. Though these reference works do not indicate specific publications, they can give you an idea of some of the businesses and organizations that may have a special interest in your topic. These works include the addresses and telephone numbers of the businesses and organizations they list, so you can write or call to get the information you need. For example, your authors were recently involved in organizing a parent volunteer program in a local elementary school. Upon checking the *Directory of Nonprofit Organizations*, we found a listing for the National School Volunteer Program, headquartered in Alexandria, Virginia. A call to their office revealed that they provide booklets, pamphlets, and other information to schools considering volunteer programs. They mailed us a kit immediately, and we had it within a week.

The time between your request for information and its arrival may be too long for you to use the information in your speech. Many students do not choose speech topics far enough in advance to make mail-order sources practical for classroom assignments. At least a week, and sometimes as much as a month, may go by before the materials arrive. However, even if their value for use in class is limited, mail-order materials may prove very useful when you have been invited well in advance of the speaking date to make a presentation.

One other drawback to mail-order information needs to be mentioned here. Private companies and organizations produce printed materials only because they have a vested interest in the field. Without saying that all such materials are inaccurate, it is probably fair to say that they are by nature one-sided. You can expect oil companies, for example, to minimize the harm oil spills can do to an environment. Therefore, you need to consider these sources carefully before using the information they provide. You should ideally have independent sources of information, which may mean writing to several organizations for information.

LIBRARY RESOURCES

The richest and most used source of supporting materials is, of course, the library. Though your college library may seem a forbidding maze, take heart from the fact that all libraries, whether the smallest village library or the huge Library of Congress, house the same sorts of materials and are organized in a similar way. Some basic general knowledge about libraries can make all of them easier to use.

Unless you already know the library you will be using, plan to spend some time becoming familiar with your library's layout and services. Some libraries offer staff-guided tours; most others will at least have floor plans and location guides available. Figure 7.1 is a good example of a thorough guide to a university library. Before you have to do research under pressure, explore the library at a leisurely pace. In your exploration, look for the location of the following five types of holdings: books, periodicals, newspapers, government documents, and reference materials.

All libraries, from the smallest village library to the Library of Congress, house the same sorts of materials and are organized in a similar way.
(Charles Feil/Stock Photos, Inc.)

<table>
<tr><td colspan="2">

HOURS OF SERVICE

Library

</td><td>

YOUR GUIDE

TO THE

</td><td colspan="2">

TELEPHONE NUMBERS

</td></tr>
</table>

HOURS OF SERVICE

Library

Fall & Spring:	8am-11pm, M-Th
	8am-10pm, F
	8am-5pm, Sat
	1pm-10pm, Sun
Summer:	7am-10pm, M-Th
	8am-5pm, F-Sat
	2pm-10pm, Sun

Media Services

| Fall & Spring: | 8am-5pm, M-F |
| Summer: | 7am-4pm, M-F |

SLAC Lab

All Year:	10am-7pm, M-W
	10am-4pm, Th-F
	5pm-9pm, Sun

Copy Center

Fall & Spring:	12n-8pm, M-Th
	10am-4pm, F
Summer:	9am-3pm, M-Th
	4pm-7pm, Sun

YOUR GUIDE

TO THE

LEARNING RESOURCES CENTER

Southwest Texas State University
San Marcos, Texas

TELEPHONE NUMBERS

AV Software (except films)	245-2328
Circulation Desk	245-3681
Government Documents	245-3836
Hours Information	245-2187
Interlibrary Loan	245-2685
KWIK-Tip (recorded info.)	245-2106
Media Services (films)	245-2319
Reference/Information	245-2686
Reserve Desk	245-2328
SLAC Lab	245-2996

Learning Resources Center
Southwest Texas State University
San Marcos, Texas 78666
**The progressive university
with a proud past**
Southwest Texas University is an affirmative action,
equal opportunity educational institution

Welcome to the Learning Resources Center! We hope this pamphlet will be helpful in orienting you to our collection and facilities. Please **ask for assistance** at any time: staff are always available to answer your questions.

The LRC is made up of (1) the Library and (2) Media Services. The Library is located on floors 3-11 of the J.C. Kellam Building and houses all materials except 16mm films. Media Services is located in the Psychology Building and provides a variety of graphics, audio and video services, as well as maintaining and circulating the 16mm films and projectors.

Also located in the Kellam Building is the Student Learning Assistance Center (SLAC), which provides tutoring, study skills courses, and related counseling.

Our Library is an **open-stack** collection. Except for the Archives/Special Collections facility, all materials are freely accessible for browsing. Books and AV materials can be checked out using your student ID card. There is no limit on the number of books you can borrow at a time. Most items can be renewed unless someone else has requested them. If you cannot find an item on the shelf, ask the Circulation staff to conduct a search for you. Overdue items can be recalled and held for you. Fines are assessed for overdue AV items, but not for books.

Service-Fees—Library photocopiers cost 5¢/page. Microfilm and microfiche can be copied at 10¢/page. IBM Selectric typewriters are available at 25¢ for 15 munites. Fees for special services are discussed below.

Interlibrary Loan—This service obtains materials not owned SWT by borrowing them from other libraries. Faculty and graduate students can use ILL at any time. Undergraduates may place requests if co-signed by an instructor. ILL processing sometimes takes several weeks, and fees may be charged by the supplying library. Ask at the Reference Desk for request forms and information.

Computer-Assisted Reference Services—Offers computer searches of over 250 bibliographic databases in a variety of subject areas. This is similar to searching print indexes, but is much faster and more flexible. The search produces a list of journal articles and other materials on your topic, which may or may not be owned by our library. The cost varies widely, but usually runs between $5 and $25. Ask at the Reference Desk for further information.

Use of Area Libraries—The Reference Dept. has holdings lists showing titles owned by other libraries in the San Antonio/Austin area. Most of these libraries can be used freely, but they do place restrictions on SWT students borrowing their materials. To borrow books from San Antonio and Seguin college libraries, you must have obtained a special authorization card from the SWT Reference Desk. The card is good for seven days and up to four books. You can get a UT-Austin courtesy borrowing card by paying a $2 fee and a $30 deposit at the Perry-Castaneda Library. The card is valid for one year. Ask at the Reference Desk for further information about using other libraries.

Disabled Student Services—For assistance in entering the Library, pick up the exterior telephone on the southwest corner of the Kellam Building (corner nearest the main entrance). The phone automatically rings the Circulation Desk, and a staff member will come to the door and accompany you upstairs. Also, SLAC offers special academic support services to disabled students.

FIGURE 7.1

Guide to a university library. (*Courtesy of Southwest Texas State University Library Resources Center*)

Books

▼
stacks
The collection of books in a library.

When you think of libraries, you generally think of books. And with good reason: Most of the floor space of a library is devoted to that library's book collections. These collections are called the **stacks.** Stacks may be either open or closed, depending on library policy.

An open-stack library means that the collections are on open shelves and available to anyone who wishes to browse through them. Open stacks give researchers the chance of making lucky finds, since books on a particular subject are shelved next to one another. For example, if you are looking for a specific book on play therapy, you may, on the same shelf, find two or three other books on the same subject. The main drawback to open stacks is that they are vulnerable to both loss of materials and the misplacement of books by careless users.

The closed-stack library is one in which only persons granted certain privileges are allowed in the stacks—most generally, librarians, library aides, faculty, and graduate students. Undergraduates and others must consult the card catalog and copy onto a retrieval card or call slip the title, author, and call number of the book they want. This card or slip is then given to a librarian at the circulation desk, who sends it to the appropriate area of the stacks. A library worker there will find the desired book and send it to circulation, where the borrower can either check it out or use it in the study area of the library.

Most of the floor space of a library is devoted to that library's book collection.
(Joseph Nettis/Photo Researchers, Inc.)

The advantages of the closed-stack library are that users are saved some legwork, and the stacks generally stay more orderly than in an open-stack system. The chief disadvantages are the length of time it can sometimes take to get materials and the impossibility of making a lucky find. Whatever the setup, you will have to adapt to the particular method your library uses.

Card Catalog

Just how do you find what you want from among those several floors in your college library? You probably have used a **card catalog** in a smaller public or school library. University libraries are no different. Even though their holdings are much larger than those of the average public library, access to books is also gained through a card catalog at university libraries.

Card catalogs may be either traditional or computerized. A traditional card catalog will usually be located on one of the first or main floors of the library, and in a college or university library it will be so large that you won't be able to miss it! Each book will be listed on at least three separate 3-by-5 cards, arranged alphabetically in file drawers. One card is filed according to the author's last name, one according to the first word in the title of the book (ignoring *a*, *an*, and *the*), and one according to subject (see Figure 7.2). There may be several subject cards if the book can be listed under more than one subject heading.

A number of libraries have computerized their card catalogs. Instead of running around a huge number of filing cabinets trying to find the drawers you need, you sit down at a screen or monitor, turn it on, and follow the directions given. If you type in a subject, author, or title, the screen will display the library's holdings for that category. Other research techniques remain the same as for traditional card catalogs; the computerized catalog simply saves space (the library's) and physical energy (yours).

The books you will find in your library will be an important source when preparing your speeches. However, books are inherently outdated. Most books are written two or three years before they are published. If your speech is on a current topic or if you want to use current examples, you will probably not find these in books. For up-to-date information, you should turn to periodicals and newspapers.

Periodicals

The term periodicals refers to both general-interest magazines, such as *Newsweek*, *Good Housekeeping*, and *Reader's Digest*, and trade and professional journals, such as *Communication Monographs*, the *Quarterly Journal of Economics*, and *Sociometry*. Both types of periodicals are useful to researchers. As we just observed, periodicals are more timely than books. Current magazines may be only a few days old.

Just as you need a card catalog to help you find books, you need similar help to decide what periodicals might be useful. Several indexes can provide such assistance.

card catalog
A file of information about the books in a library; may use an index card filing system or computerized system.

FIGURE 7.2

Sample subject, author, and title cards from a university card catalog.

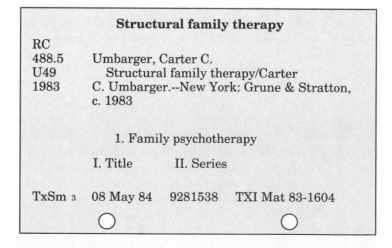

Family therapy

RC
488.5   Umbarger, Carter C.
U49   Structural family therapy/Carter
1983   C. Umbarger.--New York: Grune & Stratton,
         c. 1983

1. Family psychotherapy

I. Title   II. Series

TxSm 3   08 May 84   9281538   TXI Mat 83-1604

Umbarger, Carter C.

RC
488.5   Umbarger, Carter C.
U49   Structural family therapy/Carter
1983   C. Umbarger.--New York: Grune & Stratton,
         c. 1983

1. Family psychotherapy

I. Title   II. Series

TxSm 3   08 May 84   9281538   TXI Mat 83-1604

Structural family therapy

RC
488.5   Umbarger, Carter C.
U49   Structural family therapy/Carter
1983   C. Umbarger.--New York: Grune & Stratton,
         c. 1983

1. Family psychotherapy

I. Title   II. Series

TxSm 3   08 May 84   9281538   TXI Mat 83-1604

Periodical Indexes

A large number of indexes are published, covering a large number of general subject areas and listing most of the thousands of periodicals published on a regular basis.

The following are some of the frequently used periodical indexes.

1. The *Reader's Guide to Periodical Literature* is the oldest and most frequently consulted periodical index. It lists both popular magazines and a few trade and professional journals. Articles are alphabetized according to both subject and author. Figure 7.3 illustrates entries from a typical page in the *Reader's Guide*.

MONEY MARKETS
The economy; uncertainty isn't about to go away. K. Pennar and G. D. Wallace. il *Business Week* p52-3 F 22 '88
Financial globalization [address, November 9, 1987] B. T. Craig. *Vital Speeches of the Day* 54:230-2 F 1 '88
MONEY RATES *See* Interest (Economics)
MONEY SUPPLY
See also
Federal Reserve System (U.S.)
MONOTOMY *See* Boredom
MONSOONS
The effect of Eurasian snow cover on global climate. T. P. Barnett and others. bibl f maps *Science* 239:504-7 Ja 29 '88
MONSTER TRUCKS
Competitions
Why is Meridith Doulton considered a big wheel? 'Cause monster truck fans have a real crush on her. il por *People Weekly* 29:86 F 22 '88
MONTANA
See also
Glacier National Park (Mont.)
MONTE CARLO METHOD
Using financial tools for nonfinancial simulations [use of Poisson distribution in spreadsheets for inventory problems] J. L. Conger. bibl il *Byte* 13:291-2+ Ja '88
MONTEREY BAY (CALIF.)
Lover's Point to Seaside on Monterey's new bike-or-walk trail. il *Sunset (Central edition)* 180:45 Ja '88
MONTGOMERY, L. M. (LUCY MAUD), 1874-1942
about
A tale of twin spinsters. C. Wood. il por *Maclean's* 101:59 F 15 '88
MONTGOMERY, LUCY MAUD *See* Montgomery, L. M. (Lucy Maud), 1874-1942

MONTGOMERY BUS BOYCOTT, 1955
See Civil rights demonstrations—History
MONTHS
See also
February
MONTOYA, JUAN
about
The still of the country, a designer's Hudson River Valley residence. J. Taylor. il *Architectural Digest* 45:120-7 F '88
MONTVILLE, LEIGH
Far north of Calgary. il map *Sports Illustrated* 68 Sp Issue: 174-6+ Ja 27 '88
MOODY, FRANCES
about
Frances Moody, who compared her husband (unfavorably) to a Sciko and ticked a few people off. il pors *People Weekly* 29:44 F 22 '88
MOODY, LINDA A.
Women in seminary: any progress? *The Christian Century* 105:109-10 F 3-10 '88
MOON, SUN MYUNG
about
Rev. Moon's political moves. E. Clift and M. Miller. il por *Newsweek* 111:31 F 15 '88
MOON
See also
Eclipses, Lunar
Lunar occultation highlights for 1988. D. W. Dunham. il *Sky and Telescope* 75:68-9 Ja '88
Photographs and photography
Images [lunar crater Aristarchus photographed from Apollo 15] il. *Sky and Telescope* 75:34-5 Ja '88
Surface
Looking for lunar fractures. M.T. Kitt. il *Astronomy* 16:56-61 F '88

FIGURE 7.3

Entries from the *Reader's Guide to Periodical Literature.*

(Reader's Guide to Periodical Literature, *1988. Copyright © 1988 by the H. W. Wilson Company. Material reproduced by permission of the publisher.*)

The *Reader's Guide* is a cumulative index, published every two weeks. The volumes are combined into quarterly and annual volumes. Its cumulative structure allows the *Reader's Guide* to be available for very current materials, as well as in bound volumes for easy reference to past years.

2. The *Social Sciences Index* and the *Humanities Index* list, for the most part, professional, trade, and specialty publications dealing with the social sciences and the humanities. Originally published as the *Reader's Guide Supplement*, the *Social Sciences Index* and the *Humanities Index* are organized and cumulated like the *Reader's Guide*.

3. The *Education Index* lists not only articles about education but also articles on various subjects that are taught (think about the wide range of departments within a university, and you will have some idea of the scope). Its format is similar to that of the other periodical indexes.

4. The *Public Affairs Information Service Bulletin* indexes both periodicals and books in such subject areas as sociology, political science, and economics. Entries are listed alphabetically by subject, in much the same format as the other indexes.

Other specialized indexes may also prove valuable, depending on your topic and purpose. The *Business Periodicals Index*, the *Psychology Index*, the *Music Index*, the *Art Index*, and the *Applied Science and Technology Index* are a few of these specialized publications that you may wish to explore at one time or another.

Laser Disk Scanners

A number of computerized periodical indexes, including the *Magazine Index*, the *Business Index*, and *Infotrac*, are now available on laser disk scanners in many libraries. Their entries look much like those of the traditional indexes just discussed, but, like the computerized card catalog, the scanners save both library space and physical effort on your part. Rather than looking through several years of the *Reader's Guide*, you can simply flip on a switch, enter a subject or author, and see on the screen the listings for that heading, arranged with the most recent publications first.

The *Magazine Index* includes more than 350 popular magazines. Originally containing only very recent materials, the *Magazine Index* now indexes material dating at least as far back as the 1940s.

A more specialized scanner is the *Business Index*. It indexes a number of library materials related to business, including periodicals, books, the *New York Times* financial section, the *Wall Street Journal*, and various journals of business law. It is a valuable resource for the speaker who has chosen a topic related to business.

Infotrac indexes mainly general-interest magazines and a few specialized journals, from 1985 to the present. It is updated monthly. Like most other indexes and scanners, *Infotrac* is easily accessible by subject.

Easy to use and requiring only a fraction of the space taken up by bulky bound indexes, these and other laser disk services are likely to expand their offerings in the future.

Newspapers

Just as periodicals are more up-to-date than books, so newspapers are more current than periodicals. You may be able to find information that is only hours old by reading the latest edition of a daily newspaper. Newspapers also offer more detailed coverage of events and special stories than periodicals, simply because they are published more often. Finally, newspapers usually cover stories of local significance that most often would not appear in national newsmagazines.

Generally, libraries have only the latest newspapers in their racks. Back issues are quickly transferred to microfilm for more efficient and permanent storage. Don't let microfilm intimidate you. Microfilm readers are easy to use, and most librarians or aides working in the newspaper section will be glad to show you how to set up the reader with the film you need.

As with any research, before you can consult a newspaper, you have to know where to look. To find relevant information on your subject, you need to consult the equivalent of a catalog. Fortunately, newspapers are cataloged in much the same way as periodicals in indexes. The three major newspaper indexes are the *New York Times Index*, the *Christian Science Monitor Index*, and the *Wall Street Journal Index*, all arranged according to subject. In addition, a number of medium to large newspapers publish their own indexes; your library may carry several of these, particularly if one such newspaper is published nearby.

You might also avail yourself of the laser disk contribution to the world of newspaper indexing, called, appropriately, the *National Newspaper Index*. This service not only lists the three papers that have their own indexes—the *New York Times*, the *Christian Science Monitor*, and the *Wall Street Journal*—but also the *Washington Post* and the *Los Angeles Times*.

When doing newspaper research, keep this tip in mind: If you need information about a specific event and you know the day on which it occurred, you can simply get a copy of a newspaper for that or the following day and probably find a news story on the event.

Government Documents

Government documents can be a rich source for your speech. The federal government researches and publishes information on almost every conceivable subject.

Documents published by the government are usually housed together in a special area of the library called the government document section. The huge mass of government pamphlets, reports, and other publications presents a challenge to libraries as well as to researchers. Your best ally in learning to use this vast amount of material is a good government documents librarian who will point out the major features and holdings of his or her unique domain.

The most important listing of government documents is the *Monthly Catalog of U.S. Government Publications*. A bit more complex than the *Reader's Guide*, the *Monthly Catalog* is a rich source and well worth the time needed to learn its indexing system.

Reference Materials

All major libraries contain a specialized group of published works called reference materials. Reference materials are indexed in the card catalog. Their call numbers usually have a *ref* prefix or suffix to show that they are housed in the reference section of the library. Like periodicals, newspapers, and microfilms, they are usually available only for in-house research and cannot be checked out.

Reference materials include encyclopedias, dictionaries, directories, atlases, almanacs, yearbooks, books of quotations, and biographical dictionaries. All may, at one time or another, prove useful to the speaker. Let's examine a few of the most frequently consulted reference works.

1. *Encyclopedias*. The standard for general encyclopedias has for many years been the *Encyclopaedia Britannica*. Nearly every library will have a fairly recent set of *Britannica*, as well as several other general encyclopedias, such as the *Encyclopedia Americana* and the *World Book Encyclopedia*.

In addition, there are a number of specialized encyclopedias. Art, philosophy, psychology, and music are just a few of the fields covered by specialty encyclopedias.

2. *Dictionaries*. The foremost dictionary of the English language is the *Oxford English Dictionary*, or *OED*. Published in 12 large volumes, the *OED* provides definitions, pronunciations, etymologies, and usage histories for every word in the dictionary. No other dictionary is this comprehensive. In all likelihood, you will rarely need as much information about a word as the *OED* provides. Therefore, the unabridged *Random House Dictionary of the English Language* or a desktop *Webster's Collegiate Dictionary* will probably serve your purposes.

There are also specialty dictionaries. *Black's Law Dictionary*, which provides legal definitions, is one example. Such diverse fields as geography, music, and economics also have their own special dictionaries.

3. *Directories*. The *Encyclopedia of Associations* and the *Directory of Nonprofit Organizations* were mentioned earlier in this chapter. These and other directories, including telephone directories, are usually available in the reference section.

4. *Atlases*. An atlas is a geographical tool that provides maps, tables, pictures, and facts about the people and resources of various regions. Frequently used atlases include *Good's World Atlas*, the *Rand McNally College World Atlas*, and the *Township Atlas of the United States*. There are also specialized atlases of history and politics.

5. *Almanacs and yearbooks*. Almanacs and yearbooks are compilations of facts. The *Statistical Abstract of the United States* is published annually by the Census Bureau and contains statistics on nearly every facet of life in the United States, including birth and mortality rates, income, education, and religion. The *World Almanac* contains factual information about almost every subject imaginable. Its content ranges from facts about ruling monarchs of the eighteenth century to a list of every winner of the Kentucky Derby.

6. *Books of quotations*. These are compilations of quotes on almost every conceivable subject. Most of these books are arranged alphabetically by subject; a few are arranged according to author, with subject entered in an index. The *Oxford Dictionary of Quotations* and *Bartlett's Familiar Quotations* are two widely consulted works.

7. *Biographical dictionaries*. These are reference works that contain biographical

articles—some short, others not—on persons who have achieved some recognition. Usually, biographical dictionaries are organized alphabetically. Probably the best-known general works in this area are the *Who's Who* series, which include brief biographies of international, national, and regional figures of note. The *Dictionary of National Biography* provides biographies of famous British subjects who are no longer living; the *Dictionary of American Biography* does the same for deceased Americans of note. The *Directory of American Scholars* provides information about American academicians (you can probably find profiles of some of your current professors in this work). And if none of those just mentioned has the biography you are seeking, you might try the *Biography Index*, a quarterly publication that lists current articles and books containing biographical sketches.

Reference librarians are specialists in the field of library science. They are often able to suggest additional resources that you might otherwise overlook. A suggestion here: If you plan to use the reference section, visit the library during daytime working hours. A full-time reference librarian is more likely to be on hand and available to help you at that time than in evenings or on weekends.

Special Services

In addition to the materials just described, most libraries offer a number of special services. These include interlibrary loans, computer-assisted searches, and area library privileges.

The interlibrary loan is one way to obtain materials that you found listed but not owned by your library. You might, for example, discover in an article you are reading, a reference to a book that you might want to read. But your library does not have the book in its collection. An interlibrary loan can locate the book at another library and get it to you, usually within a few days. Most libraries charge a small fee for this service.

A number of companies have compiled computerized bibliographic databases similar to the various print indexes just discussed. A college or university library may subscribe to several hundred databases. Computer-assisted searches of these databases can provide printouts of articles and books on a variety of subjects. Information retrieval and cross-referencing can be done quickly and easily, with a reference librarian or other special-interest librarian helping you conduct the search. The only real drawback is cost—expect to pay a user's fee for a computerized search, which will vary according to the library and the databases to which it subscribes. Currently the average cost for a computer search is between $5 and $25.

It is very likely that computer searches will continue to become more widely used. Only a few years ago, the *Magazine Index*, *Business Index*, *National Newspaper Index*, and *Infotrac* were accessible only through special searches; in many libraries these four services are now available to users at no cost.

Finally, many libraries have exchange arrangements with libraries of neighboring colleges and universities. You may find that in addition to your own college library, there are two or three others within a fairly convenient radius available for your use.

HOW TO RESEARCH

You have toured the library and have a location guide in hand for future reference. You know the kinds of materials and services your library offers and how to use them. In short, you're ready to begin researching your speech. But unless you approach this next phase of speech preparation carefully and systematically, you may find yourself wasting a good deal of time and energy retracing steps to copy down bits of information you forgot the first time. Approaching research logically can make your efforts easier and more efficient. You need to (1) develop a preliminary bibliography, (2) locate materials, (3) rank or grade materials, and (4) take notes.

Develop a Preliminary Bibliography

A preliminary bibliography, or list of potentially useful sources, should be your first research goal. The preliminary bibliography may include references to any or all of the print materials we just discussed: books, periodicals, newspapers, or government documents. You will probably list more sources than you actually look at or refer to in your speech; at this stage, the bibliography simply serves as a menu of possibilities.

Unless you conduct a database search, which will give you a computer printout, you will have to find a system for recording your list of sources. The handiest items for this purpose are 3-by-5 note cards. Record one source on each card, copying down all necessary bibliographical information, which we will discuss shortly. Cards will give you the greatest flexibility. Later you can omit some of them, add others, write comments on the cards, or alphabetize them much more easily than if you had made a list on a sheet of paper. Let's see what bibliographical information needs to appear on the cards.

For a book, you will need to record the author's name, title of the book, publisher and date of publication, and the library's call number. Figure 7.4 illustrates how to transfer the information from a catalog card to a bibliography card.

The information you need to record for magazine and newspaper articles is similar to that for books. Write down the author's name (if one is listed), title of the article, name of the periodical or newspaper, volume and number (if provided) of the publication, date of publication, and page number on which the article appears. If any of this information is not immediately obvious in the index you are using or if there are abbreviations that you do not understand, check the front of the index, which will provide an explanation of all codes used. Scanners provide this information as well. Figure 7.5 shows a bibliography card for an article discovered in the *Reader's Guide*.

You may wish to include in your bibliography a government publication, pamphlet, newsletter, fact sheet, or some other specialized information format. As long as you record title, author, publisher, date, and page number, you will probably have at hand the information you might need for any print material. For a government document, you will also need to record the Superintendent of Documents classification number, available in the *Monthly Catalog of U.S. Government Publications*.

Card Catalog Card

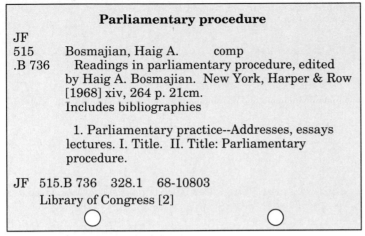

Bibliography Card

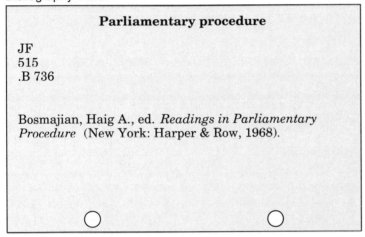

FIGURE 7.4

Sample card catalog entries.

The key to making a useful bibliography is to establish a consistent form so that at a quick glance you can find the page number, title, publisher, or some other vital fact about a publication. Following a consistent form will also help ensure that you do not accidentally leave out a crucial piece of information about the source.

How many sources should you have in a preliminary bibliography for, say, a ten-minute speech? A reasonable number might be ten or twelve. If you have a list of three books, seven articles, and two pamphlets, you might find that your library does not have a couple of them, several others are checked out, and still others are not as useful as you had hoped. If you are left with three or four sources, you will be doing well. Better spend a little extra time "padding" your bibliography now than rushing back to the library in a last-minute panic because you don't have enough material for your speech.

From *Reader's Guide*, March 25, 1988, p. 23:

MOORE, KENNY, 1943-
  The hero returns. il pors *Sports Illustrated* 68 Sp
    Issue: 252-5 Ja 27' 88

Bibliography card made from above entry

Moore, Kenny. "The Hero Returns." *Sports Illustrated*
  (January 27, 1988, pp. 252-55).

FIGURE 7.5

Sample *Reader's Guide to Periodical Literature* entry recorded on a bibliography note card.

Locate Materials

With bibliography and location guide in hand, you are now ready to look for the materials you need. Let's suppose that you decided to look first for the books you want.

In a closed-stack library, you fill out a request card to get the book you're interested in. Take the card to the circulation desk and wait nearby for your book to arrive.

In an open-stack library, you look for books yourself. To find them, you must understand the library's shelving system. Library books are shelved according to either a Library of Congress or a Dewey Decimal call number, depending on the system your particular library uses. Most larger libraries have adopted the Library of Congress system because it represents more subdivisions of subject categories. At any rate, the first letter or number of a call number indicates the general type of book—literature, social science, religion, and so on. Letters or numbers following the initial designation indicate a subcategory. Your location guide (see Figure 7.1) tells you the floor or section of the stacks that houses books carrying the call numbers in which you are interested.

Once you know where to find a book you want, go to that area and check the call number guides on the ends of the bookcases to find exactly where on the shelves your book should be. Like dictionary guide words, the call number guides indicate the call numbers of the first and last book in each bookcase. All books with call numbers between the two guide numbers will be located in that bookcase.

If the title you want is not where it should be and you think it will be an important resource for your speech, you can go to circulation and place a hold on the book. The book will then be reserved for you when it is returned by its current borrower.

Your location guide will also tell you where the library houses periodicals. Some libraries devote a floor or section just to periodicals. All the bound periodicals will be arranged on shelves there, in alphabetical order. Current issues may be displayed on magazine racks, or they may be located in a reading room or other area of the library.

Other libraries shelve their periodicals in the stacks, according to subject matter. You look up the title of the periodical in the card catalog, copy the call number, and proceed as if you were looking for a book. As a rule, periodicals cannot be checked out, so you will need to do your research at the library or copy the articles you want for further reference.

Newspapers are usually housed together in their own section of the library, although current newspapers, like current magazines, may be in a separate reading room. Older issues of newspapers are usually on microfilm. You will need to present certain information, usually the name of the newspaper and the date of the issue you want, to the librarian in charge of newspaper microfilms. The librarian will find the film and bring it to you. When you receive the microfilm, you may have to sign a card for it. You then load the microfilm into the reader and look for the article you are interested in. Inserting the film into the reader may be a little tricky, so don't hesitate to ask for help from a librarian if you are inexperienced.

The government documents section usually arranges materials according to the Superintendent of Documents classification number, which, as noted earlier, can be found in the *Monthly Catalog of U.S. Government Publications*. Government document sections may have other ways of organizing their information as well, including vertical files of materials. Again, if you do not have much experience using government documents, the librarian in that section can be very helpful.

Reference materials are usually housed together in the reference section of the library and cannot be removed from the area. You will either have to take notes or make photocopies to get the information you want.

Rank Materials

As you find the materials listed in your preliminary bibliography, review them swiftly in just enough detail to decide which ones are likely to be useful for your speech. For a book this may involve glancing over the table of contents; flipping quickly through the book to note any charts, graphs, or other visual materials that might be useful; and perhaps skimming a key chapter or two. Shorter articles, pamphlets, and fact sheets should be skimmed as well. The purpose of this quick preview is to decide on the usefulness of the sources before you begin reading more closely and taking notes.

You may wish to devise a number or letter system to rank materials according to their usefulness. The ranking code will make it easier to remember and concentrate on the materials that are most likely to yield the information you need. If you find any other useful information in the material you are previewing, note that on your card as well. It may be hard to remember after a hectic weekend which book had those great charts you could reproduce for your speech.

If none of the materials you find look particularly good, you may need to return to the bibliography building stage to try to locate more potential sources.

Take Notes

Read Carefully   Once you have made your bibliography, located materials, and previewed and rated those materials, you are ready to begin your careful reading and note taking. Start with the sources that you estimated would be the most helpful. If one of your sources is a book, read it selectively. You probably do not have time to read all of it, so read only the chapters or sections you marked as especially interesting in your earlier preview. If your source is an article, pamphlet, encyclopedia entry, or other short work, you should read the whole thing. As you read, notice the writer's point of view and main ideas. But above all, look for specific supporting material that might be useful in your speech.

Write Down Important Ideas and Information   If you find an example, statistic, opinion, or other material that might be useful in your speech, write it down. Even if you discover little specific supporting material but do find a particularly intriguing general idea or main point, write that down too. You will find it much easier to put your final speech together if you have all your ideas and supporting materials in written form at your fingertips, rather than having to scratch your head and think, "Now where did I read that?"

Use a Consistent Format   Just as you were consistent in writing your bibliography, you should also follow a consistent pattern in note taking. Having to locate and then decipher notes scratched on scrap paper, the inside of a book cover, a checkbook, and the last letter from Mom can frustrate even the most determined speechwriter. Instead, use note cards: 4-by-6 or 5-by-8 cards should be large enough for your notes. Whenever you are working on a speech, it is a good idea to carry a few cards with you. You can jot down a fleeting idea that came to mind while you were sipping coffee or note an intriguing fact in a magazine article you glanced at in a doctor's office or at a friend's house.

What should you include on a note card? The most important rule is to put only *one piece of supporting material or one idea on each card*. When you begin to organize your speech, you can physically shuffle your note cards into the order in which you plan to use the material. If you have more than one idea or fact on a note card, you will have to recopy or cross-reference the card somehow, which is time-consuming and potentially confusing.

If you copy a phrase, sentence, or paragraph verbatim from a source, be sure to put quotation marks around it when you write it down. You may need to know later in the preparation process whether it was a direct quote or a paraphrase.

In addition to copying the information itself, you also need to indicate on the

Paraphrased note taken from a book:

McCrum, Robert; Cran, William; and MacNeil, Robert.
   The Story of English (New York: Penquin Books, 1987),
   p. 19.

English has richest vocabulary of all languages: Oxford
English Dictionary lists 500,000 words
German has vocabulary of 185,000 words
French has fewer than 100,000 words

Direct quotation from a periodical article:

Kantrowitz, Barbara. "Preemies." *Newsweek* (May 16,
1988), p. 67.

"Preemies most likely to have serious problems in later
life were those who had been very ill at birth and whose
families had low education levels."

FIGURE 7.6
Paraphrased note taken
from a book and from a
periodical article.

note card the source from which it came. Again, consistency is the key. If you have a carefully coded final bibliography, you can place the source code at the top of each note card on which you have written down information or quotes from that source. You will need to add only the page number of each note. A somewhat more extended option is to use only the author's last name, title, and page number on the note card. Or you may wish to write a complete bibliographical reference on each card. This procedure takes more time but ensures that you will have vital reference information immediately at hand as you work on your speech later.

Finally, leave enough space at the top of each note card to add a heading, which should summarize the idea expressed in the note. Such headings will make it easier to find a particular bit of material quickly when you are ready to assemble the speech. Figure 7.6 illustrates good note-taking format.

There is no rule as to how many note cards you may have for each source. You may write only one note card from one article you read, five from another, and twenty from a third. The amount of useful supporting material you find will vary widely from source to source.

Note cards can also be made during an interview and even from original ideas or information you already know from firsthand experience. Use the same format as for notes taken from written material. Your goal is to write out all your supporting material. This will greatly simplify the organizational task still ahead.

RECAP

DEVELOPING A RESEARCH PLAN

1. Develop a preliminary bibliography.
2. Locate the materials you need.
3. Determine which material is most important.
4. Take notes as you read.

SUMMARY

Public speakers need to know not only what kinds of supporting materials to use in their speeches but also where and how to find them. This chapter discussed four sources of supporting materials: personal knowledge and experience, interviews, mail-order materials, and library resources.

Most speakers can provide some illustrations, explanations, definitions, or other supporting material from their own knowledge and experience. Such material has the advantage of increasing the audience's respect for the speaker's authority.

Interviewing someone who is an expert on the subject of the speech or who has a unique point of view about the subject is a second way to gather supporting materials. Interviewers may take written notes or tape their interviews; later, they will transcribe the information they gathered onto note cards.

Information about many topics is available by mail from various sources. Directories available in the reference sections of most libraries can suggest names and addresses of government agencies, businesses, and organizations that may publish relevant information. Researchers must allow ample time to order and receive such information.

Finally, most speakers rely heavily on library materials—books, periodicals, newspapers, government documents, and reference materials—as sources of supporting material. This chapter discussed how to locate these sources in libraries and also suggested several special services that speakers should consider as they search for relevant material to include in their speeches.

Once a speaker knows where to look for materials, he or she should develop a preliminary bibliography of sources, locate those sources, skim and rank materials as to their potential value for the speech, and take notes from the materials. With notes in hand, the speaker is ready to progress to the next stage in the speechmaking process.

1. Identify key sources of supporting material.
2. How do you plan an interview?
3. What are the key resources available in a typical library?
4. Identify the steps involved in conducting research.
5. What information can you find in a card catalog?
6. Name some reference materials you might use in preparing a speech.

1. Use library resources to discover the answers to the following questions:
   A. Does your library have the following periodicals? Indicate whether each is available in bound volumes or on microfilm.
      1. *American Art Journal*
      2. *Consumers Research Magazine*
      3. *Physics Teacher*
      4. *Western Political Quarterly*
      5. *Ecological Monographs*
   B. Which of the following scanner services does your library offer?
      1. *Infotrac*
      2. *Magazine Index*
      3. *National Newspaper Index*
      4. *Business Index*
   C. On the front page of the *New York Times* on November 20, 1952, was a story about the financial condition of U.S. colleges. What was the headline of that story? Who wrote the story?
   D. How many entries do you find under the heading "Liberal Education" in the 1988 *Reader's Guide*?
   E. Copy the entries you find under the heading "Philosophy, Jewish" in the *Education Index* for July 1988–June 1989.
   F. Use a quotation dictionary to find a quotation about *enthusiasm*. Write down the quotation and its source. What dictionary did you use?
   G. Who won the Academy Award for Best Actor in 1962? For what film? Where did you find the information?
   H. What is the call number for Herman Melville's *Moby Dick*?
2. For each topic below, list at least two library resources likely to yield relevant information:
   > fighting forest fires
   > Einstein and the atomic bomb
   > the lost city of Atlantis
   > the Battle of San Jacinto
   > the Devil's Triangle
   > the government's role in daycare for young children
   > the trial of Julius and Ethel Rosenberg
   > the Berlin Wall
3. Select the topic for your next classroom speech. Develop a bibliography of at least two books, one periodical article, one newspaper article, and one government document or reference work. Use 3-by-5 note cards and a consistent form in taking down the information you need.

8

Organizing Your Speech

Organized thought is the basis of organized action. (*Rene Magritte,* Personal Values, *1952. Oil on canvas, 31½ × 39". Collection Harry Torczyner, New York.*)

ALFRED NORTH WHITEHEAD

Sue went into the lecture hall feeling exhilarated. After all, Dr. Anderson was a Nobel laureate in literature. He would be teaching and lecturing on campus for at least a year. What an opportunity!

Sue took a seat in the middle of the fourth row, where she had a clear view of the podium. She opened the notebook she had bought just for this lecture series, took out one of the three pens she had brought with her, and waited impatiently for Dr. Anderson's appearance. She didn't have to wait long. Dr. Anderson was greeted by thunderous applause when he walked out onto the stage. Sue was aware of an almost electric sense of expectation among the audience members. Pen poised, she awaited his first words.

Five minutes later, Sue still had her pen poised. He had gotten off to a slow start. Ten minutes later, she laid her pen down and decided to concentrate just on listening. Twenty minutes later, she still had no idea what point Dr. Anderson was trying to make. And by the time the lecture was over, Sue was practically asleep. Disappointed, she gathered her pens and her notebook (which now contained one page of lazy doodles) and promised herself she would skip the remaining lectures in the series.

Dr. Anderson was not a dynamic speaker. But his motivated audience of young would-be authors and admirers might have forgiven that shortcoming. What they were unable to do was to unravel his hour's worth of seemingly pointless rambling—to get some sense of direction or some pattern of ideas from his talk. Dr. Anderson had simply failed to organize his thoughts.

This scenario actually happened. Dr. Anderson (not his real name) disappointed many who had looked forward to his lectures. His inability to organize his ideas made him an ineffectual speaker. You too may have had an experience with a teacher who possessed awesome knowledge and ability in his or her field but could not organize his or her thoughts well enough to lecture effectively. No matter how knowledgeable speakers may be, they must organize their ideas in logical patterns to ensure that their audience can follow, understand, and remember what was said. Our diagram of audience-centered communication shows that speeches are organized *for* audiences, with decisions about organization being based in large part on an analysis of the audience.

In the first seven chapters of this book, you learned how to plan and research a speech, based on audience needs, interests, and expectations. The planning and research process took you through five stages of speech preparation:

1. Select and narrow a topic.
2. Determine your purpose.
3. Develop a central idea.
4. Generate main ideas.
5. Gather supporting material.

Now it is time to move from planning and researching to putting the speech together—in other words, to organizing your ideas and information. The sixth stage in our audience-centered public speaking process is simply that:

6. Organize your speech.

Just as you learned to accomplish the first five steps methodically, so can you learn a systematic plan of organizing your speech. First, we will discuss the patterns of organization commonly used to arrange or structure the main ideas of a speech. Then we will discuss how to organize subpoints and supporting materials. Finally, we will talk about transitions, previews, and summaries. Chapter 9 will discuss outlining, and Chapter 10 will deal with introductions and conclusions, the final two components of the organizational stage of the preparation process.

In Chapter 5, we discussed how to generate a preliminary "skeleton outline" by seeing whether your central idea had *natural divisions*, could be supported by several *reasons*, or could be explained by a number of *steps*. The divisions, reasons, or steps became the main points of the body of your speech and fullfilled the organization task highlighted in Figure 8.1.

Now that you have researched and gathered your supporting material, do these main points still seem the best divisions of your central idea? Do you think you may have to change your purpose statement or central idea because of new information about your topic or your audience's needs, interests, and expectations? If

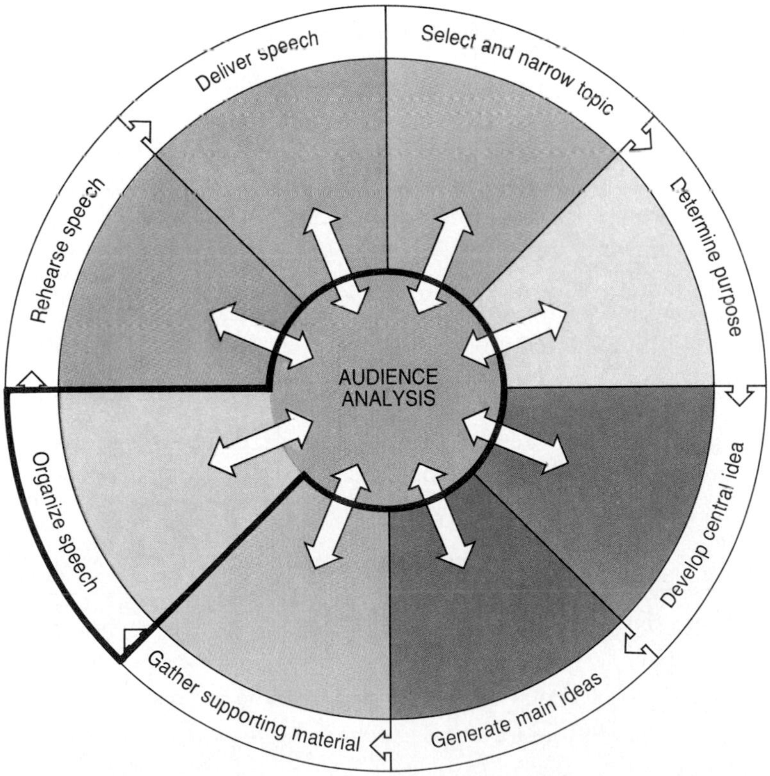

ORGANIZE YOUR MAIN POINTS

FIGURE 8.1

Organize your speech to help your audience remember your key ideas and give your speech clarity and structure.

you want to make revisions based on information discovered during your research, now is the time to do so.

After you have adjusted your skeleton outline, you are ready to consider how best to organize your main ideas. At this point you will have to make choices from among five organizational patterns: (1) chronological, (2) topical, (3) spatial, (4) causal, and (5) problem-solution. While organizing your speech, you will also have to make decisions about combining several of these patterns. One additional pattern of organization, the motivated sequence, is actually a variation of the problem-solution pattern. Because it is used almost exclusively in persuasive speeches, a detailed discussion of the motivated sequence will appear in detail in Chapter 16, "Methods of Persuasion."

Arrange Ideas Chronologically

If you decide that your central idea statement could be explained best by a number of steps, you will probably organize those steps chronologically. Chronological organization is organization by time; that is, your steps are ordered according to when each step occurred or should occur. Historical speeches and how-to speeches are the two kinds of speeches usually organized chronologically.

Examples of topics for historical speeches might include the history of the women's movement in the United States, the sequence of events that led to the 1974 resignation of President Richard Nixon, or the development of the modern Olympic Games. You may wish to organize your main points either from earliest to most recent (forward in time) or from recent events back into history (backward in time). The progression you choose depends on your personal preference and on whether you want to emphasize the beginning or the end of the sequence. According to the principle of **recency,** the event discussed *last* is usually the one the audience will remember best.

In the following speech on the crisis facing the American family farm, the speaker moves forward in time, developing his last point in detail so that it remains fresh in the minds of his audience at the end of his speech.

▼
recency
Arranging most important information last.

Purpose Statement: At the end of my speech, the audience will be able to explain how the current farm crisis has developed.

Central Idea: American family farms are facing a great crisis.

  I. The 1970s were flourishing economic times. Interest rates were low, and machinery was relatively inexpensive.

 II. In the early 1980s, farmers began to overproduce; at the same time, agricultural exports dropped.

III. In the mid-1980s, crop and land prices fell, while interest rates soared.

IV. As we enter the 1990s, farming is experiencing its worst days since the Great Depression.[1]

In another historical speech, this one discussing the factors that led to the literary renaissance in England, the speaker believes the introduction of the printing press to be the most important influence and organizes the speech backward in time:

Purpose Statement: At the end of my speech, the audience will be able to list and explain the two forces that prompted the English literary renaissance.

Central Idea: Two powerful forces for change led to the English literary renaissance, which began late in the fifteenth century:

  I. 1485—Henry VII defeated Richard III at the Battle of Bosworth Field, ascended the throne, and began the Tudor dynasty.
 II. 1476—William Caxton brought the printing press to England.

By discussing the printing press last, the speaker gives it the greatest emphasis in the speech. Chronological organization, then, refers to either forward or backward progression, depending on which end of a set of events the speaker intends to emphasize. The element common to both movements is that dates and events are discussed in sequence rather than in random order.

How-to explanations usually follow a sequence or series of steps arranged in time (first do this, next do that, then do this other thing, and finally you've got your finished product). In these speeches, you almost always move from beginning to end, from the first step to the last—forward in time. A speech explaining how to strip painted furniture might be organized as follows:

Purpose Statement: At the end of my speech, the audience will be able to list the four steps involved in stripping old paint from furniture.

Central Idea: Stripping old paint from furniture requires four steps:

   I. Prepare work area and gather materials.
  II. Apply chemical stripper.
 III. Remove stripper with scrapers and steel wool.
  IV. Clean and sand stripped surfaces.

Organize Ideas Topically

If your central idea has natural divisions, your speech can often be organized topically. Speeches on such diverse topics as factors to consider when selecting a pet, types of infertility treatments, and the three kinds of cross-country skis could all be organized topically.

Natural divisions are often fairly equal in importance. It may not matter which point is discussed first, second, or third. The order in which you arrange your main points will be a matter of personal preference. At other times, you may wish to emphasize one point more than the others. If so, you will again need to consider the principle of *recency*. As we observed a moment ago, audiences tend to remember best what they hear last. For example, if your speech is on the various living arrangements available to college students, you may decide to discuss living at home, rooming in a dorm, joining a fraternity or sorority, and renting an apartment. If you want your audience of fellow students to consider living in a dorm, at least for a year or two, you would probably discuss that possibility as the fourth and last option. Your speech might have the following structure:

Purpose Statement: At the end of my speech, the audience will be able to discuss the pros and cons of the four lifestyle options for college students.

Central Idea: College students have at least four living arrangements available to them:

   I. Living at home
  II. Renting an apartment
 III. Joining a fraternity or sorority
 IV. Living in a dormitory

▼
primacy
Arranging most important information first.

    By contrast, if your topic is controversial and you know or suspect that your audience will be skeptical or hostile toward your ideas, you may want to organize your main points according to the principle of **primacy,** or putting the most important idea first. That way you do not risk losing or alienating your audience before you can reach your most significant idea. Further, your strongest idea may so influence their attitudes that they will be more receptive to the rest of your speech.

Purpose Statement: At the end of my speech, the audience will be able to explain the advantages of federal funding for abortions.

Central Idea: Federal funding for abortions has three advantages:

   I. It prevents the birth of unwanted, potentially abused children.
  II. It eliminates the monetary barrier to equal rights.
 III. In the long run, it actually saves welfare money.

In this example, the speaker realized that advocacy of federal funding for abortions would be controversial. The three main points of the speech were therefore arranged according to primacy, advancing the most persuasive argument first.

    One other set of circumstances may dictate a particular order of the main points in your speech. If your main points range from simple to complicated, it makes sense to arrange them in order of **complexity,** progressing from the simple to the more complex. If, for example, you were to explain to your audience the mathematical functions possible with a slide rule, you might discuss them in this order:

Purpose Statement: At the end of my speech, the audience will be able to demonstrate the four functions possible on a slide rule.

Central Idea: Four mathematical functions are possible on a slide rule:

Organizing your ideas according to where they are located is called spatial *organization.*
(*Jerry W. Myers/The Stock Market*)

I. Multiplication
II. Division
III. Square roots
IV. Logarithms

Teachers from the very early elementary grades on, use order of complexity to organize their courses and individual lessons. The kindergartener is taught to trace circles before learning to print a lowercase *a*. The young piano student practices scales and arpeggios before playing Beethoven sonatas. The college freshman practices writing 500-word essays before attempting a major research paper. Most of the skills you have learned have been taught by order of complexity.

Order Ideas Spatially

Organizing your ideas according to their position in space is another pattern sometimes applied to main points. When you say, "As you enter the room, the table is to your right, the easy chair to your left, and the kitchen door straight ahead," you are organizing your ideas spatially. Spatial organization is arranging items according to their location and direction. It does not usually matter whether the speaker chooses to progress up or down, east or west, front or back, as long as ideas are developed in a logical order. If the speaker skips up, down, over, and back, he or she will only confuse the audience rather than paint a distinct word picture for them.

Speeches on such diverse subjects as the landscape of Texas, what to see in a day at the Smithsonian Institution, and the makeup of an atom, may all be organized spatially. Here is a sample outline for the first of those topics:

Purpose Statement: At the end of my speech, the audience will be able to list and describe the five most important natural features of Texas.

Central Idea: As its size might suggest, Texas is a state of diverse natural features.

   I. Forests
  II. Prairies and plains
 III. Hill country
  IV. Deserts
   V. Big Bend mountains and basins

As those familiar with Texas will recognize, the spatial organization of this outline is basically from east to west.

Arrange Ideas to Show Cause and Effect

cause and effect
Discussing first the causes of a problem and then discussing the effects of the problem

If you choose your main points by listing the reasons you think your central idea is true, you will probably organize your speech causally. Causal organization deals with **cause and effect.** A speech organized to show cause and effect may state a problem and then seek its causes. Or the speech may present a cause and then describe its effects. What you want the audience to remember will dictate which of these strategies you choose. If you wish to emphasize the causes, you will discuss the effect first and then examine its causes. A student trying to convince her audience to write a will explained the causes of *not* writing wills:

Purpose Statement: At the end of my speech, the audience will be able to explain and refute the reasons people don't write wills.

Central Idea: There are many reasons people don't write wills.

   I. Unwillingness to face death
  II. Fear that writing a will may cause us to die
 III. Ignorance of how to prepare a will[2]

If, by contrast, you wish to emphasize the effects of a situation, you generally first present the situation and then examine its effects. The following outline of a student speech on adult illiteracy examines the effects of that problem:

Purpose Statement: At the end of my speech, the audience will be able to discuss three effects of adult functional illiteracy.

Central Idea: Adult functional illiteracy is a major problem for America today.

   I. High cost to society
  II. Poverty for the illiterates
 III. Decline in readership of newspapers and public notices[3]

The causes or effects presented as main points may themselves be organized according to the principles of recency, primacy, or complexity that we discussed earlier in this chapter.

Organize Ideas by Problem and Solution

While you may organize your ideas according to a pattern of cause and effect to discuss how a problem arose, if you want to emphasize how best to *solve* the problem, you will probably use a problem-solution pattern.

In discussing cause-effect organization, we observed that you may either deal with effects first and then causes or with causes first and then effects. The problem-solution pattern can likewise be used in either order. You may sometimes wish to present a solution or a proposal and then note the problems that it will solve. An example of that approach is this outline for a speech on school volunteer programs.

Purpose Statement: At the end of my speech, the audience will be able to explain how school volunteer programs can help solve three of the major problems facing our public schools today.

Central Idea: School volunteer programs can help alleviate many of the problems faced by public schools today.

   I. Loss of financial support and inability to afford special programs
  II. Scarcity of teachers in artistic and highly technical fields
 III. Lack of continuity between learning at school and learning at home

In other instances, you may want to present a problem and then offer several possible solutions. The next speech is an example of this approach.

Purpose Statement: At the end of my speech, the audience will be able to list and explain four possible solutions to the problem of rising medical costs in the United States.

Central Idea: Skyrocketing medical costs in the United States must be contained.

   I. Voluntary cost containment by the medical community
  II. Government price regulations for medical services and supplies
 III. Proliferation of private-sector HMOs
  IV. A program of guaranteed national health care

Deciding what to emphasize can help you organize your problem-solution speech. If you wish to emphasize problems, you should present the solution first and then discuss the problems as your main ideas. If you want to emphasize the solutions, you should discuss the problem first and then present your solutions.

Causal and problem-solution patterns of organization are often combined in a speech. For example, you may identify a problem, probe its causes, and then offer one or more solutions. Because you have first examined the causes, you can tailor the solutions to them. Speaking on the need for education about AIDS, a student adopted the following organizational pattern:

Purpose Statement: At the end of my speech, the audience will be able to explain why and how education is the answer to the AIDS epidemic.

Central Idea: Society must modify its behavior in regard to AIDS.

I. Three reasons Americans have not changed their behavior
   A. Belief that science will find a quick cure
   B. Disbelief that general population is at risk
   C. Ignorance
II. Education as the solution
   A. Schools
   B. Home
   C. Media[4]

Like this speech, which combines causal and problem-solution patterns, many speeches will be organized according to some combination of the five patterns we have just discussed. None need be exclusive of the others.

RECAP

ORGANIZE YOUR MAIN IDEAS	Pattern	Description
	Chronological	Organization by time or sequence
	Topical	Organization according to the speaker's discretion, recency, primacy, or complexity
	Spatial	Organization according to location or position
	Causal	Organization by discussing first causes and then effects or first effects and then causes
	Problem-solution	Discussion of a problem and then various solutions or of a solution and then the problems it would solve

Once you decide how to organize your main points, you may need to subdivide them. For example, if you give a how-to speech on dog grooming, your first main point may be

SUBDIVIDE YOUR MAIN POINTS

    I. Gather your supplies.

"Supplies" indicates that you need more than one piece of equipment, so you add subpoints that describe the specific supplies needed:

I. Gather your supplies.
    A. Soft brush
    B. Firm brush
    C. Wide-toothed comb
    D. Fine-toothed comb
    E. Scissors
    F. Spray-on detangler

The subpoints in this example are arranged topically. Any of the five organizational patterns that apply to main points can apply to subpoints as well. It is also possible that your main points may be arranged according to one pattern and your subpoints according to another. Chances are, the main points of the speech on dog grooming will be organized chronologically. But the subpoints of point I are organized topically.

Another example of using different patterns to organize main points and subpoints can be found in this speech on the problem of modern air traffic control.

Purpose Statement: At the end of my speech, the audience will be able to explain why and how air traffic control can be improved.
Central Idea: Air traffic control needs amending today.

    I. History of the problem
   II. Effects of the problem
  III. Probable solutions[5]

The overall design of this speech combines the causal and problem-solution patterns. But the subpoints of point I are put together chronologically, as the word *history* suggests:

    I. History of the problem
    A. The Professional Air Traffic Controllers Organization (PATCO) complains to the FAA for years that there is too much stress.
    B. In 1981 PATCO and FAA negotiate for higher pay and fewer hours.
    C. PATCO refuses the FAA offer and goes on strike.
    D. President Reagan fires 13,000 air traffic controllers.
    E. FAA gradually rebuilds controller numbers.[6]

A personal computer can help you "cut and paste" as you draft and revise your speech outline.
(*Courtesy of IBM*)

Subpoints, then, can be arranged in any pattern, even if it differs from the organization of the main points of the speech.

Right now, don't worry too much about such outlining details as Roman numerals, letters, and margins. They will be covered in Chapter 9. Your goal at this time is to get your ideas and information on paper. Keep in mind, too, that until you've delivered your speech, none of your decisions are etched in stone. You may need to add, regroup, or eliminate points or subpoints at any stage in the preparation process, as you consider the needs, interests, and expectations of your audience. The Nobel prizewinning author Isaac Bashevis Singer has observed, "The wastebasket is a writer's best friend." He could just as accurately have said "speaker" instead of "writer." Many drafts indicate that you are working and reworking ideas to improve your product and make it the best you can. It does *not* mean that you are a poor writer or speaker.

INCORPORATE YOUR SUPPORTING MATERIALS

Once you have organized your points and subpoints, you are ready to flesh out the speech by inserting your supporting materials. If you have written down this material on note cards, as suggested in Chapter 7, the process of incorporating them should be fairly easy. One good method is to write each main point and subpoint on a separate note card of the same size as the ones on which you recorded your supporting materials. Arrange these note cards in the order in which you have organized your speech. Then go through your supporting-material note cards, one by one, and decide where in the speech you will use each one. The headings you wrote at the top of each card should help in this procedure. Place each supporting-material card behind the appropriate main point or subpoint.

After you have arranged all your supporting materials, read through your note cards from the beginning. At this point you are reading an outline of the *body* of the speech only (no introduction or conclusion) and have not yet included transitions, previews, or summaries (which we will discuss later in this chapter). However, you should now have a fairly complete outline of the contents of your speech.

It may be useful to have a sheet of paper and pen or pencil handy to jot down any points or subpoints that may now suggest themselves but for which you have no supporting materials. If you feel that they are important enough to be included in your speech, you will have to do some further research and note taking. Or you may come to feel that these points are not worth the trouble and will therefore eliminate them.

There is always the possibility that you may find that you have too much support. While there is no established ceiling on how much support you can have, you will probably not use more than four or five pieces to prove even a controversial point. Otherwise, you may overburden your speech and tax the patience of your listeners. What do you eliminate? In Chapter 6, we discussed such factors as relevance, appropriateness, significance, and variety as guides in choosing the best supporting materials. Using the same criteria now will help you keep the best support and eliminate any that may be insignificant, irrelevant, or repetitious.

ORGANIZE YOUR SUPPORTING MATERIALS

You have decided what supporting materials to use and where they should go in your speech. But in support of your second main point you have an illustration, two statistics, and an opinion. What order do you put these in? How do you organize the supporting materials themselves?

You can sometimes use the five standard organizational patterns to arrange your supporting materials, as well as your main points and subpoints. Illustrations, for instance, may be organized chronologically. In a speech on Boy Scouting, a student arranged several brief examples in a chronological sequence:

> Since the days of Teddy Roosevelt [every one] of our nation's presidents have been involved in Boy Scouting. President John F. Kennedy expressed his sincere belief in Boy Scouting when he said, "In a very real sense, the principles learned and practiced as Boy Scouts add to the strength of America and her ideals." President Gerald Ford shared with the American public, "I am the first Eagle Scout to become President and I thank scouting for the three great principles: Self-Discipline, Teamwork and Moral Values, which are the basic building-blocks of great leadership."[7]

At other times, however, none of the five patterns may seem suited to the supporting materials you have. In those instances, you may need to turn to an organizational strategy more specifically adapted to your supporting materials. These strategies include (1) primacy or recency, (2) specificity, (3) complexity, and (4) "soft" to "hard."

Primacy or Recency

We have already discussed how the principles of primacy and recency determine whether you may want to put material at the beginning or end of your speech. Those patterns are used so frequently to arrange supporting materials that we mention them again as major organizational strategies. Suppose that you choose three statistics to support a main point. All are relevant and significant, but one is especially gripping. The desire to emphasize this statistical information suggests that you save it for last, as did the student in this excerpt from a speech on organ transplants:

> A glance at the statistics concerning survival rates best demonstrates transplant's workability today. The *New York Times Magazine's* June 19, 1983, edition reports that the one-year survival rate for heart transplants is 65%. Liver transplant patients have a 70% survival rate according to the October 1, 1983, issue of *Science News*, with the longest surviving patient exceeding 13 years. Even more interesting is the amount of success in kidney transplants which now command a 90–97% survival rating.[8]

The speaker organized her three statistics in the order of their significance, saving her "clincher" for last. While our example is of statistics, the principles involved can also apply to groups of examples, opinions, or any combination of supporting materials.

As we mentioned earlier, only if your topic is extremely controversial and your audience is likely to be neutral or hostile should you present your most powerful supporting material first.

Specificity

Sometimes your supporting materials will range from very specific examples to more general overviews of a situation. You may either offer your specific information first and end with your general statement or make the general statement first and support it with specific evidence.

In this speech on worldwide political repression, the speaker chose to present data from individual countries first and then to conclude with a general statement from the United Nations:

> Amnesty International says there are perhaps 10,000 [prisoners of conscience] in the Soviet Union and 2,000 in Poland, 15,000 in Turkey and 10,000 spread across Africa, 5,000 in South America and some 100,000 are strung across Pakistan, Afghanistan, Iran, Iraq, South Korea and the Phillippines. Yet the numbers do not stop there. Over one-half of the 157 members of the United Nations are said to have at least some prisoners of conscience. In its most recent state of the world report, the United Nations conceded our planet is still racked with "political liquidations, mass killings and torture."[9]

Complexity

We have already discussed moving from the simple to the complex as a way to organize your subtopics. The same method of organization may also determine how you order your supporting materials. In many situations, it makes sense to start with the simplest ideas that are easy to understand and work up to more complex ones. When describing how the sun causes skin cancer, the next speaker first explains the simplest effect of sun—rapid aging of the skin—and then goes on to the more complex effect—molecular alteration:

> First, the sun can dry skin and make it less elastic. The result is premature wrinkles. Second, the sun can actually affect the molecular structure of the body, deranging DNA molecules. An immediate result is damage to our immune system and loss of our ability to fight off disease. A second, potentially more significant effect of such genetic mutation is that it may be passed on to our children and their children.[10]

"Soft" to "Hard" Evidence

Supporting materials can also be arranged from "soft" to "hard." Soft supporting materials are based mainly on opinion or inference. Hypothetical illustrations, explanations and descriptions, definitions, analogies, and opinions are usually considered soft. Hard evidence includes factual examples and statistics. Actually, it would be more accurate to think of soft and hard as two ends of a continuum, with various supporting materials falling somewhere between. The surgeon general's analysis of the AIDS crisis, for example, would be placed nearer the hard end of the continuum than would a sales pitch for batteries from an Olympic athlete, even though both are opinions. The surgeon general is a more credible speaker whose analysis is the result of his extensive knowledge of and research into the subject.

Soft-to-hard organization of supporting materials relies chiefly on the idea that the last statement will be remembered best. Speakers usually want to save their most convincing evidence until last, and most often that evidence is hard. Notice how the following speaker moves from a soft hypothetical example to a hard statistic in this excerpt from a speech on discrimination against epileptics:

> Let us look at the hypothetical life of a typical epileptic. Let's call him Steve.
>
> Steve started school, just like other children, and Steve was just a normal student. Until one day on the playground, Steve suffered an epileptic seizure. Only a few people observed the seizure but soon word spread that Steve was a freak, and with that seizure Steve became part of a national statistic. The . . . Commission for the Control of Epilepsy and Its Consequences pointed out in [its] 1978 report that "social ostracism is one of the major problems confronting children with epilepsy." The report goes on to cite a survey that reveals [that] while 60% of the teachers felt that regular classwork was best for an epileptic child, only 27% would personally want such a child in their classroom.[11]

The hypothetical example is followed by an expert opinion and then by a conclusive statistic. The speaker has arranged her supporting material from soft to hard.

RECAP

ORGANIZE YOUR SUPPORTING MATERIALS	Strategy	Description
	Primacy	Most important material first
	Recency	Most important material last
	Specificity	From specific information to general overview or from general overview to specific information
	Complexity	From simple materials to more complex ones
	"Soft" to "Hard" Evidence	From opinion or inference to fact or statistic

DEVELOP CONNECTORS

Once you have arranged your note cards, you have a logically organized, fairly complete outline of your speech. But if you tried to deliver the speech at this point, you would find yourself often groping for some way to get from one point to the next. Your audience might become frustrated or even confused by your hesitations and awkwardness. Your next organizational task is to develop connectors—words and gestures that allow you to move smoothly from one idea to the next throughout your speech, showing relationships between ideas and emphasizing important points. Three types of connectors can serve as glue to hold your speech together: transitions, previews, and summaries.

Transitions

Transitions indicate that a speaker has finished an idea and is moving to another. Transitions may be either verbal or nonverbal. Let's consider some examples of each type.

Verbal Transitions   A speaker can sometimes make a verbal transition simply by repeating a key word from an earlier statement or by using a synonym or a pronoun that refers to an earlier key word or idea. This type of transition is often used to make one sentence flow smoothly into the next (this sentence itself is an example: "This type of transition" refers to the sentence that precedes it). Other verbal transitions show relationships between ideas. These include the following transitional words and phrases:

in addition	on the one hand . . . on the other hand
not only . . . but also	however
therefore	moreover
thus	for example
in other words	finally
in conclusion	in summary

You will feel more comfortable delivering a well organized speech.
(*Nancy J. Pierce/Photo Researchers, Inc.*)

Simple enumeration (*first*, *second*, *third*) can also point up relationships between ideas and provide transitions.

One type of transition that can occasionally backfire and do more harm than good is one that signals the end of a speech. "Finally" and "in conclusion" are the two most common concluding transitions. A speaker who uses one of these should then finish the speech as quickly as possible. "Finally" and "in conclusion" give the audience implicit permission to stop listening, and they often do. If the speech has been too long or has otherwise not gone well, the audience may even audibly express relief. A famous instance of a disastrous "false conclusion" occurred at the end of Arkansas governor Bill Clinton's speech nominating Lloyd Bentsen for the vice-presidency at the 1988 Democratic national convention. Clinton's speech had run nearly twice the ten minutes he had been allotted, and delegates were already restless and irritated. The floor erupted in cheers when Clinton announced, "And in conclusion . . ." Admittedly an extreme case, Governor Clinton's experience teaches a harsh lesson: Use discretion in signaling your conclusion!

Internal previews and summaries, which will be discussed later in this chapter, are still another way to provide a transition from one point to the next in your speech. They have the additional advantage of summarizing your main ideas, thereby enabling audience members to understand and remember them.

Repetition of key words or ideas, the use of connective words or phrases, enumeration, and internal previews and summaries all provide verbal transitions from one idea to the next. You may need to experiment with several alternatives before you find one that will give you the smooth transition you seek in a given instance. If none of these alternatives seems to work well, you might consider a nonverbal transition.

RECAP

VERBAL TRANSITIONS	Description	Example
	Repeating a key word, or using a synonym or pronoun that refers to a key word	"*These problems* cannot be allowed to continue."
	Showing relationship of next idea to previous one	"*In addition to* the facts that I've mentioned, we need to consider one additional problem."
	Enumerating	"*Second*, there has been a rapid increase in the number of accidents reported."
	Using internal summaries and previews	"*Now that we have discussed the problems* caused by illiteracy, *let's look at some of the possible solutions.*"

Nonverbal Transitions   Nonverbal transitions can occur in several ways, sometimes alone and sometimes in combination with verbal transitions. A change in facial expression, a pause, an altered vocal pitch or speaking rate, or a movement may all indicate a transition.

For example, a speaker talking about the value of cardiopulmonary resuscitation began his speech with a powerful anecdote of a man suffering a heart attack at a party. No one knew how to help, and the man died. The speaker then looked up from his notes and paused, while maintaining eye contact with his audience. His next words were: "The real tragedy of Bill Jorgen's death was that it should not have happened." His pause, as well as the words that followed, indicated a transition into the body of the speech.

Like this speaker, most good speakers will use a combination of verbal and nonverbal transitions to move from one point to another through their speeches. You will study more about nonverbal communication in Chapter 11, "Delivery."

Previews

In Chapter 12, we will discuss the differences between writing and speaking styles. One significant difference which we will note here is that public speaking is more repetitive. Audience-centered speakers need to remember that the members of their audiences, unlike readers, cannot go back to review a missed point. The maxim often quoted by speech teachers is "Tell them what you're going to tell them; tell them; then tell them what you've told them." A preview fulfills the first third of that formula: "Tell them what you're going to tell them." As its name indicates, a preview is a statement of what is to come. Previews help to ensure that audience members will first anticipate and later remember the important points of a speech. Like transitions, previews also help to provide coherence.

Two types of previews are usually used in speeches: the preview statement, or initial preview, and the internal preview. The preview statement usually occurs at or near the end of the speech introduction. It is a statement of what the main points of the speech will be. In other words, it is a blueprint of the speech, revealed to the audience for the first time. A student speaking on the dangers of radon gas offered this preview statement at the end of her introduction:

> What I'd like to look at today is what radon is, how it enters our homes, the effects it has on our bodies, and most importantly, the relatively simple methods available to us to circumvent this.[12]

Her four points are clearly defined. Sometimes speakers will enumerate their main points to outline them even more clearly:

> In the next few minutes I'd first like to look at the new problem of farm suicides and how it is sweeping across the wheat and cornfields of America. Secondly, I would like to look at why the problem is occurring and finally, offer solutions for the dislocated farmer, the farmer who has had his farm foreclosed on.[13]

Notice that while the first preview statement is one sentence, the second consists of two sentences. The word *statement* does not necessarily mean one long, rambling sentence. As in the farm suicide speech, the preview statement can often consist of several short sentences.

In addition to outlining the main points of the speech, a preview statement will usually contain a speaker's central idea. It may even include a modified purpose statement. The following speaker stated her central idea as part of her preview statement:

> Illiteracy among athletes must be stopped. In order to fully grasp the significance of this problem, we will look at the root of it, and then move to [its] effects, and finally, we will look at the solution.[14]

And another speaker included an overt statement of purpose with her preview statement:

> My purpose today is to convince each of you that having a will is important by discussing why people avoid writing a will; what a will is and why we need one; and finally, how can we obtain a will.[15]

To summarize, the preview statement reveals the main points of the speech to the audience for the first time. It may also include the central idea or the speaker's purpose. Finally, the preview statement provides a smooth connection between the introduction and the body of the speech.

In addition to using previews near the beginning of their speeches, speakers also use them at various points throughout. These internal previews introduce and outline ideas that will be developed as the speech progresses. As has been noted, internal previews can serve as transitions. The following speaker, for example, had just discussed what radon gas is and how many people are exposed to it. She then provided this transitional preview into her next point: "To truly comprehend the significance of the problem, we need an understanding of how radon works."[16] Her listeners then expected her to discuss how radon works, which, of course, she did. Their anticipation increased the likelihood that they would later remember the information.

Sometimes speakers couch internal previews in the form of questions that they plan to answer. Note how the question in this example provides an internal preview:

> As John Hinckley has demonstrated, the easy accessibility of firearms in America is a national scandal.
>   We can now easily see why firearms are being used so frequently, but what can we do to solve this startling problem?
>   One of the best solutions to our problem is to have a stricter registration system on handguns.[17]

Just as anticipating an idea will help audience members remember it, so will their mentally answering a question help them plant that answer firmly in their minds.

Summaries

"Tell them what you've told them"—the final portion of the speech teacher's advice—justifies the use of summaries. Like previews, summaries provide additional exposure to a speaker's ideas and can help ensure that audience members will grasp and remember them. Most speakers use two types of summaries: the final summary and the internal summary.

A final summary occurs in or just before the end of a speech. In fact, sometimes the summary *is* the conclusion. (Conclusions will be discussed in Chapter 10.) The final summary is the opposite of the preview statement. The preview statement gives an audience their first exposure to a speaker's main ideas; the final summary gives them their *last* exposure to those ideas. Here is an example of a final summary from a speech on U.S. Customs:

> Today, we have focused on the failing U.S. Customs Service. We have asked several important questions, such as, "Why is Customs having such a hard time doing its job?" and "What can we do to remedy this situation?" When the cause of a serious problem is unknown, the continuation of the dilemma is understandable. However, the cause for the failure of the U.S. Customs Service is known: a lack of personnel. Given that fact and our understanding that Customs is vital to America's interests, it would be foolish not to rectify this situation.[18]

This final summary leaves no doubt as to the important points of the speech.

Internal summaries, as the name suggests, are those that occur within and throughout a speech. They are often used after two or three points have been discussed, to keep those points fresh in the minds of the audience as the speech progresses. Here is an example from a speech on the teacher shortage:

> So let's review for just a moment. One, we are endeavoring to implement educational reforms; but two, we are in the first years of a dramatic increase in enrollment; and three, fewer quality students are opting for education; while four, many good teachers want out of teaching; plus five, large numbers will soon be retiring.[19]

Like internal previews, internal summaries also help provide transitions. In fact, internal summaries are often used in combination with internal previews to form transitions between major points and ideas. Each of the following examples makes clear what has just been discussed as well as what will be discussed next:

> Now that we've seen how radon can get into our homes, let's take a look at some of the effects that it can have on our health once it begins to build.[20]

> We have looked at the great need. Americans are dying *now*. You and I can help.[21]

> It seems as though everyone is saying that something should be done about NutraSweet. It should be retested. Well, now that it is here on the market, what can we do to see that it does get investigated further?[22]

Transitions, summaries, and previews—all three types of connectors are the "glue" that holds the speech together. Without connectors, even a well-organized speaker would falter and hesitate. With them, the speaker can achieve a coherent flow of ideas and can help ensure that the audience will remember those ideas.

SUMMARY

In this chapter, we examined the process of organizing your speech in a logical fashion so that audience members can follow, understand, and remember your ideas. We pointed out early in the chapter that the process of organization is by nature audience-centered. Speeches are organized for audiences, with the speaker keeping in mind at all times the unique needs, interests, and expectations of the particular audience.

A speaker must first consider how best to organize the main points of the speech. We discussed five patterns and noted that any combination of them is possible. The patterns are chronological, topical, spatial, causal, and problem-solution.

Next we talked about subdividing main points and organizing those subpoints so that audience members could most readily grasp, understand, and remember them. The five patterns for organizing main points can apply to subpoints as well.

We then discussed how to incorporate supporting materials into a speech, describing a process of putting all main points, subpoints, and supporting materials on note cards and then organizing those cards.

The next task we analyzed was the arrangement of supporting materials. We observed that supporting materials may sometimes be organized according to one of the five patterns we discussed but that other organizational strategies might be primacy, recency, specificity, complexity, or "soft" to "hard" evidence.

Finally, we discussed the importance of developing various types of connectors that would pull the speech together and give it continuity: verbal and nonverbal transitions, previews, and summaries.

Chapters 9 and 10 will cover the two remaining parts of the organizational task: outlining the speech and preparing an introduction and conclusion.

QUESTIONS FOR DISCUSSION AND REVIEW

1. Identify and describe the major patterns for organizing your main ideas in a speech.
2. Identify and describe several strategies for organizing your supporting material.
3. Give an example of a verbal transition.
4. How do you incorporate supporting materials into your speech?
5. What functions do speech previews serve?

SUGGESTED ACTIVITIES

1. Read one of the speeches in Appendix C. Answer the following questions:
   a. According to what pattern are the main points organized?
   b. Identify any subpoints of the main points, and describe how they are organized.
   c. Look at the supporting materials. If two or more are used to support any one main point or subpoint, what strategy do you think the speaker used to organize them?
   d. Is there a preview statement? If so, what is it?
   e. Is there a final summary? If so, what is it?
   f. Find at least one example of each of the following:
      A verbal transition that indicates a relationship between ideas
      An internal preview
      An internal summary
2. Select three topics from the following list. For each topic, write a purpose statement, a central idea, and two to five main points. Identify the organizational strategy you would use to organize those main points.
      Possible solutions for child abuse
      Protecting endangered species
      Responsible pet ownership
      Three well-known fad diets
      Solving the problem of world hunger
      The electoral college
      History of the Panama Canal
      The funding of health care research
      High adventure in our national parks
      Being an organ donor
      History of motion pictures
      How to grow a successful garden

3. Here are some examples of central ideas and outlines of main points. Identify the organizational pattern used to organize each group of main points. If the pattern is topical, do you think the speaker also applied the principle of primacy, recency, or complexity? If so, identify which one.

Purpose Statement: At the end of my speech, the audience will be able to list and explain the three factors to consider in buying a home.

Central Idea: The prospective home buyer should consider three factors in selecting a home:

   I. Interior decorating
  II. Layout
 III. Location

Purpose Statement: At the end of my speech, the audience will be able to explain three theories about what happened to the dinosaurs.

Central Idea: There are at least three distinct theories about what happened to the dinosaurs.

   I. A large asteroid hit the earth.
  II. There was a gradual climate shift.
 III. There was a gradual change in the level of oxygen in the atmosphere.

Purpose Statement: At the end of my speech, the audience will be able to explain why provision for the mentally ill is inadequate in the United States.

Central Idea: The process of caring for the mentally ill has broken down in the United States.

   I. Fewer than half of the needed number of community-based "halfway houses" exist.
  II. Funding is inadequate.
 III. Involuntary commitment is rare.[23]

Purpose Statement: At the end of my speech, the audience will be able to describe the layout and features of the new university multipurpose sports center.

Central Idea: The new university multipurpose sports center will serve the activity needs of the students.

   I. The south wing will house an Olympic-size pool.
  II. The center of the building will be a large coliseum.
 III. The north wing will include handball and indoor tennis facilities as well as rooms for weight lifting and aerobic workouts.

9
Outlining Your Speech

Every discourse ought to be a living creature; having a body of its own and head and feet; there should be a middle, a beginning, and end, adapted to one another and to the whole. (Richard Diebenkorn, Ocean Park No. 22, 1969. Oil on canvas, 93 × 81". Virginia Museum of Fine Arts, gift of Sydney and Frances Lewis.)

PLATO

A while ago, a family decided to spend a weekend near the Texas Gulf Coast. Soon after they left home on a hot, cloudless June morning, the air conditioning in their car broke down. By late afternoon, the car was *very* hot, the family was *very* tired, and the prospect of an air-conditioned motel room was *very* welcome. The husband was driving and the wife navigating as they approached their destination. Only a few more minutes, they thought, and they would relax in the cool quiet of their room. Imagine their frustration when, a half hour later, they were still searching for the motel. "Let *me* see the map," demanded the exasperated husband.

"Here, if you think you can do better," snapped the wife. "This map is useless!"

Trying to remain cool and collected (no easy task with the temperature approaching 100 degrees), the husband studied the map. Sure enough, it looked as though they should be at the motel by now. In sweaty desperation, he finally stopped to ask for directions.

"Oh, you should've turned right four blocks back," explained a store clerk. The wife had been right. The map *was* useless because it had not shown the necessary turn in the road.

This actually happened—to our family! We experienced directly the frustration of having an inaccurate map. Just as we rely on maps to find our way on unfamiliar roads, so do we rely on outlines to be "speech maps." In Chapter 8, you learned several approaches to organizing your ideas and supporting materials. You studied how to add coherence to your speech with transitions, previews, and summaries. In Chapter 9, we will discuss how to map out, or outline, the organization you have developed, both for your use and for the benefit of your audience. Outlining your speech completes the organization stage of your audience-centered speech preparation process.

Actually, most speakers find that they may need to prepare three types of outlines: (1) a full-content outline, (2) an abbreviated-content outline, and (3) a key-word outline. Let's examine the purposes and requirements of each of these three outlines in turn.

FULL-CONTENT OUTLINE

Although few speeches should be written out in paragraph form, most speakers prepare a full-content outline. A full-content outline includes all main points, subpoints, and supporting materials to be used in the main portion, or body, of a speech. It also includes the purpose statement, central idea, introduction, conclusion, and connectors.

The full-content outline is a detailed map of your speech. Preparing one has several advantages. It allows you to judge the unity and coherence of your speech—to see how well the parts fit together and how smoothly the speech flows. You can check a full-content outline to make sure that all points and subpoints are clearly, logically related and adequately supported. You can check the appropriateness of your organizational patterns, making certain that these patterns emphasize the points you want. The outline enables you to critique your introduction and conclusion and to see whether your speech as a whole is audience-centered. When you begin to rehearse your speech, you can use the full-content outline as the basis of your delivery.

Preparing a Full-Content Outline

The following suggestions will help you prepare your full-content outline.

1. *Write your full-content outline in complete sentences, of the type you will eventually use when delivering your speech.* Unless you write complete sentences, you will have trouble judging the coherence of the speech. Moreover, complete sentences will help during your first rehearsals. Do not write cryptic phrases and count on remembering later what you meant when you wrote them down. Write all your ideas and supporting statements in complete sentences.

2. *Use correct outline form.* Although you did not have to follow a proper outline form when you generated your preliminary outline, you will need to do so now. Using the proper outline form lets you see at a glance the exact relationships that exist between the various ideas and supporting materials in your speech. It thus serves as an important critical tool. The correct outline form contains five elements.

a. **Use standard outline numbering.** Outline numbering is logical and fairly easy to learn. Based on the principle of subordination, it follows this sequence:

    I.   Main point
       A. First subpoint of I
          1. First subpoint of A
             a. First subpoint of 1
                (1) First subpoint of a
                    (a) First subpoint of (1)

Second points at each level are indicated by the second number or letter of the sequence. For example, the second subpoint of I would be indicated by the capital letter *B*. It is unlikely that you will subdivide much beyond the level of lowercase letters (*a*, *b*, etc.) in most speech outlines. If you do, you may have an excess of supporting materials and may want to consider cutting some of them.

b. **Each point has at least two subdivisions, if it has any.** Logic dictates that you cannot divide anything into one part. If you find that you have only one subpoint, you should incorporate it into the point above it. Another way to remember this principle is to remember that every capital A must have a B, every 1 must have a 2 and so on. There is no maximum limit on the number of subpoints you may have, but if you have more than five or six, you may want to consider placing several of them under another division. An audience unable to remember seven or eight subpoints may well remember those same ideas if they are divided into blocks of three or four.

c. **Points, subpoints, and supporting material must be properly indented.** Main points, indicated by Roman numerals, are written closest to the left margin:

    I.   First main point
   II. Second main point
  III. Third main point

Notice that the *periods* following the Roman numerals line up, rather than the first numerals, and therefore the initial letters of the main points line up.

Subpoint A begins directly underneath the first *word* of point I:

    I. Every speech has three parts.
      A. The first part is the introduction.

If a sentence takes up more than one line, the second line begins under the first *word* of the preceding line:

    I. Every speech has three parts.
      A. The first part, both in our discussion and in actual delivery, is the introduction.

The same rules of indentation apply at all levels of the outline.

    d. **The first word of each point at each level is capitalized.** You will probably follow this rule automatically when you write a full-sentence outline, since sentences begin with capital letters. But even if the outline consists of words or phrases, the first word at each level is still capitalized:

    I. Every speech has three parts.
      A. Introduction
      B. Body
      C. Conclusion

Notice that the preceding three subpoints are *not* followed by periods. Unless the entry is a complete sentence, it is generally is not followed by a period.

    e. **All points at the same level are parallel in structure.** In the preceding example, points A, B, and C are all single nouns. They are parallel structures. Following the same logic, since I was a complete sentence, we would expect II to be a complete sentence also:

    I. Every speech has three parts.
      A. Introduction
      B. Body
      C. Conclusion
    II. Every speech should be audience-centered.

These five rules—(a) use standard numbering; (b) make certain that each point has at least two subdivisions, if any; (c) use correct indentation; (d) capitalize the first word at each level; and (e) make sure all points at the same level have parallel structures—will serve as an easy guide and reference as you produce your full content outline.

3. *Write and label your purpose statement and central idea at the top of your full-content outline.* The purpose statement and central idea can serve as yardsticks by which to measure the relevance of each main point, subpoint, and piece of supporting material. Everything in the speech should contribute to your purpose and should directly support your central idea. A speech that meets this criterion is unified.

Unless your instructor directs you to do otherwise, do not work the purpose statement and central idea into the outline itself. Instead, label them and place them separately at the top of the outline.

4. *After you have decided on key transitions, previews, summaries, introduction, and conclusion, add these to your outline.* Place the introduction and preview statement before the outline, the conclusion after the outline, and the connectors within the outline. Follow your instructor's guidelines as to whether you should incorporate these elements into your numbering system.

RECAP

SUMMARY OF CORRECT OUTLINE FORM

Rule	Example

1. Use standard outline numbering.	I.
	  A.
	    1.
	      a.
	        (1)
	          (a)

2. Each point should have at least two subdivisions, if any.	I.
	  A.
	  B.

3. Points, subpoints, and supporting material should be properly indented.	I. First main point
	  A. Begins under word
	  B. Lines up with A
	    1. Starts under *Lines*
	    2. Lines up with 1
	II. Second main point

4. Capitalize the first word of each.	I. There are three points.
	  A. First point
	  B. Second point
	  C. Third point

5. All points at the same level should be parallel in structure.	I. This is a sentence.
	  A. A phrase
	  B. Another phrase
	II. This is also a sentence.

Sample Full-Content Outline

Now that you know how to prepare a full-content outline, let's look at an example. This speech is persuasive and would run about ten minutes. If your speeches are shorter, your outlines will be shorter too. Notice that the purpose, central idea, introduction, preview statement, transitions, and conclusion are written apart from the outlined points of the body of the speech. Again, follow your instructor's specific requirements for form.

FULL-CONTENT OUTLINE FOR STUDENT SPEECH ON TANDEM TRUCKS[1]

Purpose: The audience will use caution in driving around tandem trucks.

Central Idea: Tandem trucks present a hazard to drivers on the nation's highways.

Introduction: The mood was festive; the participants were very happy as children usually are on a bus that's taking them home from school. But their happiness soon turned to tragedy. The bus had come to a stop. Within seconds, it was struck from behind by a large tandem truck. A boy in the back of the bus was killed instantly. The bus driver and the remaining children were all injured. The truck driver saw the bus but he couldn't stop. The brakes that he'd been meaning to have repaired failed. It was this failure that shocked the small town of Tuba City, Arizona, last April. It was a failure that could have been and should have been prevented.

Preview Statement: Today I'd like to discuss the hazards of tandem trucks on our nation's highways. The first thing I want to tell you about is how Congress and the trucking industry lobbyists have seriously compromised our safety on our nation's roads and highways. The next thing I will explain is the federal government's ability, or rather inability, to deal with these unsafe trucks. Finally, I will make some suggestions as to how you and I, the public at large, can take action against and protect ourselves from these large, safety-violating trucking firms.

I. Our safety is seriously jeopardized by the presence of these trucks on our nation's roads and highways.
   A. Accidents involving tandem trucks are frequent and fatal. The Knight-Ridder newspapers, after finishing an extensive probe into the issue of truck safety, concluded that tandem trucks are involved in twice as many fatal accidents as automobiles.
   B. Thanks to Congress and the trucking industry lobbyists, you'll be seeing more of those wider, longer, and heavier trucks taking to our nation's roads and highways.
   C. These concessions will make already unbearable injuries and fatalities increase.
      1. According to the 1985 *Statistical Abstract of the United States*, 30,360 persons were killed in tandem truck–related accidents in 1982.
      2. There were 1,056,000 debilitating injuries such as paralysis, 957,000 temporary disabilities such as broken limbs, and over 99,000 permanent impairments such as loss of hearing or eyesight due to head, neck, and spinal injuries.
      3. Wage loss, medical expenses, and insurance costs were estimated to be well over $26 billion a year.

Transition: But why is it that these statistics are so high in comparison to automobiles?

  II. Trucks are an accident waiting to happen.
      A. According to Knight-Ridder on April 22, 1985, "The Motor Carrier Bureau is unable to inspect most trucking companies and is rarely able to follow up on inspections because of manpower shortages. Three out of four trucking companies have never been audited for safety."

Transition: Well, one would hope that the firms that had been audited would be safe. This hope is mere wishful thinking.

      B. Even when trucks are found to be in violation of the federal standards, the average fine per truck is only $19.
      C. Weigh stations are inadequate.
          1. There are only 144 safety inspectors to staff over 500 weigh stations and audit nearly 1000 trucking companies every year.
          2. An Associated Press article stated in April 1985, "Nearly one out of three trucks stopped by safety inspectors in 1983 was ordered out of service immediately because of safety defects that could cause an accident."

Transition: The problem is clear. We have been taken advantage of by these large trucking firms.

      D. Examples abound of accidents occurring because of unsafe trucks.
          1. *U.S. News and World Report*, May 1984, reports: "The failure of a rear spring on a tanker rig carrying 8,600 gallons of gasoline on a Philadelphia freeway caused an accident that killed two persons and engulfed the truck and three other vehicles in flames."
          2. In April 1984, a tractor-semitrailer carrying a full load of propane gas exploded, killing two persons and seriously injuring four others.
      E. The federal government has made little progress.
          1. According to the General Accounting Office, "Nevertheless, the Department of Transportation has not taken action to obtain the necessary budgeting increases to hire additional safety inspectors."
          2. Again, according to the GAO, "The Carrier Safety Bureau has been very hesitant to issue fines to unsafe truck companies."
      F. The trucking industry lobbyists are our enemy.
 III. A solution needs to be found.
      A. Write letters to Congress.
      B. Steer clear of those large trucks.
          1. Be especially cautious when passing one.
          2. Be especially cautious when one is passing you.
      C. Always wear your seat belt.

Conclusion: Safety, that's all we're asking for. To feel secure in knowing that the truck that's coming up behind you is going to stop. The bus driver in Tuba City must have surely thought that the truck coming up behind him was going to stop. This issue is especially important to you and me, as drivers who spend countless hours on our nation's roads and highways—our nation's unsafe roads and highways. How many more people must die before we, as responsible citizens, will take action?

ABBREVIATED OUTLINE

As mentioned earlier, the full-content outline allows you to put together on paper all the elements of your speech. It is your detailed map. Rarely does an instructor, speaking coach, or audience member need to see your full-content outline. It is common, however, for these individuals to desire a streamlined outline. Your instructor may want to see at a glance how you organized the speech. The members of your audience may wish to have outlines so that they can refer to your speech at a later time. The kind of outline they need is an abbreviated outline.

Preparing an Abbreviated Outline

The abbreviated outline, as the name suggests, is not as detailed as the full-content outline. Specifically, it has these characteristics:

1. It is rarely written in complete sentences. Single words and short phrases are most common.

2. An abbreviated outline still follows correct outline form, as described earlier.

3. According to the wishes of your instructor or other person who will use the outline, you may still include the purpose statement, central idea, introduction, and conclusion.

4. Most often, the abbreviated outline will not include any of your transitions or supporting materials.

Sample Abbreviated Outline

An abbreviated outline for the student speech on tandem trucks might look like this.

Purpose: The audience will use caution in driving around tandem trucks.

Central Idea: Tandem trucks are a hazard on the nation's highways.

Introduction: The mood was festive; the participants were very, very happy. Such is the spirit of children on a bus that's taking them home from school. But the happiness was soon to become tragedy. The bus had come to a stop. Within seconds, it was struck from behind by a large tandem truck. A boy in the back of the bus was killed instantly. The bus driver and the remaining children were all injured. The truck driver saw the bus but didn't stop. He couldn't stop. The brakes that he'd been meaning to have repaired failed. It was this failure that shocked the small town of Tuba City, Arizona, last April. It was a failure that could have been and should have been prevented.

Preview Statement: Today I'd like to discuss the hazards of tandem trucks on our nation's highways. First, I want to tell you how Congress and the Trucking Industry Lobbyists have seriously compromised our safety on our nation's roads and highways. Next I will explain the Federal Government's inability to deal with these unsafe trucks. Finally, I will make some suggestions as to how you and I can protect ourselves from these large, safety-violating trucking firms.

I.   Problem of tandem trucks
    A. Frequent and fatal accidents
    B. More trucks on the road
    C. Increase in injuries and casualties
II. Accident waiting to happen
    A. Rare inspections
    B. Insignificant fines
    C. Inadequate weigh stations
    D. Bad accidents
    E. Little progress
    F. Trucking lobbyists at fault
III. Solutions
    A. Letters
    B. Caution

Conclusion: Safety, that's all we're asking for. To feel secure in knowing that the truck that's coming up behind you is going to stop. The bus driver in Tuba City must have surely thought that the truck coming up behind him was going to stop. This issue is especially important to you and me, as drivers who spend countless hours on our nation's roads and highways—our nation's unsafe roads and highways. How many more people must die before we, as responsible citizens, will take action?

As you compare the abbreviated outline with the full-content outline, you will notice immediately that the abbreviated one is much shorter. Main points and subpoints are indicated by words or phrases rather than complete sentences. Supporting materials and transitions are omitted. This outline enables you to see quickly the basic structure and content of the speech.

Your public speaking instructor may ask you to turn in some version of either a full-content or abbreviated outline for each speech you give in class. He or she may have additional or slightly different requirements than those addressed here. For example, many instructors may want to see a bibliography. You should, of course, always comply with your instructor's specific requirements.

KEY-WORD OUTLINE

After preparing full-content and abbreviated outlines, you began rehearsing your speech. At first you used the full-content outline, but now you find yourself needing it less and less. Both the structure and the content of your speech are pretty well set in your mind. At this point, you are ready to prepare a key-word outline, which will become your speaking notes.

Preparing a Key-Word Outline

The following characteristics are typical of key-word outlines.

1. Abbreviations are often used. To make the outline as brief as possible, you may use any abbreviations that will be clear as you speak.

2. The key-word outline is written with single words or short phrases rather than complete sentences.

3. The introduction and conclusion are now included, but in much shortened form. The first and last sentences, however, are often written in full. You may feel more comfortable if you have them in front of you. Writing out the first sentence eliminates any fear of a "mental block" at the outset of your speech. And writing a complete last sentence ensures a smooth ending to your speech and a good final impression.

4. Like the full-content outline, the key-word outline includes supporting materials and connectors. Statistics should be written out, as should any material you will quote directly. Key transitions should also be written out. Notice the transitions between points I and II; between IIA and IIB; and between IIC and IID in the sample key-word outline. Writing key transitions in full ensures that you will not grope awkwardly for a way to move from one point to the next. After you have rehearsed the speech several times, you will know where you are most likely to falter and can add or omit written transitions as needed.

5. The key-word outline may not include a purpose statement or a written central idea unless the latter is part of the introduction or preview.

6. Standard outline form is used. As we observed earlier, the standard outline form leaves no doubt as to the relationships of the parts of your speech. If you have composed your speaking notes in correct outline form, you will find it much easier to find the exact point or piece of supporting material you are seeking when you glance down at your notes.

7. The key-word outline uniquely contains delivery cues and reminders, such as "Louder," "Pause," or "Move in front of podium." Delivery cues should be written by hand, or, if the entire outline is handwritten, in a different color ink. Imagine the embarrassment of the speaker who looks down at his notes and reads aloud, "Pause here"! Such gaffes can and have happened. Several years ago, former President Gerald Ford read the delivery cue "Look into right camera" during an address. Clearly differentiating delivery cues from speech content will help prevent such mistakes.

In short, a key-word outline contains whatever notes and cues you need to deliver your speech with confidence, but not so many that you find yourself reading the speech to your audience.

RECAP ▼

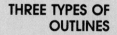

THREE TYPES OF OUTLINES	Type	Purpose
	Full-content outline	Allows speaker to examine speech for completeness, unity, coherence, and overall effectiveness. Serves as first rehearsal outline.
	Abbreviated-content outline	Permits audience to review major ideas after speech has been delivered.
	Key-word outline	Becomes speaker's final delivery outline.

Sample Key-Word Outline

Since we used the tandem truck speech for the two other outlines, let's continue with it for the key-word outline. This form differs from the two others in that the purpose statement and central idea are not included. The introduction and conclusion are present, but in shortened form. Here is the key-word outline.

Intro: The mood was festive; the participants were very, very happy. (*Pause.*) Tragedy—struck by tandem truck. Boy killed, others injured. Brake failure. Tuba City, Arizona, shocked.

Preview: Hazards of tandem trucks:
      1. Congress and lobbyists have compromised safety
      2. Federal govt's inability to deal with trucks
      3. Action and protection
  I. Danger
     A. Frequent and fatal accidents
     B. More trucks
     C. Increase in injuries and casualties
       1. 1985 *Stat. Abstracts*—30,360 killed in 1982
       2. 1,056,000 debilitating injuries
         957,000 temporary injuries
         99,000 permanent impairments (hearing, eyesight)
       3. Cost—$26 billion

Trans.: But why is it that these statistics are so high in comparison to automobiles?
 II. Accident waiting to happen
     A. Rare inspections—Knight-Ridder, April 22, 1985—"The Motor Carrier Bureau is unable to inspect most trucking companies and is rarely able to follow up on inspections because of manpower shortages. Three out of four trucking companies have never been audited for safety." (*Pause.*)

Trans.: Well, one would at least hope that the firms that had been audited would thus be safe. This hope is unrealistic.
     B. Average fine—$19
     C. Inadequate weigh stations
       1. 144 inspectors, 500 stations, 1000 trucking cos.
       2. AP, April 1985—"Nearly one out of three trucks stopped by safety inspectors in 1983 was ordered out of service immediately because of safety defects that could cause an accident."

Trans.: The problem is quite clear. We, the American people, have been taken advantage of by these large trucking firms.
     D. Examples of accidents
       1. *U.S. News*, May 1984—"The failure of a rear spring on a tanker rig carrying 8,600 gallons of gasoline on a Philadelphia freeway caused an accident that killed two persons and engulfed the truck and three other vehicles in flames."
       2. April 1984—tractor-semitrailer carrying propane exploded, killing 2 and injuring 4

    E. Little progress
       1. GAO—"Nevertheless, the Department of Transportation has not taken action to obtain the necessary budgeting increases to hire additional safety inspectors."
       2. "The Carrier Safety Bureau has been very hesitant to issue fines to unsafe truck companies."
    F. Lobbyists = enemy
III. Solutions
    A. Letters to Congress
    B. Caution
       1. When passing
       2. When being passed
    C. Seat belts

Concl.: Safety, that's all we're asking for. Tuba City. We spend countless hours on roads. How many more people must die before we, as responsible citizens, will take action?

As you rehearse the speech, you will probably continue to revise the key-word outline. You may cut the outline further, or you may add or delete delivery cues

Note cards are small enough to hold in one hand, if necessary, and stiff enough not to rustle.
(*Billy E. Barnes/Stock, Boston*)

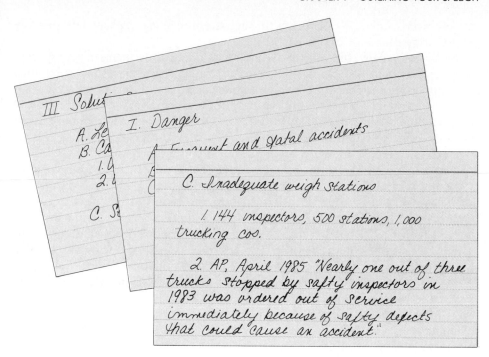

FIGURE 9.1
Your speaking notes can include your key-word outline.

or written transitions. Your goal is a delivery outline that provides enough information to ensure smooth delivery but not so much as to burden you with unnecessary notes or tempt you to look down at the notes too often during the speech.

Speaking Notes

At some point while rehearsing, you may wish to transfer the key-word outline to note cards (see Figure 9.1). Paper is difficult to handle comfortably. It has a tendency to rustle, and as a consequence may very well distract your audience.

Two or three 4-by-6 or 5-by-8 note cards will give you enough space for a key-word outline; the number of cards you use depends on the length of your speech. These cards are small enough to hold in one hand, if necessary, and stiff enough not to rustle. Type or print your outline neatly on one side of the note cards. Make sure that the letters and words on the cards are large enough so that you can see them easily. Do *not* use such ingenious schemes as flipping the note cards and reading from back to front at some point during the speech. Under pressure of delivering the speech, you may end up fumbling for the next point in your outline. Number the note cards. This will prevent fiascos resulting from out-of-order notes.

In this chapter, we examined outlining. We covered the three types of outlines most public speakers prepare: the full-content outline, the abbreviated outline, and

SUMMARY

the key-word outline. We then went through the process and explained the purpose of preparing each type of outline.

First, you prepare a full-content outline, including all the elements of your speech: purpose statement and central idea; carefully organized main points, subpoints, and supporting materials; previews, summaries, and transitions necessary for coherence; introduction; and conclusion. Each of these elements is written in complete sentences and organized according to levels of subordination. It is from this outline that you begin to rehearse your speech.

Next you prepare an abbreviated outline. If you are preparing the speech for class, you follow the directions given by your instructor. If you have not been given contrary directions or are preparing the outline for use by the members of your audience, you follow established standard outline form but rarely use complete sentences, relying instead on individual words and phrases. This outline needs to be clear and detailed enough that others can understand and follow it but not as detailed as the full-content outline. The abbreviated outline retains the purpose statement, central idea, introduction, and conclusion of your speech.

Finally, you prepare a key-word outline. This, with slight adjustments, will become your speaking notes. It need not include the purpose statement or central idea. All other ideas and materials are noted in as much detail as you will need when delivering the speech. The key-word outline also includes speaking cues. In most instances, you will eventually transfer the key-word outline to note cards.

QUESTIONS FOR DISCUSSION AND REVIEW

1. What is a full-content outline?
2. How would you prepare an abbreviated outline?
3. What do you include and what do you leave out when preparing a key-word outline?
4. What are some of the items that you should include in preparing speaking notes?

SUGGESTED ACTIVITIES

1. Select a speech from Appendix C. Prepare an abbreviated outline of that speech.
2. Discuss the pros and cons of having a speaker's outline in front of you while you are listening to the speech.
3. The following is an abbreviated outline of the body of a speech. This outline exhibits a number of errors in form. Find five flaws in the outline.

THE COLLEGE WORK-STUDY PROGRAM

I. Program eligibility
    A. There are four initial requirements for work-study students.
        1. Have need for employment
        2. Good grades
        3. Be a full-time student
        4. Be a citizen or permanent resident of the U.S.

3. Gain favorable attention for the speech
4. Establish a motivation for listening
5. Establish your credibility

Let's examine each of these five functions in more detail.

Introduce the Subject Perhaps the most obvious purpose of an introduction is to introduce the subject of a speech. Within a few seconds after you begin your speech, the audience should have a pretty good idea of what you are going to talk about. Do not get so carried away with jokes or illustrations that you forget this basic purpose. There is not much point in telling a joke or a story and then failing to relate it to your topic. Few things will frustrate your audience more than having to wait through half your speech before figuring out what you are talking about!

The best way to ensure that your introduction does indeed introduce the subject of your speech is to include a statement of your central idea in the introduction. In the introduction to a speech on geriatric medicine, the speaker left little room for doubt about the subject of her speech: After opening the speech with an illustration about her grandfather's poor health care at the hands of a doctor who misdiagnosed the disease, the speaker said that doctors "have simply not been provided with proper medical training in the care of the elderly."[1] In a speech on the importance of listening, another speaker offered this statement of her central idea near the end of her introduction: "Listening is the interpretation and evaluation of what we hear. Today I'd like to talk about listening."[2] In both cases, the speakers made certain that the subjects of their speeches were announced in the introductions.

In short, don't get so carried away with trying to open with an interesting, creative, empathetic, or funny introduction that you forget the foremost purpose of the introduction: It should introduce the subject of your speech.

The 1988 National Democratic convention featured speakers who appropriately introduced and concluded the convention.
(Robert Phillips)

Preview the Body of the Speech   The second purpose of a speech introduction is to preview the main ideas of your speech. As you saw in Chapter 8, the preview statement usually comes near the end of the introduction, often immediately following a statement of the central idea. It outlines for the audience what the main ideas of your speech will be. The preview statement "tells them what you're going to tell them." It allows your listeners to anticipate the main ideas of your speech, which in turn helps ensure that they will remember those ideas after the speech.

After opening with an illustration, a speaker talking about political prisoners of conscience offered this preview statement:

> I'll begin with a definition of a prisoner of conscience. I'll present a rough outline as to their numbers and locations. I'll examine some of the reasons for their abuse; and finally, I'll offer some solutions to ease their suffering.[3]

This preview statement makes clear to the audience what the main points of the speech are going to be.

An effective introduction not only introduces the subject of the speech, but it also previews the main ideas that will be presented in the body of the speech.

Gain Favorable Attention   You are exposed to countless verbal messages every day, both from the media and from other people. For you to focus on any one message, something about it has to grab your attention and put you in a receptive mood. So a third purpose of the speech introduction is to gain favorable attention for your speech. Because listeners form their first impressions of the speech quickly, if the introduction does not capture their attention and cast the speech in a favorable light, the rest of the speech may be wasted on them. The speaker who walks to the podium and drones, "Today I am going to talk to you about . . ." has probably lost most of the audience in those first few boring words. Some of the ways to gain the attention of audiences will be discussed later in this chapter. Most people can be "hooked" by a good illustration, humor, a startling fact or statistic, or one of the other methods we will discuss.

Why do we emphasize *favorable* attention? For one very good reason. It is possible to grab an audience's attention but in so doing to alienate them or disgust them so that they become irritated instead of interested in what you have to say. For example, a student began an antiabortion speech with a graphic description of the abortion process. She caught her audience's attention but made them so uncomfortable that they could hardly concentrate on the rest of her speech.

Another student gave a speech on the importance of donating blood. Without a word, he began by savagely slashing his wrists in front of his stunned audience. As blood spurted, audience members screamed, and one fainted. It was real blood, but not his. The speaker worked at a blood bank. Using the bank's blood, he placed a device under each arm that allowed him to pump out the blood as if from his wrists. He certainly grabbed his audience's attention! But they never heard his message. The shock and disgust of seeing such a display made that impossible. He did not gain favorable attention.

The moral of our two tales: By all means, be creative in your speech introductions. But also use common sense in deciding how best to gain the favorable attention of your audience. Alienating them is even worse than boring them.

Establish a Motivation for Listening   Even after you have captured the attention of your audience, you have to give them some reason to want to listen to the rest of your speech. An unmotivated listener quickly tunes out. You can help establish listening motivation by showing the members of your audience how the topic affects them directly.

In Chapter 6, we presented six criteria for determining the effectiveness of your supporting materials. The first of those criteria was *proximity*, the concept that listeners will be most attentive to information that affects them directly. Just as proximity is important to supporting materials, it is also important to speech introductions. "This concerns *me*" is a powerful reason to listen. Notice how this speaker involves her audience with the problem of toxic silver dental fillings:

> It's estimated that 90% of the American population has silver fillings. That's some 225 million Americans with mercury in their teeth. Because this number is so large and many of us are counted in this number, I'd like to tell you about mercury, the toxic poison, and show you why we must escape its contamination.[4]

The significance of the statistics is attention-getting, but the speaker motivates her audience to listen further by pointing out their personal susceptibility to the potential dangers.

After introducing the problem of unfair political asylum, another speaker observed:

> At this point, you are probably asking yourself: "Why should I be concerned about a problem involving only foreigners?" First of all, our government makes the decisions—it represents us. As a nation, we assumed the responsibility of political asylum. Therefore, we must deal with it, however complex. Finally and most importantly, the problem deserves our attention, because the policy serves humanity. We know that it is only right to correct the inconsistencies within the system.[5]

In this passage, the speaker made an impersonal problem—political asylum—morally relevant to her listeners. She motivated her audience by placing on them a burden of personal responsibility; she told them why the problem should be of interest to them. Demonstrating that your topic is of vital personal concern to your audience is an effective motivator.

Establish Your Credibility   **Credibility** is the attitude listeners hold toward a speaker. A credible speaker is one whom the audience judges to be a believable authority and a competent speaker. A credible speaker is also someone the audience believes in and can trust. Even though we will discuss credibility in greater detail in Chapter 16, we stress here that as you begin your speech, you should be mindful of your listeners' attitude toward you. When thinking of your listeners, ask yourself,

credibility
The attitude a listener holds toward a speaker.

"Why should they listen to me? What is my background with respect to the topic? Am I personally committed to the issues about which I am going to speak?"

Many people have so much admiration for a political or religious figure, an athlete, or an entertainer that they sacrifice time, energy, and money to be members of an audience to which one of these admired persons is speaking. When Pope John Paul II came to the United States during the summer of 1987, people traveled great distances and stood for hours in intense heat to celebrate Mass with him.

Most people cannot take their own credibility for granted when they speak. If you can establish your credibility early in the speech, it will help motivate your audience to listen. One way to build credibility in the introduction is to be well prepared and to appear confident. Speaking fluently while maintaining eye contact does much to convey a sense of confidence. If you seem to have confidence in yourself, your audience will have confidence in you.

A second way to establish credibility is to tell the audience of your personal experience with your topic. If you are an expert on your topic, don't let modesty keep you from letting the audience know. Instead of considering you as boastful, most audience members will listen to you with respect. Notice how the following speaker opened his speech on Boy Scouting:

> I come before you today representing one out of fifteen million people in over 67 countries throughout the world who belong to a very special organization, an organization designed to help prepare youth for their future life. The organization is Boy Scouting, the world's best known youth movement.[6]

Learning that the speaker was someone who was actively involved in scouting undoubtedly helped motivate the audience to listen to his point of view.

Another student opened her speech with this personal illustration:

> Within the last year, two members of my family were diagnosed by their doctors as having skin cancer, caused by the sun. In my mother's case, she had purposefully, although naively subjected herself to the sun, laying out, tanning in tanning salons, etc. In my grandmother's case, she was diagnosed by her doctor as having skin cancer from her normal exposure to the sun. This woman had never sought the sun. Both of these cases made me realize that even though I don't subject myself as my mother does, I certainly get more unintentional exposure than my grandmother. So, I came face to face with the fact that I too could contract this disease.[7]

Because she revealed her personal involvement with the topic, the speaker undoubtedly gained authority in the eyes of her audience. Her listeners would probably say to themselves, "She really knows what she's talking about." By enhancing her own credibility, the speaker established a strong motivation for the audience to listen to her.

Speech introductions, then, should introduce the subject, preview the body of the speech, gain favorable attention for the speech, establish a motivation for listening, and establish your personal credibility. All this—and brevity too—may seem impossible to achieve. But it isn't! What are some specific ways to design an effective introduction?

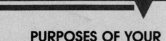

RECAP

PURPOSES OF YOUR SPEECH INTRODUCTION	**Purpose**	**Method**
	Introduce the subject	Present your central idea to your audience.
	Preview your main ideas	Tell your audience what you are going to tell them.
	Gain favorable attention	Use an illustration, a startling fact or statistic, quotation, humor, question, a reference to a historical event, a reference to a recent news event, a personal reference, a reference to the occasion, a reference to a preceding speech.
	Establish a motive for listening	Tell your listeners why they need to pay attention.
	Establish your credibility	Describe your credentials. Tell your listeners about your commitment to your topic.

Methods of Introduction

Whereas most of you, with a little practice, can write satisfactory central ideas and preview statements, it may be more difficult to gain your audience's attention and give them a reason to listen to you. Fortunately, several methods can help you develop effective introductions to your speeches. Not every method is appropriate for every speech, but chances are that you can discover among these alternatives at least one type of introduction to fit your speech topic and purpose, whatever that might be.

Specifically, we will discuss ten ways of introducing a speech:

1. Illustration
2. Startling fact or statistic
3. Quotation
4. Humor
5. Question
6. Reference to a historical event
7. Reference to a recent news event
8. Personal reference
9. Reference to the occasion
10. Reference to a preceding speech

Illustration   Not surprisingly, since it is the most inherently interesting type of supporting material, an illustration can provide the basis for an effective speech introduction. In fact, if you have an especially compelling anecdote that you had planned to use in the body of the speech, you might do well to use it instead in your introduction. A relevant story often effectively introduces a subject. An interesting illustration invariably gains an audience's attention. And a personal anecdote can help establish your credibility.

Here is how one speaker opened a speech on the problems associated with diplomatic immunity:

> In 1982, Carol Holmes was raped at gunpoint in her apartment. Three weeks after the incident, Ms. Holmes identified her offender as he walked down the street, and she then notified the New York police while her boyfriend subdued the man. After 45 minutes of questioning, Manuel Aryee, the accused assailant, was released a free man.[8]

This story has drama, is relevant, and arouses the indignation of the audience—in short, it is an effective way to open the speech.

An inherently poignant illustration was offered by this speaker in the opening of a speech on organ donation:

> On October 28, 1982, doctors told Jamie Fiske's grief stricken parents that their 11-month-old daughter could not survive until Thanksgiving. Jamie's hope lay in finding a suitable human liver donor. Only a liver transplant could save Jamie's life.
>
> Some of you may remember the name, Jamie Fiske. You may even recall the dramatic televised appeal which her father, Charles Fiske, made to the American Academy of Pediatricians that day in October. For me, and I hope for some of you, the real hero of the Jamie Fiske saga was not the famous transplant surgeon but a baby boy named Jess Bellon. Why? Because less than a week after Charles Fiske's plea for an organ donor, Jess Bellon's liver was successfully transplanted to Jamie Fiske.[9]

Here is a final example of an illustration, this one used in an introduction to a speech on the value of autopsy:

> My middle name should have been Imelda. Mother always gave her children the middle name of a godparent. Instead, I became Mary Beth. I thought of my mother's naming system when my godmother and aunt, Imelda, died last summer, an event the family viewed as a blessing. Imelda had suffered throughout her adult life from insanity. Intensive work with psychiatrists and the latest drugs failed to offer Imelda help. No one in our family really understood her plight—we only knew that she was crazy.
>
> We finally understood Imelda—after her death. Doctors performed an autopsy and found that Imelda had suffered from a rare disease in which her body's muscles grew uncontrollably, cutting off blood circulation to her brain, causing her insanity. We felt guilty about the way we had treated Imelda. We were also relieved to discover that her illness was not hereditary.[10]

This personal illustration captured the attention of the audience. In addition, the speaker established her own involvement and expertise in the subject.

Startling Fact or Statistic   A second method of introducing a speech is the use of a startling fact or statistic. Startling an audience with the extent of a situation or problem will invariably catch their attention as well as motivate them to listen further to what you have to say.

This opening of a speech on teenage pregnancy must have caused the audience to sit up and take notice:

> There's a disease lurking in this country. A disease that quietly strikes one American teenager every 30 seconds—over one million a year. A disease that could be controlled . . . hasn't been; a disease that could be eliminated . . . isn't. It will affect 40 percent of today's 14-year-olds at least once before they reach 20. It's not contagious, not incurable; but once you catch it—you'll suffer from its effects for the rest of your life. What is it? The disease is teenage pregnancy.[11]

The statistical information on teenage pregnancy is indeed startling. In addition, the speaker employed the technique of suspense, withholding the topic until she had relayed the statistics. Almost in spite of themselves, audience members must have found themselves guessing the cause of such alarming figures. And because they invested mental energy in thinking about the answer, the speaker had their attention. A similar example comes from a speech on the common cold:

> Americans get 500 million per year. This disease makes us lose 32 million days of work and makes us spend 105 million days in bed. We spend over 1 billion dollars in over-the-counter drugs to help alleviate its symptoms, which include a sore throat, runny nose, sneezing, coughing, high temperature, and headaches. What is it? It is the oldest and most common ailment known to man—the common cold.[12]

Like the methods of organization discussed in Chapter 8, the methods of introduction are not mutually exclusive. Very often, two or three are effectively combined in a single introduction. For example, the following speaker combined the methods of illustration and startling statistic for this effective introduction to a speech on geriatric medicine:

> Although my grandfather continued to struggle against dying, he did not go gentle into that good night. He died in an Arkansas hospital of what doctors officially termed as "old age."
>
> My grandfather was a member of one of the fastest growing groups in America: those over 65. Between the years 1900 and 1980, the number of people over 65 has tripled. By the year 2040, most of us will not be short of companions our age, because by then the elderly population will be at least 45%.[13]

Quotation   Using an appropriate quotation to introduce a speech is a common practice. Often a past writer or speaker has expressed an opinion on your topic that is more authoritative, comprehensive, or better stated than what you can say. In a speech on the proliferation of "superbabies," one speaker turned to Scripture to introduce her speech:

> "Happy is the man that findeth wisdom, and the man that getteth understanding, for the wisdom is more profitable than silver, and the gain she brings is better than gold."
>
> This quotation, as taken from the _New English Bible_, Proverbs, Chapter III, is the cry that was uttered to the children of the earth. Today, the cries are coming . . . from the mouths of parents.[14]

The passage quoted possesses both poetic beauty and scriptural authority, providing an interesting and effective introduction to the speech.

A different kind of quotation, this one from an expert, was chosen by another speaker to introduce a similar topic, the disappearance of childhood in America:

> "As a distinctive childhood culture wastes away, we watch with fascination and dismay." This insight of Neil Postman, author of *Disappearance of Childhood*, raised a poignant point. Childhood in America is vanishing.[15]

Because the expert was not widely recognized, the speaker included a brief statement of his qualifications. This authority "said it in a nutshell"—expressed in concise language the central idea of the speech.

Although a quote can effectively introduce a speech, do not fall into the lazy habit of turning to a collection of quotations every time you need an introduction. There are so many other interesting, and sometimes better, ways to introduce a speech that quotes should be used only if they are extremely interesting, compelling, or very much to the point.

Humor   Humor, handled well, can be a wonderful attention getter. It can help relax your audience and win their goodwill for the rest of the speech. The following anecdote, for example, could be used to open a speech on the importance of adequate life insurance:

> "If you were to lose your husband," the insurance salesman asked the young wife, "what would you get?"
> She thought for a moment, then ventured: "A parakeet."[16]

Humor need not always be the stuff of Donald O'Connor's classic "Make 'Em Laugh" routine or Three Stooges slapstick comedy. It does not even have to be a joke. It may take more subtle forms, such as irony or incredulity. Here is another quietly humorous opening of a speech on deception in education:

> Sassafras Herbert proudly displays her certificate from the American Association of Dietary Consultants. This certificate entitles Herbert to a listing in the Official Directory of Nutrition and Dietary Consultants and special rates on malpractice insurance. She'll probably need those rates. Sassafras Herbert is an 11-year-old poodle.[17]

Humor can be used in many circumstances and for many topics, but certain subjects do not lend themselves to a humorous introduction. It would hardly be appropriate to open a speech on teenage suicide, for example, with a funny story. Nor would it be appropriate to use humor in a talk on certain serious crimes. Used with discretion, however, humor can provide a lively, interesting, and appropriate introduction for many speeches.

Question   When using a question to open a speech, you will generally use a "rhetorical question," the kind you don't expect an answer to. Nevertheless, your listeners will probably try to answer mentally. Questions prompt the audience's mental participation in your introduction. Such participation is an excellent way to ensure their continuing attention to your speech.

This speaker opened a speech on geographical illiteracy with a series of questions: "Can you name the states that border the Pacific Ocean? What country lies between Panama and Nicaragua? Can you name the Great Lakes?"[18] And another speaker opened his speech on teenage suicide with this simple question: "Have you ever been alone in the dark?"[19]

Questions are commonly combined with another method of introduction. In fact, the last speaker went on to tell a poignant story about a young suicide victim and, after that, to relate some rather startling statistics about the problem. Another speaker opened a speech on the inadequacies of our current driver's license renewal system with three startling brief examples followed by a question:

> In 31 states a blind man can be licensed to drive. In 5 states, just send in your check and they will send back your renewed license, no questions asked.
> In 1916 my grandfather got his license for the first time. No exam was required; no exam has been required since. Ever wonder why our highways seem a bit unsafe today?[20]

Either by themselves or in tandem with another method of introduction, questions can provide effective openings for speeches.

Reference to a Historical Event   What American is not familiar with the opening line of Lincoln's classic Gettysburg Address: "Four score and seven years ago, our

Making a reference to a historical event as Lincoln did when he began his Gettysburg Address with "Four score and seven years ago . . ." can be an effective speech opener.
(*Bettman Archive*)

fathers brought forth on this continent a new nation, conceived in liberty, and dedicated to the proposition that all men are created equal"? Note that this opening sentence refers to the historical context of the speech. You, too, may find a way to begin a speech by making a reference to a historical event.

Every day is the anniversary of something. Perhaps you could begin a speech by drawing a relationship between a historical event that happened on this day and your speech objective. How do you discover anniversaries of historical events? Three sources should prove useful. First, consult Jane M. Hatch's *American Book of Days*; this resource lists key events for every day of the year and also provides details of what occurred.[21] Another source, *Anniversaries and Holidays*, by Ruth W. Gregory, identifies and describes key holidays.[22] Finally, many newspapers have a section that identifies key events that occurred on "this day in history." If, for example, you know you are going to be speaking on April 6, you could consult a copy of a newspaper from April 6 of last year to discover the key commemorative events for that day.

We are not recommending that you arbitrarily flip through one of these sources to crank up your speech; your reference to a historical event should be linked clearly to your speech purpose. Note how Carl Sandburg began a speech on March 4, 1961, the hundredth anniversary of Lincoln's first inaugural:

> Here one hundred years ago to the day were 10,000 people who hung on the words of the speaker of the day. Beyond this immediate audience were 30 million people in 34 states who wanted to know what he was saying. Over in the countries of Europe were more millions of people wondering whether the American Union of States would hold together or be shattered into fragments.[23]

If you, like Carl Sandburg, can use the historical context of the day to begin a speech, you will be well on your way to making your message memorable as well as attention-catching.

Reference to Recent News Event   If your topic is timely, a reference to a recent news event can be a good way to open your speech. An opening taken from a recent news story can take the form of an illustration, a startling statistic, or even a quotation, gaining the additional advantages discussed under each of those methods of introduction. Moreover, referring to a recent event will increase your credibility by showing that you are knowledgeable about current affairs.

"Recent" does not necessarily mean a story that broke just last week or even last month. An occurrence that has taken place within the past year or so can be considered recent. Even a particularly significant event that is slightly older than that, such as the 1989 removal of the Berlin Wall, can qualify. Here is how one speaker used an anecdote drawn from a contemporary news story to open a speech on amusement park safety:

> It was another beautiful day at the amusement park. Warm sunshine, the smell of cotton candy, the kids, and the rides. The roller coaster's whooshing 60 mile per hour speed was accompanied by the familiar screams of delight from kids of all ages. Another ride, the Comet, was flying gracefully through the heavens when suddenly a chain broke flinging

one of the gondolas 75 feet into the air before it crashed, killing a man and seriously injuring his son.

This accident, on May 26 in Pontiac, Illinois, was just one of many in 1984—one of many that could have been avoided.[24]

Another speaker turned to a news story for some startling statistics on kidnapping by parents:

The October 23rd, 1983, issue of the *New York Times* reported some startling facts. It reported the findings of the Gallup Poll Organization that there are about 500,000 incidents each year in which kids are kidnapped from one of their parents by the other parent. That's a half million parental kidnappings per year.[25]

The first speaker delivered his speech in 1985; the second, in 1984. These events were only several months old and therefore fresh in the minds of people who knew them. They also pointed up the fact that the problems discussed in the speeches were current and urgent ones.

Personal Reference A reference to yourself can take several forms. You may express appreciation at having been asked to speak. You may share a personal experience. Or you may reveal your authority on the subject of your speech.

British statesman Winston Churchill, whose mother was American, used this personal statement of appreciation to open his address to the U.S. Congress shortly after the bombing of Pearl Harbor in December 1941:

Members of the Senate and of the House of Representatives of the United States, I feel greatly honoured that you should have invited me to enter the United States Senate Chamber and address the representatives of both branches of Congress.

The fact that my American forebears have for so many generations played their part in the life of the United States, and that here I am, an Englishman, welcomed in your midst, makes this experience one of the most moving and thrilling in my life, which is already long and has not been entirely uneventful.

I wish indeed that my mother, whose memory I cherish across the vale of years, could have been here to see. By the way, I cannot help reflecting that if my father had been American and my mother British, instead of the other way around, I might have got here on my own. In that case, this would not have been the first time you would have heard my voice. In that case, I should not have needed any invitation; but, if I had, it is hardly likely that it would have been unanimous. So perhaps things are better as they are.[26]

Reminding his audience of his own American roots helped Churchill to establish a strong common bond on which he drew as he urged the cooperation of Congress in the war effort.

You have already read some examples of personal illustrations as speech introductions. Here is an example of a personal anecdote meant to arouse audience empathy:

As I was working my way through the public school system, I, like my peers, believed that I was receiving a fine education. I could read and write, and add and subtract—yes, all of the essentials were there. At least that's what I thought. And, then, the boom lowered: "Attention class—your next assignment is to present an oral report of your paper in front of the class next week." My heart stopped. Panic began to rise up inside. Me? In front of thirty other fourth graders giving a speech? For the next five days I lived in dreaded anticipation of the forthcoming event. When the day finally arrived, I stayed home. It seemed at the time to be the perfect solution to a very scary and very real problem. Up to that time, I had never been asked to say a word in front of anyone, and, more importantly, had never been taught anything about verbal communication skills.[27]

The third type of personal reference, that which establishes your authority, was illustrated earlier in this chapter by the introduction to the speech on Boy Scouting. In another example, a speaker draws on his military experience to establish his credibility:

After 20 years in the army during peace and war, and after having made master sergeant twice and been busted back to buck private three times, I think I learned something about military discipline. Let me tell you, it's irrational.[28]

Personal references, then, can serve a variety of purposes. But what they do most of all—in all circumstances—is establish a warm bond between you and your audience.

Reference to the Occasion   Instead of referring in your introduction to a historical event, you can refer to the occasion at hand. This way of introducing your talk is especially well suited to occasions that are noteworthy and are the reason you were asked to give your talk. For example, when a neighborhood elementary school celebrates its twenty-fifth anniversary, its first principal might open her remarks this way:

It is a special joy for me to be here this afternoon to help celebrate the twenty-fifth anniversary of Crockett Elementary School. How well I remember the excitement and anticipation of that opening day so many years ago. How well I remember the children who came to school that first day. Some of them are now your parents. It was a good beginning to a successful twenty-five years.

References to the occasion are often used at weddings, birthday parties, dedication ceremonies, and other such events. It is customary to make a personal reference as well, placing oneself in the occasion. The audience at the school probably expected the principal to do just that. The reference to the occasion can also be combined with other methods of introduction, such as an illustration or an opening question.

Reference to a Preceding Speech   Referring to an earlier speech is the sole impromptu method of introduction. It occurs most often when your speech is one of several being presented on the same occasion. The occasion might be speaking day in a speech class, a symposium, or a lecture series in which your talk is one of many.

Referring to a previous speech as a way of introducing your own is generally improvised because usually you do not know until shortly before your own speech

Referring to a previous speech is often done if the speech is one of several being presented on the same occasion.
(*Laima Druskis*)

what other speakers will say. Then you must decide on the spot whether referring to one of these previous speeches will be better than using the introduction you originally prepared. As a rule, you are better off sticking with your planned introduction. Occasionally, however, a reference to a previous speech may work well, either by itself or in combination with the prepared introduction. And sometimes it is a virtual necessity.

Few experiences will make your stomach sink faster than hearing a speaker just ahead of you speak on your topic. Worse still, that speaker may even use some of the same supporting materials you had planned to use. When this situation happens, you are better off to acknowledge the previous speaker's efforts than to "play ostrich." The audience will probably empathize with your awkward situation, and your acknowledgment of the previous speaker can help to ease tension, particularly if it is done in a good-humored way.

Another time when it might be wise to refer to a preceding speech occurs when another speaker has spoken on a topic so related to your own that you can draw an analogy. In a sense, your introduction becomes a transition from that earlier speech to yours. Here is an example of an introduction delivered by a student speaker under those circumstances:

When Juli talked to us about her experiences as a lifeguard, she stressed that the job was not as glamorous as many of us imagine. Today I want to tell you about another job that appears to be more glamorous than it is—a job that I have held for two years. I am a bartender at the Rathskeller.[29]

In summary, as you plan your introduction, remember that any combination of the methods just discussed is possible. With a little practice, you may find yourself choosing from several good possibilities as you prepare your introduction.

CONCLUSIONS

Your introduction creates an important first impression; your conclusion leaves an equally important final impression. Long after you finish speaking, your audience is likely to remember the effect, if not the content, of your closing remarks.

Unfortunately, many speakers pay less attention to their conclusions than to any other part of their speeches. They believe that if they can get through the first 90 percent of a speech, they can think of some way to conclude it. Perhaps you have had the experience of listening to a speaker who has failed to plan the conclusion. Awkward final seconds of stumbling for words may be followed by hesitant applause from an audience that is not even sure the speech is over. It is hardly the best way to leave people who came to listen to you.

Just as you learned ways to introduce a speech, you can learn how to conclude one. We will begin by considering the purposes of speech conclusions and will go on to study methods that will help you achieve those purposes.

Purposes of Conclusions

An effective conclusion has four purposes:

1. Summarize the speech
2. Reemphasize the thesis in a memorable way
3. Motivate the audience to respond
4. Provide closure

We will discuss each of these purposes in turn.

Summarize the Speech   Remember the golden rule of public speaking: "Tell them what you're going to tell them; tell them; then tell them what you've told them." Conclusions fulfill the final third of that prescription. They are a speaker's last chance to repeat his or her main ideas for the audience. Most speakers summarize their speech as the first part of the conclusion or perhaps even as the transition between the body of the speech and its end. The summary is to the conclusion what the preview statement is to the introduction.

One speaker summarized his speech on emissions tampering in an effective way, casting the summary as an expression of his fears about the problem and the actions that could solve his fears:

I'm frightened. Frightened that nothing I could say would encourage the 25% of emissions tampering Americans to change their ways and correct the factors that cause their autos to pollute disproportionately. Frightened that the American public will not respond to a crucial issue unless the harms are both immediate and observable. Frightened that the EPA will once again prove very sympathetic to industry. Three simple steps will alleviate my fear: inspection, reduction in lead content, and, most importantly, awareness.[30]

Many speakers end their speeches with a summary alone. Many others, though, combine a summary with one of the other methods of conclusion to be discussed later in this chapter.

Reemphasize the Main Idea in a Memorable Way   Another purpose of a conclusion is to restate the main idea of the speech in a memorable way. The conclusions of a number of famous speeches are among the most memorable statements we have. For example, General Douglas MacArthur's farewell to the nation at the end of his career concluded with these memorable words:

"Old soldiers never die; they just fade away." And like the old soldier of that ballad, I now close my military career and just fade away—an old soldier who tried to do his duty as God gave him the light to see that duty. Good-by.[31]

But memorable endings are not the exclusive property of great orators. With practice, most people can prepare similarly effective conclusions. Chapter 13, "Language Style," will offer you ideas for using language to make your statements more memorable. As a preliminary example of the memorable use of language, here is how a student concluded his speech on lobbying: "Mr. Lincoln, . . . you once told us government was 'by the people.' . . . I don't think you could have imagined who is now doing the 'buying' for us."[32] This speaker's clever play on Lincoln's phrase helped his audience remember the central idea of his speech.

Another way to reach a memorable conclusion is to borrow the words of someone else. The following speaker draws on two quotations to help make a final memorable point in a speech on book deterioration:

One person described such an experience [a book deteriorating in her hands] this way: "The front part of the book I took from the shelf was in my left hand, the back was in my right hand, and in between was this yellow snow drifting to the floor." That yellow snow is an idea that has been destroyed, not debunked, but destroyed. As Gilbert Highet asserts, "Books are not lumps of lifeless paper, but *minds* alive on the shelves . . . so by taking one down and opening it up, we [hear] the voice of a person far distant from us in time and space, and hear him speaking to us. Mind to mind, heart to heart." Unless, of course, that voice falls fractured to the library floor in a flurry of yellow snow.[33]

The end of your speech is your last chance to impress the central idea upon your audience. Do it in such a way that they cannot help but remember it.

Motivate the Audience to Respond   One of your tasks in an effective speech introduction is to motivate your audience to listen to your speech. Motivation is also a necessary component of an effective conclusion—not motivation to listen, but motivation to respond to the speech in some way. If your speech is informative, you may want the audience to think about the topic or to research it further. If your speech is persuasive, you may want your audience to take some sort of appropriate action—write a letter, buy a product, make a telephone call, or get involved in a cause. In fact, an *action* step is essential to the persuasive organizational strategy called the motivated sequence, which will be discussed in detail in Chapter 16.

In a speech on auto mechanic fraud, the speaker motivated her audience to wield their consumer power to stop the abuse:

> . . . with every dollar we spend, we're telling Mr. Badwrench that it's good to be bad. If we close our wallets and start spending some common sense, we can say goodbye to Mr. Badwrench . . . and get the monkey wrench out of our lives.[34]

Another speaker ended a speech on protection of child witnesses with this motivational conclusion:

> Given the increased frequency with which children appear in trials, our chance of personal involvement is likely. As relatives of children who may need to testify in court, we need to help them as they prepare for what may be a traumatic event. As potential jurors, we need to understand that a child witness can provide accurate, essential information. By protecting the child witnesses and accepting vital information they may present, we can achieve a more complete justice.[35]

Just as the conclusion is your last chance to reemphasize your main idea in a memorable way, so is it your last chance to motivate your audience to respond to your message.

Provide Closure   Probably the most obvious purpose of a conclusion is to let the audience know that the speech has ended. Speeches have to "sound finished."

You can attain closure both verbally and nonverbally. Verbal techniques include using such transitions as "finally," "for my last point," and "in conclusion." As noted in Chapter 8, you should use care in signaling your conclusion. For one thing, such a cue gives an audience unspoken permission to tune out. Notice what students do when their professor signals the end of the class session. Books and notebooks slam shut, pens are stowed, and the class generally stops listening. A concluding transition needs to be followed quickly by the final statement of the speech.

A second verbal technique will be described in more detail a little later in this chapter. It involves returning to the illustration, question, quotation, or other technique that was used to open the speech. Referring to the introduction provides closure and completes the ideas begun in the introduction.

Nonverbal closure can be achieved by such means as a pause between the body of your speech and its conclusion. You can also slow your speaking rate, move out from behind a podium to make a final impassioned plea to your audience, or signal with falling vocal inflection that you are making your final statement. The most effective closure is both verbal and nonverbal. The bottom line is, make sure your speech *sounds* finished.

RECAP ▼

PURPOSES OF YOUR SPEECH CONCLUSION	**Purpose**	**Technique**
	Summarize your main ideas	Tell them what you told them.
	Reemphasize the main ideas in a memorable way	Use a well-worded closing phrase. Provide a final example.
	Motivate the audience to respond	Urge the audience to think about the topic or to research it further. Suggest appropriate action.
	Provide closure	Use verbal and nonverbal transitions. Refer to your introduction.

Methods of Conclusion

Although summarizing a speech is a fairly straightforward task, reemphasizing the thesis in a memorable way, motivating the audience to respond, and providing effective closure to the speech may require more creative thinking and planning.

Any of the methods of introduction discussed earlier can help you conclude your speech. Quotations, for example, are frequently used in conclusions, as in this speech on geographical illiteracy:

> For in the words of Gilbert Grosvener, President of the National Geographic Society, "A knowledge of geography—where you are in relation to the rest of the world—is essential for an understanding of history, economics and politics. Without it, the prospects of world peace and cooperation, as well as a grasp of human events is beyond our reach. With it, we not only understand others, but we can better understand ourselves."[36]

You may also turn to illustrations, personal references, or any of the other methods of introduction to conclude your speech.

In addition to being able to adapt any of the methods of introduction to the conclusion, there are at least three other distinct methods of conclusion. These include a reference to the introduction, an inspirational appeal or challenge, and an appeal to action.

Reference to the Introduction   In our discussion of closure, we mentioned referring to the introduction as a way to end a speech. Finishing a story begun in the introduction, answering a rhetorical question posed in the introduction, or reminding the audience of the startling fact or statistic you presented in the introduction is each an excellent way to provide closure. Like bookends at either side of a group of books on your desk, a related introduction and conclusion provide unified support for the ideas in the middle.

The following speaker's topic dealt with personal problems caused by the current farm crisis. She had opened her speech with an illustration of an Iowan named Dale Burr, whose anguish had led to a murder-suicide. Her conclusion was this: "Just think . . . if someone had helped Dale Burr cope with the stress he was facing, maybe he and three others might not have died on that cold December day."[37]

Another speaker had begun his speech on the need for catastropic health insurance by quoting Robert Browning:

> Grow old along with me!
> The best is yet to be,
> The last of life, for which the first was made.[38]

He concluded his speech by referring to that Browning quotation:

> Robert Browning tells us the last of life is as precious as the first. While the future will always hold uncertainty, with catastrophic health insurance we can more fully prepare for whatever is yet to be.[39]

A third speaker had introduced his speech by talking about the downfalls inevitably suffered by the heroes of Greek mythology. He drew an analogy between the risks they faced and the risks inherent in the use of antibiotics—the dangers of overuse. Here is how that speaker ended his speech:

> The demise of Medusa carries with it one final message. With her death, Perseus received two drops of blood. One drop had the power to kill and spread evil; the other, to heal and restore well-being. Similarly, antibiotics offer us two opposite paths. As we painfully take stock in our hubris, in assuming that we can control the transformation of nature, we may ponder these two paths. We can either let antibiotics do the work of our immune systems and proper farm management which may return us to the times when deathly plagues spread across the world, or we can save these miracle drugs for the times when miracles are truly needed.[40]

Each of the three examples just given is quite different. In the first, the speech opened and closed with an illustration; in the second, both introduction and conclusion centered on a quotation; and in the third, beginning and ending relied on an analogy between mythology and modern medicine. What the three speeches had in common was that the conclusion of each harked back to the introduction. A reference to the introduction usually provides an effective and memorable conclusion.

Inspirational Appeal or Challenge Another way to end your speech is to issue an inspirational appeal or challenge to your listeners, rousing them to a high emotional pitch at the conclusion of the speech. The conclusion becomes the climax. One famous example comes from the "I Have a Dream" speech of Martin Luther King, Jr.:

From every mountainside, let freedom ring, and when this happens . . . when we allow freedom to ring, when we let it ring from every village and every hamlet, from every state and every city, we will be able to speed up that day when all of God's children, black men and white men, Jews and Gentiles, Protestants and Catholics, will be able to join hands and sing in the words of the old Negro spiritual, "Free at last! Thank God Almighty, we are free at last!"[41]

That King's conclusion was both inspiring and memorable has been affirmed by the growing fame of that passage through the years since he delivered the speech.

A more recent example is Ronald Reagan's farewell address delivered to the Republican national convention in August 1988. More personal than King's conclusion, it is nonetheless inspirational. Answering assertions that he was entering the twilight of his life, he concluded his speech with these words:

Twilight, you say?
    Listen to H. G. Wells: "The past is but the beginning of a beginning, and all that is and has been is but the twilight of the dawn."
    That's a new day—a sunlit new day—to keep alive the fire so that when we look back at the time of choosing, we can say that we did all that could be done.
    Never less.[42]

Appeal to Action   As noted earlier in this chapter, Chapter 16 will discuss organizing the persuasive speech, which often includes an appeal to action. Often this appeal occurs in the conclusion of a speech or at least is restated there.

An effective appeal for action comes in the conclusion of this speech on the dangers of light trucks, vans, and minivans:

The government and the industry are not looking out for us; we must protect ourselves. So often we take our mode of transportation for granted. We can no longer afford to be so foolish, especially when the price could be our lives. Only by examining the inherent dangers in these vehicles and who is responsible for them can we begin to establish safer transportation for everyone. So as you head home tonight look at the light truck you are in or those light trucks on the road beside you, consider what little protection there is, buckle up, and hope for a safe trip home.[43]

Combining a call to action with a reference to his introduction, another speaker urged his audience to act on the issue of pesticide control:

The Pied Piper fooled his prey. We are also being fooled. Fooled by the Federal Government and fooled by chemical lawn spray companies. There is no reason that 800 people should die or 800,000 people injured every year as a result of these chemical poisonings. One brief letter. One small action. These can help better insure that we are not led to our unsuspecting injuries or deaths. Meagan Connelley recovered from her chemical poisoning. But now she must hide from the Pied Piper of Pesticides as he plays on. She can only hope that legislation will be enacted to provide better control over the use of these pesticides in our lawns. For Meagan's sake, and for our own personal safety, can't we be that hope?[44]

Depending on audience, occasion, and your own interests and purposes, you can effectively and memorably end your speech by drawing on one of the methods we just discussed.

SUMMARY   In this chapter, we explored the purposes and methods of speech introductions and conclusions. We stressed the importance of beginning and ending your speech in a way that is memorable and that also provides the repetition audiences need.

A good speech introduction should perform five important functions:

1. Introduce the subject
2. Preview the body of the speech
3. Gain favorable attention for the speech
4. Provide a motivation for listening
5. Establish the speaker's credibility

Introducing the subject and previewing the body of the speech can be accomplished by including your central idea and preview statement in the introduction. Gaining favorable attention and providing a motivation for listening can be achieved by using one or a combination of the following methods:

1. Illustration
2. Startling fact or statistic
3. Quotation
4. Humor
5. Question
6. Reference to a historical event
7. Reference to a recent news event
8. Personal reference
9. Reference to the occasion
10. Reference to a preceding speech.

Concluding your speech is just as important as introducing it, for it is the conclusion that leaves the final impression. Specifically, a conclusion should accomplish four purposes:

1. Provide closure
2. Reemphasize the central idea in a memorable way
3. Motivate the audience to respond
4. Summarize the speech

Summarizing is a fairly straightforward task; achieving memorable closure and motivating audience response require somewhat more creativity. Conclusions may take any one of the forms used for introductions. In addition, three other methods are unique to conclusions:

1. Reference to the introduction
2. Inspirational appeal or challenge
3. Appeal to action

Once you have planned the introduction and the conclusion, you have completed the final organizational step of the speech preparation process.

1. Identify the functions of a speech introduction.
2. What are methods of capturing favorable audience attention at the beginning of your speech?
3. What are the functions of the conclusion of your speech?
4. Suggest several approaches that can be used to conclude a speech.

1. Examine the sample speeches in Appendix C. Identify the approach each speaker uses to begin and conclude the speech.
2. Go to the library and find a book of quotations, such as *Bartlett's Familiar Quotations*. Find interesting quotations that could be used to begin speeches on the following topics:
     The joys of raising children
     The value of an education
     We watch too much TV.
     Everyone should take a history course.
     We should be thankful to live in a free country.
3. How could you establish a motivation for your classroom audience to listen to you on each of the following topics?
     Birth control
     Jogging
     Prison reform
     Inflation
     Lee Iacocca
     Speed traps
     The history of greeting cards
     Elvis Presley
     Acid rain
4. Using the suggested topics in activity 3, write a complete introduction and conclusion for a speech. Write a brief paragraph in which you identify and explain the principles you followed in preparing your introduction and conclusion.

11

Rehearsal and Speech Delivery

OBJECTIVES

After studying this chapter, you should be able to

1. Identify three reasons delivery is important to a public speaker

2. Identify and describe four types of delivery

3. Identify and illustrate physical characteristics of effective delivery

4. Describe the steps to follow when you rehearse your speech

5. List four suggestions for enhancing the final delivery of your speech

Speak the speech, I pray you, as I pronounced it to you, trippingly on the tongue. (*Patrick Henry Addressing the House of Burgesses. Superstock.*)

WILLIAM SHAKESPEARE

While reflecting on one of his early unsuccessful speech efforts, Mark Twain once said,

> If I had those beloved and revered old literary immortals back here now on the platform at Carnegie Hall I would take that same old speech, deliver it, word for word, and melt them till they'd run all over the stage. Oh, the fault must have been with *me*, it is not in the speech at all.[1]

Twain's conclusion about the importance of delivery in contributing to a speech's success raises an important question. What's more important: what you say or how you say it? Delivery has long been considered an important part of public speaking. But is the delivery of your speech more important than the content of your message? Since ancient Greece, people have argued about the role delivery plays in public speaking.

More than 2000 years ago, some thinkers held that delivery was not an "elevated" topic of study. In his classic treatise *The Rhetoric*, written in 333 B.C., Aristotle claimed that "the battle should be fought out on the facts of the case alone; and therefore everything outside the direct proof is really superfluous." Writing in the first century, Quintilian, Roman rhetorician and author of the first book on speech training, acknowledged the importance of delivery when he said that the beginning speaker should strive for an "extempore" delivery style. His countryman, the great orator Cicero, felt that delivery was very important, for without effective delivery, "a speaker of the highest mental capacity can be held in no esteem, while one of moderate abilities, with this qualification, may surpass even those of the highest talent." Sixteen centuries later, the elocution movement carried the emphasis on delivery to an extreme. For elocutionists, speech training largely consisted of techniques and exercises for improving posture, movement, and vocal quality.

Today speech communication teachers believe that both content and delivery contribute to speaking effectiveness. A recent survey suggested that "developing effective delivery" is a primary goal of most speech teachers.[2] Considerable research supports the claim that delivery plays an important role in influencing how audiences react to a speaker and his or her message.

REHEARSING YOUR SPEECH

In previous chapters we have discussed how to develop an audience-centered message. We have guided you through the process of preparing a speech, from selecting a topic through organizing your speech. Armed with your speech outline, you are now ready to bring the speech to life. As shown in Figure 11.1, you will begin to rehearse your speech in preparation for your speech performance. This chapter reviews key principles and techniques that can help you maximize your rehearsal efficiency as you prepare to deliver your speech. Specifically, we will review methods of speech delivery and identify characteristics of your physical delivery, eye contact, facial expression, vocal delivery, and personal appearance.

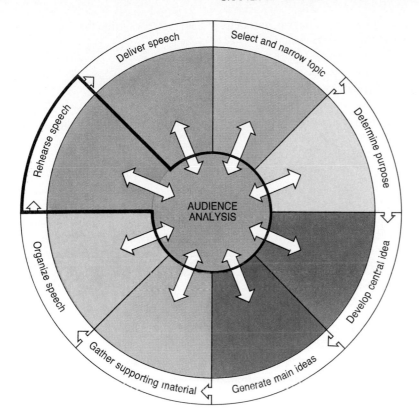

FIGURE 11.1

Rehearsing your speech delivery will help you present your speech with confidence.

Role of Delivery in Communication

IMPORTANCE OF DELIVERY

Experts tell us that nonverbal factors such as body language play a major role in the communication process. As much as 65 percent of the *social meaning* of messages is based on nonverbal signals. You cannot *not* communicate. As was noted in Chapter 1, all that you do can be interpreted as having meaning.

In a public speaking situation, nonverbal elements seem to influence perceptions of speakers' effectiveness. A study by Allen H. Monroe suggests that audience members equate effective public speaking with effective delivery.[3] In comparing good and bad speakers, Monroe found that the first six characteristics student audiences associated with an ineffective speaker were related to the speaker's delivery. A monotonous voice was rated as the most distracting, followed by stiffness, lack of eye contact with the audience, fidgeting, lack of enthusiasm, and a weak voice. Parallel to the negative findings, he observed that audiences liked direct eye contact, alertness, enthusiasm, a pleasant voice, and physical activity.

Examining the "general effectiveness" of student speeches, another researcher concluded that delivery was almost twice as important as content when students gave self-introduction speeches and three times as important when students gave persuasive speeches.[4] The way you deliver a speech does influence the way listeners will respond to your message.

Delivery, Emotions, and Attitudes

Style of delivery is particularly important in communicating feelings, emotions, attitudes, likes, and dislikes to an audience. One researcher found that as little as 7 percent of the emotional impact of a message is communicated by the words we use.[5] About 38 percent is communicated by such qualities of voice as inflection, intensity, or loudness, and 55 percent by our facial expressions. Generalizing from these findings, we may say that approximately 93 percent of emotional meaning is communicated nonverbally. Although some scholars question whether these findings can be applied to all communication settings, the research does suggest that the manner of delivery provides important information about feelings and emotions. The way you deliver your speech will influence how your listeners feel about you and your message.

Audiences Believe What They See

"I'm very glad to speak with you tonight," drones the speaker in a monotone, eyes glued to his notes. His audience probably does not believe him. When our nonverbal delivery contradicts what we say, people generally believe the nonverbal message. In this case, the speaker is communicating that he's *not* glad to be talking to this audience.

We usually believe nonverbal messages because they are more difficult to fake. Although we can monitor certain parts of our nonverbal behavior, it is difficult to control all of it consciously. Research suggests that a person trying to deceive someone may speak in a higher vocal pitch, at a slower rate, and with more pronunciation mistakes than normal.[6] Blushing, sweating, and changed breathing patterns also often belie our stated meaning. As the saying goes, "What you do speaks so loud, I can't hear what you say."

METHODS OF DELIVERY

Now that we have seen that the style of delivery plays a vital role in public speaking, let's look closely at the four methods of delivery from which a speaker can choose: (1) manuscript reading, (2) speaking from memory, (3) impromptu speaking, and (4) extemporaneous speaking. Let's consider each in some detail.

Manuscript Reading

You have a speech to present and are afraid you will forget what you have prepared to say. So you write your speech and then read it to your audience.

Reading a speech from a manuscript is usually a poor way to deliver a speech.
(*Ellis Herwig/Stock, Boston*)

Speech teachers frown on this approach, particularly for public speaking students. Reading is usually a poor way to deliver a speech. Although it may provide some assurance of not forgetting the speech, reading from a manuscript is rarely done well enough to be interesting. You have probably attended a lecture that was read and wondered, "Why doesn't he just make a copy of the speech for everyone in the audience rather than reading it to us?"

Speeches that are read from a manuscript are not interesting because we speak differently from the way we write. Spoken communication is more *informal*, *personal*, and *redundant* than written communication. It takes a very talented communicator to write and then read a speech in a conversational style.

Even though in most cases it is unwise to read your speech, there are exceptions. Some speeches should be read. One advantage of reading from a manuscript is that you can choose words very carefully, a fact that often makes it a preferred method of delivery for someone who is dealing with a sensitive and critical issue. The President of the United States, for example, often finds it useful to have his remarks carefully scripted. An awkward statement could result in serious consequences, not only for his political career but also for the security of our nation. Statements to the press by the chief executive officers of corporations under fire should be delivered from carefully crafted papers rather than tossed off casually.

You may also want to read your speech from a manuscript if you devote careful attention to the style of what you are saying. Metaphors, alliteration, and other stylistic concerns can be given greater attention in a written message than in a more extemporaneous oral one.

The key to giving an effective manuscript speech is to sound as though you are *not* giving a manuscript speech. Speak with vocal variation—vary the rhythm, inflection, and pace of your delivery. Be familiar enough with your manuscript so that you can have as much eye contact with your audience as possible. Use gestures and movement to add interest and emphasis to your message.

Speaking from Memory

"All right," you think, "since reading a speech is hard to pull off, I'll write my speech out word for word and then memorize it." You're pretty sure that no one will be able to tell, since you won't be using notes. Memorizing your speech also has the advantage of allowing you to have maximum eye contact with the audience. But while you may be able to maintain eye contact with your audience (a good thing), most memorized speeches *sound* stiff, stilted, and overrehearsed. The inherent differences between speaking and writing will be evident in a memorized speech, just as they can be heard in a manuscript speech. You also run the risk of forgetting parts of your speech and awkwardly searching for words in front of your audience. For these reasons, speech teachers do not encourage their students to memorize speeches for class presentation.

If you are accepting an award, introducing a speaker, making announcements, or delivering other brief remarks, a memorized delivery style is sometimes acceptable. As with manuscript speaking, however, you must take care to make your presentation sound lively and interesting. In general, however, we do not encourage you to memorize a speech exactly as you penned it. More than likely it will sound uninspiring and mechanical.

Impromptu Speaking

A third method of delivery is called impromptu speaking. The word *impromptu* comes from the Latin and means "in readiness" or "at hand." An impromptu speech is one delivered without any preparation or rehearsal. We sometimes describe the impromptu method as "off the cuff" or "thinking on your feet." The advantage of impromptu speaking is that the speaker can speak informally, maintaining direct eye contact with the audience. But unless the speaker is extremely talented or has learned and practiced the techniques of impromptu speaking (which will be discussed in Chapter 17), the speech itself will be unimpressive. An impromptu speech usually lacks logical organization and thorough research. There are times, of course, when we are called on to speak without advance knowledge of the invitation. But if informed of a speaking assignment, impromptu speaking should not be the method of choice.

Extemporaneous Speaking

If not manuscript, memorized, or impromptu speaking, what's left? An extemporaneous method is the approach most speech communication teachers recommend for most situations. When delivering a speech extemporaneously, you speak from a written or memorized general outline, but you do not have the exact wording in front of you or in memory. You have rehearsed the speech so that you know key ideas and their organization, but not to the degree that the speech sounds memorized. An extemporaneous style is conversational; it gives your audience the impression that the speech is being created as they listen to it, and to some extent it is. Audiences prefer to hear something live rather than something canned. Even though you can't tell the difference between a performance that is taped or live when it is broadcast on TV, you would probably prefer seeing it live. There is added interest and excitement associated with seeing something happening now. An extemporaneous speech sounds live rather than as though it were prepared yesterday or weeks ago. The extemporaneous method reflects the advantages of a well-organized speech delivered in an interesting and vivid manner.

RECAP

METHODS OF DELIVERY	Manuscript	Reading your speech from a prepared text
	Memorized	Giving a speech from memory without using notes
	Impromptu	Delivering a speech without preparing
	Extemporaneous	Knowing the major ideas, which have been outlined; the exact wording has not been memorized

You have learned the importance of effective delivery and have identified four methods of delivery. You now know that for most speaking situations, you should strive for a conversational style. But you still may have a number of specific questions about enhancing your delivery effectiveness. Typical concerns include these: "What do I do with my hands?" "Is it all right to move around while I speak?" "How can I make my voice sound interesting?" As you continue to read the text, these and other questions about the delivery of your speech will be answered. You will next consider five major aspects of delivery: (1) physical delivery, (2) eye contact, (3) facial expression, (4) vocal delivery, and (5) personal appearance.

CHARACTERISTICS OF EFFECTIVE DELIVERY

Physical Delivery

Gestures, movement, and posture are the three key attributes of physical delivery, or **body language**. Your body language will influence whether your audience sees

Putting your hands in your pocket can lend to the informality of your speech, but, if overdone, you may appear too casual.
(Bob Daemmrich/Stock, Boston)

you as credible and competent. It also helps determine whether you successfully gain and hold audience interest. A good public speaker knows how to use effective gestures, make meaningful movements, and maintain an appropriate posture while speaking to an audience.

Gestures   The next time you have a conversation with someone, notice how both of you use your hands and bodies to communicate. Important points are emphasized with gestures. You also gesture to indicate places, to enumerate items, and to describe objects. Gestures have the same functions for public speakers. Yet many people who gesture easily and appropriately in the course of everyday conversations aren't sure what to do with their hands when they find themselves in front of an audience.

Public speaking teachers often see several unusual, inappropriate, and unnatural gestures. Common problems include keeping your hands behind your back in a "parade rest" pose. We are not suggesting that you never put your hands behind your back, only that standing at parade rest during an entire speech looks awkward and unnatural and may distract your audience.

Another common position is with one hand on the hip in a "broken wing" pose. Worse than the "broken wing" is both hands resting on the hips in a "double broken wing." The speaker looks as though he or she will soon burst out in a rendition of "I'm a Little Tea Pot." Again, we are not suggesting that speakers refrain from placing their hands on their hips, only that to hold that one pose throughout a speech looks unnatural and will keep them from using other gestures.

Few poses are more awkward-looking than when a speaker clutches one arm while speaking. This position suggests that the speaker was grazed by a bullet and is holding his or her arm for relief. We might expect the speaker to call out reassuringly, "Don't worry, Ma; it's only a flesh wound."

Hands in pockets can give a casual appearance in ordinary circumstances, but, if overdone, this posture can be inappropriate in front of an audience. It makes the speaker look as if he were afraid to let go of his change or his keys.

Another interesting, albeit unnatural use of gestures occurs when a speaker clasps his hands and lets them drop in front of him in a kind of "fig leaf clutch." Gestures can distract your audience in various other ways as well. Grasping the lectern until your knuckles turn white or just letting your hands flop around without purpose or control does little to help you communicate your message.

If you don't know what to do with your hands, think about the message you want to communicate. As in ordinary conversation, your hands should simply help emphasize or reinforce your verbal message. Specifically, note the following ways in which your gestures can lend strength to what you have to say: (1) repeating, (2) contradicting, (3) substituting, (4) complementing, (5) emphasizing, and (6) regulating.

REPEATING Gestures can help you build needed redundancy by repeating your verbal message. For example, you can say, "I have three major points to talk about today," while holding up three fingers. Or you can describe an object as 12 inches long while holding your hands about a foot apart. Repeating what you say via nonverbal means can reinforce your message and make it stronger.

CONTRADICTING Since your audience will sooner believe what you communicate nonverbally than verbally, you need to monitor your gestures to make sure that you are not contradicting what you say. It is difficult to convey an image of control and confidence by using flailing gestures and awkward poses. To monitor your gestures, you will have to develop a kind of relaxed self-consciousness. You don't want to display behavior that will conflict with your intended image or message, nor do you want to appear stiff and self-conscious. So the crucial thing to keep in mind while monitoring your own behavior is to *stay relaxed*.

SUBSTITUTING Not only can your behavior reinforce or contradict what you say, but your gestures can also substitute for your message. Without uttering a word, you can hold up the palm of your hand to calm a noisy crowd. Flashing two fingers to form a *V* for victory or raising a clenched fist are other common examples of how gestures can substitute for a verbal message.

COMPLEMENTING Gestures can also add further meaning to your verbal message. A politician who declines to comment on a reporter's question while holding up his hands to augment his verbal refusal, uses his gesture to complement or provide further meaning to his verbal message.

EMPHASIZING You can give emphasis to what you say by using an appropriate gesture. A shaking fist or a slicing gesture with one or both hands help emphasize a message. So does pounding your fist into the palm of your hand. Other gestures can be less dramatic but still lend emphasis to what you say. You should try to

Winston Churchill's "V" for victory gesture is an example of substituting a nonverbal cue for a word.
(*UPI/Bettman Newsphotos*)

allow your gestures to arise from the content of your speech and your emotions.

REGULATING   Gestures can also regulate the exchange between you and your audience. If you want the audience to respond to a question, you can extend both palms to invite a response. During a question-and-answer session, your gestures can signal when you want to talk and when you want to invite others to do so.

Criteria for Effective Gestures   Although we gave examples of the way gestures relate to what we say, we have purposely not identified specific gestures to go with particular statements or feelings. Turn-of-the-century elocutionists taught their students how to gesture to communicate specific emotions or messages. Today teachers of speech act differently. Rather than prescribe gestures for specific situations, they feel that it is more useful to offer suitable criteria (standards) by which to judge effective gestures, regardless of what is being said. Here are some guidelines that you can think about when working on your delivery.

1. Gestures should be *relaxed*, not tense or rigid. Your gestures should flow with your message. Avoid sawing or slashing through the air with your hands unless you are trying to emphasize a particularly dramatic point.

2. Gestures should appear *definite* rather than as accidental brief jerks of your hands or arms. If you want to gesture, go ahead and gesture. Avoid minor hand movements that will be masked by the lectern.

3. Gestures should be *appropriate* for the verbal content of your speech. If you are excited, gesture more vigorously. But remember that prerehearsed gestures that do not naturally arise from what you are trying to say are likely to appear awkward and stilted.

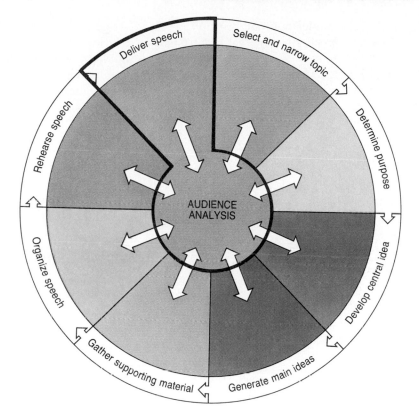

FIGURE 11.2

Even during the final step of the speechmaking process, delivering your message, you need to be audience-centered.

4. Strive for *variety* and versatility in your use of gesture. Try not to use just one hand or one all-purpose gesture. Gestures can be used for a variety of purposes, such as enumerating, pointing, describing, and symbolizing an idea or concept (such as clasping your hands together to suggest agreement or a coming-together process).

5. Gestures should appear *natural*, not artificial or contrived. The pounding fist or raised forefinger in hectoring style will not necessarily enhance the quality of your performance.

6. Gestures should be *unobtrusive*; your audience should focus not on the beauty or appropriateness of your gestures but on your message. Your purpose is to communicate a message to your audience, not to perform for your listeners in such a way that your delivery receives more attention than your message.

7. Gestures should be *well timed* to coincide with your verbal message. When you announce that you have three major points, your gesture of enumeration should occur simultaneously with your utterance of the word *three*. It would be poor timing to announce that you have three points, pause for a second or two, and then hold up three fingers.

8. Gestures must be *adapted to the audience*. In more formal speaking situations, particularly when speaking to a large audience, bolder, more sweeping, and more dramatic gestures are appropriate. A small audience in a less formal setting calls for less formal gestures.

In summary, keep one important principle in mind: Use gestures that work best for you. Don't try to be someone that you are not. Jesse Jackson's style may work for him, but you are not Jesse Jackson. Your gestures should fit your personality. We believe it is better to use no gestures than to try to counterfeit the gestures of someone else. Your nonverbal delivery should flow from *your* message.

RECAP

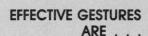

EFFECTIVE GESTURES ARE . . .

Relaxed	Natural
Definite	Unobtrusive
Appropriate	Well timed
Varied	Adapted to the audience

Movement   Should you walk around during your speech, or should you stay in one place? If there is a lectern, should you stand behind it, or would it be acceptable to stand in front of it or to the side? Is it all right to sit down while you speak? Can you move among the audience, as Phil Donahue does on his TV talk show? You may well find yourself pondering one or more of these questions while preparing for your speeches. The following discussion may help you answer them.

You may want to move about while delivering your speech, but you should take care that your movement does not detract from your message. If the audience focuses on your movement rather than on what you are saying, it is better to stand still. In short, your movement should be consistent with the verbal content of your message. It should make sense rather than appear as aimless wandering.

As you consider incorporating movement into your speech, you should also be mindful of the physical barriers that exist between you and your audience. Barriers such as a lectern, rows of chairs, a chalkboard, an overhead projector, or other audiovisual aids may act as obstacles between you and your audience. If physical barriers make you feel too far removed from your audience, move closer. Make yourself comfortable by adapting to your speaking environment.

You may also signal the beginning of a new idea or major point in your speech with movement. As you move into a transition statement or change from a serious subject to a more humorous one, movement can be a good way to signal that your approach to the speaking situation is changing.

Your use of movement during your speech should make sense. It should not be perceived as random pacing in front of your audience, nor should it appear overly dramatic.

Posture   Although few formal studies of posture in relation to public speaking have been conducted, there is evidence that the way you carry your body communicates significant information. One study even suggests that your stance can reflect on your credibility as a speaker.[7] Slouching across the lectern, for example, does not project an image of vitality and interest in your audience.

While your face and voice play the major role in communicating a specific emotion, your posture communicates the *intensity* of that emotion. If you are happy, your face and voice will reflect your happiness; your posture will communicate the intensity of your joy.

Since the days of the elocutionists, few speech teachers or public speaking texts have advocated specific postures for public speakers. Today we believe that the specific stance you adopt should come about naturally, as a result of what you have to say, the environment, and the formality or informality of the occasion. For example, it may be perfectly appropriate as well as comfortable and natural to sit on the edge of a desk during a very informal presentation. Most speech teachers, however, do not encourage students to sit while speaking for classroom speeches. In general, avoid slouched shoulders, shifting from foot to foot, or drooping your head. Your posture should not call attention to itself. It should instead reflect your interest in the speaking event and your attention to the task at hand.

Eye Contact

Of all of the delivery features discussed in this chapter, the most important one in a public speaking situation is eye contact.[8] Eye contact with your audience serves several important functions: It (1) opens communication, (2) checks on audience reactions, (3) makes you more believable, and (4) keeps your audience interested. Each of these functions contributes to the success of your delivery and thus your speech.

Making eye contact with your listeners clearly shows that you are ready to talk to them. Most people, including you, usually start a conversation by looking at the person they are going to talk to. The same process occurs in public speaking.

Once you've started talking, continued eye contact lets you know how your audience is responding to your speech. You don't need to look at your listeners continuously in a sort of fixed stare. As the need arises, you should certainly look at your notes, but you should also look at your listeners frequently, just to see what they're doing.

Most listeners will think you capable and trustworthy if you look them in the eye. Several studies document a relationship between eye contact and increased speaker credibility.[9] Speakers with less than 50 percent eye contact are considered unfriendly, uninformed, inexperienced, and even dishonest by their listeners.

While maintaining eye contact with your listeners, you help keep their interest in your speech alive. Audience members that have more than 50 percent eye contact with their speaker retain much more of the message, according to postspeech tests.[10]

As you have just seen, eye contact serves several important functions in your speech. Now let's look at some suggestions for incorporating eye contact in your delivery style. Establish eye contact with your audience even before you open your speech with your attention-catching introduction. When it's your time to speak, walk to the lectern (or the front of the audience if you're not using a lectern), pause, and look at your audience before you say anything. Eye contact nonverbally says, "I am interested in you; tune me in; I have something I want to share with you." You should have your opening sentence well enough in mind that you can deliver it without looking at your notes or away from your listeners.

Try to establish eye contact with the entire audience, not just the front row or only one or two people. Look to the back and front and from side to side of your audience, selecting an individual to focus on and then moving on to someone else. You need not rhythmically move your head back and forth like a lighthouse beacon. It's best not to establish a predictable pattern to your looking. Look at individuals, establishing person-to-person contact with them—not so long that it will make a listener feel uncomfortable but long enough to establish the feeling that you are talking directly to that individual. *Don't* look over your listeners' heads; establish eye-to-eye contact.

RECAP

GOOD EYE CONTACT . . .	Lets your audience know you are interested in them and that you want to talk to them
	Permits you to monitor audience reaction to your message in order to determine whether your audience is responding to you
	Establishes your credibility
	Helps your audience maintain interest and remember more of your message

Facial Expression

Your face plays a key role in expressing your thoughts, emotions, and attitudes. We observed earlier that as much as 55 percent of the emotion you feel is reflected on your face. Your audience sees your face before they hear what you are going to say. Thus you have an opportunity to set the emotional tone for your message before you start speaking. Though you are capable of producing over 250,000 different facial expressions, they most often express only six primary emotions: happiness, anger, surprise, sadness, disgust, and fear.

Vocal Delivery

Have you ever listened to a DJ on the radio and imagined what he or she looked like, only later to see a picture and have your image of the announcer drastically altered? Vocal clues play an important part in creating the impression we have of a speaker. Based on vocal clues alone, you make inferences about a person's age, status, occupation, ethnic origin, income, and a variety of other matters. As a public speaker, your voice is one of your most important delivery tools in conveying your ideas to your audience. Your credibility as a speaker and your ability to communicate your ideas clearly to your listeners will in large part depend on your vocal delivery.

Vocal delivery includes pitch, rate, volume, pronunciation, articulation, pauses, and general variation of the voice. A speaker has at least two key vocal obligations to an audience: (1) Speak to be understood and (2) speak with vocal variety to maintain interest.

Speaking to Be Understood   To be understood, you need to control three aspects of vocal delivery: volume, articulation, and pronunciation.

VOLUME The fundamental purpose of your vocal delivery is to speak loudly enough so that your audience can hear you. Your speech **volume** is determined by the amount of air projected through your larynx, or voice box. More air equals more volume of sound. Your diaphragm, a muscle in your upper abdomen, helps control the volume of sound by increasing the flow of air from your lungs through your voice box. If you put your hands on your diaphragm and say, "Ho-ho-ho," you will feel the muscles contract and the air being forced out of your lungs. Breathing from your diaphragm rather than increasing air flow through your lungs alone can increase the volume of sound as well as enhance the quality of your voice.

volume
The softness or loudness of a speaker's voice.

The appropriate volume of sound depends on how far you are from your audience, the amount of noise or distraction that exists, and whether you want to provide emphasis to ideas or phrases. If you are some distance from your audience without a microphone, you will obviously need to speak loudly enough to be heard. But even when you are close to the first row of your audience, you need to be mindful of your listeners in the back row. Crying babies, airplanes, lawn mowers, and restless, mumbling audience members are typical kinds of noises that you may have competing with you. Increased volume can help keep attention focused on you and your speech when noisy distractions occur. Even without such distractions, you may want to increase your volume to emphasize a word or a phase. Your increased volume, coupled with slowing down and clearly articulating each word, can help your audience understand what you are saying.

Sometimes you may want to decrease your volume of sound to gain or maintain audience attention. We know a kindergarten teacher with excellent classroom control who was much more successful in getting her students' attention by speaking softly rather than by yelling. The change in volume was attention-getting. Dropping your speech volume, while making sure your voice is still audible, may provide enough variation to gain the attention of your audience after you have spoken for a period of time with considerable volume.

ARTICULATION **Articulation** is the ability to make speech sounds clearly and distinctly. In addition to speaking loudly enough, you will need to say your words so that your audience can understand them. Without distinct enunciation or articulation of the sounds that make up words, your listeners may not understand you or may fault you for simply not knowing how to speak clearly and fluently. Here are some commonly misarticulated words:[11]

whadayado	*instead of*	what do you do
wanna	*instead of*	want to
seeya	*instead of*	see you
dint	*instead of*	didn't
lemme	*instead of*	let me
mornin	*instead of*	morning
wep	*instead of*	wept
soun	*instead of*	sound

Most errors in articulation result from an unflattering flaw: laziness. It takes more effort to articulate speech sounds clearly. We often get in a hurry to express our idea, or we just get into the habit of mumbling, slurring, and abbreviating. Such speech flaws may not keep your audience from understanding you, but poor enunciation does reflect on your credibility as a speaker.

The best way to improve your articulation of sounds is first to identify words or phrases that you have a tendency to slur or chop. Once you have identified them, practice saying the words correctly. Make sure that you can hear the difference between the improper and proper pronunciation. Your speech teacher can help you check your speech articulation.

PRONUNCIATION Whereas articulation is concerned with the production of speech sounds, **pronunciation** refers to the proper sounds that form words. Mispronouncing words can also detract from speaker's credibility. Often, however, we are not aware that we are mispronouncing a word unless someone points out our error. Here are some common pronunciation errors.

Reversing speech sounds:

hundred	*not*	hunnert
perspiration	*not*	prespiration
predicament	*not*	perdicament

Substituting an *i* sound for an *e* sound:

thin	*not*	then
since	*not*	cents
wind	*not*	wend

▼
articulation
The ability to make speech sounds clearly and distinctly.

▼
pronunciation
The ability to use the proper sounds to form words clearly and accurately.

Allowing an *r* sound to intrude into some words:

wash	*not*	warsh
yellow	*not*	yeller
tomato	*not*	tomater

Substituting an *a* sound for an *i* sound:

finger	*not*	fanger
think	*not*	thank
sink	*not*	sank

Drawling or exaggerating the *l* sound in some words:

fool	*not*	foo-ahl
school	*not*	schoo-ahl
cool	*not*	coo-ahl

Leaving out sounds that should be pronounced in the middle of a word:

curiosity	*not*	curosity
actually	*not*	actchally
naturally	*not*	natcherly

Accenting the wrong syllable:

police'	*not*	po'lice
supreme'	*not*	su'preme
Detroit'	*not*	De'troit

Speaking with Variety   Besides being understood by your listeners as a result of having sufficient volume, clear articulation, and correct pronunciation, you need to speak with variety. To speak with variety is to vary your pitch, rate, and pauses. It is primarily through the quality of our voices, as well as our facial expressions, that we communicate whether we are happy, sad, bored, or excited. If your vocal clues suggest that you are bored with your topic, your audience will probably be bored also. Appropriate variation in vocal pitch and rate as well as appropriate use of pauses can add zest to your speech and help maintain audience attention.

PITCH   Vocal **pitch** is how high or low your voice sounds. You are able to sing because you can change the pitch of your voice to produce a melody. Lack of variation in pitch has been consistently identified as one of the most distracting characteristics of ineffective speakers. A monotone is boring.

pitch
How high or low your voice sounds.

Everyone has a habitual pitch. This is the range of your voice during normal conversation. Some people have habitually high pitch, while others have a low pitch. The pitch of your voice is determined by how fast the folds in your vocal cords vibrate. The faster the vibration, the higher the pitch. Male vocal folds open and close approximately 100 to 150 times each second; female vocal cords vibrate about 200 times per second, thus giving them a higher vocal pitch.

Your voice has **inflection** when you raise or lower the pitch as you pronounce words or sounds. Your inflection is what helps determine the meaning of your utterances. A surprised "ah!" sounds different from a disappointed "ah." Different too would be "ah?" Your vocal inflection is thus an important indicator of your emotions and helps give clues as to how to interpret your speech.

inflection
The variation of the pitch of your voice.

The best public speakers vary their inflection considerably. We're not suggesting that you need to imitate a top-forty radio disk jockey when you speak. But variation in your vocal inflection and overall pitch helps you communicate the subtlety of your ideas.

If you have been accused of having a monotone, you will need to try to learn to produce meaningful variations in pitch and inflection. Record your speech as you rehearse, and evaluate your use of pitch and inflection critically. If you are not satisfied with your inflection, consider practicing your speech with exaggerated variations in vocal pitch. Not that you would deliver your speech with excessive pitch variation, but it may help you explore the expressive options available to you.

RATE How fast do you talk? Most speakers average between 120 and 180 words per minute. There is no "best" speaking rate. Great speakers use no standard rate of speech that can account for their speaking skill. Daniel Webster purportedly spoke at about 90 words per minute, Franklin Roosevelt 110, President Kennedy a quick-paced 180. Martin Luther King, Jr., started his "I Have a Dream" speech at 92 words a minute and was speaking at 145 during his conclusion.[12] The best rate depends on two factors: your speaking style and the content of your message.

You can understand words at a much faster rate than you normally speak them. Some experts have clocked our listening comprehension rate at up to 1200 words per minute.[13] Though it may be difficult to sustain attention to a speech delivered at this pace, it is technically possible for you to comprehend words delivered with such speed.

A common fault of many beginning speakers is to deliver a speech too quickly. One symptom of speech anxiety is that you tend to rush through your speech to get it over with. Relying on feedback from others can help you determine whether your rate is too rapid. Tape-recording your message and listening critically to your speaking rate can help you assess whether you are speaking at the proper speed. Fewer speakers have the problem of speaking too slowly, but a turtle-paced speech will almost certainly make it more difficult for your audience to maintain interest. Remember, your listeners can grasp information much faster than you can give it to them.

You need not deliver your entire speech at the same pace. It is normal for you to speak more rapidly when talking about something you are excited about. You slow your speaking rate to emphasize key points or ideas. Speaking rate is another tool available to you to add variety and interest to your vocal delivery. The pace of your delivery, however, should make sense in terms of the ideas you are sharing with your listeners.

PAUSES An appropriate pause can often do more to accent your message than any other vocal characteristic. President Kennedy's famous line, "Ask not what your country can do for you; ask what you can do for your country," was effective not only because of its language but also because it was delivered with a pause dividing the two thoughts. Try delivering that line without the pause; it just doesn't have the same power without it.

Effective use of pauses, also known as effective timing, can greatly enhance the impact of your message. Whether you are trying to tell a joke, a serious tale, or a dramatic story, your use of a pause can determine the effectiveness of your anecdote.

Johnny Carson, David Letterman, and Roseanne Barr are masters at timing a punch line. Radio commentator Paul Harvey is known for his flair for vocal delivery. His dramatic pauses serve as meaningful punctuation in his talks.

Beware of the vocalized pause. Many beginning public speakers are uncomfortable with silence and so rather than pausing where it seems natural and normal, they will vocalize sounds like "umm," "er," "you know," and "ah." We think you will agree that "Ask not ah what your er country can do ah for you; ask you know what you umm can do er for your uh country" just doesn't have the same impact as the unadorned original statement. Vocalized pauses will annoy your audience and detract from your credibility; eliminate them.

Silence can be a very effective tool in emphasizing a particular word or sentence. A well-timed pause coupled with eye contact can powerfully accent your thought.

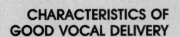

RECAP

CHARACTERISTICS OF GOOD VOCAL DELIVERY

Good Speakers	Poor Speakers
Have adequate volume	Speak too softly to be heard
Articulate speech sounds clearly and distinctly	Slur speech sounds
Pronounce words accurately	Mispronounce words
Have varied pitch	Have a monotonous pitch
Vary speaking rate	Consistently speak too fast or too slow
Pause to emphasize ideas	Rarely pause or pause too long

Personal Appearance

We have focused on such nonverbal delivery factors as gestures, movement, eye contact, facial expression, and vocal delivery. Finally, let's consider some implications of your personal appearance as you present a speech.

Most people have certain expectations about the way a speaker or other person should look. One of your audience analysis tasks is to identify what those audience expectations are. This can be trickier than it might at first seem. John T. Molloy has written two books, *Dress for Success* and *Dress for Success for Women*, in an effort to identify what the well-dressed business person should wear. But as some of his own research points out, appropriate wardrobe varies, depending on climate, custom, culture, and audience expectations. It may be improper to wear blue jeans to a business meeting, but it would be just as inappropriate to wear a business suit to a gathering of artists.

There is considerable evidence that your personal appearance affects how your audience will respond to you and your message, particularly during the opening moments of your presentation. If you violate their expectations of appearance, you will be less successful in achieving your purpose. Scholars tell us that the opening seconds of a job interview help set the tone for the interview because the interviewer is influenced by the applicant's appearance. There is every reason to believe that your audience's initial impression of you as a speaker plays an important role in determining the impact that you and your talk will have.

Styles and audience expectations change and are sometimes unpredictable. Therefore, a general rule of thumb to follow is this: When in doubt about what to wear, select something conservative. Also take your cue from your audience. You need not always mirror their appearance, but if you know that the males in your audience wear suits and ties and the females wear dresses, you would be wise to avoid dressing more casually.

REHEARSING YOUR SPEECH: SOME FINAL TIPS

Just knowing some of the effective characteristics of speech delivery will not make you a better speaker unless you can put these principles into practice. Effective public speaking is a skill that takes practice. Practicing takes the form of rehearsing. The following suggestions will help you make the most of your rehearsal time.

1. Finish drafting your speech outline at least two days before your speech performance. The more time you have to work on putting it all together, the better.

2. Before you prepare the speaking notes that you will take with you in front of your audience, rehearse your speech aloud to help you determine where you will need notes to prompt yourself.

3. Revise your speech as necessary to keep it within the time limits set by your instructor or whoever invited you to speak.

4. Prepare your speaking notes. Use whatever system works best for you. Some speakers use pictorial symbols to remind them of a story or an idea. Others use complete sentences or just words or phrases in an outline pattern to prompt them. Most teachers advocate note cards for speaking notes.

5. Rehearse your speech standing up so that you can get a feeling for your use of gestures as well as your vocal delivery. Do not try to memorize your speech or choreograph specific gestures. As you rehearse, you may want to modify your speaking notes to reflect changes that seem appropriate.

6. If you can, present your speech to someone else so that you can practice establishing eye contact. Seek feedback from your captive audience about both your delivery and your speech content.

7. If possible, tape-record or videotape your speech during the rehearsal stage so that you can observe your vocal and physical mannerisms and make changes that may be necessary. If you don't have a video, you may find it useful to practice before a mirror so that you can observe your physical delivery.

8. Your final rehearsals should try as much as possible to re-create the speaking

situation you will face. If you will be speaking in a large classroom, try to find a large classroom in which to rehearse your speech. If your audience will be informally seated in chairs in a semicircle, then this should be the context in which you rehearse your speech. The more realistic the rehearsal, the more confidence you will gain.

DELIVERING YOUR SPEECH

The day arrives and you are ready. Using information about your audience as an anchor, you have developed a speech with an interesting topic and a fine-tuned purpose. Your central idea is clearly identified. You have gathered interesting and relevant supporting material (examples, illustrations, statistics) and organized them well. Your speech has an appropriate introduction, a logically arranged body, and a clear conclusion that nicely summarize your key theme. You have rehearsed your speech several times; it is not memorized, but you are comfortable with the way you express the major ideas. Your last task is calmly and confidently to communicate with your audience. You are ready to deliver your speech.

As you approach the time for presenting your speech to your audience, consider the following suggestions to help you prepare for your successful performance.

1. At the risk of sounding like your mother, we suggest that you get plenty of rest before your speech. Last-minute, late-night final preparation can take the edge off your performance. Many professional public speakers also advocate that you watch what you eat before you speak; a heavy meal or too much caffeine can have a negative effect on your performance.

2. Review the suggestions for managing speech anxiety that we presented in Chapter 2. Remember, it is normal to feel some apprehension and nervousness about speaking to others. Use the methods we described to help you perform your best.

3. Arrive early for your speaking engagement. If your room is in an unfamiliar location, give yourself plenty of time to find it. Relax before you deliver your message; budget your time so you do not spend your moments before you speak harriedly looking for a parking place or frantically trying to attend to last minute details.

4. Visualize success. Picture yourself delivering your speech in an effective way. Also, remind yourself of the effort you have spent preparing for your speech. A final mental rehearsal can boost your confidence and help ensure success.

Even though we have identified many time-tested methods for enhancing your speech delivery, keep in mind that speech delivery is an art rather than a science. The manner of your delivery should reflect your personality and individual style.

SUMMARY

In this chapter, we discussed the importance of effective speech delivery and identified suggestions for enhancing your delivery. The way you deliver your speech affects audience attitudes; it's the primary way in which you communicate your thoughts and emotions to an audience. Audiences will believe what they see more readily than what they hear.

Of the four methods of delivery—manuscript, memorized, impromptu, and extemporaneous—the extemporaneous method is preferred. Speak from an outline without memorizing the exact words.

We have offered several suggestions for enhancing your delivery. Your gestures and movements should appear relaxed, definite, appropriate, varied, natural, unobtrusive, and well timed, and they should be adapted to your audience. Eye contact is the single most important delivery variable; looking at your audience helps control communication, checks audience reactions, establishes your credibility, and maintains audience interest. Your facial expression and your vocal clues are the primary ways in which you communicate your feelings and emotions to an audience. How loudly you speak, how clearly you articulate, and how correctly you pronounce the words you use determines how well your audience understands your thought; your vocal pitch, rate, and uses of pauses help provide variation to add interest to your talk.

The chapter concluded with several final suggestions for rehearsing and delivering your speech. We suggested that you leave at least two days to focus on your speech delivery and develop your speaking notes. As much as possible, re-create the speech environment when you rehearse. You will be rewarded with a smoother delivery style and more confidence when you deliver your message.

QUESTIONS FOR DISCUSSION AND REVIEW

1. Why do delivery variables play a major role in communicating your thoughts?
2. Describe, compare, and contrast four different methods of delivery.
3. Why is extemporaneous delivery the preferred delivery method?
4. What functions do gestures serve?
5. Identify criteria for effective gestures, posture, and movement.
6. Describe four functions of speaker eye contact.
7. Explain several characteristics of effective vocal delivery.

SUGGESTED ACTIVITIES

1. Videotape one of your speeches, either when you present your speech in front of your class or during your rehearsal. Critique your tape, focusing on your delivery. Write a 200- to 400-word analysis of your delivery strengths and weaknesses based on the principles and suggestions presented in the chapter.
2. Attend a political campaign speech presented by a politician. Pay particular attention to his or her delivery. Provide a written critique of the speaker's use of posture, gesture, eye contact, vocal clues, and appearance. If you were a campaign consultant, what advice would you give this politician?

3. While you are rehearsing your next class speech, experiment with using a new delivery style. If you seldom, if ever, use gestures, practice using more gestures than normal to experience a different, more effective delivery approach. Make a conscious effort to change your vocal delivery style; if you normally have little vocal variation, try delivering your speech with considerable variation or changes in pitch, rate, volume, and intensity. After your experiment with a new delivery style, write a brief report describing what the advantages or disadvantages of the different delivery strategies were.

12
Visual Aids

Seeing . . . , most of all the senses, makes us know and brings to light many differences between things. (John Frederick Peto (1854–1907), Letter Rack. Oil on canvas, 23½ × 19½". The Metropolitan Museum of Art, George A. Hearn Fund, 1955. (55. 176))

ARISTOTLE

Frazier walked to the front of the class and dramatically pulled a 2-foot papier-mâché model of a cockroach out of a sack. He attached a string to the "bug" and suspended it from the ceiling. Then he began his speech about how to rid a home of pests. The trouble was, no one listened to Frazier's message. His audience was obsessed with the creature dangling in midair.

The intention was good, but the execution was bad. Frazier had failed to use visual aids effectively. Visual aids are powerful tools. They can help you to communicate your ideas with greater clarity and impact than can words alone, but they can also overwhelm your speech. You need to follow the guidelines described in this chapter for maximum effectiveness.

A visual aid is any object that calls on sight to help your audience understand your point. Charts, photographs, posters, drawings, graphs, slides, movies, and videos are just some of the types of visual aids that we will discuss. Some of these, such as movies and videos, call on sound as well as sight to help you make your point.

When you are first required to give a speech using visual aids, you may scratch your head, wondering, "How can I use visual aids in an informative or persuasive speech? Those kinds of speeches don't lend themselves to visuals." As it happens, almost any speech can benefit from visual aids. An assignment that requires you to use visual aids is not as different from other types of speeches as you might at first think. Your general objective will still be to inform, persuade, or entertain. The key difference is that a speech having visual aids uses supporting material that can be seen rather than only heard by an audience.

In this chapter, we will look at visual aids as an important communication tool and will also examine several kinds. Toward the end of the chapter, we will suggest guidelines for using visual aids in your speeches.

WHY USE VISUAL AIDS?

Visual aids are invaluable to you as an audience-centered speaker. They help your audience *understand* and *remember* your message, communicate your *organization* of ideas, gain and maintain *attention*, and illustrate a *sequence* of events or procedures.

1. *Visual aids enhance understanding.* Of your five senses, you learn more from sight than the others combined. In fact, it has been estimated that over 80 percent of all information comes to you through sight. To many people, seeing is believing. We are a visually oriented society. For example, most of us learn the news by seeing it on TV. Because your audience is accustomed to visual reinforcement, it is wise to consider how you can increase their understanding of your speech by using visual aids. For example, a picture of Maui will help your listeners understand the beauty of Hawaii better than just a verbal description. As the old cliché has it, a picture is indeed worth a thousand words.

2. *Visual aids enhance memory.* Not only will your audience improve their understanding of your speech, but they will also remember what you say better as a result of visual reinforcement. It is well known that you remember most what you understand best. Researchers estimate that you remember 10 percent of what you read, 20 percent of what you hear, 30 percent of what you see, and 50 percent of what you simultaneously hear and see. During the 1988 Democratic presidential

primary, Michael Dukakis depicted his opponent Richard Gephardt in a commercial doing somersaults. Dukakis wanted people to remember Gephardt's flip-flops on the issues. When the time came to vote in the primary, many people recalled the commercial about Congressman Gephardt, who lost the primary elections.

3. *Visual aids help listeners organize ideas.* Most listeners need help understanding the structure of your speech. Even if you clearly lay out your major point, use effective internal summaries, and make clear transition statements, your listeners will welcome additional help. Listing major ideas on a chart, poster, or overhead transparency will add clarity to your talk and help your audience grasp your main ideas. Visually presenting your major ideas during your introduction, for example, can help your audience follow them as you bring them into the body of your speech. Key ideas can be displayed during your conclusion to help you summarize your message succinctly.

4. *Visual aids help gain and maintain attention.* Marsha began her speech about poverty in America by showing the face of an undernourished child. She immediately had the attention of her audience. Chuck began his speech with the flash of his camera to introduce his photography lecture. He certainly alerted his audience at that point. Midway through her speech about the lyrics in rock music, Julie not only spoke the words but also displayed a giant poster of the song lyrics so that her audience could read the words and sing along. Visual aids not only grab the attention of your listeners but can also be used to keep their interest when words alone might not.

5. *Visual aids help illustrate a sequence of events or procedures.* If your purpose is to inform an audience about a process—how to do something or how something functions—you can do this best through actual demonstrations or with a series of visuals. Whether your objective is instructing people to bake a cake or to build a greenhouse, demonstrating the step-by-step procedures will help your audience understand the processes. If you wish to explain how hydroelectric power is generated, a series of diagrams can help your listeners understand and visualize the process.

When demonstrating how to make something, such as your prize-winning cinnamon rolls, you can have each step of the process prepared ahead of time and show your audience how you go through the steps of preparing your meal. You could have the dough already mixed and ready to demonstrate how you sprinkle on the cinnamon. A climax to your speech could be to unveil a finished pan of rolls still warm from the oven. If time does not permit you to demonstrate how to prepare your rolls, you could have at hand a series of diagrams and photographs to illustrate each step of the procedure.

RECAP

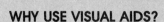

WHY USE VISUAL AIDS?	
	1. They help your audience understand your message.
	2. They help your audience remember your message.
	3. They communicate the organization of your message.
	4. They gain and maintain audience attention.
	5. They illustrate a sequence of events or procedures.

TYPES OF VISUAL AIDS

The first question many students ask when they learn they are required to use visual aids is "What type of visual aid should I use?" We will discuss various kinds, grouped into three classifications: (1) three-dimensional visual aids, (2) two-dimensional visual aids, and (3) audiovisual aids.

Three-Dimensional Visual Aids

Objects   You have played the trombone since you were in fifth grade, so now you decide to give an informative speech about the history and function of this instrument. Your trombone is an obvious visual aid, which you could show to your audience as you talk about how it works. Perhaps you might play a few measures to demonstrate its sound and your talent.

Or you are an art major and have just finished a watercolor painting. Why not bring your picture to class to illustrate your talk about watercolor techniques?

Objects add interest because they are tangible. They can be touched, smelled, heard, and even tasted, as well as seen. Objects are real, and audiences like the real thing.

If you use an object as a visual aid, make sure that it can be handled with ease. If an object is too large, it can be unwieldy and difficult to show to your audience. Tiny objects can only be seen close up. Thus it will be impossible for your listeners to see the detail on your antique thimble, the intricate needlework on your cross-stitch sampler, or the attention to detail in your miniature log cabin. Other objects can be dangerous to handle. One speaker, for example, attempted a demonstration of how to string an archery bow. He made his audience extremely uncomfortable when his almost strung bow flew over the heads of his listeners. He certainly got their attention, but he lost his credibility.

Models   Sometimes it is not possible to bring to the classroom the object you would like to show your audience. It may be too large or too small, too dangerous or illegal. If so, consider showing your audience a model. Since you cannot bring a World War II fighter plane to class, buy or build a scale model instead. To illustrate her lecture about human anatomy, one student brought a plastic model of a skeleton. An actual human skeleton would have been difficult to get and carry to class.

Most colleges and universities do not allow firearms on campus. A drawing that shows the features of a gun is much safer than using a real gun as a visual aid. If you need to show the movable parts of a gun, perhaps a papier-mâché, plastic, or wood model would serve.

As with objects, make sure that your models can be handled with ease and are large enough to be seen by all.

People   In addition to inanimate objects, people can serve as visual aids for a speech. Here are a number of examples. Susan wanted to show some of her own dress designs. She asked several women to model her clothes during her speech. Paul wanted to illustrate several wrestling holds. He used a friend to help demonstrate how he won the district wrestling championship. Linda, a dance instructor, wanted to illustrate how she teaches the latest dance steps. She arranged to have one of her dance students attend her speech to demonstrate her dance techniques. In each of these speeches, the speaker used another person to help communicate an idea.

If you plan to use people to illustrate your message, remember these key points. First, it is usually unwise to ask for spur-of-the-moment volunteers for help while you are delivering your speech. You would do much better to choose a trusted friend or colleague before your presentation so that you can fully inform him or her about what needs to be done. Rehearse your speech using your living visual aid.

Second, it is distracting to have your support person stand beside you doing nothing. If you don't need the person to demonstrate something during your opening remarks, wait and introduce the person to your audience when needed.

Third, remember that *you* can serve as a visual aid to demonstrate or illustrate major points. If you are talking about the game of tennis, you might bring your favorite racquet to class so that you can illustrate your superb backhand or simply show novices the proper way to hold this device. If you are a nurse giving a talk about medical procedures, by all means wear your uniform to establish your credibility.

And fourth, do not allow your assistants to run away with the show. For example, don't let your dance student perform the *pas de bourrée* longer than is necessary to illustrate your technique. Nor should you permit your models to prance about too provocatively while displaying your dress designs. And don't allow your buddy to throw you when you demonstrate the wrestling hold that made you champ. Remember, your visual aids are always subordinate to your speech. You must remain in control.

Two-Dimensional Visual Aids

Although tangible, three-dimensional objects, models, and people can be used to illustrate a talk, the most common visual aids are two-dimensional. Two-dimensional presentation aids include drawings, photographs, maps, graphs, charts, slides, flipcharts, overhead transparencies, and the chalkboard.

Drawings   A drawing is a popular and often-used visual aid because it is easy and inexpensive to make. Drawings can be tailored to your specific needs. To illustrate the functions of the human brain, for example, one student drew an outline of the brain and labeled it with large block letters to indicate where brain functions are located. Another student wanted to show the different sizes and shapes of leaves for trees in the area. She drew enlarged pictures of the leaves, using appropriate shades of green, to communicate the information she wished to impart.

You don't have to be a master artist to develop effective drawings. As a rule, large and simple line drawings are more effective for stage presentations than are detailed images. If you have absolutely no faith in your artistic skill, you can probably find a friend or relative who can help you prepare a useful drawing.

Photographs   Photographs can be used to show objects or places that cannot be illustrated with drawings or that an audience cannot view directly. The problem with photos, however, is that they are usually too small to see clearly. Drugstore or supermarket photo size, even the new 4-by-6 size from 35-millimeter film, is too small to see if you hold it up in front of an audience. If your listeners occupy only two or three rows, it might be possible to hold a photograph close enough for them to see a key feature of the picture. The details will not be visible, however, beyond the first row. Passing a photograph among your listeners is not a good idea either; it creates competition for your audience's attention.

The only sure way to use a printed photograph as a visual aid for a large audience is to enlarge the photograph. An enlarged photograph of your new boat could be nicely integrated into a speech about tips on purchasing a fishing boat. Some photo shops will produce poster-size color laser photocopies at a modest cost. Even though enlarging a photo will involve time and money, it may be just the visual you need to achieve your speaking objective. An alternative to a printed photograph is to take a picture of your photograph with slide film and project the image onto a large screen with a slide projector.

If you use a photograph or slide for your speech visual aid, make sure it is large enough to be seen clearly.
(*Shopper/Stock, Boston*)

Slides   Slides can help illustrate your talk if you have access to a screen and a slide projector. While a photograph of your recent vacation might be too small to be seen, a slide can be projected so that all can see the picture clearly. Remote-control features on many modern projectors help you change from one slide to the next without relying on anyone else for help. And audiences generally enjoy slides, which have an inherent attention factor that a speaker can use to his or her advantage.

But working with slides can present problems also. Many a slide-illustrated lecture has been cut short because the projector bulb burned out or a slide jammed in the projector and could not be extracted. Although slides are not exactly high-tech, they do require attention to technical details.

Moreover, with the lights out, you are less able to receive nonverbal feedback from your listeners and cannot maintain eye contact with your audience.

Giving a slide lecture requires considerable preparation. First, you have to be sure that the slides are put in the order in which they will be needed during your speech. Second, you must know in which direction the slide carousel moves to feed the projector so that you will know how to load it. Third, you must know how to operate the remote-control switch so that you can move back and forth among your slides, if you wish, for the purposes of your talk. All this, of course, requires preparation and practice. Carefully rehearse your speech using your slides and projector.

Maps   Most maps are designed to be read from a distance of no more than 2 feet. As with photographs, the details on most maps won't be visible to your audience. You could use a large map, however, to show general features of an area. Or you can use a magnified version of your map. Certain copiers are able to enlarge images as much as 200 percent. It would then be possible to enlarge a standard map of Europe, let's say, so that your listeners in the last row could see the general features of the continent. Using a dark marker, one speaker highlighted the borders on a map of Europe to indicate the countries she had visited the previous summer. She used a red marker to show the general path of her journey. To use maps effectively, you will probably need to modify your map so that your listeners can both see it and read it.

Graphs   A graph is a pictorial representation of statistical data in an easy-to-understand format. Since statistics are abstract summaries of many examples, most listeners find graphs an effective way to make the data more concrete. Graphs are particularly effective in showing overall trends and relationships among data. The four most common types of graphs are bar graphs, pie graphs, line graphs, and picture graphs.

Bar Graphs   A bar graph consists of flat areas—bars—of various lengths to represent information. The bar graph in Figure 12.1 clearly shows how family free time has recently decreased for most Americans since 1970. Figure 12.2 illustrates the sources of stress in family life. These two graphs make the information clear and immediately visible to the listeners. By comparison, words and numbers are more difficult to assimilate, especially in something so ephemeral as a speech.

Pie Graphs   A pie graph shows the general distribution of data. The two pie

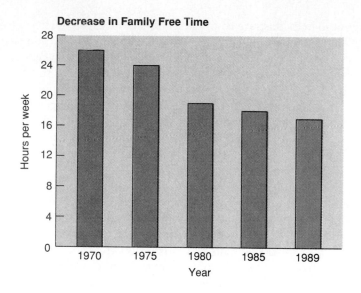

FIGURE 12.1 _____

graphs in Figure 12.3 compare American and European wake-up times. The graphs make it possible to see the most popular and least popular times for arising.

LINE GRAPHS   Line graphs show relationships between two or more variables. Like bar graphs, line graphs plot a course through statistical data to show overall

FIGURE 12.2 _____

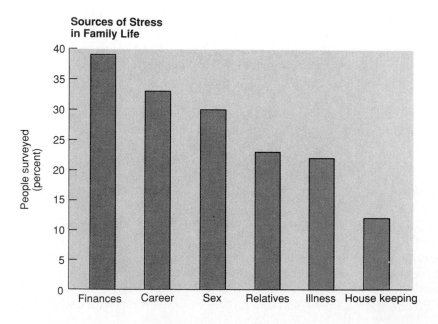

When People Wake Up

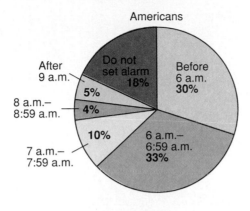

Americans

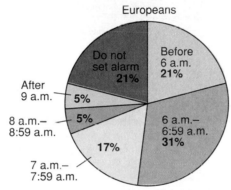

Europeans

FIGURE 12.3

trends (Figure 12.4). A line graph can cover a greater span of time or numbers than a bar graph without looking cluttered or confusing. As with other types of visual aids, a simple line graph communicates better than a cluttered one.

PICTURE GRAPHS   In place of either a line or a bar, you can use pictures to represent the data you are summarizing (Figure 12.5). Picture graphs look somewhat less formal and less intimidating than other kinds of graphs.

Charts   Charts summarize and present a great deal of information in a small amount of space (Figure 12.6). As visual aids, charts have several advantages. They are easy to use, reuse, and enlarge so as to be seen easily. They can also be displayed in a variety of ways. You can use a flipchart, a poster, or an overhead projector, which can enable you to show a giant image of your chart on a screen. As with all other visual aids, charts must be simple. Do not try to put too much information on one chart.

The key to developing effective charts is to prepare very carefully the lettering of the words and phrases you use. If the chart contains too much information, audience members may feel it is too complicated to understand, and ignore it. If your chart looks at all cramped or crowded, divide the information into several

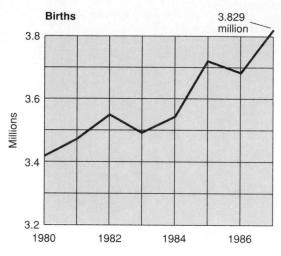

FIGURE 12.4

Source: *National Census Bureau*

charts and display each as needed. Print your letters instead of writing them in longhand. If a computer is available, consider using one that has the software capability to prepare large charts or graphs. Make sure that your letters are large enough to be seen clearly in the back row. Use simple words or phrases, and eliminate unnecessary words. Draft your visual on a small piece of paper before you transfer the information in enlarged form to your poster.

FIGURE 12.5

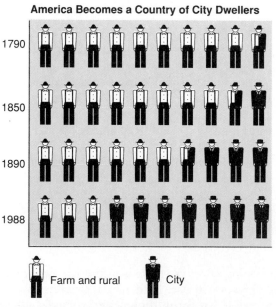

Note how few words are needed to convey the facts because of the multiple visual cues the listener is given.

Change in Leisure-Time Activities 1960-1989	
Gardening	+12%
Bicycling	+10%
Fishing	+9%
Camping	+10%
Jogging	+40%
Golfing	+30%
Opera and musical theater	-38%

FIGURE 12.6

Flipchart   Flipcharts are commonly used in business presentations and training sessions. They consist of a large pad of paper resting on an easel. You can either prepare your visuals on the paper before your speech or draw on the paper while speaking. Flipcharts are easy to use. During your presentation, you need only flip the page to reveal your next visual.

Most experienced flipchart users recommend that you use lined paper to keep your words and drawings neat and well organized. Another suggestion is to make penciled-in speaking notes on the chart that only you can see. Brief notes on a flipchart are less cumbersome than using note cards or carrying a clipboard with notes. If you do use crib notes, however, be sure that your notes are few and brief; using too many notes will tempt you to read rather than have eye contact with your audience.

Overhead Transparencies   As a student, you may be familiar with what an overhead projector looks like, but you probably have had little experience in using one yourself. This instrument projects an image drawn on clear sheets of plastic, called transparencies, onto a screen so that the image can be seen by a large group.

Overhead projectors are popular because they have several advantages. They allow you to maintain eye contact with your audience yet still see your visual by looking at the transparency on the projector. Unlike other projectors, the overhead doesn't require that you turn off the lights in the room to see the projected image. You may wish to dim the lights a bit, but most images can be seen clearly in normal room light. Overheads also permit you to prepare your transparency ahead of time and to make marks on it during your presentation. If you do write during your speech, limit your markings to a few short words or to underlining key phrases.

Consider the following suggestions when using an overhead projector.

1. If possible, practice with the overhead projector in the room in which you will be delivering your speech. That way you can be certain that the projector is the proper distance from the screen and that your image will be large enough to be seen.

Overhead projectors are popular because they have a number of advantages.
(*Gabe Palmer/The Stock Market*)

2. Turn the overhead projector off when not showing your visual so that it will not detract from your speech. One major virtue of overheads is how easy it is to control the projection of visual images. At the touch of a button, your visual appears or disappears from view.

3. Do not put too much information on one transparency. Use no more than seven lines on one sheet. Do not use a full page of typewritten material in an overhead projection.

4. Reveal one line of text at a time by blocking out the text with a sheet of paper. Say you have four key ideas that you want to highlight in your speech. Rather than revealing all four ideas at once, reveal each point as you verbally introduce each idea. This helps hold audience interest.

5. If possible, try leaving the bottom fourth of your transparency blank. Images that are projected low on the screen often are not visible to audience members in the back.

6. Consider using the overhead projector without a transparency as a spotlight to highlight something you have written on a poster or chalkboard. With a large audience, an accent light can add emphasis to other visuals.

7. Consider using color. Colored transparencies are available from most bookstores. You can also use different-colored markers to highlight key points.

8. For ease of handling, place the transparency in a cardboard frame. Such frames are available wherever transparencies are sold. A frame lessens the likelihood that the transparencies will stick together or get torn along the edges.

Chalkboard   For people in college, the most readily accessible visual aid is a chalkboard. A chalkboard has several advantages as a visual medium. It costs little. It is also simple to use; it's low-tech, so you need not worry about extension cords or special techniques. Chalkboards are also widely available. Most classrooms and lecture halls have ready-to-use chalkboards—though sometimes you may have to hunt for chalk and erasers!

Despite the advantages of chalkboards, however, many speech teachers steer their students away from them. When you write on the board, you have your back to your audience; you do not have eye contact! Some speakers try to avoid that problem by having their visual on the board before their speech starts. But if you put your chalk drawing on the board before you speak, you will encounter other problems. For one, your listeners will be looking at your visual rather than listening to your introductory remarks. Moreover, chalkboards are probably the least novel and therefore least interesting visual aid. They are not particularly effective at getting or holding audience attention.

A chalkboard is best used for only very brief phrases, a single word or two, or very simple line diagrams that can be drawn in just a few seconds. It is usually better to prepare a chart, graph, or drawing on a poster or overhead transparency than to use a chalkboard.

Audiovisual Aids

We have discussed several types of visual aids used in public speaking and making presentations. But there are also other kinds of presentational aids. These join sound to sight in communicating ideas. You are probably familiar with all of these: movies, videos, and audio aids such as tapes, records, and compact disks. Now you will encounter these familiar media in a new context. Instead of being passively entertained or instructed by them, you may actively use them to support your ideas.

Movies   Unlike some of the other visual aids we've discussed, movies are large enough to be seen by your audience. Further, they can dramatically capture and hold your audience's attention. But for student classroom speeches, movies are seldom appropriate. We don't recommend their use unless you can achieve your purpose in no other way.

One central problem is that you must turn off the lights so that the visual image can be seen clearly. A darkened room means that you will have less control over your audience; they can become restless and, if bored with the movie, doze off or fall asleep. There is nothing more embarrassing than to hear the loud buzz of someone snoring through your lecture. Remember, movies can be dull as well as interesting.

Most movies are not designed as supporting material for a speech. Usually, they are conceived as self-contained packages. Unless you show only a short excerpt, an entire movie can quickly overwhelm your speech. Instead of serving as an aid in achieving your own particular objective, the movie will take over and steal the show. Of course, if you are a skilled moviemaker, as some of you may well be, you probably have enough control over your medium to tame it and make it serve your purpose.

Movies also need special equipment. Unless you have had experience using a movie projector, you would do well to find another way to communicate your ideas.

Videotape   With the advent of videocassette recorders (VCRs), more public speakers are using videotapes to help communicate their ideas. A VCR can be hooked up to a regular TV to show brief scenes from a rented movie, an excerpt from a training film, or a video that you made yourself with a video camera. Videotapes permit instant replay and stop-action freeze-frame viewing. Some VCRs have a slow-motion function. You can also play and replay a scene several times if you want your audience to watch subtle movement or action.

A 25-inch screen is generally visible to an audience of twenty-five or thirty people. For larger audiences, you will need several TV monitors or a large projection TV system.

As with movies, don't allow the video portion of your speech to take over. Also, you will again need special equipment, so be cautious. Don't assume that all of the necessary extension cords and other hardware will be ready to go. You need to plan your use of video equipment in advance. And as with any external device, rehearse with the equipment until you can handle it smoothly.

Audio Aids   Although we have concentrated on visual aids, we need also to be aware of audio supporting material. Tapes, records, or compact disks can also communicate your thoughts, depending on your topic and speech objective. If you are an organist giving a talk about organ music, you might play a few measures of Bach's Toccata and Fugue in D Minor on tape, record, CD, or a portable electronic keyboard to illustrate some point. While showing slides of her recent Caribbean vacation, a student used a recording of steel drum music as soft background for her talk. Another student interviewed students on campus about local parking problems. Rather than reading quotes from irate drivers who couldn't find a place to park, he played a few excerpts of taped interviews.

As with movies and videos, use audio aids sparingly. You do not want your speech's electronic soundtrack to interfere with your message. Probably the easiest and least expensive audio aid to use is a tape recorder that uses cassettes. It is small enough to handle easily, can be held up to a microphone to amplify the sound to a large audience, and can be cued to start exactly where you want it to. A compact disk has excellent fidelity, can also be cued to start at a certain passage, but takes a separate amplifier and speakers to take full advantage of the increased sound quality. A record player is a bit trickier to use than tape or CD because of the difficulty of getting the needle cued exactly where you want it.

GUIDELINES FOR USING VISUAL AIDS

Make It Easy to See

Without a doubt, the most violated principle of visual aids in public speaking is "Make it big!" Countless speeches have been accompanied by writing on a chart or graph that is too small to read, an overhead projector image that is not large enough to be legible, or a graph on a flipchart that simply can't be understood from the back row. If the only principle you carry away from this chapter is to make your visual aid large enough to be seen by all in your audience, you will have gained more skill than a majority of speakers who use visual aids in speeches. *Write big!*

Select the Right Visual Aid

Because there are so many choices among visual aids, you may wonder, "How do I decide which visual aid to use?" Here are some suggestions.

1. Think of your speech objective. Don't select a visual aid until you have decided on the purpose of your speech.

2. Consider the size of your audience. If you have a large audience, do not choose a visual aid unless it can be seen clearly by all. Suit the aid to the audience.

3. Take into account your own skill and experience. Use only equipment with which you are comfortable or have had practical experience.

4. Know the room in which you will speak. If the room has large windows with no shades and no other way to dim the lights, do not consider using visuals that require a darkened room.

Prepare Your Visual Aid before You Speak

Prepare your visual aid well in advance of your speaking date. Avoid late-night, last-minute visual aid construction. Your waning hours before you give your speech should be devoted to your speech rather than to the preparation of a visual aid. Your visual aid should add strength to your speech, instead of giving the impression of being a mere afterthought.

Rehearse with Your Visual Aid

Jane had trouble. She nervously approached her speech teacher ten minutes before class asking if class could start immediately because her visual aid was melting. She planned to explain how to get various stains out of clothing. Her first point was to show how chewing gum should be removed. She had forgotten the gum, so she had to ask for a volunteer from the audience to spit out his gum so she could use it in her demonstration. The ice that she had brought to rub on the sticky gum had by this time melted. All she could do was dribble some lukewarm water on the gummed-up cloth in a valiant but unsuccessful effort to demonstrate her cleaning method. It didn't work. She was left embarrassed and on the edge of tears. It was obvious that she had not rehearsed with her visual aids.

Your appearance before your audience should not be the first time you deliver your speech holding up your chart, turning on the overhead projector, or using the flipchart. Practice with your visual aid until you feel at ease with it.

Have Eye Contact with Your Audience, Not Your Visual Aid

As do many business speakers, you may be tempted to talk to your visual aid rather than to your audience. Your focus should remain on your audience. Of course, you will need to glance at your visual to make sure that it isn't upside down or that it is the proper visual. But do not face it while giving your talk. Keep looking your audience in the eye.

Talk about Your Visual Aid, Don't Just Show It

Some speakers believe that they need not explain a visual aid. They think it's enough just to show it to their audience. Resist this approach. When you exhibit your chart showing the overall decline in the stock market, tell your audience what point you are trying to make. Visual support performs the same function as verbal support. It helps you communicate an idea. Make sure that your audience knows what that idea is. Your words should tell your listeners what you want them to focus on.

Your focus should remain on your audience, not on your visual aid.
(*Dennis Purse/Photo Researchers, Inc.*)

Don't just unceremoniously announce, "Here are the recent statistics on birth rates in the United States" and hold up your visual without further explanation. Tell them how to interpret the data. Always set your visuals in a verbal context.

Do Not Pass Objects among Your Audience

You realize that your marble collection will be too small to see, so you decide to pass some of your most stunning marbles around while you talk. Bad idea. While you are excitedly describing some of your cat's-eye marbles, you have injected a distraction into your audience. People will be more interested in seeing and touching your marbles than in hearing you talk about them. Like the football "moving pocket" play, you will have a mobile pocket of distraction as your visual aid circulates among your audience. People holding the object will be focused on the object, those who have just held it will be resettling themselves and comparing notes, those who are about ready to hold it will be full of anticipation, and those who sit behind and in front of the circulating visual will be drawn into the logistics of moving the object around. Very few people will be paying attention to you. It is not a good idea to pass objects around during your speech.

What can you do if your object is too small to see without passing it around? If no other speaker follows your speech, you can invite audience members to come up and see your object when your speech is over. If your audience is only two or three rows deep, you can even hold the object up and move in close to the audience to show it while you maintain control.

Use Handouts Effectively

Many speech instructors feel that you should not distribute handouts during a speech. Handing out papers during your presentation will only distract your audience. However, many audiences in business and other types of organizations expect a summary of your key ideas in written form. If you do find it necessary to use written material to reinforce your presentation, keep the following suggestions in mind.

1. Don't distribute your handout during the presentation unless your listeners must refer to the material while you're talking about it. Do not distribute handouts that have only a marginal relevance to your verbal message. They will defeat your purpose.

2. If you do need to distribute a handout and you see that your listeners are giving the written material more attention than they are giving you, tell them where in the handout you want them to focus. For example, you could say, "I see that many of you are interested in the second and third pages of the report. I'll discuss those items in just a few moments. I'd like to talk about a few examples before we get to page two."

3. If your listeners do not need the information during your presentation, tell them that you will distribute a summary of the key ideas at the end of your talk. Your handout might refer to the specific action you want your audience to take, as well as summarize the key information you have discussed.

Time Your Visuals to Control Your Audience's Attention

A skillful speaker knows when to show a supporting visual and when to put it away. For example, it's not wise to begin your speech with all of your charts, graphs, and drawings in full view unless you are going to refer to them in your opening remarks. Time the display of your visuals to coincide with your discussion of the information contained in them.

Jessica was extremely proud of the huge replica of the human mouth that she had constructed to illustrate her talk on the proper way to brush one's teeth. It stood over 2 feet tall and was painted pink and white. It was a true work of art. As she began her speech, she set her mouth model in full view of the audience. She opened her speech, however, with a brief history of dentistry in America. But her listeners never heard a word. Instead, they were fascinated by the model. Jessica would have done better to cover her visual with a cloth and then dramatically reveal it when she wanted to illustrate proper tooth brushing.

Here are a few more suggestions for timing your visual aids.

1. Take your visual aid away when you move to your next point, unless the information it contains will also help you communicate your next idea.

2. Have your overhead transparency already in place on the projector. When you are ready to show your visual, simply turn the projector on to reveal your

drawing. Change to a new visual as you make your next point. Turn the projector off when you are finished with your visual support.

3. Consider asking someone beforehand to help you hold your visual aid, turn the pages of your flipchart, or change the slides on the projector. Make sure that you rehearse with your assistant so that all goes smoothly during your presentation.

Keep It Simple

Simple visuals usually communicate best. Some students think that the visuals accompanying a speech have to be as complicated as a Broadway production, complete with lights and costumes. Resist trying to make your visuals complicated. Indeed, *any* complexity is too much. Words should be limited to key words or phrases. Lengthy dissertations on posterboard or an overhead usually do more harm than good. Don't cram too much information on one visual aid. If you have a great deal of information, it is better to use two or three simple charts or overhead transparencies than to attempt to put all your words on one visual.

Do Not Use Dangerous or Illegal Visual Aids

Earlier we described a speech in which the speaker accidentally caused an archery bow to shoot over the heads of his startled audience. Not only did he lose credibility because he was not able to string the bow successfully, but he also endangered his audience by turning his visual aid into a flying missile. Dangerous or illegal visual aids may shock the audience or physically endanger them. Both kinds of visuals will detract from the speaker's message. Neither is worth the risk of a ruined speech or an injured audience member.

Jim decided to bring a few of his prize pistols to class for his visual aid speech. Even though he knew that they were not loaded, audience members had no way to be sure of that. Nervous during the speech, they were clearly eager to have him finish and leave. The audience focused on the guns' continued presence and not on what Jim said.

Marty decided that the best way to warn his listeners about being slipped illegal drugs unaware was to show the drugs. His display of illegal chemicals made the entire class fidgety, uncertain whether they could be held accountable as accomplices in a possessions charge.

If your speech seems to call for a dangerous or illegal object or substance, substitute a model or some sort of picture, chart, or other representational device.

Use Animals with Caution

Most actors are unwilling to work with animals—and for good reason. At best, they may steal the show. And most often, they are unpredictable. You may *think* you have the smartest, best-trained dog in the world, but you really do not know how your dog will react to a strange environment and an unfamiliar audience. The risk of having an animal detract from your speech may be too great to make planning a speech around one worthwhile.

There have been a number of unfortunate, albeit sometimes humorous, incidents involving public speakers who attempted to use animals as visual aids. A zealous midwestern university student a few years ago decided to give a speech on cattle. What better visual aid, he thought, than a cow? He brought the cow to campus and led her up several flights of stairs to his classroom. The speech in fact went well. But the student had neglected to consider one significant problem: Cows will go up stairs but not down them.

Another student had a handsome, well-trained German Shepherd guard dog. The class was enjoying his speech and his demonstrations of the dog's prowess until the professor from the next classroom poked his head in the door to ask for some chalk. The dog lunged, snarling and with teeth bared, for the unsuspecting professor. Fortunately, he missed—but the speech was concluded prematurely.

These and other examples emphasize our point: Use animals with care, if at all.

Remember Murphy's Law

According to Murphy's Law, if something can go wrong, it will. When you use visual aids, you increase the chance that problems or snags will develop when your present your speech. The chart may fall off the easel, you may not find any chalk, the overhead projector may not be functional. We are not saying that you should be a pessimist, just that you should have a backup plan in case your best-laid plans go awry.

If something doesn't go as you had planned, do your best to keep your speech on track. If the chart falls over, simply pick it up and keep talking; don't offer lengthy apologies. If you can't find the chalk you will need and it is your turn to speak, quietly ask a friend to go on a chalk hunt in another room. A thorough rehearsal and a double check of your needed equipment (such as overhead transparencies, chalk, extension cords, extra projector bulb, or masking tape to hold your poster) can help repeal Murphy's Law.

RECAP

CHECKLIST FOR USING VISUAL AIDS

1. Is your visual aid easy to see or read?
2. Is it the right visual aid to communicate your idea?
3. Have you prepared it carefully?
4. Have you rehearsed with your visual aid?
5. Do you look at your audience when you talk rather than at your visual aid?
6. Do you talk about your visual aid rather than just show it?

7. Can you avoid having to pass around a visual aid?
8. Have you used handouts effectively?
9. Does your visual aid keep your audience's attention focused on your speech?
10. Is it simple and clear?
11. Are your visual aids legal and nonthreatening to your audience?
12. Have you weighed carefully any decision to use an animal as a visual aid?

SUMMARY

Visual aids are tools to help you communicate your ideas better than words alone can. In this chapter, we discussed how visual aids can enhance your message. We looked at different types of visual aids and reviewed general guidelines for their use.

Visual aids help influence your listeners' understanding and recollection of your ideas. They also help you communicate the organization of your ideas, help gain and maintain the audience's attention, and help you illustrate a sequence of events or procedures.

There are a variety of visual aids. Three-dimensional visual aids include objects, models, and people. Two-dimensional visual aids include drawings, photographs, slides, maps, graphs, charts, projected transparencies, flipcharts, and chalkboards. Audiovisual aids include movies and videos. Audio aids such as tapes, records, and compact disks can also be used to help communicate ideas to your listeners.

One of the basic principles of visual aids is "Make it big!" Make your visuals large enough to be seen clearly.

You should adapt your visual aid to your audience, the speaking environment, and the objective of your speech. Prepare your visual well in advance of your speech, and rehearse with the visual aid. Further suggestions include these: Talk about your visual, don't just show it; use handouts effectively; avoid passing objects among your audience; think about the proper timing of your visual; and develop only simple visuals.

QUESTIONS FOR DISCUSSION AND REVIEW

1. Name some of the ways in which visual aids can enhance a speech.
2. What are the different types of visual aids?
3. Are there disadvantages to visual aids? If so, cite some; if not, explain your answer.
4. How many different kinds of audiovisual aids are there? What are they?
5. How would you use visual aids effectively?

SUGGESTED ACTIVITIES

You will need the following materials to complete this assignment:
1. A piece of paper or posterboard measuring at least 15 by 20 inches
2. At least two felt-tip markers or a set of marking pens

3. A ruler or straightedge
4. A pencil with an eraser

Below are five speech topics, a brief description of each (as needed), and a group of statistics or other content that could be communicated with the help of a visual aid. Design and complete *two* visual aids (one on each side of your paper).

a. A demonstration speech showing the class how to make a simple recipe called peanut butter balls.

> 1/2 c. peanut butter
>
> 3 1/2 tbsp. powdered dry milk
>
> 1 tsp. honey
>
> Combine all ingredients. Roll into balls. Refrigerate the balls. Optional additions: raisins, nuts, coconut, brown sugar, sunflower seeds.

b. A speech analyzing the presidential debates of October 7, 1984. The following statistics were found in *Newsweek* for October 15, 1984: After the debate, an audience rated the candidates on several scales. For example, 37 percent rated Ronald Reagan as thoughtful and well-informed, and 45 percent rated Walter Mondale the same; 33 percent thought Reagan was confident and self-assured, and 55 percent thought Mondale was; 50 percent found Reagan more likable, and 40 percent found Mondale more likable; finally, 55 percent of the audience thought Reagan had better ideas for keeping the country prosperous, but only 35 percent thought Mondale had better ideas.

c. A speech on the importance of nonverbal communication. During a discussion of how we communicate emotion nonverbally, the speaker wants to present the figures that about 55 percent of emotion is communicated facially, about 38 percent is communicated vocally, and only about 7 percent is communicated verbally.

d. A speech on career counseling. During the speech, statistics are quoted from *Parents* magazine, in which a woman undergoing career counseling is asked to lay out her ideal plan of time allotment. She hopes to spend 35 percent of her time at a part-time job, 10 percent doing housework, 20 percent in activities with her children, 12 percent cooking, 7 percent socializing, 6 percent watching TV, and 10 percent reading and working on hobbies.

e. A speech on the importance of calcium to the diet. *Good Housekeeping* reports on the calcium contents of certain common foods: 1 cup of 2 percent milk has 352 mg, 1 cup of lowfat yogurt has 294 mg, 1 ounce of cheddar cheese has 213 mg, 1 cup of ice cream has 194 mg, and 1 cup of broccoli has 136 mg.

13

Using Words Well
Speaker Language and Style

OBJECTIVES

After studying this chapter, you should be able to

1. Compare and contrast the concepts of denotation and connotation
2. Identify four characteristics of using language effectively
3. Describe the differences between written style and oral style
4. Identify suggestions for using techniques of language style and figurative language
5. Describe ways of using language effectively in public speeches

Proper words in proper places, make the true definition of a style. (Stuart *Davis*, Blips and Ifs, *1963–1964. Oil on canvas, 71¹/₈ × 53¹/₈". Amon Carter Museum, Fort Worth. 1967. 195.*)

JONATHAN SWIFT

A sign in a clothing store window invites customers:

COME INSIDE AND HAVE A FIT.

An announcement in a church bulletin:

THURSDAY AT 5:00 PM THERE WILL BE A MEETING
OF THE LITTLE MOTHER'S CLUB.
ALL WISHING TO BECOME LITTLE MOTHERS
WILL PLEASE MEET THE MINISTER
IN HIS STUDY.

An advertisement for room service in a hotel tells you:

IF YOU WISH FOR BREAKFAST,
LIFT THE TELEPHONE AND ASK FOR ROOM SERVICE.
THIS WILL BE ENOUGH FOR YOU
TO BRING UP YOUR FOOD.

A sign at the front desk of another hotel reads:

IF YOU CONSIDER OUR HELP IMPOLITE,
YOU SHOULD SEE THE MANAGER.

Some hospitals display this sign:

NO CHILDREN ALLOWED IN THE MATERNITY WARDS.

A sign in a laundry suggests:

LADIES, LEAVE YOUR CLOTHES HERE
AND SPEND THE AFTERNOON HAVING A GOOD TIME.

A sign in a popular cocktail lounge reads:

LADIES ARE NOT TO HAVE CHILDREN IN THE BAR.

These examples clearly show that unfamiliarity with the common idiom can lead to some unintentionally funny remarks. Language can easily lead you astray. Communicating accurately and clearly is a challenge that is often not met by either private individuals or public speakers. The right word or phrase can indeed be very elusive.

In this chapter, we will focus on language and its role in communicating your ideas. Specifically, we will discuss the power of words to communicate with other people and also to confuse them. We will also suggest ways to communicate your ideas and feelings to others accurately and effectively. In the last half of the chapter, we will focus on how to speak with style—how to make what you say memorable. We will review techniques of language and end with some general recommendations for using various stylistic devices in your speeches.

Denotation and Connotation

What makes for all the difficulty in communicating? One reason is that most of language operates on two levels. These are known as denotative and connotative meanings. The **denotation** of a word is its restrictive or literal meaning. For example the word *goose* refers denotatively to a large waterfowl. The extension of the literal meaning through a process of association is known as the **connotation** of the word. In the case of *goose*, this word has the connotation of "fool," "simpleton," or "dummy," as in the phrase "silly goose."

In many instances, the context will tell you which level of meaning is intended. For example, if you heard the sentence "The mother goose led her goslings across Boston Common once again this morning," you would have no trouble figuring out which sense of *goose* was meant. If you overhead someone say, "Oh, he acted like an old goose last night," you would likewise have no difficulty recognizing the connotative meanings here.

Recognizing the old goose from its context is easy. But some contexts are not so easy and can cause unintended difficulties for the speaker. For example, if you heard someone say, "The old man called me into his office for a chat," you wouldn't be able to tell if it was an elderly man or the speaker's boss or father who called him into the office.

Connotative meanings often reflect the unique or individual associations you may have with a word, whereas the denotative meaning is usually more descriptive or literal. For example, the word *table* is defined denotatively in the dictionary as a piece of furniture consisting of a smooth flat slab affixed on legs. But when you think of the word *table*, you think of the old oak table your grandparents used to have. The word may evoke an image of you playing checkers with your grandmother. The word *table* connotes this special or unique meaning based on your past experiences.

In large measure, both the denotative and connotative meanings in our examples are public—that is, they are easily recognized by most people in our culture. But some words also have private associations or connotations in addition to their public ones. For example, the word *fireplace* has, in addition to its literal meaning, the publicly recognized connotation of warmth, friendship, hospitality, and the like. But for some individuals it may connote fire, destruction, and loss. Private meanings are difficult to predict, but as a public speaker, you should be aware of the possibility when choosing your words. This is particularly important when discussing highly emotional, controversial topics.

The Power of Language

As the students filed into the classroom, they thought it strange that their professor was handing out cookies. Yet many students accepted a crisp, tasty-looking cookie. It had every appearance of an oatmeal cookie that might well win an award at the state fair. As you would expect, the students began to munch their snack as they

THE NATURE OF LANGUAGE

denotation
The literal meaning of a word.

connotation
The individual or personal meaning of a word.

settled in for class. The professor walked to the front of the room and said, "I hope you enjoyed those cookies, which my wife baked. They're made from a special family recipe." The students smiled appreciatively.

"But there is one thing I forgot to tell you," the professor declared. "My wife did not have any oatmeal, so she used crushed dog biscuits!"

The students' faces immediately mirrored their horror. Dog biscuits? Some students began to spit their snack into the wastebasket. Others gulped hard and ran for the water fountain.

After the shock took hold, the professor confessed with a sheepish grin, "No, she really didn't use dog biscuits; she used oatmeal." He had dramatically driven home the point of the day's lecture: Even if our senses tell us that something is pleasing, words can override the sensory message. The cookies tasted fine until the students throught they contained dog biscuits instead of oatmeal.

Words have power. In a sense, they create our world. As a public speaker, your words fashion the mental images your audience "sees." Words can also affect your listeners' attitudes and behavior. Let's consider the power of words in greater detail.

Words Create Mental Images   We usually give scientists credit for "discovering" new truths and insights because they are able to translate reality into words. For example, you probably believe that Sir Isaac Newton *discovered* gravity. What he really did was *label* it. The concept "gravity" exists because Newton named it.

Some people would go so far as to say that language not only helps us to *discover* our world but actually to *invent* it. One philosopher has noted, "To name is to call into existence—to call out of nothingness."[1] In a very real sense, to name something creates it for us.

As a public speaker, you too have the power to create. Your words and phrases create mind's-eye pictures of faraway places or describe common situations with new insight. Your words can trigger images and meanings for your listeners, so take considerable care in choosing the words you use to communicate with your listeners.

Words Can Influence Attitudes   The words used to describe something can affect your attitudes and feelings about it. General Motors, for example, claims that a Cadillac does not break down, it simply "fails to proceed." Mobile home salespersons try to sell "preowned homes" rather than "used trailers." They know that the way an object is described affects your attitude toward that object.

As a speaker, your choice of words can influence the way your listeners will respond to your message. You can describe a university or college as either a "great institution of higher learning" or a "two-bit party school." To move to the national political scene, you can describe former Lieutenant-Colonel Oliver North's sale of arms to the Nicaraguan Contras in the mid-1980s as patriotic or as unlawful. Your choice of words conveys your attitudes to your audience and can also bring about a change in your listeners' attitudes. Words have the power to shape and transform ideas, values, opinions, and judgments.

Words Can Affect Behavior   What you say can also influences the way people behave. A salesperson earns his or her living by using words to affect behavior. Politicians too use words in an effort to influence your behavior—they want your vote in the next election.

A sociology professor in the 1960s wanted to illustrate the power of words in influencing behavior. He divided his class into two groups of students. To participate in the experiment, students had to have a car and a good driving record. Students in one group were told simply to drive around normally, with no changes in their driving patterns or routines. Students in the second group were given large orange-and-black bumper stickers that read, "Black Panthers." They too were told to drive as they normally would, obeying all the rules and regulations.

Within just a few days, the professor had to discontinue the study. The students who had Black Panther bumper stickers were harassed by other motorists and also received significantly more traffic tickets than students without bumper stickers.[2] The words *Black Panthers* in the 1960s influenced how other people behaved toward you.

Public speakers can wield tremendous power and influence. Nations have gone to war because of the way national leaders have influenced the attitudes and behaviors of their citizens. Franklin Delano Roosevelt's announcement of the bombing of Pearl Harbor on December 7, 1941, "a day that shall live in infamy," aroused the anger of the American people against the Japanese and strengthened their dedication to the war in the Pacific that followed. President Kennedy's inaugural address set the tone for the early months of his presidency. Ronald Reagan's nominating speech for Barry Goldwater at the 1964 Republican convention served as a key factor in catapulting Reagan to national political prominence. Carefully chosen words have often moved people to action.

USING LANGUAGE EFFECTIVELY

Language plays a major role in shaping how you see the world and in affecting your response to your surroundings. As a speaker, your challenge is to use words well so that you can communicate your intended message. As we have noted, communication is a fragile process, chiefly because people's differing experiences result in differing perceptions. As speakers, we rarely convey exactly what we intend. Yet language has the power to create images and influence attitudes and behavior. In short, the use of language deserves thoughtful attention. Every speaker is challenged to select his or her words and sentences as accurately and effectively as possible. Ideally, language should be concrete, vivid, simple, and correct. We shall discuss each of these factors.

Language Should Be Concrete

A concrete word refers to an object or describes an action or characteristic in the most specific way possible. An abstract word is more general. The word *book* is more concrete than the words *reading material*. The word *apple* is more concrete

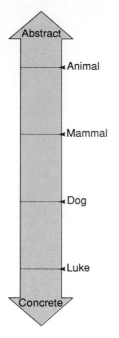

FIGURE 13.1

A "ladder of abstraction" is used by semanticists to show how a concept, idea, or thing can be described in either concrete or abstract terms.

than the word *fruit*. *Screamed* is more concrete than *said*. *Little brick schoolhouse* is more concrete than *building*. *Lamp, chimney,* and *meander* are other examples of concrete words, while *lighting fixtures, structure,* and *travel* are their abstract equivalents. Concrete words communicate more clearly than abstract words in most circumstances.

A linguistic theory known as general semantics holds that the more concrete your words, the clearer your communication. Semanticists use a "ladder of abstraction" to illustrate how a concept, idea, or thing can be described in either concrete or abstract terms. Figure 13.1 is an example. The words are most abstract at the top of the ladder and become more concrete as you move down the ladder. For maximum clarity in your communication, you should use more concrete words than abstract ones in your speeches. As Ralph Waldo Emerson noted, "Wise men pierce this rotten diction and fasten words again to visible things."

Language Should Be Vivid

Language that creates a bold and forceful image is vivid. When you speak vividly, you appeal to the senses and also engage your listeners so that they will remember what you say. Language that describes color, sound, light, textures, smells, and taste in stirring words is lively, which is what the word *vivid* means.

If you were describing your pet snake to your audience, you would do more than say it is a 3-foot-long serpent approximately 2 inches in diameter. Your audience would not be able to form much of an image of your pet from such a description. Instead, use as much sensual imagery as you can. Think of the colors and patterns on your snake. What would your listeners feel if they touched it? Would it feel cold, clammy, soft? What does the snake sound like? Describe its hiss. Describe your snake in terms that would appeal to your listeners' senses.

When searching for the right word to make your language lively, consult a thesaurus—a book that lists synonyms. But in searching for an alternative word, do not feel that you have to choose the most obscure or unusual term to vary your description. Language that is both animated and simple can very effectively evoke an image for your listeners.

Language Should Be Simple

The best language is often the simplest. Your words and sentences should be immediately understandable to your listeners. Don't try to impress them with jargon and complicated sentences. Instead, as linguist Paul Roberts advises, "Decide what you want to say and say it as vigorously as possible . . . and in plain words."[3]

In his essay "Politics and the English Language," George Orwell lists rules for clear writing. Several are worth remembering.

> Never use a long word where a short one will do. If it is possible to cut a word out, always cut it out. Never use a foreign phrase, a scientific word, or a jargon word if you can think of an everyday English equivalent.[4]

These few rules may serve as a short guide to powerful public speaking.

As an effective public speaker, you will want to eliminate words and sentences that clutter or confuse clear communication. Tape-record your practice sessions. As you play the tape back, listen for chances to say what you want with fewer words. Used wisely, simple words and simple phrases communicate with great power and precision. But don't restrict yourself to simple phrases and sentences or your speech will be choppy. A few carefully worded complex or compound sentences will add variety to your speech.

RECAP

BEWARE OF BAFFLEGAB   Do you have "bafflegab"? Here is an example of it.

> Bafflegab is multiloquence characterized by consummate interfusion of circumlocution or periphrasis, inscrutability, incognizability, and other familiar manifestations of abstruse expatiation commonly used for promulgations implementing procrustean determinations by governmental bodies.

If you are afflicted with this dread disease, read two doses of Strunk and White's *Elements of Style* and take a cold shower before going to bed.

Language Should Be Correct

A public speech is not the place to demonstrate your lack of familiarity with English grammar. Your effectiveness as a public speaker depends on a variety of factors, one of which is your ability to use the English language correctly. If you are unsure of the way to apply a grammatical rule, seek assistance. *The Handbook of Current English* by Perrin, Smith, and Corder is one classic resource that can help you resolve questions about language usage. The following discussion may also help.

1. *Confused and misused word pairs.* Archie Bunker, the central character of the TV comedy "All in the Family," became famous for his *malapropisms*. A **malapropism** is the substitution of one word for another closely resembling it in sound but having a very different meaning. Archie might call a *travelogue* a *travesty*, refer to a *subscription* as a *prescription*, and substitute *indiscretion* for *indigestion*. The humor of such confusion is obvious. But unless you want to be funny and deliberately use malapropisms, be certain to use the correct word of such pairs.

malapropism
The confusion of two words that have a similar sound but different meanings.

Another type of word pair confusion results from words that are similar in meaning but have slight differences in usage or are somewhat different grammatically. Here are some of the more common of these pairs:

a. *among/between:* These two prepositions have the same meaning but are used in different situations. Something occurs *between* two people, places, or things. But the same situation occurs *among* three or more. Consider these examples:

The relationship *between* the two brothers is strong.
The relationship *among* the seven brothers is strong.

b. *can/may:* Most people have studied this word pair since elementary school, but many are still uncertain or just careless about the distinction between the two words. So one more time: *Can* means "able." *May* indicates that permission is given.

He *can* swim the length of the pool.
He *may* go swimming today.

c. *farther/further: Farther* expresses literal distance or measurement. *Further* indicates figurative advancement.

They live *farther* from us than they used to.
He can go no *further* in his present job.

d. *fewer/less: Fewer* refers to objects that can be separated and observed individually. *Less* refers to a portion of a mass, such as a gas or a liquid.

There are *fewer* people here than I expected.
There is *less* punch left over than we had estimated.

e. *imply/infer:* Writers and speakers imply; readers and listeners *infer.*

She *implied* that the final exam would be difficult.
He *inferred* from the paper that the regents' action was justified.

The five commonly confused word pairs just discussed are by no means the only ones of their kind. But they are among the pairs most commonly misused by speakers. Learning them so that you can easily and quickly choose the correct word of each pair will improve your ability to use language correctly.

2. *Dangling and misplaced modifiers.* Concern about where to place modifying words, phrases, and clauses is somewhat unique to English-speaking people. Most other languages rely on word endings to indicate certain grammatical keys to determining modifications. The English language relies almost solely on placement in the sentence.

A dangling modifier is a word, phrase, or clause that does not logically qualify, limit, or describe anything in a sentence. Here is an example:

Arriving early for class, the door was still locked.

Arriving early for class does not connect with anything in the sentence. Its placement would suggest that it modifies door, but that possibility does not make sense. The sentence should be rewritten so that it reads, "Arriving early for class, I found the door still locked." Now it is clear that the phrase modifies the pronoun *I.*

A similar error occurs when a word, phrase, or clause seems to modify a word in the sentence, but the relationship is not what the speaker intended. A misplaced modifier can be found in this sentence:

The instructor handed out the papers *with few words*.

The placement of the phrase *with few words* indicates that it describes the papers. What the speaker really meant was that the instructor did not say much when returning the papers. A more accurate sentence would be, "With few words, the instructor handed out the papers."

3. *Subject-verb agreement*. **Agreement** is the grammatical term used to describe the correct relationship between a subject and its verb. Simply stated, a singular subject takes a singular verb, and a plural subject takes a plural verb.

In English, most verbs have only two forms in the present tense (the third person singular adds *s*, as in "he speaks") and only one in the past tense. Subject-verb agreement becomes a challenge in only a few specific kinds of situations, including these:

a. *Compound subjects*: If two or more subjects are joined by *and*, they usually require a plural verb:

George and Martha *visit* their children frequently. (Remember, a plural verb, unlike a plural noun, is the form *without* an *s* on the end.)

If compound subjects are joined by *or* or *nor*, the verb must agree with the subject nearest it:

Either the coach or the players *are* responsible for that prank. (In this sentence, *are*, the plural form of *be*, agrees with the plural subject *players*.)

Neither his parents nor he *plans* to visit that area again soon. (In this case, the singular verb *plans* agrees with the singular pronoun *he*.)

b. *Collective nouns*: A collective noun that refers to a group as a whole requires a singular verb:

The class *plans* to attend the special legislative session.

If the collective noun refers to a group acting individually, a plural verb is used:

The class *plan* to adopt a number of special projects for the semester.

c. *Indefinite pronouns: Somebody, anybody, everybody, nobody, someone, anyone, everyone, no one, either, neither,* and *each* are singular indefinite pronouns and require singular verbs:

Anybody *is* able to understand the problem when you explain it that way.
Each of her friends *plans* to contribute to the special fund.

d. *Relative pronouns*: The verb following the relative pronoun *who, which*, or *that* agrees with the antecedent of the pronoun (the noun to which it refers):

agreement
The grammatical term used to describe the correct relationship between a subject and its verb or a pronoun and its antecedent.

This is one of those instances that *confuse* me. (*Confuse* agrees with *instances*.)
There are many people who *support* him. (*Support* agrees with *people*.)

4. *Pronoun-antecedent agreement*. Just as a subject must agree in number with its verb, so must a pronoun agree with its antecedent, the noun to which it refers. Pronoun-antecedent agreement is not generally difficult but may confuse a speaker in the following instances.

a. *Separation of pronoun and antecedent*: If the pronoun and its antecedent are separated in the sentence, it is easy to become confused and make the pronoun agree with some intervening word:

Many citizens believe with great fervor that the government owes *them* a living. (*Them* agrees with its antecedent, *citizens*.)
Before I had a chance to read his manuscript and consider his unique ideas, I was not sure *it* should be published. (*It* agrees with its antecedent, *manuscript*.)

b. *Compound antecedents*: If two or more antecedents are joined by *and*, the pronoun is always plural:

Betty and Janice are going to study together for *their* history exam.

If antecedents are joined by *or* or *nor*, the pronoun will agree with the antecedent closest to it (just as a verb will agree with it nearest subject):

Neither Mark nor his parents are certain what course of action *they* should take.
The children or their teacher is going to accept *her* award.

c. *Collective antecedents*: If a collective antecedent (*mob, group, class, team*) is being considered as a whole, the pronoun will be singular. If a collective antecedent refers to the members as individuals, any pronoun referring to the noun will be plural.

The team received *its* trophy during a special assembly.
The team received *their* ribbons from the track meet today.

d. *Indefinite pronouns:* Just as they cause problems with subject-verb agreement, singular indefinite pronouns often confuse pronoun-antecedent agreement. The singular indefinite pronouns *somebody, anybody, everybody, nobody, someone, anyone, everyone, no one, each, either*, and *neither* are considered singular antecedents.

Anybody can boost his or *her* grade point average by taking that class.
Everybody thinks *he* knows how to listen well without being taught.

If any of the four areas of English usage just discussed are weak points for you, be especially aware of them as you practice your speeches. Tape and listen to your oral delivery. Check your language so that you can pick out errors and correct them. If you feel overwhelmed by the rules of grammar and usage, take heart:

There are a number of guides to writing well that you can use, even though there are some marked differences between speaking styles and writing styles.

RECAP

USING WORDS WELL   To make your language concrete, use specific words.

To make your language vivid, choose words that appeal to your listeners' senses.

To make your language simple, avoid a long word when a short one will do.

To make your language correct, learn the differences between certain word pairs, avoid dangling and misplaced modifiers, and monitor subject-verb and antecedent-pronoun agreement.

ORAL STYLE VERSUS WRITTEN STYLE

When you think of someone's having "style," you probably first think of the way he or she dresses. Well, language is very much like clothing. You "dress" your ideas in the words you choose. And just as your wardrobe can give you a distinctive and attractive style, so your choice of words can give your thought a distinctive and attractive form of expression. In the last analysis, style—whether in clothing or language—is a way of expressing yourself.

Your speech has memorable style when you use words and phrases that are distinctive. Most everyday speech lacks a distinctive style. Most sentences consist of a subject-verb or subject-verb-object form of construction. Sometimes, though, you, like most of us, may say something in a way that is different from the normal phrasing of a sentence. You must use a word or phrase in a way that is unique and original with you. That is speaking with a distinctive style. Before identifying some techniques to add style to your speeches, let's note some general differences in style between the way you talk and the way you write.

Your instructor has probably told you not to write your speech out word for word. The professor has said this because of the differences between writing and talking. There are at least three major differences between a written style and an oral style of language.

1. *An oral style is more personal.* When speaking, you can look your listeners in the eye and talk to them directly. If you see that they don't like or don't understand what you are saying, you can adjust your statements and explanations to gain greater acceptance. In other words, you and your audience can interact, something a writer and reader cannot do. This interaction provides you, the public speaker, with personal contact and exchange of warmth with your audience, an experience not available to the writer working alone in seclusion. That warmth and personal contact affects your speech and your verbal style. As a speaker, you are likely to use more

pronouns (*I*, *you*) than you would in writing. You are also more likely to address specific audience members by name.

2. *An oral style is less formal.* Written communication often uses a somewhat formal language and structure. If should be noted that memorized speeches usually sound like they were written because the words and phrases are longer, more complex, and more formal than those used by most speakers. Spoken communication, by contrast, is usually less formal, characterized by shorter words and phrases and less complex sentence structures. Speakers generally use many more contractions and colloquialisms than writers. Oral language is also much less varied than written language, with only fifty words accounting for almost 50 percent of what we say. Finally, spoken language is often less precise than written language. Speakers are more likely than writers to use somewhat vague quantifying terms, such as *many*, *much*, and *a lot*.

3. *An oral style is more repetitious.* When you don't understand something you are reading in a book or an article, you can stop and reread a passage, look up unfamiliar words in the dictionary, or ask someone for help. When you're listening to a speech, those opportunities usually aren't available. For this reason, an oral style is and should be more redundant. When you study how to organize a speech, you learn to provide an overview of major ideas in your introduction, develop your ideas in the body of the speech, and summarize key ideas in the conclusion. You build in repetition to make sure that your listener will grasp your message. Even during the process of developing an idea, it is sometimes necessary to state it first, restate it in a different way, provide an example, and finally summarize it. Your English professor probably warned you not to repeat yourself as you write. But oral presentations *should* have greater redundancy than written presentations.

Of course, there are great variations in both written and oral styles. Spoken language may sometimes be quite formal and written language may at times be informal, so that the demarcation between the two verbal styles is not always pronounced. You have only to compare the writing styles of William Faulkner and Ernest Hemingway or the speaking styles of Ronald Reagan and Jimmy Carter to glimpse a small part of the variations that are possible. Faulkner's work, for example, is characterized by long, complex sentences and sophisticated vocabulary, as in this description of the Grierson family home from his short story "A Rose for Emily":

> It was a big, squarish frame house that had once been white, decorated with cupolas and spires and scrolled balconies in the heavily lightsome style of the seventies, set on what had once been our most select street. But garages and cotton gins had encroached and obliterated even the august names of that neighborhood; only Miss Emily's house was left, lifting its stubborn and coquettish decay above the cotton wagons and the gasoline pumps—an eyesore among eyesores.[5]

In comparison, a passage from Hemingway's *The Sun Also Rises* conforms more closely to the style that we have described as oral. He frequently writes in the first person and relies on much shorter, simpler sentences and vocabulary:

> Someone asked Georgette to dance, and I went over to the bar. It was really very hot and the accordion music was pleasant in the hot night. I drank a beer, standing in the doorway and getting the cool breath of wind from the street. Two taxis were coming

down the steep street. They both stopped in front of the Bal. A crowd of young men, some in jerseys and some in their shirtsleeves, got out.[6]

Just as writing styles vary widely, so too do speaking styles. Note the use of personal pronouns, contractions, and relatively short sentences in this excerpt from a 1984 speech by Ronald Reagan:

> We've also offered to increase significantly the amount of U.S. grain for purchase by the Soviets, and to provide the Soviets a direct fishing allocation off U.S. coasts. But there's much more we could do together. I feel particularly strongly about breaking down the barriers between the peoples of the United States and the Soviet Union, and between our political, military, and other leaders.[7]

In contrast, the style of Jimmy Carter's announcement of the 1980 Russian grain embargo conforms more closely to what we have described as a typical written style: fewer personal pronouns and longer and more complex sentences:

> These actions will require some sacrifice on the part of all Americans, but there is absolutely no doubt that these actions are in the interest of world peace and in the interest of the security of our own nation, and are also compatible with actions being taken by our own major trading partners and others who share our deep concern about this new Soviet threat to world stability.[8]

The point here is that there is no definitive boundary between written style and oral style. The personality of the speaker or writer, the subject of the discourse, the audience, and the occasion all affect the style of the language used. In general, however, it is correct to say that oral style is usually more personal, less formal, and more repetitious than written style.

RECAP

ORAL STYLE VERSUS WRITTEN STYLE	Oral Style	Written Style
	More personal, facilitating interaction between speaker and audience	Less personal with no immediate interaction between writer and reader
	Less formal	More formal
	More repetitious	Less repetitious

The President of the United States is scheduled to make an important speech in your hometown. Since you have never seen or heard a president, you decide to attend the speech. You find his thirty-minute presentation both interesting and

TECHNIQUES OF LANGUAGE STYLE

informative. In the evening, you turn on the news to see how the networks cover his address. All three major networks excerpt the same ten-second portion of his speech. Why? What is it that makes certain portions of a speech quotable or memorable? What techniques do speech writers, as well as advertisers, use to add emphasis and pizzazz to their language? As we observed earlier, a memorable style deviates from the usual sentence arrangement and word choice. We'll examine seven stylistic devices that can help make speeches memorable by varying from the normal way we use language.[9]

Omission

▼
ellipsis
Dropping a word or phrase the listener expects to hear.

Omission is a stylistic technique that boils an idea down to its essence. When you drop a word or phrase that we expect to hear, you are using **ellipsis**, another word for omission. Telegrams often use an economy of words, since you are charged by the word and the more you can leave out, the cheaper will be your cost. But of course the words you leave out must be understood by your listeners or readers. For example, a captain of a World War II Navy destroyer used omission to inform headquaters of his successful efforts at sighting and sinking an enemy submarine. He spared all details when he cabled back to headquarters: "Sighted sub—sank same." Using as few words as possible, he communicated his message in a memorable way. About 2000 years earlier, another military commander had informed his superiors in Rome of his conquest of Gaul with the economical message: "I came, I saw, I conquered." That commander was Julius Caesar.

Advertisers love to use omission. They first coin a slogan, then repeat it again and again until the public know it so well that they will mentally finish the phrase when they see or hear the first part of it. The omission of the word or phrase causes the listener to take a more active role in the advertisement and, the advertiser hopes, to think more about the product. Here are some famous examples:

"You can take Salem out of the country, but . . . you can't take the country out of Salem."
"When you say Budweiser, . . . you've said it all."
"Just say no . . . to drugs."

In each case, the part of the slogan after the ellipsis points was eventually dropped from the advertisement.

Inversion

▼
inversion
Reversing the normal word order of a phrase or sentence.

Inversion is the technique of reversing the normal word order of a phrase or sentence. It is commonly used in poetry. Within a few lines of *Paradise Lost*, Milton refers to "Spirits damn'd" and "Creatures rational,"[10] inverting the usual English adjective-noun pattern to a less common noun-adjective pattern. Speakers, too, use inversion to make their remarks memorable. In his 1852 eulogy for Daniel Webster, clergyman Theodore Parker asked, "Do men now mourn for him, the great man eloquent?"[11] And John F. Kennedy inverted the usual subject-verb-object sentence pattern to object-subject-verb in this brief declaration from his 1961 inaugural address: "This much we pledge . . ."[12]

Suspension

When you read a mystery novel, you are held in suspense until you reach the end and learn who "done it." The stylistic technique of verbal **suspension** does something similar. It occurs when you use a key word at the end of a sentence, rather than at the beginning. When Abraham Lincoln left Springfield, Illinois, for Washington, D.C., in the winter of 1861, he told his friends, "To this place, and the kindness of these people, I owe everything."[13] The more usual, but less memorable, structure would have been, "I owe everything to this place and the kindness of these people."

Advertisers use the technique of suspension frequently. A few years ago, the Coca-Cola Company used suspension as the cornerstone of its worldwide advertising campaign. Rather than saying, "Coke goes better with everything," the copywriter decided to stylize the message by making *Coke* the last word in the sentence. The slogan became "Things go better with Coke." Again, the stylized version was more memorable because it used language in an unexpected way.

Parallelism

Parallelism occurs when two or more clauses or sentences have the same pattern. For example, a speaker may pattern two or three consecutive sentences subject-verb-object or subject-verb–prepositional phrase. The result is rhythmical and conveys a sense of balance that makes the parallel structures memorable.

When he delivered the Phi Beta Kappa oration at Harvard in 1837, Ralph Waldo Emerson cast these simple expressions in parallel structures:

> We will walk on our own feet; we will work with our own hands; we will speak our own minds.[14]

Another example of parallel structures occurs in Frederick Douglass's rousing address commemorating the Declaration of Independence and condemning slavery in 1852:

> The feeling of the nation must be quickened; the conscience of the nation must be quickened; the propriety of the nation must be startled; the hypocrisy of the nation must be exposed.[15]

parallelism
Occurs when two or more clauses or sentences have the same pattern.

Antithesis

▼
antithesis
A sentence or phrase which uses parallel structure with one section contrasting with the other.

The word **antithesis** means "opposition." In language style, antithesis is a sentence having a parallel structure, but with the two parts contrasting each other. One part balances the other. The Salem cigarette commercial discussed earlier is one famous example: "You can take Salem out of the country, but you can't take the country out of Salem." This slogan was derived from the maxim "You can take the boy out of the country, but you can't take the country out of the boy."

Speakers have long realized the dramatic potential of antithesis. In Franklin Roosevelt's first inaugural address, he declared, "Our true destiny is not to be ministered unto but to minister to ourselves and to our fellow men."[16] Both in meaning and structure, his words foreshadowed the more famous remark of John F. Kennedy nearly thirty years later: "Ask not what your country can do for you, rather ask what you can do for your country."[17] We will examine Kennedy's statement in great detail later in this chapter.

Antithesis is not restricted to politicians and ad makers. When William Faulkner accepted the Nobel prize for literature in 1950, he spoke the now famous antithetical phrase: "I believe that *man will not merely endure*: *he will prevail*."[18] An antithetical statement is a good way to end a speech. The parallel structure provides a comforting sense of closure to a presentation.

Repetition

Repetition of a key word or phrase gives rhythm, power, and structure to your message. At the climax of Patrick Henry's "Liberty or Death" speech in 1775 was this passionate use of repetition: "The war is inevitable—and let it come! I repeat it, sir, let it come!"[19] Franklin D. Roosevelt's first inaugural address is powerful and memorable for a variety of reasons, one of which is his use of repetition. His repeated use of the phrase "It can be helped" exemplified his rhetorical skill in providing hope to a depression ravaged nation:

> The task can be helped by definite efforts to raise the values of agricultural products and with this power to purchase the output of our cities.
> It can be helped by preventing realistically the tragedy of the growing loss, through foreclosure, of our small homes and our farms.
> It can be helped by insistence that the Federal, State and Local governments act forthwith on the demand that their cost be drastically reduced.
> It can be helped by the unifying of relief activities which today are often scattered, uneconomical and unequal.
> It can be helped by national planning for and supervision of all forms of transportation and of communications and other utlities which have a definite public character.[20]

▼
alliteration
The repetition of a consonant sound (usually the first consonant) several times in a phrase, clause, or sentence.

Alliteration

Alliteration is the repetition of a consonant sound (usually an initial consonant) several times in a phrase, clause, or sentence. Alliteration adds rhythm to a thought.

Two mid-twentieth-century orators who favored alliteration were Franklin Roosevelt and Winston Churchill. Roosevelt called for "discipline and direction" in his first inaugural address;[21] little more than a week later, in his first fireside chat, he urged weary listeners to have "confidence and courage."[22] Churchill, rousing Englishmen to resist the Nazi onslaught in 1940, used the alliterative phrase "disaster and disappointment."[23] Addressing the Congress of the United States a year later, he praised "virility, valour and civic virtue."[24] Too much alliteration can sound forced and can actually detract from your message, but used sparingly, alliteration can add rhythm to your rhetoric.

A Second Look at Language Style Techniques

We'd like to illustrate all seven techniques of language style with one final example.[25] If you asked almost anyone for the most quoted line from President Kennedy's speeches, that quote would probably be "Ask not what your country can do for you; ask what you can do for your country." Besides expressing a noble thought, a prime reason this line is so quotable is that it uses all seven stylistic techniques.

"Ask not . . ." is an example of omission. The subject, *you,* is not stated.

"Ask not" is also an example of inversion. In casual, everyday conversation, we

"Ask not what your country can do for you; ask what you can do for your country," illustrates a number of stylistic devices.

(*UPI/Bettmann Newsphotos*)

would usually say "do not ask" rather than "ask not." The inversion makes the opening powerful and attention-grabbing.

The sentence also employs the technique of suspension. The key message of the phrase is suspended or delayed until the end of the sentence: "ask what you can do for your country." If the sentence structure had been reversed, the impact would not have been as dramatic. Consider: "Ask what you can do for your country rather than what your country can do for you."

Kennedy uses parallelism and antithesis. The sentence is a parallel construction of two clauses, one in opposition to the other.

He also uses the technique of repetition. He uses a form of the word *you* four times in a sentence of seventeen words. In fact, he uses only eight different words in his seventeen-word sentence. Only one word, *not* occurs only once in the entire sentence.

Finally, Kennedy adds alliteration to the sentence with the words *ask*, *can*, and *country*. The alliterative *k* sound is repeated at more or less even intervals.

RECAP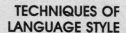

TECHNIQUES OF LANGUAGE STYLE

Omission	Drop words that are obviously understood from phrases; boil an idea down to its essence.
Inversion	Reverse the expected order of words and phrases.
Suspension	Place a key word at the end of a phrase or sentence.
Parallelism	Use the same word structure to begin several sentences or phrases.
Antithesis	In a parallel structure, oppose one part of a sentence to another.
Repetition	Repeat a key word or phrase several times for emphasis.
Alliteration	Use the same initial consonant sound several times in a phrase or sentence.

USING FIGURATIVE LANGUAGE

figure of speech
Using language which deviates from the expected meaning of words to make a description or comparison unique, vivid, or memorable.

metaphor
An implied comparison between two dissimilar things.

Besides using the specific techniques we have just reviewed, you can also add style to your message by using figures of speech. A **figure of speech** deviates from the ordinary, expected meanings of words, to make a description or comparison unique, vivid, and memorable. Figures of speech include metaphors, similes, and personification.

Metaphor

A **metaphor** is an implied comparison. By equating two words or phrases not usually considered alike, it compares two dissimilar things, as in the following examples:

She is a beautiful flower.
This exam was a real bear.
Life is a river.

Speakers use metaphors to paint vivid, concrete images in the minds of their audiences. In the 1837 Harvard address cited earlier, Ralph Waldo Emerson declares: "The dread of man and the love of man shall be a wall of defense and a wreath of joy around all."[26] Emerson's metaphors, "wall of defense" and "wreath of joy", give concreteness to the abstract concepts of defense and joy. Listeners can more easily visualize a wall and a wreath.

Elizabeth Cady Stanton's stirring 1848 address to the first women's rights convention contains this metaphorical proclamation: "In the degradation of woman the very fountains of life are poisoned at their source."[27] Stanton's metaphor, equating life with a fountain, vividly expresses the injustice and peril inherent in the degradation of woman. In that same speech, Stanton goes on to coin such metaphors as "flowers of popular applause," "thorns of bigotry and prejudice," "dark storm clouds of opposition," and "stormy bulwarks of custom and authority." Like alliteration, metaphor should be used with discretion. By today's standards, her use of metaphor seems flowery and excessive. But to the audiences of her day, who delighted in such language, Stanton must have seemed a great speaker indeed.

Simile

A **simile** is also a comparison. More overt than a metaphor, a simile includes the word *like* or *as*. Here are some examples:

simile
An overt comparison between two dissimilar things, which uses the word *like* or *as*.

Life is like a river.
She has a personality like a shining star.
He is as grumpy as a bear before breakfast.

Similes, used sparingly and with creativity, can help you communicate your ideas in an interesting manner.

General Douglas MacArthur, in his address to Congress on April 19, 1951 (the "Old Soldiers Never Die" speech), observed: "Like a cobra, any new enemy will more likely strike whenever it feels that the relativity in military or other potential is in its favor."[28] MacArthur's choice of simile works well. The serpentine image is graphic, and his specific choice of *cobra* suggests the possibility of sudden and swift death. The further the comparison can be extended, the better the simile or metaphor works.

Personification

Personification is the attribution of human qualities to inanimate things or ideas. Like metaphor and simile, if used thoughtfully and sparingly, personification can

personification
The attribution of human qualities to inanimate things or ideas.

help create vivid imagery for an audience. In his eulogy for Daniel Webster, Theodore Parker proclaims, "Massachusetts, the dear old mother of us all! Oh! let her warn her children to fling away ambition."[29]

By vesting a state with the human quality of motherhood, Parker implies a beloved, protective guardian. Franklin Roosevelt's oratorical skill was noted earlier. Roosevelt makes nature a generous provider in this statement from his first inaugural: "Nature still offers her bounty and human efforts have multiplied it. Plenty is at our doorstep."[30]

EFFECTS OF USING STYLISTIC TECHNIQUES

Using the stylistic techniques we have discussed can have important benefits for you as a public speaker. But stylistic devices should not be used to camouflage lack of content. Nor should your speech be so stylized that it sounds like flowery poetry rather than a speech. That said, the discreet use of stylistic devices can have positive effects in public speaking.

1. An effective speaking style helps gain and maintain attention. Since by definition a verbal style is language used in a way that deviates from the usual way we talk, a properly styled speech can help add interest and keep your audience tuned in to what you want to say.

2. An effective speaking style helps your listener understand your message. Sometimes using a metaphor or a simile is the most effective way of helping your audience understand the idea you want to communicate. Using a figure of speech can make what you have to say meaningful to your listener.

3. An effective speaking style helps your audience remember your message. Using the verbal techniques we discussed here can help your audience recall an idea more easily. As we have noted, advertisers want you to remember their product. They use slogans, jingles, and phrases that incorporate effective principles of style to help you remember and ultimately purchase their product. As a public speaker, you can assist your audience in recalling your message, particularly its key ideas, if you too incorporate the principles of style discussed in this chapter.

SUGGESTIONS FOR USING LANGUAGE EFFECTIVELY

We have explored several ways to add interest and power to your language by describing how to incorporate stylistic devices in your speech. The techniques of omission, inversion, suspension, parallelism, antithesis, repetition, alliteration, metaphor, simile, and personification can be of great benefit to you as you seek to make your speeches interesting, understandable, and memorable. We end this chapter by reviewing some key principles that can help you use these techniques with skill.

1. Do not overstylize your speech. Even though we have made great claims for the value of style, do not overdo it. Including too much highly stylized language can put the focus on your language rather than on your content. Use style sparingly.

2. Consider using stylistic techniques in your opening sentences, statement of key ideas, and conclusion. Save your use of stylistic devices for times during your speech when you want your audience to remember your key ideas or when you wish to capture their attention. Some kitchen mixers have a "burst of power" switch to help you churn through difficult mixing chores with extra force. Think of the stylistic devices that we have reviewed as opportunities to provide a burst of power to your thoughts and ideas.

3. Seek opportunities to use short, common words effectively. Long words give style to language because we usually use short words in our everyday speech. But short words are more forceful than long ones. Think of cursewords—the most forceful words in any language. Think of those monosyllabic commands—Sit! March! Stop! When a technical term is too unusual or cumbersome, find a way to describe the concept with another word, or use a simile or a metaphor. To talk about the process of floccinaucinihilipipification (the action or habit of estimating something as worthless) may make an interesting speech, but the word itself probably will not add to your audience's ability to remember it.

4. Use stylistic devices to economize. When sentences become too long or complex, see if you can recast them with antitheses or suspensions. Also remember the possibility of omission.

5. Become aware of style in messages. As you watch TV, listen to the radio, or read newspapers and magazines, look for effective examples of the use of style in language. When you watch the evening news, see if the "sound bites" from politicians' speeches or the quotes from experts illustrate uses of stylistic techniques. You'll be surprised at how many of the commercials and excerpts from speeches employ principles of style.

6. Practice using style in your messages. Seek ways to apply the principles that we have discussed here to your speeches. Chances are that your everyday conversation already has some style. When you want to give a command to someone, you probably use the technique of omission ("Come here" rather than "You come here"). When you are trying to memorize something, you know the value of repetition. Repeating something over and over helps you remember it. Since you were in grade school, you have probably used name calling, a form of metaphor, either to persuade or to catch attention ("Hey, smarty pants"). Now channel these and the other stylistic techniques to work for you in your public speaking.

In this chapter, we suggested ways to use words that can give you ideas maximum impact. We began by discussing the imprecise nature of language; it is sometimes difficult to communicate exactly what you mean. We also observed that language is powerful. Words have the ability to create powerful images in the minds of your listeners. Words can affect attitudes as well as behavior.

To be effective, language should be concrete, vivid, simple, and correct. We explored principles of usage that can help you speak clearly and correctly.

SUMMARY

It is not a good idea to write your speech out word for word. As we discussed in Chapter 11, reading a polished speech from a manuscript will make you sound stilted. In this chapter, we noted that there is a difference between the way we talk and the way we write when it comes to our use of language. In general, oral style is more personal, less formal, and more repetitious than written style.

The last part of this chapter focused on how to use language in an interesting way to express your ideas forcefully and memorably. We provided definitions and examples of the techniques of omission, inversion, suspension, parallelism, antithesis, repetition, and alliteration. We also made suggestions for using such figures of speech as metaphor, simile, and personification.

Effective speakers take great care in wording their speeches. Time invested in using words well can help you gain and maintain the attention of your listeners, help your audience understand your message, and help them remember what you say.

QUESTIONS FOR DISCUSSION AND REVIEW

1. What criteria determine effective language use?
2. Compare and contrast oral style with written style.
3. Provide examples of the techniques of language style.
4. Differentiate among the uses of metaphor, simile, and personification.
5. Why stylize a message?
6. Make suggestions for using language effectively.

SUGGESTED ACTIVITIES

1. Consult *Roget's Thesaurus*, a comprehensive collection of synonyms for words, and find a different word to express each of the following:

cry	rich
clumsy	love
error	smooth
cold	surprise
frightened	restore
great	full
little	increase

2. The following phrases are memorable portions of famous speeches. Compare and contrast these phrases with an ordinary way of expressing the same thought.[30]

   "an iron curtain"

   "Give me liberty or give me death!"

   "The only thing you have to fear is fear itself."

   "I have but one lamp by which my feet are guided, and that is the lamp of experience."

"Speak softly, and carry a big stick."

"You shall not crucify mankind upon a cross of gold."

3. Find examples of omission, inversion, suspension, parallelism, antithesis, repetition, and alliteration in the speeches in Appendix C.

4. Identify examples of attention-catching use of language in TV, radio, or magazine advertisements.

14

Speaking to Inform

OBJECTIVES

After studying this chapter, you should be able to

1. Identify the four goals of speaking to inform
2. Describe five different types of informative speeches
3. Discuss defining, describing, and narrating as methods of informing
4. Explain the four-part structure of most narratives
5. List and explain ten principles for preparing an informative speech

Not only is there an art in knowing a thing, but also a certain art in teaching it. (*Sir Lawrence Bragg*, Christmas Lecture On Electricity, *1961. Royal Institute, London. Superstock*)

CICERO

As you are raking leaves in your front yard, a car pulls over and a bewildered woman pokes her head out of the window. "How do you get to Interstate Seventy from here?" she yells.

Your history professor has asked each student to give an oral report describing one battle from the Civil War. You decide to review the Battle of Gettysburg.

Each Thanksgiving you send your aunt a fruitcake made from your unique prize-winning recipe. This Thanksgiving, when she comes for her annual visit, she asks you to tell her how to make your special cake.

In each of these situations, your task is to give information to someone. Whether in a chance conversation or a formal speech, you will often find that your speaking purpose is to inform. To inform is to teach someone something you know. You have probably heard more informative speeches than any other type of speech. From your first days of watching "Sesame Street," "Mr. Rogers," and "Captain Kangaroo" (if you grew up in the 1960s or 1970s), up through the English lecture you attended yesterday, you have listened to and learned from informative speaking. In the course of many everyday events, you have given information as well. Now you will learn to impart knowledge and understanding to others in a planned, formal way.

Conveying information to others is a useful skill in almost all walks of life. You may find that informing others will be an important part of your job, perhaps as a regional manager of a national corporation reporting the sales figures from the last fiscal quarter or as an accountant teaching your secretary how to organize your files. Other activities, such as teaching a Chinese cooking class or chairing monthly meetings of the Baker Street Irregulars, can also require you to provide information.

In this chapter, we will suggest ways to build on your experience and enhance your skill in informing others. First, we will identify the goals of informative speaking. Next, we will examine different types of informative tasks. We will then discuss specific methods of informing others. Finally, we will present some general principles of making informative presentations.

GOALS OF INFORMATIVE SPEAKING

When you are required to inform others, you have a challenging task. The information you communicate to someone else is rarely, if ever, completely understood as you intended it. As we discussed in Chapter 4, one day after hearing your presentation, most audiences will remember only about half of what you told them. And they will recall only about 25 percent two weeks later. Your job is to ensure as much retention of what you have conveyed as possible by presenting the information as effectively as you can. Remember to keep your speech centered on your audience. Your key objectives are to make your ideas clear, accurate, vivid, and interesting to your listeners.

1. *Your message should be clear.* Can you decipher the following examples of "technospeak"?

Avian species of identical plumage congregate.

Freedom from incrustations of noxious substances is contiguous with conformity to divine prescription.

Male cadavers are unyielding of testimony.

How much easier to say "Birds of a feather flock together," "Cleanliness is next to godliness," and "Dead men tell no tales"![1]

Clarity comes from using the words, phrases, examples, and visual aids that best convey your idea to your listeners. A clear statement should be easy to understand. It should be free of jargon, "flowery expressions," and complex sentence patterns. Communication is a process of creating meaning in a listener. To accomplish this, use verbal and nonverbal symbols that your listener can understand and remember.

2. *Your message should be accurate.* Three guidelines should help you avoid the potential embarrassment of inaccurate information:

    a. Double-check the facts and figures you present to your listeners.

    b. Eliminate rumors and hearsay.

    c. Instead of relying solely on your recollection of an event, person, process, or idea, consult dictionaries, encyclopedias, newspapers, and other research sources to confirm the accuracy of your information.

3. *Your message should be vivid.* Earlier we noted the challenge you face in making your message memorable. In addition to being clear and accurate, a memorable thought must be expressed in language that comes alive. As we pointed out in Chapter 13, the words you choose should paint unforgettable pictures in the minds of your listeners.

Most of us can easily spot vivid language. Of each pair of words below, which is the livelier one?

blow, howl

dog, beagle

cook, broil

noise, rumble

In each case the second word conjures up a more specific, vivid, and memorable image.

Speakers sometimes turn to figurative language to enliven their speeches. William Jennings Bryan's speech to the Democratic National Convention in Chicago on July 8, 1896, is known today by the metaphor he employed in his conclusion: ". . . you shall not crucify mankind upon a cross of gold."[2] The "Cross of Gold" speech aroused the convention delegates and ensured Bryan's nomination for the presidency. To use vivid language requires an effort of the imagination, but it helps ensure memorability.

4. *Your message should be interesting.* Your listeners can be interested in your topic for a variety of reasons. It can affect them directly, it can add to their knowledge, it can satisfy their curiosity, or it can entertain them. These are not mutually exclusive, of course. For example, if you were talking to a group of business people about the latest changes in local tax policies, you would be discussing something that

If you grew up in the 1960s or 1970s, you have listended to and learned from informative speaking since your earliest days of watching "Sesame Street." (© 1985, Children's Television Workshop)

would affect them directly, add to their knowledge, and satisfy their curiosity. But your listeners' primary interest would be in how taxes would affect them. By contrast, if you were giving a lecture on fifteenth-century Benin sculpture to a middle-class audience at a Y, your listeners would be interested because your talk would add to their knowledge, satisfy their curiosity, and provide them with entertainment. Your talk on African sculpture can also affect your listeners directly by making *them* more interesting to others. In both instances, your speech arouses interest because it offers your audience a benefit—in the first example, practical; in the second, cultural. If your audience feels that they will benefit from your speech in some way, your speech will interest them. And an interesting speech commands attention as well as respect.

TYPES OF INFORMATIVE SPEECHES

There are several types of informative speeches, which can be classified according to the subject areas they cover. By classifying these speeches, you can systematically develop ideas for particular speech topics. Informative speeches are most often about (1) ideas, (2) objects, (3) procedures, (4) people, or (5) events.

Speeches about Ideas

Speeches about ideas are usually more abstract than the other types of speeches. Principles, concepts, and theories are at the heart of idea speeches. These might be subjects of idea speeches:

> Principles of communication
> Freedom of speech
> Evolution
> Theories of aging
> Hinduism
> Communal living
> Trickle-down theory of economics

Most speeches about ideas are organized topically (by logical subdivisions of the central idea) or according to complexity (from simple ideas to more complex ones). The following example illustrates how one student organized an idea topic into an informative speech:

Topic: Liberation theology
General Purpose: To inform
Specific Purpose: At the end of my speech, the audience should be able to discuss the definition and origin of liberation theology in Latin America.

I.   Definition of liberation theology
   A. Theological concepts

  B. Sacramental innovations and explanations
  C. Social theories
 II. Intellectual origins of liberation theology
  A. In Christian tradition and thought
  B. In Marxism minus atheism

This student decided that the most logical way for her to explain liberation theology was to talk first about the *definition of liberation theology* and second about its *origins*. Her organization is *topical*—a logical division of available information about liberation theology (see Chapter 8 for more information on topical organization).

Speeches about Objects

A speech about an object might be about anything tangible—anything you can see or touch. You may or may not show the actual object to your audience while you are talking about it. (Chapter 12 provides suggestions for using objects as visual aids to illustrate your ideas.)

 Objects that could form the basis of an interesting speech might include these:

A collection of yours (rocks, record albums, plants, etc.)
Cars
Musical instruments
Personal computers
Videotape recorders
Compact disks
Antiques

 The time limit for your speech will determine the amount of detail you can share with your listeners. Even in a 30- to 45-minute presentation, you cannot talk about every aspect of any of the objects listed. So you will need to focus on a specific purpose. Here's a sample outline for a speech about an object.

Topic: Rocks
General Purpose: To inform
Specific Purpose: At the end of my speech, the audience should be able to discuss the appearance, origins, locations, and uses of the three great rock groups.

 I. Igneous rock
  A. What it looks like
  B. How it is formed
  C. Where it is found
  D. Industrial and commercial uses
 II. Sedimentary rock
  A. What it looks like
  B. How it is formed

        C. Where it is found
        D. Industrial and commercial uses
III.   Metamorphic rock
        A. What it looks like
        B. How it is formed
        C. Where it is found
        D. Industrial and commercial uses

Speeches about objects may be organized topically (the speech on the three great rock groups is practically self-organizing, according to the three groups themselves). This type of speech may also be organized chronologically. A speaker might, for example, focus on the history and development of the piano. That speech would probably be organized chronologically.

Notice that subpoint B for each type of rock in the outline is a discussion of how the rock was formed. If a how or how-to discussion becomes the central focus of a speech, it then becomes a speech about a procedure.

Speeches about Procedures

A speech about a procedure discusses how something, for example, the human circulatory system, works or describes a process that produces a particular outcome, such as how grapes become wine. At the close of such a speech, your audience should be able to describe, understand, or perform the procedure you have described. Here are some examples of procedures that could make effective informative presentations:

> How state laws are made
> How the U.S. patent system works
> How a rotary engine works
> How to refinish furniture
> How to give a speech
> How to bake
> How to avoid long lines at registration

Notice that all these examples start with the word *how*. A speech about a procedure usually focuses on how a process is completed or how something can be accomplished.

Here's a sample speech purpose and outline for a speech about a procedure:

Topic: How to hang wallpaper
General Purpose: To inform
Specific Purpose: At the end of my speech, the audience should be able to describe how to hang wallpaper.

I.   Materials needed to hang wallpaper
   A. Wallpaper
   B. Paste
   C. Straightedge
   D. Brush
II. Steps involved in hanging wallpaper
   A. Prepare the walls.
   B. Decide where to begin.
     1. Find a hidden corner.
     2. Drop a plumb line.
   C. Prepare the wallpaper.
     1. Measure walls and paper.
     2. Cut the paper.
     3. Paste the paper.
     4. Fold the paper.
   D. Hang the wallpaper.
     1. Hang from the top.
     2. Match seams and patterns.
     3. Smooth the paper.
     4. Trim the paper.

This speech, like most other speeches about a procedure, consists of a chronological progression or a series of steps. Notice this speaker's organizational strategy. Instead of listing a dozen parallel steps, she grouped her ideas into two main points, the second of which has four subpoints. This organization of her speech will make it much easier for her audience to remember her directions than if she had listed a dozen separate steps without any organizational strategy.

   Another speaker, describing how to make German chocolate brownies, used an organizational strategy that grouped some of her steps together like this:

I.   Add dry ingredients.
   A. Sugar
   B. Flour
   C. Salt
   D. Baking powder
II. Add liquid ingredients.
   A. Milk
   B. Vanilla
   C. Water
   D. Eggs
III. Mix the ingredients.
   A. Dry ingredients
   B. Liquid ingredients
   C. Dry and liquid ingredients together
IV. Bake the ingredients.

Her audience will remember the four general steps much more easily than they could have hoped to recall each ingredient as a separate step.

Many speeches about procedures include visual aids (see Chapter 12). Whether you are teaching people how to hang wallpaper or how to bake brownies, showing them how to do something is almost always more effective than just telling them how to do it.

Speeches about People

A biographical speech could be about someone famous or about someone you know personally. Most of us enjoy hearing about the lives of real people, whether famous or not, living or dead, who had some unique quality about them. The key to presenting an effective biographical speech is to be selective. Don't try to cover every detail of your subject's life. Relate the key elements in the person's career, personality, or other significant life features so that you are building to a particular point rather than just reciting facts about an individual. Perhaps your grandfather was known for his generosity, for example. Mention some key experiences from his philanthropic adventures to make a point about sharing. If you are talking about a well-known personality, pick information or a period that is not widely known, such as the person's childhood or private hobby.

One speaker gave a memorable speech about his neighbor.

> To enter Hazel's house is to enter a combination greenhouse and zoo. Plants are every-where; it looks like a tropical jungle. Her home is always warm and humid. Her dog Peppy, her cat Bones, a bird named Elmer and a fish called Frank can be seen through the philodendron, ferns, and pansies. While Hazel loves her plants and animals, she loves people even more. Her finest hours are spent serving coffee to her friends and neighbors, playing Uno with family until late in the evening, and just visiting about the good old days. Hazel is one of a kind.

Note how the speech captures Hazel's personality and unique charm. Speeches about people should give your listeners the feeling that the person is a unique, authentic individual.

Most of us would think we'd talk about the life of a person in chronological order—birth, school, career, marriage, achievements, death. However, if you are interested in presenting a specific theme, for example, "Winston Churchill, master of English prose," you may decide instead to organize those key experiences top-ically—Churchill first as a brilliant orator whose words alone stood up against German steel in 1940, then as a cub reporter in South Africa during the Boer War of 1899 to 1902.

Speeches about Events

Where were you on January 28, 1986—the day the *Challenger* space shuttle exploded and killed all seven astronauts on board? Chances are that you clearly remember

A major event, such as the explosion of the Challenger, can form the basis of a fascinating informative speech.
(*NASA*)

where you were and what you were doing on that and other similarly fateful days. Major events punctuate our lives and mark the passage of time.

A major event can form the basis of a fascinating informative speech. You can choose to talk about an event that you have either witnessed or researched. Your goal is to describe the event in concrete, tangible terms and to bring the experience to life for your audience. Have you ever experienced a hurricane? Have you witnessed the inauguration of a president, governor, or senator? Were you in New York City for the Statue of Liberty centennial celebration? Or you may want to re-create an event that your parents or grandparents lived through. What was it like to be in Pearl Harbor on December 7, 1941?

You may have heard a recording of the famous radio broadcast of the explosion and crash of the dirigible *Hindenburg*. The announcer's ability to describe both the scene and the incredible emotion of the moment has made that broadcast a classic. As that broadcaster was able to do, your purpose as an informative speaker describing an event is to make that event come alive for your listeners and to help them visualize the scene.

Most speeches built around an event follow a chronological arrangement. But a speech about an event might also describe the complex issues or causes behind the event and be organized topically. For example, if you were to talk about the Civil War, you might choose to focus on the three causes of the war:

I.   Political
II. Economic
III. Social

Although these main points are topical, specific subpoints may be organized chronologically. However you choose to organize your speech about an event, your audience should be enthralled by your vivid description.

RECAP ▼

TYPES OF INFORMATIVE SPEECHES		
	Speeches about ideas	Include a discussion of principles, concepts, and theories
	Speeches about objects	Discuss something tangible
	Speeches about procedures	Review how something works or describe a process
	Speeches about people	Describe either famous people or personal acquaintances
	Speeches about events	Describe an actual occurrence

METHODS OF INFORMING

We have discussed the kinds of topics that are appropriate for an informative speech. Let us now consider the key methods of informing others: (1) defining, (2) describing, and (3) narrating. These methods were also discussed in Chapter 6.

Defining

Your basic responsibility as a public speaker is to make sure that the words and phrases you use are clearly understood by the audience. Definitions are the means whereby you can explain words and phrases that may be unfamiliar to your listeners.

With swift changes occurring in every area of life, new words appear in our vocabulary almost daily. *Entropy, Contras, AIDS, paper profits, digital recording,* and *compact disk* are just a few of the terms we have learned recently. The second edition of the unabridged *Random House Dictionary of the English Language*, published in 1987, contains 50,000 words and 75,000 definitions more than the first edition, published in 1966.[3] It is therefore not surprising that skill in defining terms is an important asset when giving information in a speech.

There are several ways to inform through definition, including these:

1. Quote a dictionary.
2. Identify the origin of the word.
3. Put the definition in your own words.
4. Define with examples.
5. Use an operational definition.

When deciding which kind of definition to use, think of the complexity of the word or phrase, the audience's knowledge of the subject, and the kinds of definition appropriate for that particular term. Do not rely unquestioningly on dictionary definitions alone.

Describing

When you describe, you provide new information. Generally, descriptions provide more detail than do definitions. Descriptions answer the questions *who, what, where, why,* and *when. Who* is your subject? *What* is the process, place, idea, or event that you want to describe? *Where* and *when* did the event take place? *Why* did it happen, or *why* is it important to the audience? (Of course, not all of these questions apply to every description.)

Word pictures were defined in Chapter 6 as lively descriptions that help your listeners form a mental image by appealing to their senses of sight, taste, smell, sound, and touch. The following suggestions will help you construct effective word pictures.

1. Form a clear mental image of the person, place, or object before you try to describe it.

2. Describe the appearance of the person, place, or object. What would your listeners see if they were looking at it? Use lively language to describe the flaws and foibles, bumps and beauties of the people, places, and things you want your audience to see. Make your description an invitation to the imagination—a stately pleasure dome into which your listeners can enter and view its treasures with you.

3. Describe what your listeners would hear. Use colorful, onomatopoetic words, such as *buzz, snort, hum, crackle,* or *hiss*. These words are much more descriptive than the more general term *noise*. Imitate the sound you want your listeners to hear with their "mental ear." For example, instead of saying, "When I walked in the woods, I heard the sound of twigs breaking beneath my feet and the wind moving

Barbara Bush often reads to children, adding interest to her stories by paying careful attention to details and descriptions.
(*Carol Powers/The White House*)

the leaves above me in the trees," you might say, "As I walked in the woods, I heard the crackle of twigs underfoot and the rustle of leaves overhead."

4. Describe smells, if appropriate. What fragrance or aroma do you want your audience to recall? Such diverse subjects as Thanksgiving, nighttime in the tropics, and the first day of school all lend themselves to olfactory imagery. No Thanksgiving would be complete without the rich aroma of roast turkey and the pungent, tangy odor of cranberries. A warm, humid evening in Miami smells of salt air and gardenia blossoms. And the first day of school evokes for many the scents of new shoe leather, unused crayons, and freshly painted classrooms. In each case, the associated smells greatly enhance the overall word picture.

5. Describe how an object feels when touched. Use words that are as clear and vivid as possible. Rather than saying that something is rough or smooth, use a simile, such as "the rock was rough as sandpaper" or "the pebble was as smooth as a baby's skin." These descriptions appeal to both the visual and tactile senses.

6. Describe taste, one of the most powerful sensory cues, if appropriate. Thinking about your grandmother may evoke for you memories of her rich homemade noodles; her sweet, fudgy, nut brownies; and her light, flaky, buttery pie crust. Descriptions of these taste sensations would be welcome to almost any audience, particularly your fellow college students subsisting mainly on dormitory food or their own cooking! More important, such description can help you paint an accurate, vivid image of your grandmother.

7. Describe the emotion that a listener might feel if he or she were to experience the scene you describe. If you experienced the scene, describe your own emotions. Use specific adjectives rather than general terms such as *happy* or *sad*.

One speaker, talking about receiving her first speech assignment, described her reaction with these words: "My heart stopped. Panic began to rise up inside. Me? . . . For the next five days I lived in dreaded anticipation of the forthcoming event."[4]

Note how effectively her choice of such words and phrases as "my heart stopped," "panic," and "dreaded anticipation" describe her terror at the prospect of making a speech—much more so than if she had said simply, "I was scared."

The more vividly and accurately you can describe emotion, the more intimately involved in your description the audience will become.

Narrating

When you are selecting supporting materials for a speech, you would do well to remember: *Everyone likes to hear a story*. You may tell a story or use an extended illustration because it has a point, objective, moral, or punch line. The anecdote or illustration helps your listeners visualize what they hear. When telling your story, make it interesting by paying careful attention to details and descriptions.

Garrison Keillor, creator of the imaginery town of Lake Wobegon, had for many years a successful radio program called "A Prairie Home Companion." Having devoted some portion of each broadcast to oral storytelling, Keillor observed that the key to telling a story well is to furnish enough information to set the scene and move the action along but not so much detail that the words get in the way of a listener's imagination. He wanted his listeners to re-create the story in their own minds.[5]

Just how does one set the scene and move the action along? Most good stories follow a four-part structure: (1) the opening, (2) the complications, (3) the climax, and (4) the resolution. These four steps follow a chronological pattern. Let's look at each of these steps more closely.

1. *Opening*. The opening of a story should set the stage for the action you are about to describe. You need to provide a word picture. What should your listeners see, hear, or feel as the curtain goes up on your story? One student set the following scene for her listeners:

> Sandy is a kindergartner. Her classroom is a typical kindergarten classroom where the children greet each other every morning in loud voices and throughout the day are anxious to share with their friends their new discoveries. They are an active, happy group of children who talk while they learn.[6]

2. *Complication*. Since the ancient Greeks, authors and playwrights have known that the key to riveting an audience's attention is conflict or complication. Once you have set the scene, you should describe some difficulty, conflict, or problem to arouse interest and develop the drama. After introducing Sandy, our student speaker complicated her story in the following way:

> When Sandy first entered the classroom, she stayed apart from all the other children and cried if asked to speak. When I first met Sandy in her classroom, she came close to tears

when I asked her her name and could only whisper it in her teacher's ear. An untrained observer would not know that Sandy has no physical disability and is intelligent—in fact, an early reader.

3. *Climax*. After you have started your story and described the conflict, you need to develop the complication to a climax. Although you may hint at the eventual outcome, one way to maintain the attention of your listeners is to add the element of suspense as you reach your climax. Sandy's story was climaxed this way:

> Sandy's teacher recognizes that Sandy is an elective mute . . . a child who chooses not to speak . . . what communication scholars term a "quiet child." For Sandy, the sounds to which she is most accustomed in the classroom are "sounds of silence."

4. *Resolution*. The fourth stage of narration or storytelling is the resolution, in which you finish the story and tie up the loose ends to provide a satisfying ending. The listeners who had been following Sandy's plight were relieved to hear this optimistic conclusion:

> Sandy's teacher has informed herself, has researched quiet students widely, and has adapted her classrooms to meet the needs of children such as Sandy. Now whenever Sandy speaks in the classroom, her classmates applaud. Each time she speaks audibly a scoop of popcorn is added to a jar. On Halloween, Sandy's class celebrated her progress with a popcorn party. Now Sandy whispers with her friends and has even led her class in a calendar activity, calling on other children. Before, Sandy had only one choice in the classroom . . . to talk with her silence. Because her teacher cared, Sandy now has another option. . . . Sandy is no longer a child "talking without speaking."

Several additional techniques may improve your storytelling still further. Humor, for example, can make a speech memorable and help maintain audience attention.

Dialogue is yet another memorable element of a well-told story. In a story about a family living through a tornado, note how the following speech excerpt uses dialogue to heighten the drama.

> When my father sighted the funnel cloud my brothers and sister could tell something terrible was about to happen. "Quick! Run to the storm cellar," yelled Dad. The howling wind was so loud that we didn't hear his warning. "I can't hear you," I shouted above the whine of the wind. "Take cover now!" he demanded. The next thing I remember was waking up in the hospital.

You do not need to have the narrative brilliance of Mark Twain to be a good storyteller. If you cannot think of an original story, you can find numerous stories on television or in movies, plays, magazines, or the newspaper. If you borrow a story from one of these sources, you should cite it in your speech. Also, unless your sole purpose is to entertain, use your story to help you achieve your speaking objective. Link your story to your major idea. Be certain that the audience understands the point you are trying to make.

RECAP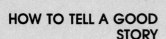

HOW TO TELL A GOOD STORY	1. Present the opening.	Set the stage for action. Provide a picture for your listeners to see.
	2. Describe the complications.	Present a situation that involves conflict or a predicament for one or more of the characters in your story.
	3. Build to a climax.	Develop the plot so that the audience is eager to see how the story is resolved.
	4. Present the resolution.	Resolve the complications; tie up all of the loose ends of the story.

PRINCIPLES OF INFORMING

Who is the best teacher you ever had? He or she was most probably a good lecturer with a special talent for making information interesting and memorable. Like teachers, some speakers are better than others at presenting information. What makes some talks more interesting and memorable than others? The application of a few principles can help. Let's review some of these principles.

1. *Present information that relates to your listeners*. Throughout this book we have encouraged you to develop an audience-centered approach to public speaking. Being an audience-centered informative speaker means that you are aware of information that your audience can use. If, for example, you are going to teach your audience pointers about trash recycling, be sure to talk about specific recycling efforts on your campus or in your own community. Adapt your message to the people who will be in your audience.

In Chapter 6, we introduced the concept of *proximity*—choosing supporting materials that might influence or happen to your listeners. Proximity or closeness is basic to informative speaking, as it is to all public speaking, and helps explain why one of the first steps in preparing a speech is to analyze the audience. Once you know their needs and interests, you will be able to choose a relevant topic or adapt the one you have.

Another basis for adapting your topic to your audience is to find out why *you* are interested in the topic. Using your own interests and background as a start, you can then find ways to establish common bonds with your audience. This will help make your topic relevant to your listeners.

2. *Establish a motive for your audience to listen to you*. Most audiences will probably not be waiting breathlessly for you to talk to them. You will need to motivate them to listen to you.

Some situations have built-in motivations for listeners. A teacher can say, "There will be a test covering my lecture tomorrow. It will count toward fifty percent of your semester grade." Such threatening methods may not make the teacher popular, but they certainly will motivate the class to listen. Similarly, a boss might say, "Your ability to use these sales principles will determine whether you keep your job." As with the teacher, your boss's statement will probably motivate you to learn the company's sales principles. By contrast, you will rarely have the power to motivate your listeners with such strong-arm tactics, and you will therefore need to find more creative ways to get your audience to listen to you.

One way to arouse the interest of your listeners is to ask them a question. Speaking on the high cost of tuition, you might ask, "How many of you are interested in saving tuition dollars this year?" You'll probably have their attention. Then proceed to tell them that you will talk about several approaches to seeking low-cost loans and grants.

"Who would like to save money on their income taxes?" "How many of you would like to have a happier home life?" "How many of you would like to learn an effective way of preparing your next speech?" are other examples of questions that could stimulate your listeners' interest and motivate them to give you their attention. Besides using rhetorical questions, you can begin with an anecdote, a startling statistic, or some other attention-grabbing device.

Don't assume that your listeners will be automatically interested in what you have to say. Pique their interest with a question. Capture their attention. Motivate them to listen to you. Tell them how the information you present will be of value to them. As the British writer G. K. Chesterton once said, "There is no such thing as an uninteresting topic; there are only uninterested people."

3. *Build in redundancy.* It is seldom necessary for writers to repeat themselves. If readers don't quite understand a passage, they can go back and read it again. When you speak, however, it is useful to repeat key points. As we have noted before, audience members generally cannot stop you if a point in your speech is unclear or if their minds wandered; you need to build in redundancy to make sure that the information you want to communicate will get across. As noted in Chapter 8, most speech teachers advise their students to structure their speeches as follows:

   a. *Tell them what you're going to tell them.* In the introduction of your speech, provide a broad overview of the purpose of your message. Identify the major points you will present.
   b. *Tell them.* In the body of your speech, develop each of the main points mentioned during your introduction.
   c. *Tell them what you've told them.* Finally, in your conclusion, summarize the key ideas discussed in the body.

4. *Use simple ideas rather than complex ones.* Your job as a public speaker is to get your ideas over to your audience, not to see how much information you can cram in. What you want to do is communicate your ideas in such a way that your audience will remember what you said. The simpler your ideas and phrases, the greater the chance that your audience will remember them.

Let's say you decide to talk about state-of-the-art personal computer hardware. Fine—just don't try to make your audience as sophisticated as you are about computers in a five-minute speech. You would make better use of your time if you discuss only major features and name one or two leaders in the field, rather than offer too much detail. Be a severe editor of your own material.

5. *Organize your speech in a logical way.* Your audience will more readily understand your information if you organize your major points logically. Regardless of the length or complexity of your speech, you must always follow a logical pattern in order to be understood.

In Chapter 8, we presented several organizational patterns. Almost any topic, we observed, can be divided into logical divisions, reasons, or steps. For example, a speech about climate might be organized around the four seasons (logical divi-

sions). You could organize a speech about the need for increased tuition by identifying why more income is needed (reasons). Your speech about raising minks
can be structured to follow the chronological sequence of the endeavor (steps).
The main ideas resulting from your division of the topic can then be arranged
chronologically, spatially, topically, or according to order of complexity. As you
may recall, in chronological order, ideas are arranged in a time sequence. A topical
structure organizes ideas by subtopics or subdivisions. The spatial pattern organizes
information by location in space. And organizing ideas according to complexity
involves arranging information from the easiest to the most difficult. Whatever
pattern you choose, make sure that your organizational strategy makes sense to
your listeners.

6. *Use connecting phrases to move from one idea to the next*. Once you have your
ideas logically arranged, you need to provide smooth transitions from one to the
next. If your information moves logically from one idea to the next, the likelihood
that your audience will understand what you tell them is increased. Unless you
purposely build in suspense, your listeners should not wonder where you are or
where you're headed at any point in your speech.

As we noted in Chapter 8, there are several ways to move smoothly from one
idea to the next. One method is to give a brief summary of what you've covered
so far, followed by a brief preview of key themes yet to be discussed. The rhetorical
question is another device for moving from one idea to the next. You could say,
for example, "Now that I've talked about the causes of AIDS, you may be wondering,
'What are the methods of treating AIDS?' That brings me to my next point."

Transitions are a useful tool in speeches. However, do not get carried away with
them. Transitions should smooth the flow of ideas, not impede it.

7. *Reinforce key ideas verbally*. You can reinforce an idea by using such phrases
as "This is the most important point" or "Be sure to remember this next point;
it's the most compelling one." Perhaps you have four suggestions for helping your
listeners avoid a serious sunburn. Your last suggestion is the most important. Make
sure your audience knows that. How? Just tell them. "Of all the suggestions I've
given you, this last tip is the most important one. Here it is: The higher the PABA
level on your sunscreen, the better." Be careful not to overuse this technique. If
you claim that every other point is a key point, your audience will soon not believe
you.

8. *Reinforce key ideas nonverbally*. You can also signal the importance of a point
with nonverbal emphasis. Gestures serve the purpose of accenting or emphasizing
key phrases, as italics do in written communication.

A well-placed pause can provide emphasis and reinforcement to set off a point.
Pausing just before or just after making an important point will focus attention on
your thought. Raising or lowering your voice can also reinforce a key idea.

Movement can also help you emphasize major ideas. Moving from behind the
lectern to tell a personal anecdote can signal that something special and more intimate
is about to be said. As we discussed in Chapter 11, your movement and gestures
should be meaningful and natural, rather than seemingly arbitrary or forced. Your
need to emphasize an idea can provide the motivation to make a meaningful movement.

9. *Pace your information flow*. Organize your speech so that you present an even
flow of information, rather than bunch up a number of significant details around
one point. If you present too much new information too quickly, you may overwhelm your audience. Their ability to understand may falter.

You should be especially sensitive to the flow of information if your topic is new or unfamiliar to your listeners. Make sure that your audience has time to process any new information you present. Your use of supporting materials can both help clarify new information and slow down your presentation.

Again, do not try to see how much detail and content you can cram into a speech. Your job is to present information so that the audience can grasp it, not to show off how much you know.

10. *Relate new information to old.* Most people learn by building on what they already know. We try to make sense out of our world by associating the old with the new. Your understanding of calculus is based on your knowledge of algebra. Even when you meet someone for the first time, you may be reminded of someone you already know.

When presenting new information to a group, help your audience associate your new idea with something that is familiar to them. Use an analogy or a comparison. Tell bewildered college freshmen how their new academic life will be similar to high school and how it will be different. Describe how your raising cattle over the summer was similar to taking care of any animal; they all need food, water, and shelter. By building on the familiar, you help your listeners understand how your new concept or information relates to their experiences.

RECAP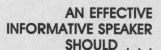

AN EFFECTIVE INFORMATIVE SPEAKER SHOULD . . .

Present information that relates to the listeners
Establish motivation to listen
Build in redundancy
Use simple ideas rather than complex ones
Organize the speech logically
Use clear transitions
Reinforce key ideas verbally and nonverbally
Pace the information flow
Relate new information to old

SUMMARY

To inform is to teach someone something you know. In this chapter, you have studied the goals, types, methods, and principles of informing others.

There are four goals of informative speeches. First, your message should be clear. Use words and phrases that the listener can understand. Second, your message should be accurate. Don't rely solely on your memory of the facts. Consult dictionaries and other resource materials to ensure an accurate presentation. Third, your message should be vivid. By making your message lively, you help your listener remember your key ideas. Fourth, your message should be interesting to your listeners. Consider your audience's interests, needs, likes, and dislikes.

In this chapter, we examined the five basic types of informative speeches. Speeches about *ideas* are often abstract and generally discuss principles, concepts, or theories.

Object speeches are about tangible things. Speeches about *procedures* explain a process or describe how something works. Speeches about *people* can be about either the famous or the little-known. Speeches about *events* describe major occurrences or personal experiences.

We also reviewed three major methods of informing others: defining, describing, and narrating. The chapter concluded with a discussion of ten principles that will help you prepare and present a clear, accurate, vivid, and interesting message.

QUESTIONS FOR DISCUSSION AND REVIEW

1. What are the goals of informative speaking?
2. What are the different types of informative speaking?
3. Compare and contrast the following methods of informing: defining, describing, and narrating.
4. How would you reinforce your main ideas?
5. Describe how to relate new information to familiar information.

SUGGESTED ACTIVITIES

1. From the following list of suggested topics for an informative speech, select five and develop a specific purpose sentence for each. For one of those topics, identify two to four major ideas. Organize them topically, chronologically, or according to some other logical pattern of organization.

How to get a better grade in public speaking	How to buy a color TV
The spread of terrorism in the Middle East	Surrogate parenthood
How our Constitution was written	Safe-driving principles
A historical person I wish I could meet	How the stock market works
What makes a good teacher	
The best way to lose weight	CB radios

2. Replace each of the following words with a livelier one:

cat	airplane	house
work	light	eat
walk		

3. Look up the origin of the following words in a comprehensive dictionary, such as the *Oxford English Dictionary* or the *Etymological Dictionary of Modern English*.

logic	pillow
communication	teacher
dance	

4. Write a word picture, a vivid, colorful description that appeals to the senses, for one of the following scenes:

   Christmas morning when you were 6
   A visit to your grandparents'
   Your first day at college
   Your most frightening experience
   Your most memorable Fourth of July celebration

5. Select a true story from a magazine such as *Reader's Digest* or a story from the writings of Mark Twain, Bill Cosby, or Garrison Keillor. Identify and analyze (a) the opening, (b) the complication, (c) the climax, and (d) the conclusion.

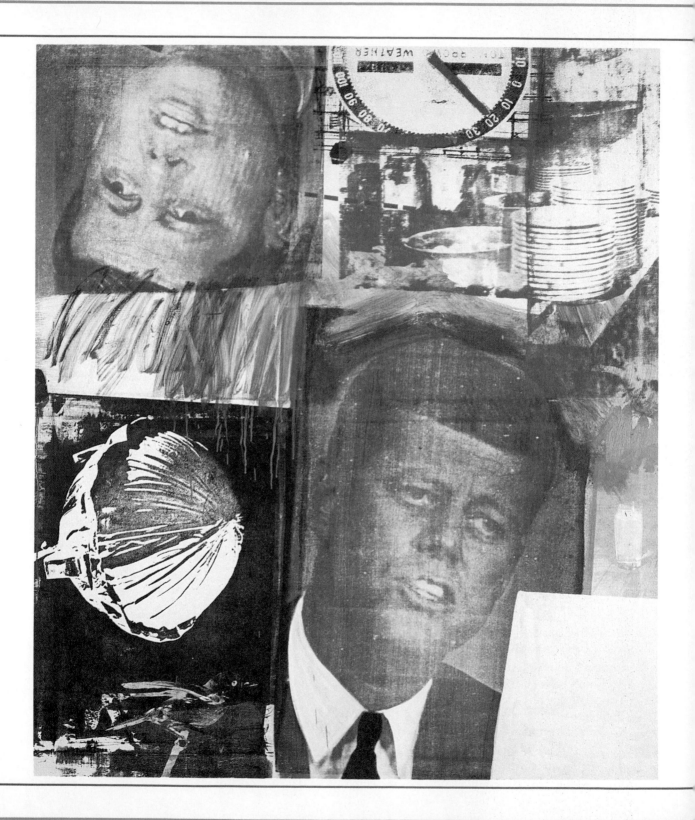

15

Principles of Persuasive Speaking

▼

OBJECTIVES

After studying this chapter, you should be able to

1. Define persuasion
2. Describe dissonance theory
3. Identify Maslow's five levels of needs, which explain how behavior is motivated
4. Select and develop an appropriate topic for a persuasive speech
5. Identify four principles of persuasive speaking

. . . the power of speech, to stir men's blood. (Robert Rauschenberg, Untitled, 1964. Oil on canvas, 58 × 50". Leo Castelli Gallery, New York.)

WILLIAM SHAKESPEARE

It happens over six hundred times each day. It appears as commercials on TV and radio; as advertisements in magazines, newspapers, and billboards; and as fund-raising letters from politicians and charities. It also occurs when you are asked to give money to a worthy cause or to donate blood. "It" is persuasion. Efforts to persuade you occur at an average rate of once every $2\frac{1}{2}$ minutes each day.[1] Because it's such an ever-present part of your life, it is important for you to understand how persuasion works. What are the principles of an activity that can shape your attitudes and behavior? What do car salespersons, advertising copywriters, and politicians know about how to change your thinking and behavior that you don't?

In this chapter, we are going to discuss several concepts that explain how persuasion works. Such information can sharpen your own persuasive skills and can also help you become a more informed receiver of the persuasive messages that come your way. In this chapter, we will define persuasion and discuss the psychological principles underlying all or most efforts at persuading others. We will also discuss some of the factors you should consider when selecting a persuasive speech topic and developing arguments for your speeches. In Chapter 16, we will examine some of the specific techniques of crafting a persuasive speech.

WHAT IS PERSUASION?

persuasion
The process of changing or reinforcing attitudes, beliefs, values, or behaviors.

Persuasion is the process of changing or reinforcing attitudes, beliefs, values, or behavior. Trying to get a person to sign up for a new class, to exercise more, to eat less, to stop smoking, to oppose abortions, and to favor legalizing marijuana are all examples of efforts to persuade. You are trying to get your listener to think, feel, or behave in a predetermined manner. Note that our definition of persuasion is not limited to changing ideas or behavior. You can also reinforce or strengthen existing attitudes or behaviors persuasively. A minister who encourages his congregation to continue to contribute to the church knows that they have given before; he wants them to keep on giving. He wants to reinforce their existing behavior.

Persuasive and Informative Speaking

In Chapter 14, we discussed several strategies for informative speaking, the oral presentation of new information to listeners so that they will understand and remember what is communicated. The purposes of informing and persuading are interrelated. Why inform an audience? Why give new information to others? We often provide information to give listeners new insights that may affect their attitudes and behavior. Information alone has the potential to convince others, but if information is coupled with strategies to persuade, the chances of success increase. Persuasive speakers intentionally try to influence their listeners' point of view or behavior. If you want your listeners to respond to your persuasive appeal, you will need to think carefully about the way you structure your message to achieve your specific purpose.

Because of the interrelationships between persuasive speaking and informative speaking, you need not discard the principles of informative speaking that you studied in Chapter 14. Your speech will still need to be well organized, with interesting supporting material, well-chosen language, smooth transitions, and fluent delivery. But now your speech purpose will target change or reinforcement of your audience's attitudes, beliefs, values, or behavior. As a persuasive speaker, you will need to develop arguments and evidence to support your speech's objective.

At this point, we should take a short digression to offset any possible confusion. The word *argument* here is not used to mean "quarrel" or "disagreement." In our context, *argument* means "reason for believing something," and *evidence* is the proof that supports the reason. Arguments and evidence always go together, and together they make a rational process.

Now let us return to our discussion. Your credibility as a speaker is even more important when your objective is to persuade than when you are only interested in giving information. To be fully persuasive, you will also need to appeal to your listeners' emotions as you try to change or reinforce their ideas and behavior. In short, the art of persuading others involves appeals to reason and emotion.

Attitudes, Beliefs, and Values

Look at our definition of persuasion once again: the art or process of changing or reinforcing attitudes, beliefs, values, and behavior. While behavior is self explanatory, let's take a closer look at *attitudes*, *beliefs*, and *values* to learn more about how to approach the process of persuading others.

attitude
A learned predisposition to respond favorably or unfavorably toward something; likes and dislikes.

Attitudes   An **attitude** is learned predisposition to respond favorably or unfavorably toward something. What does this mean? It refers to the way you have learned to respond to your world, based on your past associations and experiences. For example, what is your attitude toward snakes? What would happen if a friend of yours sneaked up behind you right now while you were reading this book and without warning thrust a snake in your face? Given the fear most people have of the slithering reptiles, you would probably recoil in horror. In this case, you have a learned predisposition to dislike snakes. As a persuasive speaker, you will need to know your listeners' attitudes toward your speech topic so that you can anticipate their responses and develop strategies to change or reinforce those attitudes.

Attitudes reflect or express your likes and dislikes. What's your attitude toward chocolate cake? If you like it, you have a positive attitude toward it. If you hate it and it makes you break out in a rash, you have a negative attitude toward it. Or perhaps you have no strong feelings about chocolate cake; you can take it or leave it. You are neutral toward it; your attitude is one of indifference.

Your attitudes toward persons, places, and things, then, can be classified as positive, negative, or indifferent. If you want to persuade a listener to buy a set of encyclopedias, you would be wise to know what his or her existing attitudes are about encyclopedias, books, salespersons, and education. The more you know about your listeners' attitudes and how they developed those attitudes, the better able you will be to adapt your message to them.

belief
A way we structure reality to accept something as either true or false.

value
An enduring concept of good and bad, right and wrong.

Beliefs   A **belief** is the way in which you structure reality to accept something as either true or false. If you believe in something, you are convinced it exists. You have structured your sense of what is real and what is unreal to account for the existence of whatever you believe in. If you believe in God, you have structured your sense of what is real and unreal to include the existence of God. Undoubtedly you believe that the sun will rise again in the morning and set in the evening. Based on your experience, this is what you believe to be true. You believe something to be true or false depending on your past experience or the evidence you have available. As a public speaker, it is very important to understand the key beliefs of your audience, especially if your goal is to change or reinforce listener beliefs.

Values   A **value** is a concept of intrinsic good and bad, right and wrong. Helping those in need, for example, is intrinsically good—that is, it is good in and of itself, without reference to anything else. What do you value? For most Americans, it would be things like honesty, trustworthiness, freedom, loyalty, marriage, family, and money. If you value something, you classify it as good or desirable. If you do not value something, you think of it as bad or wrong. Values form the basis of your life goals and the motivating force behind your behavior. Understanding what your listeners value can help you refine your analysis of them and adapt the content of your speech to those values.

Why is it useful to make distinctions among attitudes, beliefs, and values? Since the essence of persuasion is to change or reinforce these three qualities, it is very useful to know exactly what you are concerned with. Of the three qualities, audience values are the most stable. Most of us have acquired our values when very young and have held on to them into adulthood. Our values, therefore, are generally deeply ingrained. It is not impossible to change the values of your listeners, but it is much more difficult than trying to change a belief or an attitude. Political and religious points of view, which are usually based on long-held values, are especially difficult to modify.

A belief is more susceptible to change than a value, but it is still difficult to change. Beliefs are changed by evidence. You will have a difficult time, for example, trying to change someone's belief that the world is flat; existing evidence supports a different conclusion. It takes a great deal of evidence to change a belief and alter the way your audience structures reality.

Attitudes (our likes and dislikes) are much easier to change than either beliefs or values. Today we may approve of the President of the United States; tomorrow we may disapprove because of a recent action he has taken. We may still believe that the country is financially stable, and we may still value a democratic form of government, but our attitude toward the President has changed because of his recent policy decision.

As illustrated in Figure 15.1, values are most basic; they change least frequently. Beliefs change, but not as much as attitudes. Trying to change an audience's attitudes is easier than attempting to change its values. We suggest that you think carefully about your purpose in making a persuasive speech. Know with certainty whether your objective is to change or reinforce an attitude, belief, or value. Then decide what you have to do to achieve your objective.

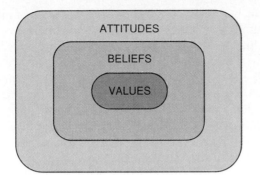

FIGURE 15.1
Values are more central
than beliefs and attitudes.

MOTIVATION

It's late at night, and you're watching your favorite talk show before going to bed. The program is interrupted by a commercial extolling the virtues of ice cream. Suddenly, you remember that you have the flavor advertised, royal rocky road. You apparently hadn't realized how hungry you were for ice cream until the ad reminded you of the lip-smacking goodness of the cool, creamy, smooth treat. Before you know it, you are at the freezer, doling out a couple of scoops of ice cream.

If the sponsor of that commercial knew how effective it had been, he or she would be overjoyed. The ad was persuasive and changed your behavior. How does persuasion work? What principles explain why you were motivated to dig through the freezer at 11:30 at night for a bowl of ice cream? Let's look at three attempts to explain why we respond to efforts at persuasion.

Dissonance Theory

Dissonance theory is based on the principle that you strive to be consistent in your thoughts and actions.[2] The theory assumes that you operate from an organized, logical set of concepts about yourself, others, and everything with which you come into contact. According to the theory, you are a rational person. Whenever you are presented with information that is inconsistent with your current attitudes, beliefs, values, or behavior, you experience discomfort called **cognitive dissonance.** The word *cognitive* has to do with our ways of knowing and understanding ourselves and our world. *Dissonance* means "lack of harmony or agreement." When you think of a dissonant chord in music, you probably think of a series of sounds that are unpleasant or not in tune with the melody or other chords. Cognitive dissonance, then, means that you are experiencing a way of thinking that is inconsistent and uncomfortable. Your discomfort with your incompatible thoughts prompts you to change your attitudes, beliefs, values, or behavior so that balance or consistency is reestablished.

The need to restore balance is common. We have all experienced it at one time or another. If you are walking down a flight of stairs too fast and start to lose your balance, you will probably grab for the handrail to restore your balance so you won't fall. You normally want to keep your balance. This is the same process that,

cognitive dissonance
The sense of disorganization that prompts a person to change when new information conflicts with previously organized thought patterns.

according to dissonance theory, occurs psychologically when information you hear causes you discomfort—you lose your balance. Someone who is trying to persuade you usually tries first to identify an existing problem or need. For example, the need could be your desire for a bedtime snack. The persuader then claims that his or her solution or suggestion can best solve the problem or meet the need. The solution to your problem is to eat some ice cream. Thus the persuader first attempts to "create" dissonance and then seeks to relieve it by suggesting a change that will restore balance. The change itself is the persuader's objective.

A local political candidate who wants to be mayor usually first tries to make his or her audience aware of the various problems that exist in the community; the contender usually blames the current mayor for most of the problems. Once dissonance has been created, the candidate then suggests that these problems can be solved or at least managed better if he or she were to be elected as the city's next mayor. Using the principles of dissonance theory, the mayoral candidate first upsets the audience, then restores its balance and feeling of comfort by providing a solution to the city's problems, his or her election as mayor. By following the candidate's advice, the audience achieves cognitive consistency.

Vonda Ramey, calling for more attention to children who cannot read, created dissonance in the minds of her listeners when she documented the widespread problem of illiteracy in her prize-winning oration "Can You Read This?"

> Approximately two-thirds of U.S. colleges and universities have to provide remedial reading and writing courses for students. The University of California at Berkeley, which gets the top one-eighth of all high school students, has to put almost half of the freshmen in remedial composition classes.
>
> Instructional materials used by the armed forces look like comic books, with pictures and simple language to help new recruits who have a problem reading. One manual has five pages of just pictures to show a soldier how to open the hood of a truck.[3]

When you are confronted with dissonant information, there are a number of options available to you besides following the suggestion of the speaker.[4] Persuasion is not just a process of simply creating dissonance and then suggesting a solution to the problem. Let's now look at those options.

Ways of Restoring Balance

ATTACK THE CREDIBILITY OF THE SOURCE   Instead of believing everything a speaker has said, you could choose to discredit the speaker. Let's assume you now drive a Ford. Possibly interested in buying a new car, you approach a Chevrolet salesman, who begins to talk about what awful cars Fords are and what fine ones Chevys are. You could agree with him, or you could find that your salesman is ill-informed and attack his competence. Instead of changing your attitude about Fords, you have changed your attitude about the salesman. As a persuasive speaker, you need to be perceived as credible so that your audience accepts your conclusion rather than rejects you.

REINTERPRET THE MESSAGE   A second way in which your listeners may overcome cognitive dissonance and restore balance is to hear what they want to hear. They may choose to focus on the parts of your message that are consistent with

An effective salesperson understands your motives and needs.
(*L. L. T. Rhodes/StockPhotos, Inc.*)

what they already believe and ignore the more unfamiliar or controversial parts. Your job as an effective public speaker is to make your message as clear as possible so that your audience will not reinterpret your message. A clearly worded message with simple, vivid examples will help make your point and keep your listeners from hearing what they want to hear.

SEEK NEW INFORMATION   Another way of trying to cope with cognitive dissonance when confronted with a distressing argument is to seek more information on the subject. You look for additional information to support your position and to refute the arguments of the person who created the dissonance. As the owner of a minivan, you experience dissonance when you hear a speaker describe the recent rash of safety problems with minivans. You turn to your friend and whisper, "Is this true? Are minivans really dangerous? I've always heard they were safe." Your question to your companion is a request for new information to validate your ownership of a minivan. When you hear a political speech that tries to change your view, you may seek new information to help justify your stand on the issues.

STOP LISTENING   Some messages are so much at odds with our attitudes, beliefs, and values that we decide to stop listening. Most of us do not seek opportunities to hear or read messages that oppose our opinions. It is unlikely that a staunch Democrat would attend a fund raiser for the state Republican party. The principle of selective exposure suggests that we tend to pay attention to situations that are consistent with our points of view and to avoid those that are not. When we do find ourselves trapped in a situation in which we are forced to hear a message that doesn't support our beliefs, we tend to tune the speaker out. We stop listening to avoid the dissonance.

CHANGE ATTITUDES, BELIEFS, VALUES, OR BEHAVIOR   A fifth way to respond to dissonant information is to do as the speaker wishes us to. We can change our attitude and thereby reduce the dissonance that we experience. After listening to a life insurance sales presentation in which you are told that when you die, your family will have no financial support (you experience dissonance), you decide to take out a $100,000 policy to protect your family. You've restored the balance of ideas. After hearing a candidate for president deliver a campaign speech in which the economic problems of the country are discussed (you experience dissonance), you decide that he or she is the best person to deal with the problems. The goals of advertising copywriters and political candidates are similar in that they want you to experience dissonance so that you will change your attitudes, beliefs, values, or behavior.

Needs as Motivators: Scratching the Itch

When you have an itch, you usually need to scratch. The same principle operates when trying to motivate a listener to respond as you wish. The more you understand what your listeners need, the greater the chances are that you can gain and hold their attention and ultimately get them to do what you want. The classic theory that outlines our basic needs was developed by Abraham Maslow.[5] Maslow suggests that there is a hierarchy of needs that motivates the behavior of all of us. Basic needs (such as food, water, and air) have to be satisfied before we can be motivated to respond to higher-level needs. Figure 15.2 illustrates Maslow's five levels of needs, with the most basic at the bottom. When attempting to persuade an audience, a public speaker attempts to stimulate these needs in order to change or reinforce attitudes, beliefs, values, or behavior. Let's examine these needs in some detail.

FIGURE 15.2
Maslow's hierarchy of needs.

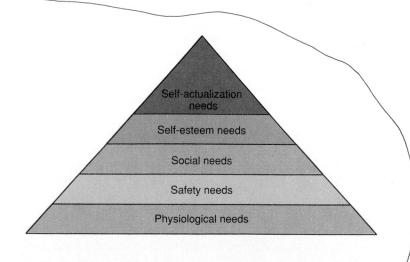

Physiological Needs   The most basic needs for all humans are physiological: air, water, and food. According to Maslow's theory, unless those needs are met, it will be difficult to motivate a listener to satisfy other needs. If your listeners are hot, tired, and thirsty, it will be more difficult to persuade them to vote for your candidate, buy your insurance policy, or sign your petition in support of local pet leash laws. As a public speaker, you should be sensitive to the basic physiological needs of your audience so that your appeals to higher-level needs will be heard.

Safety Needs   Once basic physiological needs are met, your listeners are concerned about their safety. We have a need to feel safe, secure, and protected, and we need to be able to predict that the need for safety of ourselves and our loved ones will be met. The classic sales presentation from insurance salespersons includes appeals to our need for safety and security. Many insurance sales efforts include photos of wrecked cars, anecdotes of people who were in ill health and could not pay their bills, or tales of the head of a household who passed away, leaving the basic needs of his or her family unmet. Appeals to use seat belts, stop smoking, start exercising, and use condoms all play to our need for safety and security.

In a speech titled "Emissions Tampering: Get the Lead Out," John Ryan appealed to his listeners' need for safety and security when he began his speech with these observations:

> A major American producer is currently dumping over 8,000 tons of lead into our air each year, which in turn adversely affects human health. The producers of this waste are tampering with pollution control devices in order to cut costs. This tampering ecalates the amount of noxious gases you and I inhale by 300–800%. That producer is the American motorist.[6]

Social Needs   We all need to feel loved and valued. We need contact and reassurance from others that they care about us. According to Maslow, these social needs translate into our need for a sense of belonging to a group (fraternity, religious organization, friends). Powerful persuasive appeals are based on your need for social contact. We are encouraged to buy a product or support a particular issue because others are buying the product or supporting the issue. The message is, to be liked and respected by others, you must buy the same things they do or support the same position they support.

Self-esteem Needs   The need for self-esteem reflects our desire to think well of ourselves. Jesse Jackson is known for appealing often to the self-worth of his listeners by inviting them to chant, "I am somebody." This is a direct appeal to his listeners' need for self-esteem. Advertisers also appeal to our need for self-esteem when they encourage us to believe that we can be noticed by others or stand out in the crowd if we purchase their product. Commercials promoting luxury cars usually invite you to picture yourself in the driver's seat with a beautiful person next to you while you receive looks of envy from those you pass on the road. The powerful need for self-esteem fuels many persuasive messages.

As a Light Fighter in today's Army you'll always be learning, moving, thinking on your feet.
Time and time again you'll meet the greatest challenge of them all — yourself. You'll learn to face the tough problems, to think them through, and find the solution. Being an Army Light Fighter means adventure, pride and confidence. And that gives you a real edge on life. What's more, if you qualify, you can earn up to $25,200 through the Montgomery GI Bill plus the Army College Fund.
For more information call 1-800-USA-ARMY, or see your local Army recruiter. **ARMY. BE ALL YOU CAN BE.**

**MEET THE GREATEST CHALLENGE OF THEM ALL.
YOURSELF.**

Self-actualization describes our need to achieve our highest potential.
(*U.S. Army Recruiting Command*)

▼
self-actualization
The need to achieve our highest potential; to "be all that we can be."

Self-actualization Needs   At the top of Maslow's hierarchy is the need for **self-actualization.** This is the need to achieve our highest potential. The U.S. Army uses the slogan "Be all that you can be" to tap into the need for self-actualization. Calls to be the best and the brightest are appeals to self-actualization. According to the assumption that our needs are organized into a hierarchy, the other four need levels must be satisfied before we can be motivated to achieve the ultimate in personal satisfaction.

Motivating through Appeals to Fear

Brother says to sister: "If you don't stop what you're doing, I'm going to tell Mom!" Whether that sibling realized it or not, he was using a persuasive technique called a *fear appeal*. One of the oldest methods of trying to change someone's attitude or behavior, the use of a threat is also one of the most effective. In essence, the appeal to fear takes the form of an "if-then" statement. If you don't do *X*, awful things will happen to you. A persuader builds an argument on the assertion that a need will not be met unless the desired behavior or attitude change occurs. The principal reason that appeals to fear continue to be made in persuasive messages is that they work. A variety of research studies support the following principles for using fear appeals.[7]

1. A strong threat to a loved one tends to be more successful than a fear appeal directed at the audience members themselves. A speaker using this principle might say, "Unless you are able to get your children to wear seat belts, they could easily be injured or killed in an auto accident."

2. The more competent, trustworthy, or respected the speaker, the greater the likelihood that an appeal to fear will be successful. A speaker with less credibility will be more successful with moderate threats. The surgeon general of the United States will be more successful in convincing people to use condoms to avoid the risk of AIDS than you will.

3. Fear appeals are more successful if you can convince your listeners that the threat is real and will probably occur unless they take the action you are advocating. For example, you could dramatically announce, "Last year, thirty percent of smokers developed lung cancer and eventually died. Unless you stop smoking, there is a high probability that you could develop lung cancer, too."

The effectiveness of fear appeals is based on the theories of cognitive dissonance and Maslow's hierarchy of needs. The fear aroused creates dissonance, which can be reduced by following the recommendation of the persuader. Appeals to fear are also based on targeting an unmet need. Fear appeals depend on a convincing insistence that a need will go unmet unless a particular action or attitude change occurs.

RECAP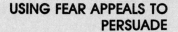

USING FEAR APPEALS TO PERSUADE

1. Fear appeals involving loved ones are often more effective than appeals directed to audience members themselves.
2. The greater your credibility, the more likely your fear appeal will be effective.
3. You must convince your audience that the threat is real and could actually happen.

Dissonance theory, needs hierarchy theory, and fear appeals help us understand how listeners are persuaded to change their attitudes, beliefs, values, and behaviors. Realize, however, that persuasion is not as simple as these approaches may lead you to believe. There is no precise formula for motivating and convincing an audience. Attitude change occurs differently in each individual; it's not something that occurs automatically if the right words are used. There are no magic words, phrases, or appeals. Persuasion is an art that draws on science. Sensitivity to listeners' emotions, as well as to their needs and the techniques of public speaking, is necessary for persuasive messages to be effective.

Now that you understand what persuasion is and how it works, let's turn our attention to the task of preparing a persuasive speech. One of your first challenges when asked to present a persuasive speech is to choose an appropriate topic.

DEVELOPING YOUR PERSUASIVE SPEECH

Selecting Your Persuasive Speech Topic

The best persuasive speech topic is one about which you feel strongly. What attitudes, beliefs, values, and behaviors do you hold dear? If your listeners sense that you are not committed or excited about your topic, they won't be, either. Many of the mechanics of delivery and presentation can be defined more readily if you are speaking about a topic with passion and conviction. So the first step in choosing a persuasive topic is to inventory your own attitudes, beliefs, and values. Use the brainstorming method that we discussed earlier in your effort to identify your interests and convictions.

Besides your own interests and feelings about a topic, controversial issues make excellent sources for persuasive topics. A controversial issue is a question about which people disagree. Here are several: Should the university increase tuition so that faculty members can have a salary increase? Should the United States build the Star Wars defense system? Should the United States and the Soviet Union agree to a freeze on midrange nuclear weapons? You need to be audience-centered—know the local, state, national, or international issues that interest your listeners.

We recommend that you, as a student of public speaking, pay attention to the media to help keep you current on the important issues of the day. If you're not already doing so, you should read at least one newspaper every day. Take a look at a national newsmagazine like *Time*, *Newsweek*, or *U.S. News and World Report* to keep in touch with issues and topics of interest. The editorial page of the newspaper is also a good place to see what issues are of interest to people. Another interesting source of controversial issues is talk radio programs. Both national and local radio call-in programs may give you some ideas that are appropriate for a persuasive speech. Even if you already have a clear idea of your speech topic, keeping up with the media can give you additional ideas to help narrow your topic or find interesting and appropriate supporting material.

The following list may help you choose issues or topics for a persuasive speech. Remember, there is a difference between selecting a speech topic and determining your speech purpose. These topics will need to be narrowed to fit your time limit and adapted to your specific audience.

Persuasive Speech Topics

Why you should buy a U.S.-built car
The dangers of weight lifting
We should reduce our sugar intake
We should reduce our salt intake
We should reduce our fat intake
We should reduce our body weight
Spend more leisure time doing [something]
Volunteer for [something]
The electoral college system for electing presidents should be changed

Every U.S. citizen should spend two years in mandatory community service
State drug laws should be changed
The income tax system should be changed
All undergraduate courses should be graded on a pass-fail basis only
Everyone should take a foreign language
There is too much violence in cartoons
Everyone should read a weekly newsmagazine regularly
Everyone should be required to take a communication course
Couples should (or should not) live together before marriage
We devote too much attention to college athletics
Don't invest in the stock market
The United States should have a tougher trade policy
All farmers should be given low-interest loans
Women should (or should not) be ordained as ministers
The government should provide health care for all
Divorce laws should be changed
Spend more time listening to music
Spend less time watching TV
Casino gambling should (or should not) be legalized in this state
The legal drinking age should be changed
Birth control pills should (or should not) be dispensed by state-supported schools
The federal court system needs to be changed
A college education should be available to all citizens at no cost
Teachers should be paid more
Students should grade their professors

Developing Your Persuasive Speech Purpose

Once you have decided on a topic for your persuasive speech, your next step is to develop a specific purpose for your speech. In Chapter 5, we discussed techniques that could be used in narrowing your topic to fit your time limit.

Besides knowing your time limit, you also need to know your audience to help formulate your specific objective. Your specific purpose should be developed with the attitudes, beliefs, and values of your listeners in mind. If you know, for example, that your audience is strongly opposed to legalizing abortion, it would be unwise to try to convince them to reverse their position in a five- to seven-minute speech. As we discussed in Chapter 4, you may want to develop a survey or a questionnaire to assess the points of view held by your audience. Your specific objective will reflect audience attitudes, your ultimate goal, and the time limit imposed on you.

The following work sheet can help you develop a specific purpose for your persuasive message.

Persuasive Speech Work Sheet

Topic:_____

Analysis of Your Point of View

What are *your* feelings about your topic?   ____Favorable
                                                 ____Neutral
                                                 ____Unfavorable

What beliefs support your point of view?

What values support your attitudes and beliefs about the topic?

Analysis of the Audience's Point of View

What are the unmet needs of your audience?

What are the general audience attitudes about your topic?   ____Favorable
                                                               ____Neutral
                                                               ____Unfavorable

What are the audience beliefs about the topic?   ____It is significant to the broader society.
                                                    ____It is important only to members of the audience.

                                                    ____It is a direct and personal threat.

What underlying values support your listeners' feelings about the topic?

What current audience members' behaviors or practices suggest that they either agree or disagree with your point of view?

What is the specific attitude, belief, or value you want your audience to have following your speech?

What kind of action do you want your audience to be able to take following your speech?

What is the time limit for your speech?

Summarize your message in one sentence.

What is the specific purpose of your speech? At the end of my speech, audience members should be able to

We have identified some of the factors that can motivate an audience and have provided some clues for formulating a specific purpose for your speech. We conclude this chapter by discussing some general principles to help you link the theory of persuasion with the practice of persuasion.

PUTTING PERSUASIVE PRINCIPLES INTO PRACTICE

1. Persuasion will be more likely to occur if you try to change an audience member's point of view gradually rather than suddenly. Rarely does a listener hear a single thirty-second commercial and then purchase the product advertised. Dramatic changes of attitude, belief, values, and behavior can occur after just a brief exposure to a persuasive message, but it usually takes time and repeated exposure to bring about permanent attitude changes in your listeners. Political candidates and advertisers usually develop a prolonged campaign to help achieve their ultimate goal of getting your vote or your dollar. There may be several intermediate objectives that they want to achieve, such as having you recognize the name of the product or the candidate. They know that decisions to support a political candidate for office are based on a variety of factors, including the candidate's appearance, the attitudes of others, and our understanding of the candidate's view of the issues.

In the course of developing your speech, lay the groundwork for your objective early in your effort at persuasion. Identify what you and your listeners already agree on. Show your listeners that you understand their attitudes and values before trying to change their minds and behavior.

2. Persuasion will occur more easily if your goal is consistent with the attitudes, beliefs, values, and behavior of your listeners. As noted earlier in this chapter, people strive for consistency. You will be a more successful advocate if your speech objective can be seen as compatible with the views already held by your audience. Again we remind you to be audience-centered. One theory suggests that when we are con-

fronted with a persuasive message, our response can be classified into one of three categories: latitude of acceptance (we generally agree with the speaker), latitude of rejection (we disagree), and latitude of noncommitment (we're not sure how to respond).[8] As a persuasive speaker, it is in your interest to gain as much latitude of acceptance as you can while you are trying to change your audience's views. Your goal, of course, is to have your message fully accepted by your listeners. To do that, you will need to know where they stand on the issues before you craft your message so that you can adapt to their position.

3. Persuasion will be more likely to occur if the advantages of your proposal are greater than the disadvantages. Your job as a persuasive speaker is to convince your listeners that the benefits of your proposal are much greater than the listeners' current point of view or course of action. Whenever you make a decision to buy something, you do a brief cost-benefit analysis. You consider the cost of the item (a new computer at $1500), and you also think of the benefits the purchase will bring (better grades, less time spent typing because editing is so easy). If the benefits of purchasing the new computer outweigh the costs, you decide to make the purchase. In a similar fashion, your job is to convince your listeners that the benefits or advantages of adopting your point of view will outweigh whatever costs or disadvantages are associated with your proposal. Most salespersons are taught not to reveal what an item will cost until they are sure you understand the benefits of whatever they are selling. They want you to visualize owning and enjoying the product first. If you conclude that the benefits outweigh the costs, you will probably buy the product.

4. Persuasion will be more likely to occur if your proposal meets your listeners' needs. We have already described Maslow's hierarchy of needs and how we are motivated to satisfy more basic needs first and then satisfy higher-level needs such as self-esteem and self-actualization. In the early stages of developing your persuasive message, identify how your proposal or viewpoint will satisfy the needs of your audience. What do your listeners need that they currently do not have? How can you adapt your message to tie into their unmet needs? Answering these questions can give you some useful and powerful strategies for developing your persuasive objective and speech.

The principles described in this chapter should give you some insight into the way persuasion works. Our overview of the approaches to persuasion should help you choose a persuasive topic and formulate a specific speech purpose. In Chapter 16, we will build on the principles reviewed here and suggest specific strategies for developing your persuasive message.

SUMMARY

In this chapter, we discussed some general theories that explain how persuasion works to change or reinforce attitudes, beliefs, and values, which are the determinants of behavior. We then described how you can build this theoretical knowledge into your speech preparation so as to deliver a persuasive message.

Persuasion is the process of changing or reinforcing attitudes, beliefs, values, and behavior. Attitudes are learned predispositions to respond favorably or unfavorably toward something. A belief is the way you structure what is true and what is false. A value is a conception of right and wrong.

We examined three theories that explain how persuasion works. First, we discussed the concept of cognitive dissonance, which holds that we all strive for balance or consistency in our thoughts. When a persuasive message invites us to change our attitudes, beliefs, values, or behavior, we respond by trying to maintain intellectual balance or cognitive consistency.

A second theory explains why we are motivated to respond to persuasion by proposing that we wish to satisfy our needs. Abraham Maslow identified a five-level hierarchy of needs: physiological, safety, social, self-esteem, and self-actualization.

A third theoretical approach that helps us understand how persuasion works is called fear appeals. Fear can motivate us to respond favorably to a persuasive suggestion. To avoid pain or discomfort, we may follow the recommendation of a persuasive speaker.

Preparing and presenting a persuasive speech requires the same approach as preparing any other kind of speech. A key first concern is choosing an appropriate topic. We discussed some methods for developing a persuasive speech topic.

The chapter concluded by describing the application of the broad principles of persuasion to preparing a persuasive speech.

In Chapter 16, we will discuss specific techniques that build on the principles that we looked at in this chapter.

---

1. What is persuasion?
2. What is dissonance theory, and how does it explain the way persuasion functions?
3. How would you describe and illustrate Maslow's hierarchy of needs?
4. What principles underlie the use of fear appeals to motivate an audience?
5. What would be your chief concerns in selecting a persuasive speech topic?

QUESTIONS FOR DISCUSSION AND REVIEW

---

1. Collect four or five magazine advertisements for various products. Analyze the persuasive strategies in each ad. Look for applications of cognitive dissonance, Maslow's hierarchy of needs, or fear appeals. Which theory do you see being illustrated most often?
2. Write a short essay noting similarities and differences in preparing and presenting an informative speech and a persuasive speech.
3. Select a controversial topic such as abortion, gun control, multilingualism, or use of contraceptives by teenagers. For the topic you select, analyze your own attitudes, beliefs, and values. What do you like and dislike about the issue? What do you believe is true or not true? What key values do you hold that lead you to your point of view?

   After you have analyzed your attitudes, beliefs, and values on the topic, do a similar analysis projecting attitudes, beliefs, and values that your classmates may hold toward the issue. You could also analyze the attitudes, beliefs, and values of your parents.
4. Identify fear appeals that have been successful in motivating you to change your attitudes, beliefs, values, or behavior.
5. Prepare and deliver a five-minute persuasive speech in which you argue against your own attitudes, beliefs, or values. Did your audience believe you?

SUGGESTED ACTIVITIES

16
Methods of Persuasion

OBJECTIVES

After studying this chapter, you should be able to

1. Identify strategies to improve your initial, derived, and terminal credibility

2. Use principles of effective reasoning to develop a persuasive message

3. Employ effective techniques of using emotional appeal in a persuasive speech

4. Adapt your persuasive message to receptive, neutral, and unreceptive audiences

5. Identify strategies for effectively organizing a persuasive speech

Speech is power: Speech is to persuade, to convert, to compel. (*Anton von Werner* (*1843–1915*), The Diet of Worms in 1521: Luther facing the emperor Charles V: "Here I stand. I can do no other." *Staatsgalerie Stuttgart. ARCHIV/Photo Researchers, Inc.*)

RALPH WALDO EMERSON

The ancient Greek philosopher Aristotle defined *rhetoric* as the process of discovering the "available means of persuasion." What are these "available means" that can help you persuade an audience? In Chapter 15, we focused on the principles of persuasion. These were intended to give you a general understanding of how persuasion works. In this chapter, we will discuss methods that can help you prepare your persuasive speech. Specifically, we will suggest how to gain credibility, develop well-reasoned arguments, and move your audience with emotion. We will also discuss how to adapt your specific message to your audience, and we will end with some suggestions for organizing your persuasive message.

PERSUADING WITH CREDIBILITY, LOGIC, AND EMOTION

credibility
The attitude that a listener has toward a speaker.

Persuading with Credibility

If you were going to buy a new car, to whom would you turn for advice? Perhaps you would ask a trusted family member, or you might seek advice from *Consumer Reports*, a monthly publication that reports studies of various products on the market, among them automobiles. In other words, you would probably turn to a source that you consider knowledgeable, competent, and trustworthy—a source you think is credible.

Credibility is the attitude that a listener has toward a speaker. As a public speaker, especially one who wishes to persuade an audience, you hope that your listeners will have a favorable attitude toward you. Current research points clearly to a relationship between credibility and speech effectiveness: The more believable you are to your listener, the more effective you will be as a persuasive communicator.

Aristotle thought that a public speaker should possess good character, have common sense, and be concerned for the well-being of the audience. Quintilian, a Roman teacher of public speaking, also felt that an effective public speaker should be a person of good character. Quintilian's advice was that a speaker should be "a good man speaking well." The importance to a speaker of a positive public image has been recognized for centuries. But don't get the idea that credibility is something that a speaker literally possesses or lacks. Credibility is a mind-set that a listener has toward a speaker. Your audience, not you, determines whether you have credibility or lack it.

Credibility is not just a single factor or a single view of you by your audience. It is many factors and many views. Aristotle's speculations as to the factors that influence a speaker's ethical character have been generally supported by modern experimental studies.

competence
The factor of a speaker's credibility that refers to being perceived as informed, skilled, or knowledgeable.

trustworthiness
The factor of a speaker's credibility that refers to being perceived as believable and honest.

One clear factor in credibility is **competence**—the speaker should be considered informed, skilled, or knowledgeable about the subject he or she is talking about. If a used-car salesman sings the virtues of a car on his lot, you want to know what qualifies him to give believable information about the car.

A second major factor that influences your audience's response to you is **trustworthiness.** You trust people whom you believe to be honest. While delivering your speech, you have to convey to your audience your honesty and sincerity. Your audience will be looking for evidence that they can trust you, that you are believable.

A third factor in credibility is the speaker's **dynamism** or energy. A speaker's dynamism is often projected through delivery. **Charisma** is a form of dynamism. A charismatic person possesses charm, talent, magnetism, and other qualities that make the person attractive and energetic. Presidents Franklin Roosevelt and Ronald Reagan were considered charismatic speakers; Jesse Jackson is a dynamic speaker.

Credibility has three phases, the first of which is *initial credibility*. This is the opinion your listeners have about you even before you speak. The second phase, *derived credibility*, is the opinion of you they form as you present yourself and your message. The last phase, called *terminal credibility* or *final credibility*, is the opinion of you they have when you finish your speech.

dynamism
The factor of a speaker's credibility that refers to being perceived as energetic.

charisma
Characteristic of a talented, charming, attractive speaker.

Enhancing Initial Credibility: Improving Your Image before You Speak   Here are some suggestions for being seen as a credible speaker even before you say your first word.

1. *Give careful thought to your appearance.* The way you look should satisfy the expectations of your listeners. If they expect you to "dress for success," don't come dressed in blue jeans or a sweatsuit.

The way you look should satisfy the expectations of your listeners.
(*Bob Daemmrich/Stock, Boston*)

2. *Prepare a brief description of your credentials and accomplishments*. Have a biographical paragraph written so that the person who introduces you can use it in his or her introductory remarks. Even if you are not asked for a statement beforehand, be prepared with one.

3. *Establish eye contact before you speak*. When introduced to your audience, don't rush up to the lectern and begin your speech without first establishing eye contact, slowly but surely. The confidence you communicate before you speak will pay dividends in establishing your credibility.

Enhancing Derived Credibility: Improving Your Image during Your Speech

1. *Maintain eye contact with your audience*. Looking at your listeners during your speech signals that you are interested in talking to them.

2. *Use appropriate vocal variation*. Your vocal inflection should be appropriately varied in pitch and rate to project your interest, enthusiasm, and sincerity.

3. *Use appropriate posture, movement, and gestures*. Your physical delivery should communicate your interest in your topic and your audience. Don't slouch, slump, or lean on the lectern or table.

4. *Establish a common ground with your audience*. In your opening remarks, indicate that you share the values or concerns of your audience. Only after common ground has been established should you launch into your persuasive effort.

5. *Present a well-organized message*. Preview your main concepts in your introduction, clearly identify your major ideas in the body of your speech, and summarize your key points during your concluding remarks.

6. *Use clear transitions*. Identifying your major ideas with internal summaries, signposts, and enumeration will add organizational clarity to your speech.

7. *Use appropriate language*. Your word choice reflects your intelligence, education, and overall competence.

8. *Pronounce words clearly*. Give careful attention to the way you articulate and pronounce words. Mispronunciation detracts from your image of competence and dynamism.

9. *Support your key arguments with evidence*. Use appropriate facts, examples, statistics, and expert opinions to support your conclusions. Convince your audience that you are knowledgeable and informed by using credible, unbiased sources.

Enhancing Final Credibility: Developing a Lasting Positive Image

1. *End with eye contact*. Do not start leaving the lectern or the speaking area until you finish your closing sentence; deliver your last line with eye contact.

2. *Be prepared for questions*. Even if there is no planned question-and-answer period following your speech, be ready to respond to questions from interested listeners after the formal program.

RECAP

HOW TO ENHANCE YOUR CREDIBILITY

Initial Credibility: *Improving your image before you speak*

Give careful consideration to your appearance.

Prepare a brief description of your credentials and accomplishments that can be read to the audience.

Establish eye contact with the audience before you begin speaking.

Derived Credibility: *Improving your image during your speech*

Look at your listeners.

Use appropriate vocal variation.

Use appropriate posture, movement, and gestures.

Present a well-organized speech.

Use clear transitions.

Use appropriate diction.

Pronounce words clearly.

Support your arguments with evidence.

Final Credibility: *Developing a lasting positive image*

End with eye contact.

Be prepared for questions.

Persuading with Logic

Besides competence, trustworthiness, and dynamism, a major factor in making a strong, persuasive speech is presenting logical, well-reasoned arguments supported by credible evidence. What is logic? **Logic** is a formal system of rules for making inferences. When used rigorously, logic can make your argument absolutely convincing. It can also clarify your own thinking and help make your points clear to your audience. In essence, logic is central to all reasoning.

Developing Logical Arguments **Reasoning** is the process of drawing a conclusion from evidence. Evidence consists of the facts, examples, statistics, and expert opinions that you use to support the points you wish to make. It is your task, when advancing an argument, to prove your point. **Proof** consists of evidence plus the conclusion you draw from that evidence. Let's consider the two key elements of proof in greater detail. Specifically, we will look at types of reasoning and tests of evidence.

logic
The formal system of using rules to make an inference.

reasoning
The process of drawing a conclusion from evidence.

proof
Evidence that establishes the validity of a conclusion or assertion.

If your arguments are structured in a rational way, you have a greater chance of persuading your listeners.
(*Stacy Pick/Stock, Boston*)

Types of Reasoning   Developing well-reasoned arguments for persuasive messages has been important since antiquity. If your arguments are structured in a rational way, you have a greater chance of persuading your listeners. There are three major ways to structure an argument to reach a logical conclusion: inductively, deductively, and causally.

INDUCTIVE REASONING   **Inductive reasoning** is a way to arrive at a general conclusion from specific instances or examples. Using this reasoning approach, you reach a general conclusion based on specific examples, facts, statistics, and opinions. For example, you recently bought a foreign car that gave you trouble. Your cousin, you just learned, also bought a foreign car that did not live up to its promise. Finally, your English professor told you that her foreign car has broken down several times in the past few weeks. Based on these specific examples, you reach a general conclusion that foreign cars are poorly made.

As a persuasive speaker, your job is to construct a sound argument. That means basing your generalization on evidence that you can find. When you listen to a persuasive message, notice how the speaker tries to support his or her conclusion. To judge the validity of a generalization arrived at inductively, keep the following questions in mind.

1. *Are there enough specific examples to support the conclusion?* Are three examples of problems with foreign cars enough to prove your point that all foreign cars are inferior to American-made cars? Of the several million foreign cars that are manufactured, three cars are not a large sample. If those examples were supported by

additional statistical evidence that over 50 percent of foreign car owners complained of serious engine malfunctions, compared to only 10 percent of owners of U.S. cars, the evidence would be more convincing.

2. *Are the specific instances typical?* Were the three examples that you cited representative of all foreign cars manufactured? How do you know? What are the data on the performance of foreign cars? Also, are you, your cousin, and your professor typical of most car owners? The three of you may be careless about routine maintenance of your autos.

3. *Are the instances recent?* If the foreign cars that you are using as examples of poor quality are over three years old, you cannot reasonably conclude that today's foreign cars are inferior products. Age alone may explain the poor performance of your sample.

Reasoning by analogy is a special type of inductive reasoning. An **analogy** is a comparison. This form of reasoning compares one thing, person, or process with another to predict how something will perform and respond. When you observe that two things have a number of characteristics in common and that a certain fact about one is likely to be true of the other, you have drawn an analogy and reasoned from one example to reach a conclusion about the other. If you try to convince an audience that mandatory seat belt laws in Texas and Florida have reduced highway deaths and therefore should be instituted in Kansas, you are reasoning by analogy. You would also be reasoning by analogy if you claimed that capital punishment reduced crime in Brazil and therefore should be used in the United States as well. But as with reasoning by generalization, there are questions that you should ask to check the validity of your conclusions.

1. *Do the ways in which the two things are alike outweigh those in which they are different?* Can we compare the crime statistics of Brazil to those of the United States and claim to make a valid comparison? Are the data collected in the same way in both countries? Are there other factors besides the seat belt laws in Texas and Florida that could account for the lower automobile accident death rate? Maybe differences in the speed limit or the types of roads in those states can account for the difference.

2. *Is the assertion true?* Is it really true that capital punishment has served as a deterrent to crime in Brazil? Is it really true that mandatory seat belt laws in Florida and Texas have reduced auto highway deaths? You will need to give reasons the comparison you are making is valid, and evidence that will prove your conclusion to be true.

DEDUCTIVE REASONING   **Deductive reasoning** is reasoning from a general statement or principle to reach a specific conclusion. This is just the reverse of inductive reasoning. Deductive reasoning can be structured in the form of a syllogism. A **syllogism** is a way of organizing an argument. It has three elements: a major premise, a minor premise, and a conclusion. To reach a conclusion deductively, you start with a general statement that serves as the **major premise.** "All communication professors have excellent teaching skills" is an example of a major premise. The **minor premise** is a more specific statement about an example that

analogy
A special type of inductive reasoning in which you compare one thing, person, or process with another to predict how something will perform and respond.

deductive reasoning
A process of reasoning from a general statement or principle to reach a specific conclusion.

syllogism
A three-part way of developing an argument; it has a major premise, a minor premise, and a conclusion.

major premise
A general statement that is the first element of a syllogism.

minor premise
A specific statement about an example that is linked to the major premise; it is the second element of a syllogism.

is linked to the major premise. "John Smith is a communication professor" is an example of a minor premise. The *conclusion* is based on the major premise and the more specific minor premise. In reasoning deductively, you need to ensure that the major and minor premises are true and can be supported with evidence. The conclusion to our syllogism is "John Smith has excellent teaching skills." The persuasive power of deductive reasoning derives from the fact that the conclusion cannot be questioned if the premises are accepted as true.

To test the truth of an argument organized deductively, consider the following questions.

1. *Is the major premise (general statement) true?* Is it really true that *all* communication professors have excellent teaching skills? What evidence do you have to support this statement? The power of deductive reasoning hinges in part on whether your generalization is true.

2. *Is the minor premise (the particular statement) also true?* If your minor premise is false, your syllogism can collapse right there. In our example, it is easy enough to verify that John Smith is a communication professor. But not all minor premises can be verified as easily. For example, it would be difficult to prove the minor premise in this example:

All gods are immortal.
Zeus is a god.
Therefore, Zeus is immortal.

We can accept the major premise as true because immortality is part of the definition of *god*. But proving that Zeus is a god would be very difficult. In this case, the truth of the conclusion hinges on the truth of the minor premise.

▼

casual reasoning
A process of reasoning in which two or more events are related in such a way as to conclude that one or more of the events caused the others.

CAUSAL REASONING   A third type of reasoning is called **causal reasoning.** When you reason by cause, you relate two or more events in such a way as to conclude that one or more of the events caused the others. For example, you might argue that Gary Hart dropped out of the race for president in 1987 *because* of the allegations that he was having an affair.

There are two ways to structure a causal argument. First, you can reason from cause to effect, moving from a known fact to a predicted result. You know, for example, that interest rates have increased in the past week. Therefore, you might argue that *because* the rates are increasing, the Dow Jones Industrial Average will decrease. In this case, you move from something that has occurred (rising interest rates) to something that has not yet occurred (decreases in the stock market). Weather forecasters use the same method of reasoning when they predict the weather. They base a conclusion about tomorrow's weather on what they know about today's meteorological conditions.

A second way to frame a causal argument is to reason backward, from known effect to unknown cause. You know, for example, that a major earthquake has occurred (known effect). To explain this event, you propose that the cause of the earthquake is a shift in the fault line (unknown cause). You cannot be sure of the cause, but you are certain of the effect. A candidate for president may claim that the cause of current high unemployment (known effect) is mismanagement by the present administration (unknown cause). He then constructs an argument to prove that his assertion is accurate. To prove his case, he needs to have evidence that the present administration mismanaged the economy. The key to developing strong causal arguments is in the use of evidence to link something known with something unknown. An understanding of the appropriate use of evidence can enhance inductive, deductive, and causal reasoning.

RECAP

TYPES OF REASONING	Type	Definition	Example
	Inductive reasoning	Thought pattern that moves from specific information to a general conclusion	When tougher drug laws went into effect in Kansas City and St. Louis, drug traffic was reduced. The United States should therefore institute tougher drug laws.
	Deductive reasoning	Thought pattern that moves from a general statement to a specific conclusion	All bachelors are unmarried men. Frank is a bachelor. Therefore, Frank is an unmarried man.
	Causal reasoning	Thought pattern that relates two or more events to prove that one or more of the events caused the other	Since the 65-mile-per-hour speed limit went into effect, traffic deaths have increased. The increased highway speed has caused an increase in highway deaths.

Supporting Your Reasoning with Evidence You cannot simply state a conclusion without proving it. Proof consists of the structure of your argument plus the evidence to support your conclusion. Evidence in persuasive speeches consist of facts, examples, statistics, and expert opinions. Let's take a closer look at the major types of evidence and identify tests to make sure that your evidence is valid.

FACTS It's a fact that the world is round, that the moon is not made of green cheese, and that Alaska is the largest state in the Union. Those facts are not controversial. But you often hear the assertion "It's a fact that . . ." hurled in debates. What makes a fact a fact? A **fact** has been directly observed to be true. The spherical shape of the world, the composition of the moon, and the size of the states of the Union have all been directly observed or measured. Without direct measurement or observation, we can only make an inference. An **inference** is a conclusion based

fact
Something that has been directly observed to be true.

inference
A conclusion based on available evidence.

on available evidence. So it is a fact that the sun rose yesterday, but it is not a fact that the sun will rise tomorrow. It probably will, and we can make a strong case for believing so, but unless something has been directly observed or tested, it is inappropriate to label it a fact.

To test the validity of facts used in supporting a persuasive argument, ask the following questions:

1. Do people who observed the fact argue about whether it actually happened or existed?
2. Are there contrary facts?
3. Is the report of the fact made by someone who observed the occurrence directly?

example
An illustration used to dramatize or clarify a fact.

EXAMPLES   An **example** is an illustration that is used to dramatize or clarify a fact. Only true examples can be used validly to help prove a point. A hypothetical example, one that is fabricated just to illustrate a point, should not be used to reach a conclusion. It should only be used to clarify. In Chapter 6, we commented on the value of real or personal examples as a means of adding concrete interest to your speech.

When using examples to support an argument, there are several questions that you should ask about the validity of your evidence.

1. Is the example typical?
2. Is the example significant or important?
3. Is the source of the example reliable?
4. Are there contrary examples?
5. Has the truth of the example been checked and verified?

opinion
Testimony or quotation that expresses attitudes, beliefs, or values of someone else.

OPINIONS   An **opinion** is a personal judgment, usually made by an expert, that you quote to add credibility to your conclusion. The best opinions are made by an expert or authority who is known to be unbiased, fair, and accurate. Even so, opinions are usually most persuasive if they are combined with evidence, such as facts or statistics, that support the position of the expert.

The following questions can help you evaluate the validity of the opinions you cite and those cited by others.

1. Is the source of the opinion reliable and reputable?
2. Is the source an expert or authority in the field under discussion?
3. What are the expert's credentials?
4. Is the source biased?
5. Is the opinion consistent with other statements made by the expert?
6. Is the opinion consistent with other statements made by other experts?

statistic
Numerical data that summarize facts and examples.

STATISTICS   A **statistic** is a number used to summarize concisely several facts or samples. If statistics did not exist, you would have to enumerate countless individual examples to support arguments based on quantity, such as whether the economy is moving up or down. It is simply neither practical nor often possible to list a volume of facts and examples in order to make a supportable generalization. Just as with other types of evidence, you need to be sure that your statistics are accurate and support the point you want to make. As was observed in Chapter 6, more than any other type of evidence, statistics are abused, misused, and often misgathered. The following questions can help you determine the value of the statistics that you use in supporting your arguments.

1. Is the source of the statistics reliable?
2. Are the statistics recent?
3. Is the source of the statistics unbiased?
4. If the statistics represent a sample from a large population, are they representative of the whole population?
5. Is the sample size from which the statistics were drawn adequate?
6. Are there contrary statistics?

Reasoning Fallacies We have emphasized the importance of developing sound, logical arguments supported with appropriate evidence. Not all people who try to persuade you will use sound arguments to get you to vote for them, buy their product, or donate money to their cause. Many persuaders use inappropriate techniques called fallacies. A **fallacy** is false reasoning that occurs when someone attempts to persuade without adequate evidence or with arguments that are irrelevant or inappropriate. You will be both a better speaker and a better listener if you are aware of the following fallacies.

fallacy
False reasoning that occurs when someone attempts to persuade without adequate evidence or with arguments that are irrelevant or inappropriate.

CAUSAL FALLACY The Latin term for this fallacy is *post hoc, ergo propter hoc,* which translates as "after this, therefore, because of this." It refers to making a faulty causal connection. Simply because one event follows another does not mean that the two are related. If you declared that your school's football team won this time because you sang your school song before the game, you would be guilty of a causal fallacy. There are undoubtedly other factors that explain why your team won, such as good preparation or facing a weaker opposing team. For something to be a cause, it has to have the power to bring about a result. "That howling storm last night knocked down the tree in our back yard" is a logical causal explanation.

CIRCULAR REASONING If you hear an advertiser say that Spiffy laundry detergent cleans clothes better because it gets clothes cleaner, you have heard a circular argument. Circular reasoning uses different words to make the same point.

BANDWAGON FALLACY Someone who argues that "everybody thinks it's a good idea, so you should too" is using the bandwagon fallacy. Simply because someone says that "everyone" is "jumping on the bandwagon" or supporting a particular point of view does not make the point of view correct.

STRAW MAN This fallacy occurs when a skillful persuader sets up a weak argument (a straw man) against his or her own point of view and then proceeds to refute it, thereby leaving the original point of view seemingly untouched. The weak argument is like a straw man that the persuader knows can easily be knocked down.

EITHER-OR Someone who argues that there are only two approaches to a problem is trying to oversimplify the issues. "It's either vote for higher property taxes or close the library," asserts Daryl at a public hearing on tax increases. Such a statement ignores a variety of other solutions to a complex problem.

HASTY GENERALIZATION   A person who reaches a conclusion from too little evidence or nonexistent evidence is making a hasty generalization. For example, simply because one person became ill after eating the meatloaf in the cafeteria does not mean that everyone eating in the cafeteria will contract serious health problems because of food poisoning.

ATTACKING THE PERSON   Also known as *ad hominem*, Latin for "to the man," this involves attacking irrelevant personal characteristics about the person who is proposing an idea rather than attacking the idea itself. When George assails Janice's credibility after she presents her idea, rather than critiquing the idea itself, he is committing this fallacy. A statement such as "We know Janice's idea won't work because she has never had a good idea yet" does not really deal with the idea, which may be perfectly valid. Don't dismiss an idea solely because you have been turned against the person who presented it.

RED HERRING   The red herring fallacy takes place when someone attacks an issue by using irrelevant facts or arguments as distractions. This fallacy gets its name from an old trick of dragging a red herring across a trail to divert the dogs who may be following. Speakers use a red herring when they want to distract an audience from the real issues. For example, a politician who had been accused of taking bribes while in office calls a press conference. During the press conference, he talks about the evils of child pornography rather than addressing the charge against him; he is using the red herring technique to divert attention from the real issue—did he or did he not take the bribe?

APPEAL TO MISPLACED AUTHORITY   When ads use baseball catchers to endorse automobiles and TV heroes to sell political candidates, we are faced with the fallacious appeal to misplaced authority. Although we have great respect for these people in their own fields, they are no more expert than we are in the areas they are advertising. As both a public speaker and a listener, you must recognize what is valid expert testimony and what is not. For example, a physicist who speaks on the laws of nature or the structure of matter could reasonably be accepted as an expert. But if the physicist speaks on politics, the opinion expressed is not that of an expert and is no more significant than your own.

NON SEQUITUR   If you argue that a new parking garage should not be built on campus because the grass has not been mowed on the football field for three weeks, you are guilty of a non sequitur (Latin for "it does not follow"). Grass growing on the football field has nothing to do with the parking problem. Your conclusion simply does not follow from your statement.

Persuading with Emotion

Each year during Labor Day weekend, Jerry Lewis hosts a telethon designed for one purpose: to raise money for muscular dystrophy. Some persuasive effort is made using logical appeals (facts and figures are cited to document the seriousness of the disease). Because celebrities are used to ask for donations, the sponsors of the show rely on the credibility granted famous people to gain your dollars. But the chief method of getting your money is through various emotional appeals. You see scores of crippled or ill children who have been stricken by the disease. Emotionally charged minispeeches are delivered to arouse your sympathy for those with muscular dystrophy. Music and stories are also used to get you and the rest of the audience to donate funds. Appeals to the emotions of listeners are a powerful and effective way of getting a desired response from an audience.

A speaker who resorts to emotional appeals to persuade an audience uses generalizations, examples, opinions, and statistics as well as visual and auditory stimuli to trigger the desired feelings in his or her listeners. Whereas logical arguments may appeal to your reason, emotional arguments generally appeal to nonrational sentiments.

One theory suggests that your emotional responses can be classified along three dimensions.[1] First, you respond with varying degrees of *pleasure or displeasure*. Pleasurable stimuli consist of such things as smiling, healthy babies or daydreams about winning $1 million in a sweepstakes. Stimuli causing displeasure may be TV images of dead and mangled bodies in Beirut or news stories of child abuse.

A second dimension of emotional responses exists on a continuum of *arousal-nonarousal*. You become aroused emotionally at such things as seeing a snake in your driveway, or you may be lulled into a state of nonarousal by a boring lecture.

The third dimension of emotional responses is one's feeling of *power or powerlessness* when confronted with some stimulus. When thinking about the destructive force of nuclear weapons or the omnipotence of God, you may feel insignificant and powerless. Or perhaps you feel a sense of power when you imagine yourself conducting a symphony or winning an election.

These three dimensions—pleasure, arousal, and power—form the bases of all our emotional responses. The theory predicts that if listeners feel pleasure and are also aroused by something, such as a political candidate or a product, they will tend to form a favorable view of the candidate or product. A listener's feeling of being powerful or powerless has to do with being in control and having permission to behave as he or she wishes. A listener who feels powerful is more likely to respond to the message.

As a public speaker trying to sway your listeners to your viewpoint, your job is to use emotional appeals to achieve your goal. If you want to persuade your listeners that abortion should be outlawed, you would try to arouse feelings of displeasure and turn them against abortion. Advertisers selling soft drinks typically strive to arouse feelings of pleasure when you think of their product. Smiling people, upbeat music, and good times are usually part of the formula for selling soda pop.

Though the underlying theory of emotions may help you understand how emotions work, as a public speaker your key concern is "How can I ethically use emotional appeals to achieve my persuasive purpose?" Let's consider several methods.

1. *Use concrete examples that help your listeners visualize what you describe.* Using a concrete example of an emotionally moving scene can create a powerful response in your audience. Describing what it was like after a tornado destroyed the town

of Saragosa, Texas, can evoke strong emotions in your listeners. The images used to evoke the emotions can also help communicate the power of nature and the value of taking proper precautions when a storm warning is sounded.

> The town is no more. No homes in the western Texas town remain standing. The church where twenty-one people perished looks like a heap of twisted metal and mortar. A child's doll can be seen in the street. The owner, four-year-old Maria, will no longer play with her favorite toy; she was killed along with five of her playmates when the twister roared through the elementary school.

2. *Use emotion-arousing words.* Words and phrases can trigger emotional responses in your listeners. *Mother, flag, freedom,* and *slavery* are among a large number of emotionally loaded words. Patriotic slogans, such as "Remember the Alamo" or "Remember Pearl Harbor," have produced strong emotional responses.

3. *Use nonverbal behavior to communicate your emotional response.* The great Roman orator Cicero believed that if you want your listeners to experience a certain emotion, you should first model that emotion for them. If you want an audience to feel anger at a particular law or event, you must display anger and indignation in your voice, movement, and gesture. As we have already noted, delivery plays the key role in communicating your emotional responses. If you want your audience to become excited about and interested in your message, you must communicate that excitement through your delivery.

4. *Use selected appeals to fear.* The threat that harm will come to your listeners unless they follow your advice is an appeal to fear. As was discussed in Chapter 15, listeners can be motivated to change their behavior if appeals to fear are used appropriately. Research suggests that high fear arousal ("You will be killed in an auto accident unless you wear a seat belt") is more effective than moderate or low appeals if you are a highly credible speaker. However, there may be a risk in arousing so much anxiety in your listeners that they find what you have to say so exaggerated that they stop listening to you. Hence, unless you are a highly credible speaker, moderate fear appeals directed toward your listeners or their loved ones seem to work best.

5. *Consider using appeals to several emotions.* Appealing to the fears and anxieties of your listeners is one of the most common types of emotional appeals used to persuade, but you could also elicit several other emotions to help achieve your persuasive goal.

> *Hope.* Listeners could be motivated to respond to the prospect of a brighter tomorrow. When Franklin Roosevelt said, "The only thing we have to fear is fear itself," he was invoking hope for the future.
> *Pride.* "The pride is back" is a slogan used to sell cars. An appeal to pride can also be used to motivate listeners in a persuasive speech. The appeal to achieve a persuasive objective based on pride in oneself or one's country, state, or hometown can be very powerful. President Bush's first televised speech to the nation emphasized that we will be able to take pride in America if we can eliminate illegal drugs in our society.
> *Courage.* Challenging your audience to take a bold stand or to step away from the crowd can emotionally charge your listeners to take action. Referring to courageous men and women as role models can help motivate your listeners to

take similar actions. Patrick Henry's famous "Give me liberty, or give me death!" speech appealed to his audience to take a courageous stand on the issues before the people.

Reverence. The appeal to the sacred and the revered can be an effective way to motivate. Sacred traditions, revered institutions, or cherished and celebrated individuals can be used to help inspire your audience to change or reinforce attitudes, beliefs, values, or behavior. Mother Teresa, holy writings, and the Congress of the United States are examples of revered people or things that may be perceived as sacred by your listeners. As an audience-centered speaker, however, you need to remember that what may be sacred to one individual or audience may not be sacred to another.

Regardless of which emotions you use to motivate your audience, you have an obligation to be ethical and forthright. Making false claims, misusing evidence to arouse emotions, or relying only on emotions without any evidence to support a conclusion violates ethical standards of effective public speaking.

Your credibility, reasoning, and emotional appeals are the chief ways to persuade an audience. Now you need to refine your technique. Your use of these persuasive strategies depends on the composition of your audience. As we have observed several times before, an early task in the public speaking process is to analyze your audience. This is particularly important in persuasion. Audience members are not just sitting there waiting to respond to every suggestion a speaker makes.

STRATEGIES FOR ADAPTING IDEAS TO PEOPLE AND PEOPLE TO IDEAS

One definition of persuasive communication nicely summarizes the importance of adapting your message to your audience. "Rhetoric," suggests Donald C. Bryant, "is the process of adjusting ideas to people and people to ideas."[2] Your appeals to reason, emotion, and your own credibility are all dependent on the attitudes, beliefs, and values of your listeners.

Audience members may hold differing views of you and your subject. Your task is to find out if there is a prevailing viewpoint held by a majority of your listeners. If they are generally friendly toward you and your ideas, you need to design your speech differently than if your listeners are neutral, apathetic, or hostile. Research studies as well as seasoned public speakers can offer some useful suggestions to help you adapt your approach to your audience. We will discuss three general responses your audience may have to you: receptive, neutral, and unreceptive.

Persuading the Receptive Audience

It is always a pleasure when the audience you face is already supportive of you and your message. In speaking to a receptive group, you can explore your ideas in greater depth than otherwise. Here are some suggestions that may help you make the most of your speaking opportunity.

1. *Identify with your audience.* If you are a college student speaking to other college students with similar backgrounds and pressures, point to your similar backgrounds and struggles. Emphasize the similarities between you and your audience. What other common interests do you have? The introductory portion of your speech is a good place to mention your common interests and background.

2. *Clearly state your speaking objective.* We have stressed several times how important it is to provide an overview of your major point or purpose. This is particularly so when speaking to a group that will support your point of view.

3. *Tell your audience exactly what you want them to do.* Besides telling your listeners what your speaking objective is, you can also tell them how you expect them to respond to your message. Be explicit in directing your listeners' behavior.

4. *Ask listeners for an immediate show of support.* Evangelists usually speak to favorable audiences. Evangelist Billy Graham, for example, always asks those who support his Christian message to come forward at the end of his sermon. Asking for an immediate show of support helps to cement the positive response that you have developed during your speech.

5. *Use emotional appeals liberally.* You can usually move a favorable audience to action with strong emotional appeals while also reminding it of the evidence that supports your conclusion. If the audience already supports your position, you need not spend a great deal of time on lengthy, detailed explanations or factual information. You can usually assume that your listeners are already in possession of much of that material.

Persuading the Neutral Audience

Think how many lectures you go to with an attitude of indifference. Probably quite a few. Many audiences will fall somewhere between wildly enthusiastic and unreceptive; they will simply be neutral or indifferent. They may be neutral because they don't know much about your topic or because they just can't make up their minds whether to support your point of view. They may also be indifferent because they don't see how the topic or issue affects them. Regardless of the reason for your listeners' indifference, your challenge is to make them interested in your message. Let's look at some approaches to gaining their attention and keeping their interest.

1. *Capture your listeners' attention early in your speech.* All introductions should try to get your audience's attention, but this is particularly important when speaking to an audience that is indifferent. What can you do to get your listeners to pay attention to your message?

2. *Refer to beliefs that many listeners share.* When speaking to a neutral audience, identify common concerns and values that you plan to address. Martin Luther King's "I Have a Dream" speech (Appendix C) illustrates a reference to his listeners' common beliefs.

3. *Relate your topic not only to your listeners but also to their family, friends, and loved ones.* You can capture the interest of your listeners by appealing to the needs of people they care about. Parents will be interested in ideas and policies that affect

their children. People are generally interested in matters that may affect their friends, neighbors, and others with whom they identify, such as members of their own religion or economic or social class.

4. *Be realistic in what you can accomplish.* Don't overestimate the response you may receive from a neutral audience. People who start with an attitude of indifference are probably not going to become as enthusiastic as you are after hearing just one speech. Persuasion does not occur all at once or at a first hearing of arguments.

Persuading the Unreceptive Audience

One of the biggest challenges is to persuade audience members who are against you or your message. If they are hostile toward you personally, your job is to seek ways to enhance your acceptability and persuade them to listen to you. If they are unreceptive to your point of view, there are several approaches that you can use to help them listen to you.

1. *Don't immediately announce that you plan to change their minds.* If you immediately and bluntly tell your listeners that you plan to change their opinions, it can make them defensive. It is usually better to take a more subtle approach when announcing your persuasive intent.

2. *Begin your speech by noting areas of agreement before you discuss areas of disagreement.* Once you help your audience understand that there are issues on which you agree (such as agreeing that the topic you will discuss is controversial), your listeners may be more attentive when you explain your position.

3. *Don't expect a major shift in attitude from a hostile audience.* Set a realistic limit on what you can achieve. A realistic goal might be to have your listeners hear you out and at least consider some of your points.

4. *Acknowledge the opposing points of view that members of your audience may hold.* Summarize the reasons individuals may oppose your point of view. Doing this communicates that you at least understand the issues. Your listeners will be more likely to listen to you if they know that you understand their viewpoint. Of course, after you acknowledge the opposing point of view, you will need to cite evidence and use arguments to refute the opposition and support your conclusion.

5. *Establish your credibility.* Being thought credible is always an important goal of a public speaker, and it is especially important when talking to a hostile audience. Let your audience know about the experience, interest, knowledge, and skill that give you special insight into the issues at hand.

Is there one best way to organize a persuasive speech? The answer is no. Specific approaches to organizing speeches depend on audience, message, and desired objective. But how you organize your speech does have a major effect on your listeners' response to your message.

**ORGANIZING
PERSUASIVE MESSAGES**

Organizational Strategies

Several general principles can help you organize your speech for maximum persuasive effect.

1. *Make the audience aware of the problem before you present the solution.* Don't introduce your recommendations for change until your audience understands the issues. Making your audience aware of the problem helps gain and maintain interest and helps your audience understand why you reached the conclusion you did.

2. *Present both sides of an issue rather than just the advantages of the position you advocate.* If you don't acknowledge arguments that your listeners have heard, they will probably think about them anyway. Make some reference to the counterarguments, and then refute them with your own evidence and logic.

3. *Tell your audience what you want them to do at the end of your speech.* If you need to state specific conclusions to move your audience to action, it is better to do so toward the end of your speech than in the beginning.

4. *If you feel that your audience may be hostile to your point of view, advance your strongest arguments first.* If you save your best argument for last, your audience may have already stopped listening.

The Motivated Sequence

The motivated sequence is a five-step organizational plan that has proved successful for several decades. Developed by Alan Monroe, this simple yet effective strategy for organizing speeches incorporates principles that have been confirmed by research and practical experience.[3] It also uses the cognitive dissonance approach, which we discussed in Chapter 15: First disturb your listeners and then point them toward the specific change you want them to adopt. The five steps are attention, need, satisfaction, visualization, and action.

1. *Attention.* Your first goal is to get your listeners' attention. In Chapter 10, we discussed specific attention-catching methods of beginning a speech. Remember the particular benefits of using a personal or hypothetical example, a startling statement, an unusual statistic, a rhetorical question, or a well-worded analogy. The attention step is, in essence, the introduction to your speech.

Vic Vieth began his prize-winning speech titled "Prisoners of Conscience" with this dramatic, attention-catching description:

> Tenzin Chodrak lived on nine ounces of grain a day as he was forced to work a rock-hard soil beneath a beating sun. In time, his hair fell out and his eyebrows fell off. Tortured by his hunger he ate rats and worms and, eventually, his leather jacket.[4]

2. *Need.* After getting the attention of your audience, now establish why your topic, problem, or issue should concern your listeners. Arouse dissonance. Tell your audience why the current program, politician, or whatever you're attempting to change is not working. There is a need for a change. You must also convince your listeners that this need for a change affects them directly. During the need

step, you should develop logical arguments backed by ample evidence to support your position.

To document the need for greater involvement in human rights issues around the world, Vic Vieth established the need for concern in his "Prisoners of Conscience" speech with the following:

> There is no accurate estimation of the number of the world's prisoners of conscience. [Prisoners of conscience are people who have been jailed for beliefs and convictions that challenge their government.] Human rights organizations are overburdened and understaffed and what estimates they do provide us are only the roundest of guesses. Still, Amnesty International says there are perhaps 10,000 in the Soviet Union and 2,000 in Poland, 15,000 in Turkey and 10,000 spread across Africa, 5,000 in South America and some 100,000 are strung across Pakistan, Afghanistan, Iran, Iraq, South Korea and the Philippines. . . . In its most recent state of the world report, the United Nations conceded [that] our planet is still racked with "political liquidations, mass killings and torture."[5]

3. *Satisfaction.* After you present the problem or need for concern, you next briefly identify how your plan will satisfy the need. What is your solution to the problem? At this point in the speech, you need not go into great detail. Present enough information so that your listeners have a general understanding of how the problem may be solved.

Vic Vieth established the satisfaction step in his speech when he noted: "First, we must recognize that human rights is a worthy objective. . . . Second, once we recognize human rights as a worthy objective, we can move to make it once again a part of our foreign policy."[6]

4. *Visualization.* Now you need to give your audience a sense of what it would be like if your solution were or were not adopted. You could take a *positive visualization* approach: Paint a picture with words to communicate how wonderful the future will be if your solution is adopted. You could take a *negative visualization* approach: Tell your listeners how awful things will be if your solution is not adopted. If they think things are bad now, just wait; things will get worse. Or you could present both a positive and negative visualization of the future: The problem will be solved if your solution is adopted, and the world will be a much worse place if your solution is not adopted.

In moving to this step for his "Prisoners of Conscience" speech, Vic Vieth used a positive visualization approach when he said, "If we can muster the moral decency to defend political freedom, we may one day achieve political freedom for everyone, everywhere."[7]

He could have had an even stronger visualization step by noting the specific benefits of supporting his solution. He could have helped his audience visualize the specific joy men and women will have once they are set free. Martin Luther King's moving "I Have a Dream" speech (Appendix C) provided strong positive visualization:

> I have a dream that one day this nation will rise up and live out the true meaning of its creed, "We hold these truths to be self-evident, that all men are created equal."
>   I have a dream that one day on the red hills of Georgia the sons of former slaves and the sons of former slaveowners will be able to sit down together at the table of brotherhood.

I have a dream that one day even the state of Mississippi, a state sweltering with the heat of injustice, sweltering with the heat of oppression, will be transformed into an oasis of freedom and justice.

I have a dream that my four little children will one day live in a nation where they will not be judged by the color of their skin but by the content of their character. I have a dream today.

I have a dream that one day, down in Alabama, with its vicious racists, with its governor having his lips dripping with the words of interposition and nullification, one day right there in Alabama little black boys and black girls will be able to join hands with little white boys and white girls as sisters and brothers. I have a dream today.

I have a dream that one day every valley shall be exalted, every hill and mountain shall be made low, the rough places will be made plane and the crooked places will be made straight, and the glory of the Lord shall be revealed, and all flesh shall see it together.[8]

5. *Action.* This last step forms the basis of your conclusion. You tell your audience the specific action they can take to implement your solution. Identify exactly what you want your listeners to do. Give them simple, clear, easy-to-follow steps to achieve your goal. For example, you could give them a phone number to call for more information, provide an address so that they can write a letter of support, hand them a petition to sign at the end of your speech, or tell them whom to vote. Outline the specific action you want them to take.

In the "Prisoners of Conscience" speech, Vic Vieth identified some specific actions his audience could take:

It's up to us to support the work of organizations such as America's Watch and Amnesty International, chapters of which are on almost every campus, and it's up to us to elect, this election year, a government which places high on its list of priorities the defense of human rights.[9]

Modify the motivated sequence to suit the needs of your topic and audience. If, for example, you are speaking to a favorable audience, you do not have to spend a great deal of time on the need step. They already agree that the need is serious. They may, however, want to learn about some specific actions that they can take to implement a solution to the problem. Therefore, you would be wise to emphasize the satisfaction and action steps.

Conversely, if you are speaking to a hostile audience, you should spend considerable time on the need step. Convince your audience that the problem is significant and that they should be concerned about the problem. You would probably not propose a lengthy, detailed action.

If your audience is neutral or indifferent, spend time getting their attention and inviting their interest in the problem. The attention and need steps should be emphasized.

The motivated sequence is a guide, not an absolute formula. Use it and the other suggestions about speech organization to help you achieve your specific objective. Be audience centered; adapt your message to your listeners.

Aristotle defined rhetoric as the process of gathering the available means of persuasion. In this chapter, we have described some of the means that are available to you.

RECAP ▼

THE MOTIVATED SEQUENCE	Step	Purpose	Method
	1. Attention	To get the audience to listen to your message	Use rhetorical question, startling fact or statistic, quotation, analogy, personal example, hypothetical example, story, or illustration.
	2. Need	To describe the problem and relate it to the need for a change	Use facts, statistics, and other evidence to prove that a problem exists.
	3. Satisfaction	To present a solution that satisfies the need	Tell the audience how the problem can be solved.
	4. Visualization	To show the audience how the solution will solve the problem	*Positive*: Show the audience how great it will be if your solution is adopted. *Negative*: Show the audience how terrible it will be if your solution is not adopted.
	5. Action	To call for a personal response	Present specific, detailed instructions describing how your audience can take action.

Means of persuasion are techniques that can help you convince your listeners to follow your recommendations. In this chapter, we emphasized how to persuade with credibility, logic, and emotion.

Credibility is the view that a listener has of a speaker. The three factors of credibility are competence, trustworthiness, and dynamism. We also identified specific strategies for enhancing your credibility before, while, and after you speak.

Using effective logical arguments hinges on the proof you employ. Proof consists of evidence plus the reasoning that you use to draw conclusions from evidence. The three types of reasoning discussed were inductive reasoning from specific instances or examples to reach a general conclusion, deductive reasoning from a general statement to reach a specific conclusion, and causal reasoning relating two or more events in such a way as to conclude that one or more of the events caused the others. We also presented suggestions for using four types of evidence: facts, examples, opinions, and statistics. We concluded our section on developing logical arguments by identifying several fallacies that you should avoid.

SUMMARY

Sacred traditions, revered institutions, or celebrated individuals can inspire an audience to change or reinforce attitudes, beliefs, values, or behavior.
(*AP/World Wide Photos*)

We noted that emotion theory has identified three dimensions of emotional response to a message: pleasure-displeasure, arousal-nonarousal, and power-powerlessness. Specific suggestions for appealing to audience emotions included examples, emotion-arousing words, nonverbal behavior, and selected appeals to fear, hope, pride, courage, or the revered.

To persuade skillfully, you need to adapt your message to your audience. We reviewed strategies for adapting to receptive, neutral, and unreceptive audiences.

The chapter ended with specific suggestions for organizing a persuasive speech. The five steps of the motivated sequence (attention, need, satisfaction, visualization, and action) can be an effective pattern for organizing a persuasive speech. We suggested that you adapt the motivated sequence to your specific audience and persuasive objective.

QUESTIONS FOR DISCUSSION AND REVIEW	1. What is credibility? 2. Describe methods of enhancing your credibility before, while, and after you speak. 3. Define, compare, and contrast the following types of reasoning: inductive, deductive, and causal. 4. How can you determine if your evidence is valid? 5. Name several common reasoning fallacies. 6. In what ways can emotional appeals be used in a speech?

7. Cite strategies for speaking to a receptive, neutral, or unreceptive audience.
8. Describe the steps of the motivated sequence.

---

1. Identify three nationally known credible speakers. Identify methods and strategies that the speakers use to establish their credibility in a speaking situation. **SUGGESTED ACTIVITIES**
2. Listen to a talk radio program, and attempt to identify the types of reasoning used to develop a persuasive argument. Also, identify reasoning fallacies that you hear on call-in talk radio programs.
3. Identify a speaking situation during which the speaker effectively used emotional appeals. Describe the strategies that were used effectively to obtain an emotional response from the audience.
4. Develop strategies for presenting the same persuasive speech objective to three different audiences: an unreceptive audience, a neutral audience, and a receptive audience. Note the different strategies that you used in attempting to adapt your message to different listeners.
5. Watch or, if possible, videotape several TV commercials. Attempt to identify the five steps of the motivated sequence used in the commercials. Which steps were emphasized? Why?

17

Special-Occasion Speaking

OBJECTIVES

After studying this chapter, you should be able to

1. Identify and apply four principles for delivering an impromptu speech
2. Explain how to use a microphone for a public speech
3. Identify the five types of special-occasion speaking
4. List and describe the six types of ceremonial speeches
5. Describe the characteristics of a speech to entertain

Eternal truths will be neither true nor eternal unless they have fresh meaning for every new social situation. (The Timid Brute, *1938. Oil and govache on canvas, 22¼ × 29". Private collection, New York.*)

FRANKLIN DELANO ROOSEVELT

In a sense, any occasion that requires you to speak in public is a special occasion. Even the day you speak in class is a special occasion—a unique audience, environment, and set of circumstances in which to deliver a speech. Certain situations and occasions, however, stand out as special or distinctive. It is to these beyond-the-ordinary speech situations that we refer when we discuss special-occasion speaking. Most special-occasion speeches are given to celebrate, commemorate, entertain, or inspire. They are important enough and occur often enough to merit study.

We will first discuss two circumstances frequently encountered by special-occasion speakers. Then we will look at particular types of special-occasion speeches: introductions, ceremonial speeches, reviews of drama and literature, on-the-job speaking, and speaking to entertain. Keep in mind that one important requirement of public speaking remains constant, whether the situation is fairly standard or special: The speech must be audience-centered.

SPECIAL CIRCUMSTANCES FOR SPECIAL OCCASIONS

You are probably reading this chapter near the end of your semester or quarter of study and have probably already delivered several speeches. At this point, you are more confident than you had been about speaking extemporaneously from the front of a classroom or lecture hall. But sometime in the future, you may be faced with a number of special occasions that will call on you to exercise one or two skills that you may not have practiced yet. The first is delivering impromptu, or off-the-cuff speeches; the second is using a microphone.

Delivering the Impromptu Speech

"And the winner of this year's Founder's Award is (your name)!" Although it is usually a delightful surprise, the unexpected announcement of an award can also be a moment of panic as you struggle to collect your thoughts on the way to the podium to receive the award and make some appropriate remarks of gratitude. Or the president of your fraternal organization whispers to you just seconds before the program is to begin that he would like you to introduce the guest speaker. Or you have witnessed an accident, participated in a sports activity, or been involved in planning a major project that has attracted the press. At some point in the proceedings, a reporter thrusts a microphone in front of you and asks for a statement. What do you say?

Most of this book has been concerned with teaching you how to become an effective extemporaneous speaker. But most of us are also called on at one time or another to deliver a spur-of-the-moment or impromptu speech. As you learned in Chapter 11, impromptu delivery occurs when a speaker has only a very brief period in which to gather thoughts and then present them to an audience. Preparation time is practically nonexistent, ranging from a few seconds to a few minutes.

Impromptu speeches are always challenging and can be nerve-racking, particularly if you are asked to speak on a controversial or urgent matter. However, certain guidelines can help ease you through an impromptu speech.

1. Consider your audience and the occasion.
2. Be brief.
3. Speak honestly, but with reserve, from personal experience and knowledge.
4. Organize!

1. *Consider your audience*. Just as you have learned to do in other speaking situations, when you are called on for impromptu remarks, think first of your audience. Who are the members of your audience? What are their common characteristics and interests? What do they know about your topic? What do they expect you to say? What is the occasion of your speech? A quick mental check of these questions will help ensure that even the most impromptu remarks are audience-centered.

2. *Be brief.* When you are asked to deliver an off-the-cuff speech, your audience knows the circumstances and will not expect or even want a lengthy discourse. One to three minutes is a realistic time frame for most impromptu situations. Some spur-of-the-moment remarks, such as press statements, may be even shorter.

However, you might have to speak for more than a few minutes if you were to find yourself in a situation in which you needed to stall for time. For example, if you were chairing a program and the guest speaker had not shown up when it was time to begin, you might have to prolong the preliminaries. Such circumstances, however, need not be entirely impromptu. If you know that such a delay is possible, be prepared with some ideas or materials that could be stretched if needed.

Most of us are called upon at one time or another to deliver a spur-of-the-moment or impromptu speech.
(*Bob Daemmrich/Stock, Boston*)

3. *Speak honestly, but with reserve, from personal experience and knowledge.* Because there is no opportunity to conduct any kind of research before delivering an impromptu speech, you will have to speak from your own experience and knowledge. Remember, audiences almost always respond favorably to personal illustrations, so use any appropriate and relevant ones that come to mind. Of course, the more knowledge you have about the subject to be discussed, the easier it will be to speak about it off the cuff. But do *not* make up information or provide facts or figures about which you are not certain. An honest "I don't know" or a very brief statement is more appropriate.

Another word of caution: No matter how much knowledge you have, if your subject is at all sensitive or your information is classified, be careful when discussing it during your impromptu speech. If asked about a controversial topic, give an honest but noncommittal answer. You can always elaborate later, but you can never take back something rash you have already said. It is better to be cautious than sorry!

4. *Organize!* Off-the-cuff remarks need not falter or ramble. Effective impromptu speakers still organize their ideas into an introduction, body, and conclusion.

The introduction can use any of the methods discussed in Chapter 10. If you are often asked to speak on the spur of the moment, you would be wise to keep in the back of your mind several interesting illustrations or analogies that you can relate to a number of topics. A case in point is an introduction that a student speaker developed several years ago for impromptu speaking. She described the march of the lemmings, little mammals who herd together and, for some mysterious reason, follow one another into the sea to drown. Her brief anecdote became an analogy for human behavior related to a variety of social problems—pollution, discrimination, child abuse, suicide. All the student needed to adapt was a statement linking the march of the lemmings to human ignorance and inaction. A repertory of similarly flexible illustrations would serve any speaker well.

The body of the speech should have at least one main point. This can be brief, but it should have some support. Again, your personal experience is the kind of support that is easiest to call up and is also the best liked by most audiences.

The most effective way to conclude impromptu speeches is to refer to the introduction. For example, the coordinator of a school volunteer program was unexpectedly asked to describe that program for a group of community leaders. Her impromptu remarks went something like this:

> Some of you may have seen the movie *Field of Dreams* in the early summer of 1989. This was the movie in which a young farmer built a baseball diamond in the middle of his cornfield so that Shoeless Joe Jackson could return from beyond the grave to play baseball again. If you saw the movie, you probably remember the shivers of mystery you felt when, during the first half hour or so, the farmer heard a haunting voice wherever he turned—a voice that promised, "If you build it, he will come."
>
> Now, even though I am an incurable romantic, I will not claim to have heard the voice. But the philosophy, "If you build it, he will come," pretty well describes the optimism with which Crockett principal Pat Curtin and I began to organize a volunteer program at Crockett Elementary in the fall of 1987. We sincerely felt that if we could assess teachers' needs, actively recruit volunteers, assign volunteers to meaningful jobs, and recognize volunteers throughout the school year, they would come.
>
> And come they did. During the 1987–88 school year, thirty-five volunteers contributed eighteen hundred hours to Crockett's classrooms and support areas. During the 1988–89 school year, Travis Elementary began a volunteer program patterned after the one

we had started at Crockett. Sixty-five volunteers worked twenty-five hundred hours in the two schools. As we begin the 1989–90 school year, we expect to have programs in place in all six of San Marcos's prekindergarten-through-sixth-grade schools, and it is not unreasonable to expect that we will see approximately two hundred volunteers working as many as eight thousand volunteer hours. It is an exciting prospect and one that can ultimately make a great difference in the education of our children in this school district.

"If you build it, he will come." We built it—and the volunteers came. They are still coming, and we are only in the bottom of the first inning.

The introduction of this example is one of several "stock introductions" the speaker had gathered for the frequent presentations she must make about the school volunteer program. The statistics in the third paragraph are ones she knows well, having been instrumental in the organization and development of the program from its inception. And the conclusion refers briefly to the introduction.

As with other kinds of speeches, practice and experience will make impromptu speaking easier. If you commit to memory the four suggestions we just discussed, you will have a guide for times when you are unexpectedly called on to speak, however infrequently that may occur. Rather than groping blankly for something to say, you will be able to deliver a "put-together" talk, no matter how short the notice.

Using a Microphone

Using a microphone is certainly not restricted to special-occasion speaking, but it is in such speeches that you will most likely find yourself using one. And using the microphone requires special care. No matter how polished your speech, if you are inaudible or use a microphone awkwardly, your speech will not have the desired effect.

There are three kinds of microphones, only one of which demands much technique. The **lavaliere microphone** is the clip-on type often used by newspeople and interviewees. Worn on the front of a shirt or dress, it requires no particular care other than not thumping it or accidently knocking it off. The **boom microphone** is used by makers of movies and TV shows. It hangs over the heads of the speakers and is remote-controlled, so the speaker need not be particularly concerned with it. The third kind of microphone, and the most common, is the **stationary microphone.** This is the type that is most often attached to a podium, sitting on a desk, or standing on the floor. Generally, the stationary microphones used today are multidirectional. You do not have to remain frozen in front of a stationary mike while delivering your speech. However, you do need to take some other precautions when using one.

First, if you have a fully stationary microphone, rather than one that converts to a hand mike, you will have to remain behind the microphone, with your mouth about the same distance from the mike at all times, to avoid distracting fluctuations in the volume of sound. You can turn your head from side to side and use gestures, but you will have to limit other movements.

Second, microphones amplify sloppy habits of pronunciation and enunciation. Therefore, you need to speak clearly and crisply when using a mike.

lavaliere microphone
A microphone that can be clipped on an article of clothing to amplify your voice; may also be worn on a string from around your neck.

boom microphone
A microphone that is suspended from a bar and moved to follow the speaker; often used in movies and TV.

stationary microphone
A microphone attached to a podium or at the end of a rod that is usually located within 12 inches of a speaker's mouth.

Third, if you must test a microphone, count or ask the audience whether they can hear you. Blowing on a microphone produces an irritating noise!

Finally, do not tap, pound, or shuffle anything near the microphone. These noises too will be heard by the audience loudly and clearly. If your notes are on cards, quietly slide them aside as you progress through your speech. Notes on paper are more difficult to handle quietly, but do so with as little shuffling as you can manage.

Under ideal circumstances, you will be able to practice with the type of microphone you will use before you speak so that you can figure out where to stand for the best sound quality and how sensitive the mike is to extraneous noise. Practice will accustom you to any voice distortion or echo that might occur so that these sound qualities do not surprise you during your speech.

Modern microphones are not hard to use, but they require some practice and skill. Learn to use them to your advantage.

TYPES OF SPECIAL-OCCASION SPEECHES

Introductions

Most of us have heard poor introductions. A nervous speaker making an introduction stands up and mispronounces the main speaker's name. Or the introducer says something like, "Although we'll probably never have another speaker as good as we had last month, let me introduce tonight's speaker."

An introductory speech is much like an informative speech. The speaker delivering the introduction provides information about the main speaker to the audience. The ultimate purpose of an introduction, however, is to arouse interest in the speaker and his or her topic. When you are asked to give a speech of introduction for a featured speaker or an honored guest, your purposes are similar to those of a good opening to a speech: You need to get the attention of the audience, build the speaker's credibility, and introduce the speaker's general subject. You also need to make the speaker feel welcome while revealing some personal qualities to the audience so that they can feel they know the speaker more intimately. There are two cardinal rules of introductory speeches.

1. *Be brief.* The audience has come to hear the main speaker or honor the guest, not to listen to you.

2. *Be accurate.* Nothing so disturbs a speaker as having to begin by correcting the introducer. If you are going to introduce someone at a meeting or dinner, ask that person to supply you with relevant biographical data beforehand. If someone else provides you with the speaker's background, make sure that the information is accurate. Be certain that you know how to pronounce the speaker's name and any other names or terms you will need to use.

This short speech of introduction adheres to the two criteria we have just suggested: It's brief and it's accurate.

This evening, friends, we have the opportunity to hear one of the most innovative mayors in the history of our community. Mary Norris's experience in running her own real estate business gave her an opportunity to pilot a new approach to attracting new businesses to our community, even before she was elected mayor in last year's landslide victory. She was recently recognized as the most successful mayor in our state by the Good Government League. Not only is she a skilled manager and spokesperson for our city, but she is also a warm and caring person. I am pleased to introduce my friend, Mary Norris.

Finally, keep the needs of your audience in mind at all times. If the person you are introducing truly needs no introduction to the group, do not give one! Just welcome the speaker and step aside. "Friends" (or "Ladies and gentlemen"), "please join me in welcoming our guest speaker for tonight, the former chairman of this club, Mr. Daniel Jones." Note that the President of the United States is always introduced simply: "Ladies and gentlemen, the President of the United States."

Ceremonial Speeches

Ceremonial speeches make up a broad class of speeches delivered on many kinds of occasions. In this chapter, you will explore six types of ceremonial speeches: award presentations, acceptances, keynote addresses, commencement addresses, commemorative addresses, and eulogies.

Award Presentations   Presenting an award is somewhat like introducing a speaker or a guest: You need to remember that the audience did not come to hear you but to see and hear the winner of the award. Nevertheless, presenting an award is an important responsibility, one that has several distinct components.

First, when presenting an award, you should refer to the occasion of the presentation. Awards are often given to mark the anniversary of a special event, the completion of a long-range task, the accomplishments of a lifetime, or high achievement in some field.

Next, you should talk about the history and significance of the award. This section of the speech may be fairly long if the audience knows little about the award; it will be brief if the audience is already familiar with the history and purpose of the award. Whatever the award, a discussion of its significance will add to its meaning for the person who receives it.

The final section of the award presentation will be naming the person to whom it has been given. The longest part of this segment is the description of the achievements that contributed to receiving the award. That description should be in glowing terms. Hyperbole is appropriate here. If the name of the person getting the award has already been made public, you may refer to him or her by name throughout your description. If you are going to announce the individual's name for the first time, you will probably want to recite the achievements first and leave the person's name for last. Even though some members of the audience may recognize from your description the person about whom you are talking, you should still save the drama of the actual announcement until the very last moment.

Nominating speeches are similar enough to award presentations to warrant being discussed here. They too involve noting the occasion and describing the purpose and significance of, in this case, the office to be filled. The person making the nomination should explain clearly why the nominee's skills, talents, and past achievements serve as qualifications for the position. And the actual nomination should come at the end of the speech.

Acceptances   For every award, there must be an acceptance and, at least, a brief speech. Acceptance speeches have received something of a bad name because of the lengthy, emotional, rambling, and generally boring speeches many people have heard from winners of such awards as the film industry's Oscars. Speeches of acceptance can actually be quite insightful, even inspiring, and should leave the audience feeling no doubt that the right person won the award. Acceptance speeches need not be overly long. For some occasions, the shorter the acceptance speech, the better.

As we noted earlier in this chapter, acceptance speeches are often impromptu, since you may not know that you have won until the award is presented. A fairly simple three-part formula should help with even a spur-of-the-moment acceptance speech.

First, you should thank the person making the presentation and the organization that he or she represents. It is also gracious to thank a few people who have contributed greatly to your success—but not a long list of everyone you have ever known, down to the family dog.

Next, you should comment on the meaning or significance of the award to you. In what has become one of the most often quoted acceptance speeches ever made, novelist William Faulkner, accepting the Nobel prize for literature in 1950, declared:

> I feel that this award was not made to me as a man, but to my work—a life's work in the agony and sweat of the human spirit, not for glory and least of all for profit, but to create out of the materials of the human spirit something which did not exist before.[1]

You should also reflect on the larger significance of the award to the people and ideals it honors. In an eloquent acceptance speech, Elie Wiesel, Holocaust survivor, author, and lifelong advocate of human rights, began his acceptance speech for the 1986 Nobel peace prize with these words:

> It is with a profound sense of humility that I accept the honor you have chosen to bestow upon me. I know your choice transcends me. This both frightens and pleases me.
>
> It frightens me because I wonder: Do I have the right to represent the multitudes who have perished? Do I have the right to accept this great honor on their behalf? I do not. That would be presumptuous. No one may speak for the dead, no one may interpret their mutilated dreams and visions.
>
> It pleases me because I may say that this honor belongs to all the survivors and their children, and through us, to the Jewish people with whose destiny I have always been identified.[2]

Finally, try to find some meaning the award may have for your listeners—people who respect your accomplishments and who may themselves aspire to similar achievements. Faulkner directed his remarks to "the young men and women already dedicated to the same anguish and travail, among whom is already that one who will some day stand here where I am standing."[3]

An acceptance speech should be brief, particularly if other awards are being made on the same occasion. Your audience will appreciate a heartfelt note of thanks; they may resent a lengthy oration.

Keynote Addresses Keynote addresses are usually presented at or near the beginning of conferences or conventions and are intended to set the theme and tone for the remainder of the scheduled speakers. In essence, the keynote address states the central idea of the gathering—not for one speech but for many different ones.

The hardest task the keynote speaker faces is being specific enough to arouse interest. The very concept of a keynote address suggests generalities. The keynote speaker also needs to set a tone and an example for the speeches to come. A dull keynote speaker foreshadows a dull conference, and other speakers will have to work hard to combat the audience's preconception.

The closing sentences of Barbara Jordan's keynote address to the 1976 Democratic national convention, delivered when Jordan was a congresswoman from Texas, set a high tone for the rest of the week:

> Now, I began this speech by commenting to you on the uniqueness of a Barbara Jordan making the keynote address. Well I am going to close my speech by quoting a Republican President and I ask you that as you listen to these words of Abraham Lincoln, relate them to the concept of a national community in which every last one of us participates: "As I would not be a slave, so I would not be a master." This expresses my idea of Democracy. Whatever differs from this, to the extent of the difference, is no Democracy.[4]

The text of the entire speech is included in Appendix C.

Commencement Addresses Every graduation must have a speech—sometimes several. This unwritten but binding law means that the commencement address should take its place among other types of special-occasion speeches. Sometimes the commencement speaker is an outstanding member of the faculty or administration of the school; often the speaker is someone invited from outside the school. However the speaker is selected, the commencement speaker must fulfill two important functions.

First, a commencement speaker should praise the graduating class. Since the audience includes the families and friends of the graduates, the commencement speaker can gain their goodwill (as well as that of the graduates themselves) by pointing up the significance of the graduates' accomplishments. Beverly Chiodo of Southwest Texas State University congratulated the graduates of that university in the opening remarks of her 1987 commencement address: "This is a [historic] day. Graduates, we, your family, friends, and professors, we are glad we are here; and we rejoice in your accomplishments."[5]

The second function of the commencement speaker is to turn graduates toward the future. A commencement address is not the proper forum in which to bemoan the world's inevitable destruction or the certain gloomy future of today's graduates. Only political satirist Art Buchwald could get away with the comments he made some years ago to the graduates of Georgetown University:

"I have examined your grades. Your collective entry into the world of business marks the end of the free enterprise system as we know it. Thank you."[6]

Buchwald's irony was undoubtedly appreciated, but few others could replicate his success with similar remarks! Instead, a commencement speaker should set new, bright goals and inspire the graduates to reach for them. New York Governor Mario Cuomo did just that when he addressed the Harvard class of 1985:

> Even if you don't travel around with a scarlet letter *H* emblazoned on your sweater, or sound like you're from Boston, or order your clothes from L. L. Bean, people are going to discover soon enough where you went to school.
> They'll know because of what you'll do, the learning and intellect you'll bring to bear on your work, the depth and breadth of your talents.
> They'll know from your ambition. To be recognized. To distinguish yourselves. To be successful. To measure up to Harvard's standards: To be the best.[7]

Commemorative Addresses   Commemorative addresses are those delivered during special ceremonies held in memory of something or someone. The Fourth of July, your grandparents' fiftieth wedding anniversary, and the celebration of your state's admittance to the Union are examples of commemorative occasions that usually call for a speech.

The commemorative speaker is, in part, an informative speaker. He or she needs to present some fact about the person or event being celebrated. Then the speaker builds on that fact to urge the audience to let past accomplishments inspire them to seek new goals. "Remember the Alamo," the famous battle cry that inspired the Texans who fought for independence at San Jacinto, at once commemorated those massacred at the mission in San Antonio and drew on their sacrifice for inspiration. Daniel Webster's address at Bunker Hill on the fiftieth anniversary of that battle was both a memorial and an inspiration:

> We are among the sepulchres of our fathers. We are on ground distinguished by their valor, their constancy, and the shedding of their blood. . . .
> But there remains to us a great duty of defense and preservation; and there is open to us also a noble pursuit to which the spirit of the times strongly invites us. Our proper business is improvement. Let our age be the age of improvement. In a day of peace let us advance the arts of peace and the works of peace. Let us develop the resource of our land, call forth its powers, build up its institutions, promote all its great interests, and see whether we also, in our day and generation, may not perform something worthy to be remembered.[8]

▼
eulogy
A speech of tribute delivered to memorialize someone who has died.

Eulogies   **Eulogies,** speeches of tribute delivered when someone has died, are especially difficult commemorative addresses because of the emotional nature of the occasion. When you deliver a eulogy, you should mention, indeed, linger over, the achievements of the person to whom you are paying tribute and, of course, express a sense of loss. Adlai Stevenson delivered a eulogy for Winston Churchill in an appropriately formal, poetic style:

> Today we meet in sadness to mourn one of the world's greatest citizens. Sir Winston Churchill is dead. The voice that led nations, raised armies, inspired victories, and blew

fresh courage into the hearts of men is silenced. We shall hear no longer the remembered eloquence and wit, the old courage and defiance, the robust serenity of indomitable faith. Our world is thus poorer, our political dialogue is diminished, and the sources of public inspiration run more thinly for all of us. There is a lonesome place against the sky.[9]

It is also proper in a eulogy to include personal, even tastefully humorous recollections of the person who has died. Stevenson offered the following personal insight into Churchill's bond with both the United States and Great Britain:

He used to say that he was half American and all English. But we put that right when the Congress made him an honorary citizen of his mother's native land, and we shall always claim a part of him. I remember once years ago during a long visit at his country house he talked proudly of his American Revolutionary ancestors and happily of his boyhood visits to the United States. As I took my leave I said I was going back to London to speak to the English-Speaking Union and asked if he had any message for them. "Yes," he said, "tell them that you bring greetings from an English-Speaking Union."[10]

Finally, turn to the living, and encourage them to transcend their sorrow and sense of loss and feel instead gratitude that the dead person had once been alive among them. Again we turn to Stevenson's craftsmanship:

We are right to mourn. Yet in contemplating the life and the spirit of Winston Churchill, regrets for the past seem singularly insufficient. One rather feels a sense of thankfulness and of encouragement that throughout so long a life, such a full measure of power, virtuosity, mastery, and zest played over our human scene.[11]

Reviews of Drama and Literature

Oral reviews of books, plays, or movies are often presented as programs for club meetings, luncheons, and other fairly informal gatherings. Their purpose is at once informative, persuasive, and entertaining. Reviewers are expected to furnish information about the work being reviewed, to convince listeners that the work has either much or little value, and to entertain the audience. It is a large job, but fortunately, a well-chosen subject provides the means by which to accomplish it.

It is most common for reviewers to choose the work they will examine. Just as any speaker needs to be audience-centered, so does a reviewer when selecting material to be reviewed. Reviewers need to consider the interests and expectations of their audience, as well as the occasion for the review. They should also trust their own personal tastes. When reviewers are genuinely excited about the material, their excitement is often contagious, and the audience responds with enthusiasm about both the presentation and the work being reviewed.

Reviewers have many options for structuring their reviews. They may organize their thoughts according to plot, character, or theme. Or they may move chronologically, from cover to cover, or from opening curtain to closing.

Audiences expect reviewers to interpret the works being examined as well as to provide synopses. Various questions can be asked when judging a work. How does it compare with other works within the same genre? With other works by the same author or, in the case of a play or movie, by the same director? Are plot, character, and theme unique or conventional? If conventional, is there a unique angle or point of view? Whatever his or her opinions, a reviewer should always support them with carefully chosen excerpts from the work itself.

On-the-Job Speaking

If you intend to enter, or have already entered, a profession such as teaching or public relations, you now know that public speaking will be an almost daily part of your job. What you may not realize is that nearly every job involves the use of some public speaking skills. Audiences may range from a group of three managers to a huge auditorium filled with company employees. Presentations may be reports to corporate executives or public relations speeches to people outside your company. The occasions and opportunities are many, and chances are good that you will be asked or expected to do some on-the-job public speaking in the course of your career.

Job Interviews   Facing a prospective employer may be one of your most challenging, yet important speaking tasks. Though employment interviews are not usually public speaking events, using your audience-centered speaking skills can enhance your employability.

As with any speaking event, you need to prepare for your job interview. As we have emphasized throughout the book, consider your audience. In this case, it may

Facing a prospective employer may be one of your most challenging, yet important speaking tasks.
(*Steven Marks/StockPhotos, Inc.*)

be an audience of one—your interviewer. The more you can find out about the individual or individuals who will be interviewing you, the better prepared you can be. Your "speech topic" for a job interview is *you*. The interviewer wants to learn more about you and whether you will be able to meet his or her needs. Job search speaking is a combination of informing and persuading. You want to inform your listener about who you are and persuade him or her that you are the best person for the job. You will need to gather supporting material to help you communicate your objective. Research the company or organization to which you are applying. What are the organization's goals? How old is the company? What can you find out about the specific job for which you are interviewing?

Besides gathering information about the organization or company, you need to gather information about yourself. Personal information is usually presented on a **résumé.** A résumé should include your name, address, and phone number, a summary of your educational background, a brief employment history, a brief description of any special awards and honors, and a list of names, phone numbers, and addresses of individuals who could vouch for your expertise and character. Résumés should be impeccably typed and edited. They should also be brief. One-page résumés are usually sufficient for most entry-level jobs.

You need not draft an interview outline as you do a formal speech, but most interviews do follow a general organizational pattern. The introductory part of an interview sets the tone for the meeting. The body of the interview is when the key information about you, as well as about the organization, is shared. The concluding portion of an interview summarizes the key points, and you will usually be given an opportunity to ask questions toward the end of an employment interview.

In learning about public speaking, you studied speech delivery. In a job interview situation, how you deliver your message is crucial to making a successful presentation. Your nonverbal delivery may determine whether you are hired or not. We encourage you to be audience-centered as you make decisions about how to prepare and present yourself for a job interview. Most interviewers will expect you to dress up; a conservative suit and tie for men and a tasteful dress for women are appropriate. (Of course, if you were interviewing for a night janitorial position, a three-piece suit would be inappropriate!) Good eye contact and vocal delivery are just as important for job interviews as they are for public speaking. And your posture should communicate your interest in the job and the interviewer.

résumé
A carefully written and organized summary of your educational background, employment history, awards, honors, name, address, and phone number; used when you apply for a job, to present your credentials in a positive way.

Reports   One of the most common types of on-the-job presentations is the report. You may be asked to provide a report on how to increase sales in the next quarter or to report on a market survey your division has conducted in the past several months. Whatever the specific objective of the report, the general purpose is to communicate information or policy, sometimes ending with a persuasive appeal to try some new course of action.

Most successful reports are structured in a manner similar to the following outline:

1. *Need or problem.* The speaker discusses the need or problem that brought about the study or report in the first place. This part of the report is usually brief, because most of the people in the room are probably aware of the problem or need.

A key need for many business reports is simply to share information with other employees.

2. *Procedures for research or study.* The speaker explains how the shared information was gathered. The speaker could also discuss what the research group decided to do to explore the problem or present possible solutions to the problem, if the report is a problem-solving one.

3. *Findings.* The speaker reveals the results of the research.

4. *Relationship of the findings to the need or problem.* The speaker makes clear how the results of the research or study either clarify the need or suggest possible ways to fill it.

5. *Policy and recommendations.* For some reports, the most important part is the final section, which may outline new courses of action or changes in present policy based on the findings of the study. Not all reports, however, make policy recommendations. Many simply summarize information for those who need to know.

In addition to listening to the presentation, audience members usually receive a written copy of the report.

Public Relations Speeches People who work for professional associations, blood banks, utility companies, government agencies, universities, churches, or charitable institutions are often called on to speak to an audience about what their organization does or about a special project the organization has taken on. These speeches can be termed public relations speeches. Most public relations speeches follow this general pattern:

1. *Need or problem.* The speaker discusses the need or problem to which the organization addresses itself.

2. *Solution.* The speaker explains how the company or organization is working to meet the need or solve the problem.

3. *Anticipated objections.* The speaker may suggest and counter potential problems or criticisms, especially if past presentations have encountered some opposition to the policy or program. The speaker should emphasize the positive aspects of the policy or program and take care not to become unpleasantly defensive. The speaker wants to leave the impression that the company or organization has carefully worked through potential pitfalls and drawbacks.

Speaking to Entertain

There is great variety among speeches meant to entertain. Entertaining speeches can range from zany slapstick (Steve Martin) to sophisticated humor (Alan Alda). Occasions for such speeches can also vary, from a stand-up comedy routine for two thousand college students to an after-luncheon speech for twenty-five local Rotarians. Whatever the context, speeches to entertain share several characteristics and follow certain guidelines. These characteristics can be classified under the headings of comic devices and organizational strategies.

Comic devices are techniques that make a speech amusing. Above all, the comic speaker must master timing. Judging when and how long to pause is a skill requiring both instinct and learning that professional comics polish with experience. Pausing just before or just after a punch line can make the difference between an indifferent reaction and a roar of laughter from the audience. If you are concerned about timing, you couldn't do better than study such masters of the art as Jay Leno, Roseanne Barr, and Johnny Carson.

Facial expression is a second comic device. Verbal comedy can be funny, but being able to watch an entertainer's face can add immeasurably to the humor. Bill Cosby and Dom de Luise can evoke peals of laughter just by ringing changes in their facial expressions. Of course, the all-time master of this device was Charlie Chaplin.

The third class of comic devices is verbal. Such techniques as exaggeration and understatement, puns and malapropisms, satire, and, of course, jokes and amusing stories can all help make a speech more entertaining. If you do not have an endless supply of funny stories at your disposal, you may be comforted to learn that sourcebooks of humor are available. Organized alphabetically by subject, these books are easy to use.

In addition to using comic devices, an entertaining speaker should carefully plan the organization of the speech. Most entertaining speeches are organized somewhat loosely around a central theme. Erma Bombeck's talks, like her essays, are organized in such a manner. A second strategy is the chronological narrative, which relates events as they happened (for example, a typical day in the life of the average American family).

It is true that some people seem to be "naturally" funny. Humor is their usual style. If you are not a funny person—if, for example, you cannot get a laugh from even the funniest joke—you will need to practice an entertaining speech a number of times. Do so in front of people before trying to deliver it to your audience.

SUMMARY

We began this chapter by discussing how to deliver an impromptu speech. When presenting an impromptu speech, you should consider your audience, be brief, speak honestly from personal experience, and organize your thoughts quickly and simply.

For many special-occasion speeches, you will need to use a microphone. When using a microphone, remember to stay close to the mike, monitor your pronunciation and articulation, test the amplification system before you speak, and beware of shuffling notes, tapping, pounding, or making other sounds that, when amplified, will interfere with your talk.

We devoted the rest of the chapter to describing different types of special-occasion speeches.

Speeches of introduction should be brief and accurate.

Ceremonial speeches include award and nomination presentations and acceptances, keynote addresses, commencement addresses, commemorative addresses, and eulogies.

Reviews of drama and literature can be informative, persuasive, and entertaining all at once.

We briefly discussed three types of on-the-job speaking: job interviews, reports, and public relations speeches.

The final type of special-occasion speech we discussed was the speech to entertain. Your use of timing, facial expressions, exaggeration, puns, satire, and humorous narratives, as well as your organizational strategy, are key tools in presenting effective speeches to entertain listeners.

QUESTIONS FOR DISCUSSION AND REVIEW

1. Offer advice to someone who may be called on to deliver an impromptu speech.
2. What are the key points to keep in mind when using a microphone?
3. Provide a brief description of the six major classes of special-occasion speeches that were presented in this chapter.

SUGGESTED ACTIVITIES

1. Deliver an impromptu speech to your public speaking class on one of the following topics.

   Your first date
   Presidential politics
   What you liked best about elementary school
   The best book you ever read
   The best movie you ever saw
   The best TV program you ever saw
   Your favorite food
   Exercise is good for you
   Your most embarrassing moment
   Your first day of college
   Your favorite vacation spot
   What you like best about your hometown
   What you like least about your hometown
   Personal computers
   Your parents
   Your favorite museum
   Your favorite relative
   How you met your best friend
   Foods you hate
   Your favorite hobby

2. Each student should bring a common object to class. The object should be small enough to fit into a large grocery bag. Your instructor will gather the objects, place them in a bag, and ask you and your classmates to select an object. You are to deliver an impromptu persuasive speech, following the steps of the motivated sequence, in which you try to sell the object to your audience.

3. Attend a special-occasion speaking event, such as a school commencement, an award ceremony, or a luncheon for the retiring editor of your school newspaper. Write a critique of the speeches given, and evaluate the speeches based on the criteria presented in this chapter.

4. Pair up with another student in the class to discuss your common interests, vocational goals, and hobbies. Discover something your partner does well, and invent an award that you could give your colleague. Deliver a short presentation speech in which you bestow your award (e.g. "Best Short Story Written in English Class," "Best Piano Player in the Community"). The recipient of the award should then deliver a short acceptance speech.

18

Speaking in Small Groups

OBJECTIVES

After studying this chapter, you should be able to

1. Define small group communication
2. State the advantages and disadvantages of working in small groups
3. Organize group problem solving, using the steps of reflective thinking
4. Participate effectively in a small group
5. Identify three leadership styles and describe what leaders do to accomplish the group goal

Groups are incalculably important in the life of every human being. (*A detail from Alex Katz,* February 5:30 P.M., *1972. Oil on canvas, 72 × 144". Courtesy, Marlborough Gallery.*)

DAVID W. JOHNSON

It has been estimated that more than 11 million meetings are held every day in the United States. Groups are an integral part of our lives. Work groups, family groups, therapy groups, committees, and group projects for classes are just a few of the groups in which we may participate at one time or another. Chances are that you have had considerable experience in communicating in small groups.

In this chapter, we will concentrate on problem-solving and decision-making groups.[1] It is important to learn about group problem solving and decision making for at least two reasons. First, you will spend a major part of your work time in small groups. Up to 15 percent of a typical organization's total personnel budget is spent on group work. Middle managers generally spend up to 35 percent of their time working in groups. Most senior managers work in groups up to 60 percent of their working day.[2] A second reason to learn about groups is that it can help reduce some of the uncertainty and anxiety you may have about group deliberations. Many people don't like working in groups. If they knew more about group processes, their skill at working in groups would be enhanced, and so would their enjoyment of this activity.

In this chapter, you will learn some key communication principles and skills to help you work in groups. This will make you a useful and productive member of a team. Specifically, you will discover what small group communication is, learn to identify the advantages and disadvantages of working in groups, describe ways to improve group problem solving, recognize leadership skills, and become an effective group participant. By the end of the chapter, you will be able to use various formats for reporting group findings to others.

WHAT IS SMALL GROUP COMMUNICATION?

Small group communication occurs when a group consists of three to around a dozen people who communicate face to face, share a common purpose or goal, feel a sense of belonging to the group, and influence one another. This definition of group communication needs to be explored further.

Group Size

How many people constitute a group? Researchers in group communication generally study human interaction in groups of three to twelve people. With more than twelve, communication resembles public speaking rather than group interaction. The ideal size for a group depends on the specific task to be performed. Groups of five to seven members seem to be best.

Face-to-Face Communication

Small group communication requires that you interact with others in person. Since the advent of computers, teleconferencing, and other forms of electronic communication, it is entirely possible to exchange information without actually being

Group communication occurs when you can respond immediately to both the verbal and nonverbal communication of other people.
(*Steven Marks/StockPhotos, Inc.*)

in the presence of others. Group communication occurs, however, when you can respond immediately to both the verbal and nonverbal communication of other people.

A Common Purpose

Is a collection of five strangers waiting to get on an elevator a small group? Not according to our definition. To be a group, the members must share a *common* goal. The individuals waiting to get on the elevator may all want to get to another floor, but they do not all want to go to the same place; they don't share a common purpose. To be an effective team, all group members should share the same goals. Typical group goals include solving a problem, raising money, or making a decision.

A Sense of Belonging to the Group

One of the most satisfying aspects of group membership is the sense of belonging that a group usually engenders. The alternative feeling for individuals is often a sense of isolation. Groups are generally supportive of their members, and this tends to foster group cohesiveness. Most groups, however small, have a vivid sense of themselves as a community. This gives their members a feeling of security. The overriding feeling can be summarized as "We're in this together, and if we pull together, we'll come out OK."

Mutual Influence

Your very presence in a group can affect other group members and the group process. There are several ways in which this can occur. You may contribute ideas and share information or keep the group focused on its task. Managing conflict, telling jokes to relieve tension, watching the clock to keep your group on schedule, and taking notes are other ways in which you can have an impact on a group. You may think of leadership as one person influencing others, but leadership may be any behavior that affects others and helps a group achieve its goal. Each person in a group can influence group outcomes and can potentially be a leader. You'll learn more about leadership skills later in the chapter.

ADVANTAGES AND DISADVANTAGES OF WORKING IN GROUPS

When students find out that a group project is part of a course requirement, some feel instant despair; they have had miserable experiences working on such projects in the past. These students are all too familiar with the disadvantages of working collectively. Yet other students find group work pleasant and rewarding. They enjoy the fellowship and challenge afforded by working with others. Learning the advantages of working in groups can help you improve group productivity and communication. Knowing the potential disadvantages can help you manage problems before they become disruptive.

Advantages of Working in Groups

1. *Groups have more knowledge and information.* Because of the varied experiences and backgrounds of group members, your group has a greater chance of developing effective solutions to problems than if you were to try to do so alone. Two heads are better than one.

2. *Groups are more creative in solving problems.* Not only do groups have more information, but because of the collective experience of the group, they can often develop more ingenious methods of dealing with tough issues. Sometimes it's not just having more information but having new insight into a problem that can help resolve an issue. More people provide more points of view.

3. *You learn more when you work in a group than when you work by yourself.* Teachers know that they learn more about a subject when they teach it, rather than when passively reading or studying a topic by themselves. Understanding is improved when you take part in the give-and-take of group discussions.

4. *Group participation increases member satisfaction.* Generally, you are more likely to accept a recommendation if you had a hand in shaping that recommendation. Participating in decision making increases the likelihood that all members of a group will support the group's course of action.

Disadvantages of Working in Groups

1. *Group members may pressure others to conform.* Most of us try to avoid conflict. In our efforts to get along with others, we run the risk of agreeing with others to prevent quarrels. The members of a group may agree to undertake something just

to avoid dissension. Sociologists call this phenomenon *groupthink*—when group members agree merely to prevent conflict.

2. *One person may dominate group discussions*. Some people like to take charge. But in doing so, they may squelch others. Thus a group may lose the advantages of greater information and creativity in problem solving if one person talks too much.

3. *Group members may rely too much on other members to do the work*. It is tempting just to blend in and let someone else carry the burden of group work. As in the fable of the Little Red Hen, there may be few willing to do the work but many who want to benefit from the work of others. Lack of attendance at group meetings and nonparticipation when members are present indicate that the workload needs to be distributed more evenly.

4. *Making decisions in groups takes longer*. A key reason many people dislike group work is the amount of time it takes to accomplish a task. To achieve the advantages of working in a group, you must be patient with the extra time it takes to get things done.

RECAP

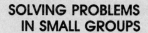

SOLVING PROBLEMS IN SMALL GROUPS

Advantages

Groups have more knowledge and information to share.
Groups have greater access to creative approaches to solving problems.
Learning increases when you work in groups.
People are more satisfied with a solution they help develop.

Disadvantages

Group members may pressure others to conform.
One person can monopolize the group.
Group members may rely too much on others to get the job done.
Working in groups takes longer than working by oneself.

A central purpose of many groups is solving problems. Problem solving is a means of finding ways of overcoming obstacles to achieve a desired goal. How can we raise money for the new library? What should be done to improve the local economy? How can we make higher education affordable for everyone in our state? Each of these questions implies that there is an obstacle (lack of money) blocking the achievement of a desired goal (new library, more local income, affordable education).

One method of organizing the problem-solving process is called **reflective thinking.** Originally a description of the way people solve problems, it has also been used to guide and structure problem-solving discussions. Although not every prob-

SOLVING PROBLEMS IN GROUPS

lem-solving discussion has to follow these steps, reflective thinking does provide a helpful blueprint that can relieve some of the uncertainty that exists when groups try to solve problems. There are five steps in the reflective thinking process.

1. Identify and Define the Problem

The first step in reflective thinking is to identify the problem clearly and to define it so that all group members have a common understanding of it and the purpose of the group meetings. Groups work best when a common goal is identified early in the group's history.

To help identify and define the problem, the group should consider the following questions:

1. What is the specific problem that we are concerned about?
2. What terms, concepts, or ideas do we need to understand in order to solve the problem?
3. Is anyone harmed by the problem?
4. Who is harmed?
5. When do the harmful effects occur?

Questions of policy are useful ways in which to identify and define problems. A policy question is phrased in such a way as to identify the course of action that should be taken to solve a problem or reach a decision. Policy questions typically begin with the words "What should be done about . . ." or "What could be done to improve . . ." Well-worded policy questions imply that there is a specific problem to be solved and are limited in scope. Here are some examples:

What should be done to improve security on our campus?
What should be done to improve the tax base in our state?
What steps can be taken to improve the United States' trade balance with other countries?

2. Analyze the Problem

Once the group understands the problem and has a well-worded question, the next step is to analyze the problem. **Analysis** is a process of examining the causes, effects, symptoms, history, and other background information that will help a group eventually reach a solution. In analyzing a problem, a group should consider the following questions:

1. What is the history of the problem?
2. How extensive is the problem?
3. Can the problem be subdivided for further definition and analysis?
4. What are the causes, effects, and symptoms of the problem?

5. What methods do we already have for solving the problem?
6. What are the limitations of those methods?
7. What new methods can we devise to solve the problem?
8. What obstacles keep us from reaching a solution?

Besides discussing these questions, the group should also develop practical **criteria** for evaluating an acceptable solution. Criteria are standards for making judgments. Useful criteria will help you recognize a good solution when you encounter one; criteria help the group focus on the goal of the group. Unless you know the guidelines your solution must follow, you will not be able to evaluate the acceptability of your solution. Here are some typical criteria for acceptable solutions:

1. The solution should be implemented on schedule.
2. The solution should be attainable within a given budget.
3. The solution should be agreed to by all group members.
4. The solution should remove the problem.

3. Suggest Possible Solutions

With the problem identified, defined, and analyzed, the group is now ready to try for possible solutions. You may recall that brainstorming was introduced in Chapter 5 as a method of generating speech topics. Many groups use brainstorming techniques to generate solutions.

Brainstorming is a way of enhancing individual and group creativity by calling up uncensored ideas. It includes the following steps:

1. Group members must understand that the goal of brainstorming is to generate solutions to a problem by whatever means. The members must also be aware of the specific problem that needs to be solved.

2. Group members must withhold all judgment and criticism. Criticism and faultfinding stifle creativity. This is one of the most difficult aspects of brainstorming to carry out. If group members find withholding judgment difficult, have the individual members write suggestions on paper first and then share the ideas with the group. Members should understand that the essential feature of brainstorming is the suspension of judgment—the only inadmissible suggestion is censorship.

3. With the goal and ground rules of brainstorming understood, the group then thinks of as many possible solutions to the problem as it can. All ideas are acceptable, even wild and crazy ones. All members must come up with at least one idea.

4. Piggyback off ideas. Expect a wild and outlandish idea to trigger another idea, either from someone else or the person with the original idea. Don't hold back.

5. Have a member of the group record all the ideas that are mentioned. Use a flipchart or chalkboard, if possible, so that all ideas can be seen and responded to.

6. After a set time has elapsed, evaluate the ideas, using the criteria that have been discussed previously. Approach the solutions positively.

Brainstorming can be used as part of the reflective-thinking process or at any time when a group needs creative ideas.

4. Select the Best Solution

The last part of the brainstorming process moves the group to the stage of choosing the best possible solution to its problem. Using the established criteria, the group can match the suggested solutions with the problem. At this point, the group may need to modify its criteria or even its definition of the problem. To help the group evaluate the solution, consider the following questions:

1. Which of the suggested solutions deals best with the obstacles?
2. What would be the long-term and short-term effects if this solution were adopted?
3. Does the suggestion solve the problem?
4. What are the advantages and disadvantages of the suggested solution?
5. Does the solution meet the established criteria?
6. Should the group revise its criteria?
7. What is required to implement the solution?
8. When can we implement the solution?
9. What result will indicate success?

5. Test and Implement the Solution

The group's work is not finished when it has identified a solution. "How can we put the solution into practice?" and "How can we evaluate the quality of the solution?" have yet to be addressed. The group may want to develop a step-by-step plan that describes how the solution will be implemented, a time frame for implementation, and a list of individuals who will be responsible for carrying out the tasks required by the solution.

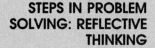

RECAP

STEPS IN PROBLEM SOLVING: REFLECTIVE THINKING

1. Identify and define the problem.
2. Analyze the problem.
3. Suggest possible solutions.
4. Select the best solution.
5. Test and implement the solution.

To be an effective group participant, you have to understand how to manage the problem-solving process. Just knowing the problem-solving steps is not enough, however, to help you with the group discussion process. You need to come to meetings prepared, evaluate evidence, effectively summarize the group's progress, listen courteously, and be sensitive to conflict.

Come Prepared for Group Discussions

To make a contribution at group meetings, you need to be informed about the issues. Prepare for group discussions by researching the issues. If the issue before your group is the use of asbestos in school buildings, for example, research the most recent scientific findings about the risks of this hazardous material. Chapter 7 described how to use the library to gather information for your speeches. Use those library research techniques to prepare for group deliberations as well. Bring your research notes to the group; don't just rely on your memory or your personal opinion to carry you through the discussion. Without research, you will not be able to analyze the problem adequately.

Do Not Suggest Solutions before Analyzing the Problem

Once a problem has been identified, most group members are eager to start suggesting solutions to it. Research suggests that it is better to analyze a problem thoroughly before trying to zero in on a solution.[3] In our culture, we are results- and solutions-oriented. Resist the temptation to settle quickly on one solution until your group has systematically analyzed the causes, effects, history, and symptoms of a problem.

Examine Evidence for Opinions and Assumptions

One study found that a key difference between groups that make successful decisions and those that don't lies in the ability of the group members to examine and evaluate evidence.[4] Ineffective groups are more likely to reach decisions quickly without considering the validity of evidence (or sometimes without any evidence at all). In those instances, they usually reach flawed conclusions.

Help Summarize the Group's Progress

Because it is easy for groups to get off the subject, group members need to summarize frequently what has been achieved and to point the group toward the goal or task at hand. One research study suggests that periodic overviews of the discussion's progress can help the group stay on target.[5] Such overviews should focus on the discussion process rather than on the topic under consideration. "Where are we now?" "Could someone summarize what we have accomplished?" and "Aren't we getting off the subject?" are examples of questions that may need to be examined.

Listen and Respond Courteously to Others

One of the key functions of a good group member is listening to others. Chapter 3's suggestions for improving listening skills are useful when you work in groups, as they are in other communication contexts. But understanding what others say is not enough. You also need to respect their points of view. Even if you disagree with someone's ideas, you should keep your emotions in check and respond courteously. Being closed-minded and defensive usually breeds group conflict.

Help Manage Conflict

In the course of exchanging ideas and opinions about controversial issues, interpersonal conflict may arise. Be prepared to help manage conflict when it appears. The following conflict management suggestions will prove helpful.

1. Keep discussion focused on issues, not personalities.
2. Rely on facts rather than just on personal opinions for evidence.
3. Seek ways to compromise; don't assume that there must be a winner and a loser.
4. Try to clarify misunderstandings in meaning.
5. Be descriptive rather than evaluative and judgmental.
6. Keep emotions in check by speaking slowly and calmly when tempers flare.

Individuals who understand how small groups operate and who apply the basic principles of effective group participation usually become valued members of the problem-solving groups in which they take part.

LEADERSHIP IN SMALL GROUPS

To lead is to influence others. To understand leadership principles in small groups is to understand how individuals influence the group to achieve its goal. Leaders can be described by the types of behavior, or leadership styles, that they exhibit as they influence the group to help achieve its goal.

Leadership Styles

Are you a take-charge kind of person, giving orders and expecting others to follow you? Or do you, as a leader, have the group vote on the course of action to follow? Or maybe you don't try to influence the group at all. Perhaps you prefer to hang back and let the group work out its own problems. Leaders have distinctive styles

To understand leadership principles in small groups is to understand how individuals
influence the group to achieve its goal.
(*Michael Manheim/The Stock Market*)

that set the tone for their entire group. A leadership style is a relatively consistent
pattern of behavior that reflects the beliefs and attitudes of the leader.

There are three general leadership styles: *authoritarian*, *democratic*, and *passive*.
Authoritarian leaders assume positions of superiority, giving orders and assuming
control of the group's activity. Although authoritarian leaders can usually organize
group activities with a high degree of efficiency and virtually eliminate uncertainty
about who should do what, most problem-solving groups prefer democratic leaders.
The reasons are obvious.

Having more faith in their groups than do authoritarian leaders, democratic
leaders involve their groups in the decision-making process rather than dictating
what should be done. In democratic groups, all topics and procedures are matters
for group discussion. Democratic leaders focus more on guiding discussion than
on issuing commands.

The passive leadership style is characterized by allowing a group complete freedom in all aspects of the decision-making process. The passive leader does little to
help the group achieve its goal. This style of leadership (more accurately, non-
leadership) often leaves a group frustrated because it lacks guidance and has to
struggle with organizing the work.

What is the most effective leadership style? Research suggests that no one style
is most effective in all group situations. Sometimes a group needs a strong authoritarian leader to make decisions quickly so that the group can achieve its goal.
Although a democratic leadership style is preferred by most groups, leaders sometimes need to assert their authority to get the job done. The best leadership style
depends on the nature of the group task, the power of the leader, and the relationship
between the leader and his or her followers.

RECAP

LEADERSHIP STYLES	Authoritarian	Democratic	Passive
	1. All determination of policy made by leader.	1. All policies are a matter of group discussion and decision, encouraged and assigned by the leader.	1. Complete freedom for group or individual decisions; minimum leader participation.
	2. Techniques and activity steps dictated by the authority, one at a time; future steps are always largely uncertain.	2. Discussion period yields broad perspectives; general steps to group goal are sketched out; when technical advice is needed, leader suggests alternative procedures.	2. Leader supplies various materials, making it clear that he or she can supply information when asked but taking no other part in the discussion.
	3. Leader dictates specific work tasks and teams.	3. Members are free to work with anyone; group decides on division of tasks.	3. Complete nonparticipation of leader.
	4. Leader tends to be personal in praise or criticism of each member; remains aloof from active group participation except when directing activities.	4. Leader is objective or fact-minded in praise and criticism, trying to be a regular group member in spirit without doing too much of the work.	4. Leader offers infrequent spontaneous comments on member activities and makes no attempt to appraise or control the course of events.

Leadership Responsibilities

Some groups have an appointed leader. Other groups do not have an appointed leader, but a leader nevertheless emerges because the group needs someone to organize its activities. For years it was assumed that all leaders shared certain traits. You either had these traits or you didn't. Our understanding of leadership today suggests that leading a group involves certain learned behaviors. Group leaders help organize work, help get tasks accomplished, and help maintain the social climate of a group.

Leaders Help Organize Work   One function of leaders is to help the group get its work done by organizing the group's activities. These are some of the specific procedural tasks:

1. Setting the group's agenda
2. Taking notes during meetings
3. Determining when a meeting starts and stops

4. Preparing handouts
5. Distributing information to group members before meetings
6. Running errands
7. Rearranging the seating

Leaders Help Get Tasks Accomplished   Another key function of a leader is to assist the group in accomplishing its task. As we just noted, leaders who help organize the work help the group develop procedures to get the job done. But leaders can do more than just help the group with procedures; they can seek information, give opinions, evaluate ideas, and perform other tasks that help the group accomplish its goal. Group task roles include these:[6]

1. The *initiator* proposes new ideas or approaches to group problem solving.
2. The *information seeker* asks for facts or other information that helps the group deal with the issues and may also ask for clarification of ideas or obscure facts.
3. The *opinion seeker* asks for clarification of the values and opinions expressed by group members.
4. The *information giver* provides facts, examples, statistics, and other evidence that help the group achieve its task.
5. The *opinion giver* offers opinions about the ideas under discussion.
6. The *elaborator* provides examples to show how ideas or suggestions would work.
7. The *evaluator* makes an effort to judge the evidence and the conclusion the group reaches.
8. The *energizer* tries to spur the group to further action and productivity.

These various leadership roles can be taken on by many members of the group, particularly if no group leader has been officially appointed. Or because of expertise in a particular area, one member may emerge as the leader to accomplish a specific task.

Leaders Help Maintain the Social Climate of a Group   A third function of a group leader is to develop a peaceful, harmonious group climate by helping to maintain amiable interpersonal relationships in a group. A friendly environment is conducive to a frank exchange of ideas. During group deliberations, it is important that all members fully express their views of what is being said. This can sometimes lead to negative reactions to a suggestion. A warm, accepting atmosphere can cushion the blow and limit the possibility of conflict. Leaders who influence the group climate positively perform some of the following functions[7]:

1. The *encourager* offers praise, understanding, and acceptance of others' ideas.
2. The *harmonizer* mediates disagreements that occur between group members.
3. The *compromiser* attempts to resolve conflicts by trying to find an acceptable middle ground between disagreeing group members.
4. The *gatekeeper* encourages the participation of less talkative group members and tries to limit lengthy contributions of other group members.

Anyone who influences the group's climate may perform any one of the roles listed. Some individuals may be good gatekeepers but would prefer to leave the harmonizer role to someone else. Maintenance functions are rarely assigned to anyone in informal group settings. We don't begin meetings by saying, "OK, Bob, you're in charge of solving all the group conflict. Trish, your job is to encourage group members when they feel frustrated." Usually these maintenance roles emerge, based on the needs of the group and the personality, skills, sensitivity, and past experiences of the group members who are present.

RECAP

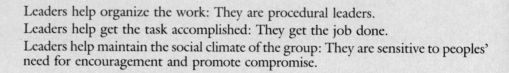

Leaders help organize the work: They are procedural leaders.
Leaders help get the task accomplished: They get the job done.
Leaders help maintain the social climate of the group: They are sensitive to peoples' need for encouragement and promote compromise.

REPORTING GROUP RECOMMENDATIONS

Most problem-solving or decision-making groups need to report the results of their deliberations to others. The report may be oral, written, or both. The standard formats in which group recommendations are made include symposium presentations, group forums, panel discussions, and written reports.

Symposium Presentation

symposium
A public discussion in which a series of short speeches is presented to an audience.

A **symposium** is a public discussion in which a series of short speeches is presented to an audience. The members of the group share the responsibility of presenting information to a larger group. Usually a moderator and the group members are seated in front of the audience, each prepared to deliver a brief report. Each speaker should know what the others will present so that the same ground is not covered twice. At the end of the speeches, the moderator can summarize the key points that were presented. The audience can then participate in a question-and-answer session or a forum presentation.

Forum Presentation

forum presentation
A discussion that usually follows a group discussion or symposium that allows audience members to respond to ideas.

A **forum presentation** consists of an audience directing questions to a group and group members responding with short impromptu speeches. Here again, the group members are seated in front of the audience. The word *forum* originated with the

A symposium is a public discussion in which a series of short speeches is presented to an audience.
(*Laima Druskis*)

Romans. The forum was originally a marketplace where Roman citizens went to shop and discuss the hot issues of the day. It later became a public meeting place where political speeches were often delivered.

A forum presentation may be the only format used, or it may follow a more structured presentation, such as a symposium or a prepared speech by one group member. Forum presentations work best when all group members know the issues and are prepared to respond unhesitatingly to questioners.

Panel Discussion

A **panel discussion** is a presentation by the members of a group to an audience to inform them about a problem, issues, or recommendations. Usually a panel discussion is led by an appointed chairperson or moderator, who organizes the presentation. He or she keeps the discussion on track and generally opens the session by announcing the topic that will be discussed. Panelists and the moderator sit in front of the audience, often behind a table. The individuals on the panel may use notes containing key facts or statistics, but they do not present formal speeches as in the symposium format. Panel discussions are more impromptu than symposium presentations.

An effective moderator gets all the panelists to participate, summarizes their statements, and serves as a gatekeeper to make sure that no member of the panel dominates the discussion. At the conclusion of the discussion, the moderator sum-

panel discussion
A group discussion designed to inform an audience about issues or a problem or to make recommendations.

marizes the main points made by the participants. Often, panel discussions are followed by a question-and-answer period.

Written Report

Written reports summarize the key deliberations of a group and emphasize the final recommendations that have been made. These reports often accompany public group discussions like the symposium, forum, or panel discussion.

In addition to the report format described in Chapter 17, reflective-thinking steps can provide a way to organize the written report. Begin the report by describing the group members; then present the definition of the problem the group discussed. Following the problem definition, include the problem analysis, criteria that were established, possible solutions, the best solution, and suggestions for implementing the solution. For the sake of clarity, use headings and subheadings liberally throughout the report. The length of the report will vary with the significance of the problem and the length of time the group has spent together. The report should include a bibliography of the sources used to reach the group's conclusion.

SUMMARY   Whether working with others is the bane of your existence or one of the joys of your life, you will spend a considerable part of your working life in groups. Small group relations involve face-to-face communication among a small number of people who share a common purpose or goal, feel a sense of belonging to the group, and influence one another.

Working in groups to solve problems and make decisions has several advantages over attempting to work individually. Group members have more diverse knowledge and information, can enhance creative approaches to problem solving, may stimulate improved comprehension, and often afford greater satisfaction in solving problems. But working with others in groups may have some disadvantages. Pressures to conform, excessive domination by a group member, too much dependence on others, and inefficient use of time are some of the drawbacks to working in a group.

We suggested that a useful way to organize problem-solving group discussions would be to follow the five steps of the reflective-thinking process: (1) identify and define the problem, (2) analyze the problem (including establishing criteria), (3) find possible solutions by using brainstorming techniques, (4) select the best solution, and (5) test and implement the solution.

Research has identified several characteristics of effective group members. Effective participants in groups are prepared, evaluate evidence, summarize, listen well, and help manage group conflict.

Leaders of small groups adopt one of three styles: authoritarian, democratic, or passive. The best style depends on the group task, the leader's authority, and the leader's relationship with other group members. Leaders perform the useful functions of organizing the work, helping to achieve the task, and maintaining the social climate of the group.

We concluded the chapter by briefly identifying several popular formats for reporting the results of group deliberations. A symposium presentation is really a series of short speeches made by the group members. A forum presentation usually takes the form of a question-and-answer session between a group and an audience. Panel discussions are spontaneous presentations of the issues in front of an audience. Finally, we observed that a written report, following the steps of reflective thinking, can be a useful format to summarize the group's accomplishment.

QUESTIONS FOR DISCUSSION AND REVIEW

1. What characteristics make a group a group?
2. Discuss the advantages and disadvantages of working in a group.
3. Describe the steps to follow when solving a problem as a group.
4. What are characteristics of effective group members?
5. Compare and contrast three leadership styles.
6. What are the key responsibilities of small group leaders?
7. What are typical ways in which groups report their recommendations to others?

SUGGESTED ACTIVITIES

1. Identify five groups to which you belong, and indicate how each group engages in small group communication as defined in this chapter.
2. For each of the problems listed, cite possible criteria for a solution.
     Capital punishment
     Violence on TV
     Casino gambling
     Defense spending
     Child abuse
     State liquor laws
     Polygraph tests
     Health care benefits
3. Working with a group of other students, use the brainstorming method of generating possible solutions for the following problems:
     Lack of parking space on campus
     High college tuition costs
     Declining reading scores in elementary grades
     Student apathy on campus
4. Following a group meeting, check the roles you performed, using the following list:

     Group Task Roles

     Initiator
     Information seeker
     Opinion seeker
     Information giver
     Opinion giver
     Elaborator

Evaluator
Energizer

Group Maintenance Roles

Encourager
Harmonizer
Compromiser
Gatekeeper

5. Compare the advantages and disadvantages of using the following methods for reporting group recommendations:

Symposium presentation
Forum presentation
Panel discussion
Written report

Epilogue

Now that you are about to complete your public speaking course, you may barely be able to resist the temptation to pat yourself on the back. Before taking this course, you, like the survey population we mentioned in Chapter 2, may have feared public speaking more than death! But you have survived and perhaps even excelled. Now you can file away your notes and never have to give another speech, right? Wrong!

There is indeed life after public speaking class—a life that will demand frequent practice and sharpening of the skills to which you have been introduced in this course. Your classroom experience has taught you how to become a better public speaker. We hope that it has also taught you to become your own best critic—able to say, "I need more eye contact" or "I need a statistic to prove this point" or "I need a transition here." But one course cannot make you a polished speaker. Unlike learning to apply a mathematical formula or learning to place commas in sentences, learning to speak in public is an ongoing process rather than a static goal.

In the years to come, both in college and beyond, you will use and continue to develop your public speaking skills in many areas of your professional and personal life. In Chapter 1 of this text, we discussed some of the skills you would learn and practice as a public speaker: organization, audience analysis and adaptation, research, effective presentation, and critical listening. Certainly you will find yourself applying these skills to numerous situations—to speaking opportunities, of course, but also to other situations that require critical listening and analytical thinking. As you take other courses, apply for a job, prepare a report for your company, attend city council meetings, and go about your day-to-day personal business, you will find yourself using the skills you learned in your public speaking class.

Your completion of this course is the commencement of your continuing development as a public speaker.
(*Bob Daemmrich/Stock, Boston*)

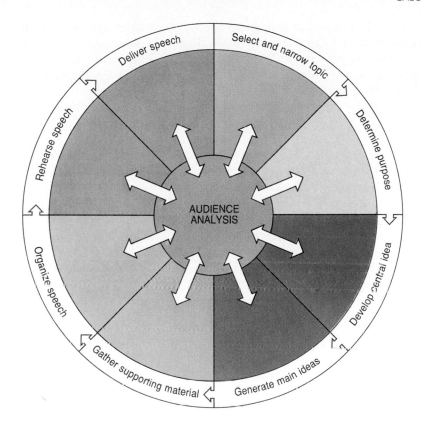

Remember: To be effective, public speaking must be audience-centered.

Of course, chances are that you will also find yourself in a number of actual public speaking situations. Perhaps you will give few "laboratory" speeches like those you have given in your speech class. But you will undoubtedly deliver one or more of the types of special-occasion speeches that we discussed in Chapter 17. You will introduce a speaker, present or receive an award, deliver a speech to commemorate a person or an occasion, give a book review, or make a sales pitch. And you will look back to this course for guidance.

Realistically, you will not remember every detail of the course or of this text. But we hope that you will remember the bottom line: that to be effective, public speaking must be *audience-centered*. As is graphically represented by the model we have used throughout this text, every step of the public speaking process, from selecting and narrowing the topic through preparing the speech to final delivery of the speech, must be approached with the audience in mind. If the audience does not understand your message or does not respond as you had hoped, your speech cannot be a success, regardless of the hours of research or rehearsal you may have dedicated to the task.

One final note about the audience-centered approach is in order here: Being audience-centered is not the same as being manipulative. If you adapt to your audience to the extent that you abandon your own values and sense of truth, you have become an unethical speaker rather than an audience-centered one. An audience-centered speaker does not tell an audience only what they want to hear. Rather, the audience-centered speaker adjusts his or her topic, purpose, central idea, main ideas, supporting materials, organization, and even delivery of the speech in such a way that the audience is most likely to listen and to come away from the speaking situation, if not persuaded, feeling at least thoughtful rather than offended or hostile.

One of the types of special-occasion speeches we discussed in Chapter 17 was the commencement address. Your completion of this course is also the commencement—the beginning—of your continuing development as a public speaker. The traditional theme of the commencement speaker is "Go forth. You have been prepared for the future." With what better thought can we leave you? Go forth. You have been prepared for the future.

A

The Classical Tradition of Rhetoric

Thomas R. Burkholder

Published by permission of Thomas R. Burkholder.

Preparing and delivering a speech always seems to be a very personal task. You must research your own topic. You must analyze and attempt to adapt to the particular audience you will face. You must find a way to cope with your own nervousness. When you confront those problems, it is sometimes helpful to remember that countless others have done so before you. And for as long as people have been giving speeches, they have been looking for ways to make them better. In fact, the study of speeches and speech making, or the study of rhetoric, dates back to the earliest years of Western civilization, hundreds of years before the birth of Christ. So in a way, your own efforts are a continuation of that classical tradition.

Speech making is probably as old as language itself. And speech criticism is probably as old as listening! But perhaps the earliest recorded evidence of "rhetorical consciousness," the awareness of excellence in speech making, appears in the writing of Homer, the ancient Greek poet. His *Iliad*, written before 700 B.C., contains numerous well-organized, well-written speeches or orations. They appear in scenes depicting debates between humans and gods, in councils of military leaders, and so forth. And they demonstrate that the ancient Greeks had a clear sense of rhetorical excellence.

THE EARLIEST TEACHERS OF RHETORIC

We will probably never know who first offered advice to another person who was preparing to deliver an oration. But many ancient writers credit a teacher named Corax with the "invention" of rhetoric sometime around 476 B.C. Corax was a resident of the city of Syracuse on the island of Sicily. He developed a "doctrine of general probability," to be used by speakers in the courts. Imagine a small man being brought into court and accused of beating a much larger, stronger man. According to the doctrine of general probability, the small man should defend himself by saying something like: "It is surely unlikely (not probable) that I would beat this man. After all, he is much larger and stronger than I. I would be crazy to risk making him angry by hitting him." But the larger man could resort to the same doctrine in response: "Of course people would think it unlikely that he would hit me. That is exactly why he felt safe in doing it!"

Another similar exchange was the basis of the most famous story about Corax and his student, Tisias. Tisias refused to pay Corax for his lessons in rhetoric, so Corax sued him in court. Corax addressed the judges: "Tisias must pay me regardless of your decision. If he wins the case, that proves the lessons I taught him were valuable and I deserve payment. And if he loses, the court will force him to pay. So either way, he must pay." But Tisias responded: "I shall pay nothing. If I lose the case, that will prove the training I received from Corax was worthless and he does not deserve payment. But if I win the case, the court will decree that I owe him nothing. So either way, I shall not pay." The judges quickly tired of such banter and threw the case out of court with the admonition, "*Mali corvi malum ovum*," or "a bad egg from a bad crow!" Legend has it that Tisias promptly left Syracuse and opened his own school of rhetoric in Greece.

Whether Tisias actually went to Greece is unknown. But by the middle of the fifth century B.C., schools of rhetoric flourished in the Greek city states. Citizens often spoke in the assemblies or legislatures, and because there were no lawyers, they presented their own cases in the courts. It was soon apparent that the most skilled speakers prevailed in the assembly and won in court. Speech teachers were in great demand. The Greeks called these teachers "Sophists," a term which literally means "wisdom bearer." The rhetorical training offered by these teachers varied greatly. Some, such as Antiphon (480–411 B.C.) and Lysias (459–380 B.C.), were actually logographers. They merely wrote speeches to be delivered by their clients and made no effort to provide training in rhetoric. Others, like Protagoras (481–411 B.C.) and Gorgias (485–380 B.C.), advertised themselves as teachers of eloquence, or the art of effective speaking.

Protagoras is often considered to be the originator of academic debating, because he required his students to argue opposing sides of issues. He believed that each side of important questions had merit, and that humans could never be certain of the "truth." Thus, he encouraged his students to build the strongest possible case for the side of the issue they were assigned to debate. Such training, he felt, would best prepare his students to conduct their affairs in the assembly and the courts. Gorgias was perhaps the first teacher of rhetoric to encourage careful use of language. He believed that speakers would be more persuasive if their speaking style was embellished. He encouraged the use of stylistic devices familiar to modern writers, like assonance, alliteration, antirhesis, and parallelism.

One of the most famous Sophists was Isocrates (436–338 B.C.). Unlike Protagoras and Gorgias, who taught only rhetoric, Isocrates claimed to train citizens to be statesmen. He made rhetoric the center of a more fully developed course of study designed to make his students wise as well as eloquent. Isocrates believed that three qualities were necessary for a person to be a great orator and statesman. First, that person must possess natural ability. Second, that ability must be developed and refined through practice and experience. Finally, to be a great orator and statesman, a person must be well educated, not just in rhetoric, but in philosophy as well. While no one can teach natural ability, Isocrates endeavored to provide his students with practice, experience, and philosophical education.

Although the Sophists attracted many students, and many Sophists became wealthy from their teaching efforts, they were not without their critics. Many felt that the training provided by the Sophists was worthless, if not dangerous. Teachers like Gorgias were accused of providing worthless training by emphasizing florid language with no regard for substance. Teachers like Protagoras were accused of training speakers to "make the worse case appear the better" by urging speakers to develop strong speeches on both sides of any issue. And Sophists in general were often criticized for failing to make their students better, more virtuous people. Without question, the most severe critic of the Sophists was the great Greek philosopher, Plato (427–347 B.C.).

BEGINNING OF THE GREEK TRADITION: THE SOPHISTS

PLATO

Plato was the student of Socrates (469–399 B.C.), and he went on to become one of the most profound and influential thinkers in history. In 385 B.C., Plato founded the famous Academy in Athens. The Academy attracted the best and brightest students and teachers in all of Greece, and remained in operation for almost nine hundred years. Plato's writings were a major influence in the development of Western philosophy and culture. His *Republic* was a blueprint for the ideal political state ruled over by a philosopher-king. His other writings covered a wide variety of subjects, including psychology, logic, and rhetoric. Most of his writings were "dialogues" which resembled plays in which the characters discussed important issues. In many of Plato's dialogues, Socrates was the chief character.

In a typical dialogue, Plato had Socrates attempt to determine the truth relevant to the issue at hand by engaging other characters in a series of questions and answers. That approach is now frequently called the "Socratic method" or the "Platonic method." It illustrated the process of "dialectic," which Plato believed was the means of discovering truth. The dialogues were often named after the characters who opposed Socrates in the discussion. Two of the dialogues, *Gorgias* and *Phaedrus*, named after those Sophists, dealt explicitly with rhetoric.

Plato's dialogues are complicated and often difficult to understand fully. Scholars have debated their meaning for centuries. Some have argued that *Gorgias* and *Phaedrus* presented inconsistent and conflicting views of rhetoric; that Plato condemned rhetoric in *Gorgias* and then praised it in *Phaedrus*. In fact, when taken together the two dialogues presented Plato's clear and coherent view of the nature and function of rhetoric.

In *Gorgias*, Plato, through the character of Socrates, condemned rhetoric *as practiced* by many Sophists of his day. He said that the rhetoric of the Sophists was merely a "knack" or a form of flattery, intended only to please the ears of listeners much like cookery pleases the palate. He condemned the Sophists for using florid language, pleasant to the ear, to "make the worse case appear the better." And he accused them of first claiming to impart wisdom and thus to make their students more just and virtuous, and then of failing to do so. But these charges were leveled at rhetoric as the Sophists practiced it, not at rhetoric itself.

In *Phaedrus*, once again through the character of Socrates, Plato praised rhetoric as it *ought to be practiced*. The Sophists focused their attention on speaking in assemblies and courts. But Plato saw the true rhetoric as a means of using language to influence the minds of listeners, wherever they might be. Going further, he saw rhetoric as a means of influencing the very souls of listeners, thus making them more virtuous. The difference between the Sophistic and Platonic ideas of rhetoric grew from Plato's understanding of "truth."

In Plato's view, truth, or knowledge, existed on several levels. The lowest, least reliable, yet most common level was called *doxa*. This sort of knowledge was the product of the human senses, of what people observed. It was least reliable because it was so easily corrupted; the senses were easily misled. Thus, Plato's condemnation of the rhetoric of the Sophists grew from its aim of pleasing (and often, he felt, misleading) the senses of listeners. On the other end of Plato's scale was *episteme*, or true knowledge. It was the product not of sensory observation, but rather of philosophical inquiry. For Plato, rhetoric as it ought to be practiced was grounded in *episteme*. Only this "true" rhetoric could be trusted to influence the souls of listeners.

The idea of rhetoric based upon truth is appealing. But before we award too much praise to Plato, we must know also that he thought most people were not capable of achieving true knowledge. Only philosophers could attain true knowledge, and thus, in the ideal political state described in his *Republic*, only the philosopher-king was allowed to use rhetoric, for the good of the state. Such uses of rhetoric are frightening. Seen in that light, the Sophists' idea that both sides of important issues should be debated in public seems preferable indeed.

ARISTOTLE

Plato's most famous student was Aristotle (384–322 B.C.). Of all ancient scholars, including Plato, no other was more influential than Aristotle. He wrote extensively on subjects as diverse as philosophy, drama, natural science, and rhetoric. Like his teacher, Aristotle had a profound effect on the development of Western culture.

Throughout his life, Aristotle was directly associated with the most brilliant and important people of his time. His father, Nicomachus, was physician in the court of Amyntas II, king of Macedon and father of Philip the Great. When Aristotle was seventeen, he was sent to Athens to study in the Academy. There he remained until Plato's death. In 343 B.C., he was summoned back to Macedon to become tutor to Philip's son, Alexander the Great. Aristotle returned to Athens in 335 B.C. and eventually founded his own school, the Lyceum. After the death of Alexander in 323 B.C., he came under suspicion in Athens because of his prior close association with Macedon. Aristotle fled to the city of Chalcis where he died the next year.

Aristotle's *Rhetoric* is the earliest systematic discussion of speech-making of which we have record. It probably existed first as his own notes for lectures he gave to students in the Lyceum. Legend has it that his students edited and published those notes after Aristotle's death. His approach to rhetoric was influenced by the philosophy of Plato. But his practical suggestions for speakers demonstrate that Aristotle was influenced by the Sophists as well. In effect, he was able to transcend both Plato and the Sophists and form a distinctive theory of rhetoric. The impact of his work continues today. Indeed, much of what appears earlier in this textbook originated with Aristotle.

Like Plato, Aristotle believed in true or ultimate knowledge. Also like Plato, he believed that only through philosophical inquiry, which was beyond the ability of most people, could true knowledge be attained. But Plato viewed rhetoric as a means through which, for the good of the state, philosopher-kings might manipulate those incapable of gaining true knowledge. Aristotle took a very different position. He believed that even those who could not attain true knowledge could, nevertheless, be persuaded to the good. Thus, persuasion was an acceptable, although inferior, substitute for true knowledge. In Plato's ideal state, only the philosopher-king could employ rhetoric because in the hands of the unenlightened, rhetoric could do great harm. In contrast, Aristotle believed that rhetoric was a morally neutral art. He did not restrict the use of rhetoric to rulers alone because he believed that, in any dispute, good would prevail provided both sides were equally well prepared; that is, provided both sides were equally well trained in rhetoric.

Aristotle envisioned rhetoric as an art, as a system which could be taught. He defined rhetoric as "the faculty of discovering, in any given case, the available means of persuasion." These means of persuasion he classified into three types: *Ethos*, or ethical appeals, based upon the degree of credibility awarded to a speaker by listeners; *Logos*, or logical appeals; and *Pathos*, or appeals to listeners' emotions. The *Rhetoric* offered speakers extremely detailed suggestions for discovering, understanding, and implementing each means of persuasion.

Aristotle also classified the different situations, or "given cases," in which speeches might be given. Those were: Deliberative, or legislative speaking; Forensic, or speaking in the courts; and Epideictic, or what he called the "ceremonial oratory of display." Today, we would call that last type "special occasion" speaking. According to Aristotle, those types were determined by the role listeners must play in each case; by the sort of "decision" they must make after hearing a particular speech. In that regard, Aristotle, like this textbook, took an "audience-centered approach" to speechmaking.

In Aristotle's system of classification, those who hear deliberative speeches were asked to render a decision regarding the most expedient course for future action. Those who heard forensic speeches were asked to judge the justice or injustice of a person's past action. And those who heard epideictic speeches were asked to award either praise or blame to the subject (usually a person) of the speech, and to judge the orator's skill as well. The *Rhetoric* offered speakers detailed suggestions for demonstrating the expedience or inexpediency of proposed courses of action, the justice or injustice of a person's deeds, and those qualities worthy of praise or blame. Aristotle also allowed for considerable overlap between the three types, indicating that while one type would predominate, elements of all three might appear in a single speech.

His discussions of expediency, justice, and qualities worthy of praise or blame, made Aristotle's *Rhetoric* more than a simple "handbook" for speakers. Those discussions provided a philosophical or ethical foundation for speechmaking. But its practical suggestions made the *Rhetoric* an extremely useful manual for public speaking as well.

THE ROMAN TRADITION

The Greek tradition of rhetoric had its most immediate, and perhaps its greatest, influence in the Roman educational system. In the second century B.C., Rome's military might extended the Republic to the east. There, Romans became familiar with Greek culture and the Greek educational system. Much of what they discovered was incorporated into Roman society, and that included training in rhetoric. In fact, rhetorical training eventually became the center of Roman education.

The Roman education system was designed to prepare citizens to participate in the affairs of the state. Primarily, that meant citizens must be prepared to speak in the legislatures and the courts. Rhetorical instruction began in the Roman grammar schools. There, students engaged in a progressive series of written and spoken exercises called the *Progymnasmata*. The lessons built upon each other, with each more difficult than the one which preceeded it. Near the end of the program of instruction, students were assigned a thesis which required them to develop arguments on a given theme, such as whether it was more noble to be a soldier or a lawyer. The series of lessons culminated in exercises in which students were required to speak for and against an existing law.

With grammar school instruction completed, most students moved on to schools of rhetoric. Instruction there was more broad in scope, but it continued to focus on preparing students to be productive citizens of Rome; that is, to be effective speakers. Students were required to learn a vast body of rhetorical theories and concepts based upon centuries of oratorical study. They were taught that the art of rhetoric consisted of five separate arts: *invention*, which involved gathering and analyzing facts and physical evidence; *arrangement*, or organization; *style*, or the eloquent and effective use of language; *memory*, or recollection of the speech for presentation; and *delivery*. These five classical "canons" of rhetoric are familiar to today's students of public speaking. The exercises in which students participated were of two types, *suasoria* and *controversia*. *Suasoria* were exercises in legislative speaking. Students debated hypothetical questions of public policy, laws, and so forth. *Controversia* were exercises in forensic or legal speaking. Students argued opposing sides of hypothetical court cases, much as present-day law students do in "moot court" contests.

Following their training in schools of rhetoric, Roman students were often apprenticed to practicing rhetoricians, such as legislators or lawyers. There the students were given opportunities to learn by observing other speakers in legislative and judicial situations. Thus, the entire Roman educational system was designed to prepare citizens to assume roles as orators in the society. Rome produced many scholars who contributed to the rhetorical tradition. Two of the most important were Cicero (106–43 B.C.) and Quintilian (35–95 A.D.).

Marcus Tullius Cicero was the child of an upper middle-class family from central Italy. Social custom dictated that he pursue his education in Rome, where he studied with the leading rhetoricians of his day. According to many, he became the greatest orator in all of Rome. His most famous works on the theory and practice of rhetoric were: *De Inventione*, written when he was approximately twenty years old; *De Oratore*, published in 55 B.C.; and *Brutus*, and *Orator*, both written in approximately 46 B.C. Cicero's aim in these works was to gather, synthesize, and expand upon the greatest teachings of previous Greek and Roman rhetoricians. He was appalled by the emphasis given to style and delivery in some schools of rhetoric, and felt the true orator should be a fully educated person. Cicero saw rhetoric as far more than courtroom pleading. Rather, he believed that the ideal orator was the learned philosopher-statesman, who used his talent for the good of the state. In his view, the true orator should be able to speak with eloquence and wisdom on any important subject.

Marcus Fabius Quintilianus was born in the part of the Roman Empire which is now Spain. Like Cicero, he was the product of a traditional Roman education. But unlike Cicero, Quintilian lived in a time when oratory began to be repressed. Tyrants ruled the Roman Empire; the legislative speaking, and even the legal speaking, which characterized Cicero's time, were greatly restricted. Despite that fact, or perhaps because of it, Quintilian's aim as a teacher of rhetoric was to educate the perfect orator. His most famous rhetorical treatise was *Institutio Oratoria*, which emphasized the moral and ethical uses of rhetoric. For Quintilian, the ideal orator was "a good man speaking well." Unfortunately, that dictum has been much abused by many modern rhetorical scholars, often to justify the study of the speaking and speeches of only highly successful political figures who were usually white and male. In fact, Quinitilian urged those who would become great orators to pursue not only eloquence, but excellence in morality and ethical character as well—qualities which are certainly not limited to, or perhaps even characteristic of, successful politicians!

CONCLUSION

The rhetorical tradition which began with the ancient Greeks and Romans has been a significant influence in Western civilization. Their theories and guidelines for successful rhetorical practice have been analyzed, refined, and extended by countless scholars for thousands of years. This textbook is a part of that tradition. Many of the rhetorical principles and suggestions for effective speech making which appear in this book can be traced through the ages back to such classical rhetoricians as Isocrates, Plato, Aristotle, Cicero, and Quintilian. Throughout history, other rhetorical scholars have made important contributions as well. But as you work to prepare your own speeches, to be delivered in class or in other settings, it is interesting and perhaps even comforting to know that your efforts are a continuation of a classical tradition of rhetoric which is as old as our Western culture.

The Classical Tradition of Rhetoric

Rhetoricians	Dates	Contributions
The First Teachers		
Corax and Tisias	476 B.C.	Doctrine of general probability
The Greek Tradition		
The Sophists		
Protagoras	481–411 B.C.	Originator of academic debate
Gorgias	485–380 B.C.	Effective language use
Isocrates	436–338 B.C.	The orator-statesman
Plato	427–347 B.C.	*Gorgias* and *Phaedrus;* Philosopher-king as orator
Aristotle	384–322 B.C.	*Rhetoric;* philosophical and practical guide for orators; rhetoric as a teachable art
The Roman Tradition		Rhetoric as the central element in education
Cicero	106–43 B.C.	*De Inventione, De Oratore, Brutus,* and *Orator;* Rome's greatest orator; philosopher-statesman as the ideal orator
Quintilian	35–95 A.D.	*Institutio Oratoria;* Eloquence combined with moral and ethical excellence; the good man speaking well

Aristotle. *Rhetoric and Poetics.* W. Rhys Roberts and Ingram Bywater, translators. New York: The Modern Library, 1954.

Black, Edwin. "Plato's View of Rhetoric." *Quarterly Journal of Speech* 44 (December 1958): 361–74.

Clark, Donald Lemen. *Rhetoric in Greco-Roman Education.* New York: Columbia University Press, 1957.

Guthrie, W. K. C. *The Sophists.* Cambridge: Cambridge University Press, 1971.

Kauffman, Charles. "The Axiological Foundations of Plato's Theory of Rhetoric." *Central States Speech Journal* 33 (Summer 1982): 353–66.

REFERENCES

Kennedy, George. *The Art of Persuasion in Greece* Princeton, New Jersey: Princeton University Press, 1963.

Murphy, James J., ed. *A Synoptic History of Classical Rhetoric*. Davis, California: Hermagoras Press, 1983.

_____, ed. *Quintilian On The Teaching Of Speaking And Writing*. Translations from Books 1, 2, and 10 of *Institutio Oratoria*. Carbondale: Southern Illinois University Press, 1987.

Plato. *The Collected Dialogues of Plato*. Edith Hamilton and Huntington Cairns, eds. Princeton New Jersey: Princeton University Press, 1961.

Watson, J. S., trans. *Cicero On Oratory and Orators*. Carbondale: Southern Illinois University Press, 1970.

B
Suggested Speech Topics

One of the more challenging tasks for beginning speakers is deciding what to talk about. We identified several suggestions in Chapter 5 to help you select and narrow your topic. Specifically, we suggested you should:

1. Consider the audience
2. Consider the demands of the occasion
3. Consider yourself

We also described three techniques to help you with your topic selection hunt:

1. Brainstorm—free associate topics until you have a long list before you start to critique your topics.
2. Listen to the media and read; keep current on the news of the day.
3. Scan lists and indexes.

To help prime your creative pump we have included the following list of topics.[1] As presented here, most of the topics are appropriate for an informative speech. Depending upon your point of view, they could also be adapted for persuasive speech topics.

The causes of unrest in the Gaza Strip.
The history and significance of the Panama Canal
What's happening in Honduras?
Why are so many farmers going broke?
What exactly happened on Black Monday?
What's the current role of Health Education?
History and purpose of campus Greek Societies.
The evolution of the musician as a popular hero.
What are the facts on world hunger?
What are the facts on the homeless in the U.S.?
Who is a powerful contemporary writer?
What is subliminal advertising?
The social/economic problems in Mexico.
What the experts say about choosing a career.
Present trends in animal conservation.
What goes into making a record album?
What ever happened to Laetrile?
What's the U.S. doing about littering?
What's happening with the ERA movement?
What diets really work?
What is socialized medicine?
What do primary elections tell us?
What are the goals of General Studies courses?

What's going on with nuclear energy?
What is the privacy act?
Is censorship going on in the U.S.?
What's involved in being an organ donor?
What are the standards used to get credit cards?
The history of the Persian Gulf situation.
The last decade in Nicaragua.
How do we choose a President?
What are the current odds on the Presidential candidates?
How does the stock market work?
What's being done to find a cure for AIDS?
What's being done for American Indians?
Pop music as cultural expression.
Do we have any ecological crises?
What are the job forecasts for the future?
What's the background to the problems in Ireland?
What's the media's role in shaping the news?
What's the New Age Movement?
The latest in genetic engineering.
Technology in the 20th century.
The changing job market.
What is "sexist" language?
New trends in advertising.

The facts on child abuse.

What the experts say about apartment vs. dorm life.

New discoveries in health care.

What's the current status on finances for U.S. education?

What's happening with solar energy?

The facts on religious cults.

What's happening with the draft?

What are the rights of adopted children?

The facts about legalized prostitution.

How happy are marriages without children?

What is involved in being a blood donor?

What has the 55 mph speed limit done for safety?

What's being done to save National Parks?

Who gets guaranteed student loans and why?

What are new methods in waste disposal?

Why people become vegetarians.

Tips on bicycle safety and protection.

How can you adopt animals from zoos?

What ever happened to UFO's?

Is there life on other planets?

What exactly are money market funds?

What the experts say about crime prevention.

The facts about diet pills.

What happens in drug therapy clinics?

What does your Alumni Association do?

The history of Jazz music.

What is electro-shock therapy?

The history of cable TV.

How do unions work?

Living together.

Success of designated smoking area laws.

The history of cremation customs.

How does cloning work?

What are the current child custody laws?

Test tube baby births.

The facts about teenage alcoholism.

New breakthroughs for the handicapped.

What is the Consumer Protection Agency?

How are scholarships awarded?

What is the "Sunset Law" for government agencies?

What are the impact of the new immigration laws?

What has been the impact of recycling centers?

What does English as official language mean?

How are movie ratings determined?

What are the facts about legalized gambling?

Are there any new concepts in mass transportation?

What is the role of the A.C.L.U.?

The impact of the instant replay in sports.

How are maps made?

What is the latest in stereophonic technology?

What does the Postmaster General do?

How does the rate of inflation get determined?

The effect of the falling rate of the Peso.

How is a loudspeaker made?

How are "mild" and "medium" jalapeños grown?

The history of Coca Cola.

The effect of telephone deregulation.

The history of the _____ River.

The history of the _____ building.

What do people in Alaska do for fun in January?

What's the future for real estate?

The history of Blue Laws.

How can you test yourself for blood/alcohol level?

What's being done about TV violence?

What can/cannot a chiropractor do for you?

What is the foreign exchange student program?

What kinds of work do volunteers do?

Tips on fire prevention.

What vitamins do for you.

How can college students invest?

Basics of dental care.

What's the Adopt-a-Grandparent program?

Alternative approaches to grades in school.

When should you begin to worry about retirement?

What the experts say about relieving stress.

Children's books and sex roles.

What goes on in a dog show?

What are the effects of the sun?

What's the future of the space program?

Public worker strikes.

What are the rules for adoption?

Population control programs.

Wildlife preserves.

New prison reform policies.

How does the welfare system work?

The effect of rising insurance rates.

How is your IQ determined?

What's National Health Insurance?

How early are people retiring these days?

What is the U.S.'s role in the United Nations?

What are the current U.S. policies on giving foreign aid?

What is first aid for a severe cut?

How does the system of bail work in Texas?

What exactly does the CIA do?

What rights do gays have in contemporary society?

What is the current status of the Ku Klux Klan?

Does the U.S. aid corporations that have money troubles?

What is the electoral college system?

What is ghost surgery?

What are advertising endorsements?

What skills are most needed in today's job market?

New advances in computer software programs.

What does the Surgeon General do?

What's happening on the U.S./Mexican border?

How is the U.S. dollar doing against the Yen these days?

Is there such a thing as a solar car?

What exactly are fiber optics?

How far can obscenity go now on radio and television?

The history of _____.

Is there anyplace in the world that has an ideal climate?

Are there any archaeological digs in your county?

What is the new growth area in the U.S.?

C
Speeches for Analysis and Discussion

I HAVE A DREAM[1]

Martin Luther King, Jr.

Washington, D.C.,
August 28, 1963

I am happy to join with you today in what will go down in history as the greatest demonstration for freedom in the history of our nation.

Five score years ago, a great American, in whose symbolic shadow we stand today, signed the Emancipation Proclamation. This momentous decree came as a great beacon light of hope to millions of Negro slaves, who had been seared in the flames of withering injustice. It came as a joyous daybreak to end the long night of their captivity.

But one hundred years later, the Negro is still not free. One hundred years later, the life of the Negro is still sadly crippled by the manacles of segregation and the chains of discrimination. One hundred years later, the Negro lives on a lonely island of poverty in the midst of a vast ocean of material prosperity. One hundred years later, the Negro is still languished in the corners of American society and finds himself an exile in his own land. And so we've come here today to dramatize a shameful condition.

In a sense we've come to our nation's Capitol to cash a check. When the architects of our republic wrote the magnificent words of the Constitution and the Declaration of Independence, they were signing a promissory note to which every American was to fall heir. This note was a promise that all men—yes, black men as well as white men—would be guaranteed the unalienable rights of life, liberty, and the pursuit of happiness.

It is obvious today that America has defaulted on this promissory note insofar as her citizens of color are concerned. Instead of honoring this sacred obligation, America has given the Negro people a bad check—a check which has come back marked "insufficient funds."

But we refuse to believe that the bank of justice is bankrupt. We refuse to believe that there are insufficient funds in the great vaults of opportunity of this nation. And so we've come to cash this check—a check that will give us upon demand the riches of freedom and the security of justice.

We have also come to this hallowed spot to remind America of the fierce urgency of now. This is no time to engage in the luxury of cooling off or to take the tranquilizing drug of gradualism. Now is the time to make the real promises of democracy. Now is the time to rise from the dark and desolate valley of segregation to the sunlit path of racial justice. Now is the time to lift our nation from the quicksands of racial injustice to the solid rock of brotherhood. Now is the time to make justice a reality for all of God's children.

It would be fatal for the nation to overlook the urgency of the moment. This sweltering summer of the Negro's legitimate discontent will not pass until there is an invigorating autumn of freedom and equality. Nineteen sixty-three is not an end, but a beginning. Those who hope that the Negro needed to blow off steam and will now be content will have a rude awakening if the nation returns to business as usual. There will be neither rest nor tranquillity in America until the Negro is granted his citizenship rights. The whirlwinds of revolt will continue to shake the foundations of our nation until the bright day of justice emerges.

But there is something that I must say to my people, who stand on the warm threshold which leads into the palace of justice. In the process of gaining our rightful place, we must not be guilty of wrongful deeds. Let us not seek to satisfy our thirst for freedom by drinking from the cup of bitterness and hatred.

We must forever conduct our struggle on the high plane of dignity and discipline. We must not allow our creative protest to degenerate into physical violence. Again and again we must rise to the majestic heights of meeting physical force with soul force.

The marvelous new militance which has engulfed the Negro community must not lead us to a distrust of all white people. For many of our white brothers, as evidenced by their presence here today, have come to realize that their destiny is tied up with our destiny. They have come to realize that their freedom is inextricably bound to our freedom. We cannot walk alone.

As we walk, we must make the pledge that we shall always march ahead. We cannot turn back. There are those who are asking the devotees of civil rights, "When will you be satisfied?" We can never be satisfied as long as the Negro is the victim of the unspeakable horrors of police brutality. We can never be satisfied as long as our bodies, heavy with the fatigue of travel, cannot gain lodging in the motels of the highways and hotels of the cities. We cannot be satisfied as long as the Negro's basic mobility is from a smaller ghetto to a larger one. We can never be satisfied as long as our children are stripped of their selfhood and robbed of their dignity by signs stating "For Whites Only." We cannot be satisfied as long as a Negro in Mississippi cannot vote and a Negro in New York believes he has nothing for which to vote. No, no, we are not satisfied, and we will not be satisfied until justice rolls down like waters, and righteousness like a mighty stream.

I am not unmindful that some of you have come here out of great trials and tribulations. Some of you have come fresh from narrow jail cells. Some of you have come from areas where your quest for freedom left you battered by the storms of persecution and staggered by the winds of police brutality. You have been the veterans of creative suffering. Continue to work with the faith that unearned suffering is redemptive.

Go back to Mississippi, go back to Alabama, go back to South Carolina, go back to Georgia, go back to Louisiana, go back to the slums and ghettos of our Northern cities, knowing that somehow this situation can and will be changed. Let us not wallow in the valley of despair.

I say to you today, my friends, so even though we face the difficulties of today and tomorrow, I still have a dream. It is a dream deeply rooted in the American dream.

I have a dream that one day this nation will rise up and live out the true meaning of its creed, "We hold these truths to be self-evident, that all men are created equal."

I have a dream that one day on the red hills of Georgia the sons of former slaves and the sons of former slaveowners will be able to sit down together at the table of brotherhood.

I have a dream that one day even the state of Mississippi, a state sweltering with the heat of injustice, sweltering with the heat of oppression, will be transformed into an oasis of freedom and justice.

I have a dream that my four little children will one day live in a nation where they will not be judged by the color of their skin but by the content of their character. I have a dream today.

I have a dream that one day, down in Alabama, with its vicious racists, with its governor having his lips dripping with the words of interposition and nullification, one day right there in Alabama little black boys and black girls will be able to join hands with little white boys and white girls as sisters and brothers. I have a dream today.

I have a dream that one day every valley shall be exalted, every hill and mountain shall be made low, the rough places will be made plane and the crooked places will be made straight, and the glory of the Lord shall be revealed, and all flesh shall see it together.

This is our hope. This is the faith that I go back to the South with. With this faith we will be able to hew out of the mountain of despair a stone of hope. With this faith we will be able to transform the jangling discords of our nation into a beautiful symphony of brotherhood. With this faith we will be able to work together, to pray together, to struggle together, to go to jail together, to stand up for freedom together, knowing that we will be free one day.

This will be the day—this will be the day when all of God's children will be able to sing with new meaning, "My country 'tis of thee, sweet land of liberty, of thee I sing. Land where my fathers died, land of the Pilgrims' pride, from every mountainside, let freedom ring." And if America is to be a great nation, this must become true.

So let freedom ring from the prodigious hilltops of New Hampshire. Let freedom ring from the mighty mountains of New York. Let freedom ring from the heightening Alleghenies of Pennsylvania!

Let freedom ring from the snowcapped Rockies of Colorado! Let freedom ring from the curvaceous slopes of California!

But not only that. Let freedom ring from Stone Mountain of Georgia!

Let freedom ring from Lookout Mountain of Tennessee!

Let freedom ring from every hill and molehill of Mississippi. From every mountainside, let freedom ring.

And when this happens, when we allow freedom to ring—when we let it ring from every village and every hamlet, from every state and every city—we will be able to speed up that day when all of God's children, black men and white men, Jews and Gentiles, Protestants and Catholics, will be able to join hands and sing, in the words of the old Negro spiritual, "Free at last! Free at last! Thank God almighty, we are free at last!"

WHO THEN WILL SPEAK FOR THE COMMON GOOD?

Barbara Jordan

Keynote Address,
Democratic National Convention,
July 12, 1976

One hundred and forty-four years ago, members of the Democratic Party first met in convention to select a Presidential candidate. Since that time, Democrats have continued to convene once every four years and draft a party platform and nominate a Presidential candidate. And our meeting this week is a continuation of that tradition.

But there is something different about tonight. There is something special about tonight. What is different? What is special? I, Barbara Jordan, am a keynote speaker.

A lot of years passed since 1832, and during that time it would have been most unusual for any national political party to ask that a Barbara Jordan deliver a keynote address . . . but tonight here I am. And I feel that notwithstanding the past, my presence here is one additional bit of evidence that the American Dream need not forever be deferred.

Now that I have this grand distinction, what in the world am I supposed to say?

I could easily spend this time praising the accomplishments of the party and attacking the Republicans, but I don't choose to do that.

I could list the many problems which Americans have. I could list the problems which cause people to feel cynical, angry, frustrated: problems which include lack of integrity in government; the feeling that the individual no longer counts; the reality of material and spiritual poverty; the feeling that the grand American experiment is failing or has failed. I could recite these problems and then I could sit down and offer no solutions. But I don't choose to do that either.

The citizens of America expect more. They deserve and they want more than a recital of problems.

We are a people in a quandary about the present. We are a people in search of our future. We are a people in search of a national community.

We are a people trying not only to solve the problems of the present—unemployment, inflation—but we are attempting on a larger scale to fulfill the promise of America. We are attempting to fulfill our national purpose: to create and sustain a society in which all of us are equal.

Throughout our history, when people have looked for new ways to solve their problems, and to uphold the principles of this nation, many times they have turned to political parties. They have often turned to the Democratic Party.

What is it, what is it about the Democratic Party that makes it the instrument that people use when they search for ways to shape their future? Well, I believe the answer to that question lies in our concept of governing. Our concept of governing is derived from our view of people. It is a concept deeply rooted in a set of beliefs firmly etched in the national conscience, of all of us.

Now what are these beliefs?

First, we believe in equality for all and privileges for none. This is a belief that each American regardless of background has equal standing in the public forum, all of us. Because we believe this idea so firmly, we are an inclusive rather than an exclusive party. Let everybody come.

I think it no accident that most of those emigrating to America in the nineteenth century identified with the Democratic Party. We are a heterogeneous party made up of Americans of diverse backgrounds.

We believe that the people are the source of all governmental power, that the authority of the people is to be extended, not restricted. This can be accomplished only by providing each citizen with every opportunity to participate in the management of the government. They must have that.

We believe that the government which represents the authority of all the people, not just one interest group, but all the people, has an obligation to actively underscore, actively seek to remove those obstacles which would block individual achievement—obstacles emanating from race, sex, economic condition. The government must seek to remove them.

We are a party of innovation. We do not reject our traditions, but we are willing to adapt to changing circumstances, when change we must. We are willing to suffer the discomfort of change in order to achieve a better future.

We have a positive vision of the future founded on the belief that the gap between the promise and reality of America can one day be finally closed. We believe that.

This, my friends, is the bedrock of our concept of governing. This is a part of the reason why Americans have turned to the Democratic Party. These are the foundations upon which a national community can be built.

Let's all understand that these guiding principles cannot be discarded for short-term political gains. They represent what this country is all about. They are indigenous to the American idea. And these are principles which are not negotiable.

In other times, I could stand here and give this kind of exposition on the beliefs of the Democratic Party, and that would be enough. But today that is not enough. People want more. That is not sufficient reason for the majority of the people of this country to vote Democratic. We have made mistakes. In our haste to do all things for all people, we did not foresee the full consequences of our actions. And when the people raised their voices, we didn't hear. But our deafness was only a temporary condition, and not an irreversible condition.

Even as I stand here and admit that we have made mistakes, I still believe that as the people of America sit in judgment on each party, they will recognize that our mistakes were mistakes of the heart. They'll recognize that.

And now we must look to the future. Let us heed that voice of the people and recognize their common sense. If we do not, we not only blaspheme our political heritage, we ignore the common ties that bind all Americans.

Many fear the future. Many are distrustful of their leaders and believe that their voices are never heard. Many seek only to satisfy their private work wants, to satisfy private interests.

But this is the great danger America faces. That we will cease to be one nation and become instead a collection of interest groups: city against suburb, region against region, individual against individual, each seeking to satisfy private wants.

If that happens, who then will speak for America?

Who then will speak for the common good?

This is the question which must be answered in 1976.

Are we to be one people bound together by common spirit sharing in a common endeavor, or will we become a divided nation?

For all of its uncertainty, we cannot flee the future. We must not become the new puritans and reject our society. We must address and master the future together. It can be done if we restore the belief that we share a sense of national community, that we share a common national endeavor. It can be done.

There is no executive order; there is no law that can require the American people to form a national community. This we must do as individuals, and if we do it as individuals, there is no President of the United States who can veto that decision.

As a first step, we must restore our belief in ourselves. We are a generous people, so why can't we be generous with each other? We need to take to heart the words spoken by Thomas Jefferson: "Let us restore to social intercourse that harmony and that affection without which liberty and even life are but dreary things."

A nation is formed by the willingness of each of us to share in the responsibility for upholding the common good.

A government is invigorated when each of us is willing to participate in shaping the future of this nation.

In this election year we must define the common good and begin again to shape a common future. Let each person do his or her part. If one citizen is unwilling to participate, all of us are going to suffer. For the American idea, though it is shared by all of us, is realized in each one of us.

And now, what are those of us who are elected public officials supposed to do? We call ourselves public servants, but I'll tell you this: We public servants must set an example for the rest of the nation. It is hypocritical for the public official to admonish and exhort the people to uphold the common good if we are derelict in upholding the common good. More is required of public officials than slogans and handshakes and press releases. More is required. We must hold ourselves strictly accountable. We must provide the people with a vision of the future.

If we promise as public officials, we must deliver. If we as public officials propose, we must produce. If we say to the American people it is time for you to be sacrificial—sacrifice. If the public official says that, we—public officials—must be the first to give. We must be. And again, if we make mistakes, we must be willing to admit them. We have to do that. What we have to do is strike a balance between the idea that government should do everything and the idea, the belief, that government ought to do nothing. Strike a balance.

Let there be no illusions about the difficulty of forming this kind of a national community. It's tough, difficult, not easy. But a spirit of harmony will survive in America only if each of us remembers that we share a common destiny. If each of us remembers, when self-interest and bitterness seem to prevail, that we share a common destiny.

I have confidence that we can form this kind of national community.

I have confidence that the Democratic Party can lead the way. I have that confidence. We cannot improve on the system of government handed down to us by the founders of the Republic; there is no way to improve upon that. But what we can do is to find new ways to implement that system and realize our destiny.

Now, I began this speech by commenting to you on the uniqueness of a Barbara Jordan making the keynote address. Well, I am going to close my speech by quoting a Republican President, and I ask you that as you listen to these words of Abraham Lincoln, relate them to the concept of a national community in which every last one of us participates: "As I would not be a slave, so I would not be a master. This expresses my idea of Democracy. Whatever differs from this, to the extent of the difference is no Democracy."

INAUGURAL ADDRESS

John F. Kennedy

*Washington, D.C.,
January 20, 1961*

Mr. Chief Justice, President Eisenhower, Vice-President Nixon, President Truman, revered clergy, fellow citizens, we observe today not a victory of party, but a celebration of freedom—symbolizing an end, as well as a beginning—signifying renewal, as well as change. For I have sworn before you and Almighty God the same solemn oath our forebears prescribed nearly a century and three quarters ago.

The world is very different now. For man holds in his mortal hands the power to abolish all forms of human poverty and all forms of human life. And yet the same revolutionary beliefs for which our forebears fought are still at issue around the globe—the belief that the rights of man come not from the generosity of the state, but from the hand of God.

We dare not forget today that we are the heirs of that first revolution. Let the word go forth from this time and place, to friend and foe alike, that the torch has been passed to a new generation of Americans—born in this century, tempered by war, disciplined by a hard and bitter peace, proud of our ancient heritage—and unwilling to witness or permit the slow undoing of those human rights to which this Nation has always been committed, and to which we are committed today at home and around the world.

Let every nation know, whether it wishes us well or ill, that we shall pay any price, bear any burden, meet any hardship, support any friend, oppose any foe, in order to assure the survival and the success of liberty.

This much we pledge—and more.

To those old allies whose cultural and spiritual origins we share, we pledge the loyalty of faithful friends. United, there is little we cannot do in a host of cooperative ventures. Divided, there is little we can do—for we dare not meet a powerful challenge at odds and split asunder.

To those new States whom we welcome to the ranks of the free, we pledge our words that one form of colonial control shall not have passed away merely to be replaced by a far greater iron tyranny. We shall not always expect to find them supporting our view. But we shall always hope to find them strongly supporting their own freedom—and to remember that, in the past, those who foolishly sought power by riding the back of the tiger ended up inside.

To those peoples in the huts and villages across the globe struggling to break the bonds of mass misery, we pledge our best efforts to help them help themselves, for whatever period is required—not because the Communists may be doing it, not because we seek their votes, but because it is right. If a free society cannot help the many who are poor, it cannot save the few who are rich.

To our sister republics south of our border, we offer a special pledge—to convert our good words into good deeds, in a new alliance for progress, to assist free men and free governments in casting off the chains of poverty. But this peaceful revolution of hope cannot become the prey of hostile powers. Let all our neighbors know that we shall join with them to oppose aggression or subversion anywhere in the Americas. And let every other power know that this hemisphere intends to remain the master of its own house.

To that world assembly of sovereign states, the United Nations, our last best hope in an age where the instruments of war have far outpaced the instruments of peace, we renew our pledge of support—to prevent it from becoming merely a forum for invective—to strengthen its shield of the new and the weak—and to enlarge the area in which its writ may run.

Finally, to those nations who would make themselves our adversary, we offer not a pledge but a request: that both sides begin anew the quest for peace, before the dark powers of destruction unleashed by science engulf all humanity in planned or accidental self-destruction.

We dare not tempt them with weakness. For only when our arms are sufficient beyond doubt can we be certain beyond doubt that they will never be employed.

But neither can two great and powerful groups of nations take comfort from our present course—both sides overburdened by the cost of modern weapons, both rightly alarmed by the steady spread of the deadly atom, yet both racing to alter that uncertain balance of terror that stays the hand of mankind's final war.

So let us begin anew—remembering on both sides that civility is not a sign of weakness, and sincerity is always subject to proof. Let us never negotiate out of fear. But let us never fear to negotiate.

Let both sides explore what problems unite us instead of laboring those problems which divide us.

Let both sides, for the first time, formulate serious and precise proposals for the inspection and control of arms—and bring the absolute power to destroy other nations under the absolute control of all nations.

Let both sides seek to invoke the wonders of science instead of its terrors. Together let us explore the stars, conquer the deserts, eradicate disease, tap the ocean depths, and encourage the arts and commerce.

Let both sides unite to heed in all corners of the earth the command of Isaiah—to "undo the heavy burdens and to let the oppressed go free."

And if a beachhead of cooperation may push back the jungle of suspicion, let both sides join in creating a new endeavor, not a new balance of power, but a new world of law, where the strong are just and the weak secure and the peace preserved.

All this will not be finished in the first hundred days. Nor will it be finished in the first thousand days, nor in the life of this administration, nor even perhaps in our lifetime on this planet. But let us begin.

In your hands, my fellow citizens, more than in mine, will rest the final success or failure of our course. Since this country was founded, each generation of Americans has been summoned to give testimony to its national loyalty. The graves of young Americans who answered the call to service surround the globe.

Now the trumpet summons us again—not as a call to bear arms, though arms we need; not as a call to battle, though embattled we are; but a call to bear the burden of a long twilight struggle, year in, and year out, "rejoicing in hope, patient in tribulation"—a struggle against the common enemies of man: tyranny, poverty, disease, and war itself.

Can we forge against these enemies a grand and global alliance, North and South, East and West, that can assure a more fruitful life for all mankind? Will you join in that historic effort?

In the long history of the world, only a few generations have been granted the role of defending freedom in its hour of maximum danger. I do not shrink from this responsibility—I welcome it. I do not believe that any of us would exchange places with any other people or any other generation. The energy, the faith, the devotion which we bring to this endeavor will light our country and all who serve it—and the glow from that fire can truly light the world.

And so, my fellow Americans, ask not what your country can do for you; ask what you can do for your country.

My fellow citizens of the world: Ask not what America will do for you, but what together we can do for the freedom of man.

Finally, whether you are citizens of America or citizens of the world, ask of us the same high standards of strength and sacrifice which we ask of you. With a good conscience our only sure reward, with history the final judge of our deeds, let us go forth to lead the land we love, asking His blessing and His help, but knowing that here on earth God's work must truly be our own.

DEVELOPING YOUR CAPACITIES

T. Richard Cheatham

Graduate School Commencement Address, Southwest Texas State University, August 12, 1988

An erudite professor decided to have a little fun at the expense of his unlearned guide as they paddled their canoe down an Arkansas river. "My good man," queried the professor, "have you ever measured the viscosity of the river water?" "Nope, can't say as I have," responded the bewildered guide. "Then you've missed half your life," snorted the professor. A few moments later the professor again broke the silence of the serene environment. "Tell me, Sir, can you correctly identify the genus and species of the flora and fauna inhabiting the shores of this river?" "Nope, can't say as I can," the guide replied. "Then you've missed half your life," snapped the professor. About that time the canoe struck a large rock hidden just below the surface, and both men were thrown to the mercy of the river's current. As the guide was swimming to shore, he heard the professor say, "I can't swim!" as he disappeared below the murky water. The guide sadly replied, "Then you've missed all your life!"

Graduates, in the words of the popular commercial, "We only go around once in life." We don't want to miss half or any portion of our lives. A recent article by Barrie Grieff of Harvard University lists five capacities which must be developed if we are to achieve success in life. Permit me to share those five capacities with you and to supplement Professor Grieff's words with the observations of successful individuals ranging from King Solomon to H. Ross Perot.

According to Professor Grieff, we must develop our capacity to love, learn, labor, laugh, and leave.

The Capacity to Love   The ancient Greeks knew the importance of love in all aspects of living. They spoke of *eros*, erotic love; of *storge*, family love; of *phileo*, friendship love; and of *agape*, unselfish and sacrificial love. In short, they knew the value of loving consorts, kin, comrades and causes!

Samual A. Cypert's recent bestseller, *Believe and Achieve*, reminds us that "unless you are a hermit living on a tropical island, you need others and others need you to be successful." Hundreds of years earlier the English poet John Donne expressed a similar thought: "No man is an island, entire of itself; every man is a piece of a continent, a part of the main."

The California Department of Mental Health recently published a report entitled *Friends Can Be Good Medicine*. Regardless of age, gender, or ethnic group, social support was praised as an enhancer of wellness and a buffer against disease. Mice injected with cancer cells and isolated developed tumors more rapidly than those animals remaining with their mates.

The late Vince Lombardi in an address before the American Management Association summed it up in this way: "I don't necessarily have to like my associates, but as a person I must love them. Love is loyalty. Love is teamwork. Heartpower is the strength of your corporation."

Coach Grant Teaff of Baylor University loves to tell the story of his first dismal season at the helm of the Baylor football program. After losing almost every game that year, Grant and one of his most loyal assistant coaches decided to get away from it all for a while—to take up the offer of an old man who had said they could come out and hunt on his property any time they chose. They got up early one Saturday morning and drove out to the property near McGregor. When they arrived at the property Grant jumped out of the pickup and ran up to the front door of the old man's house to let him know they had arrived. The old gentleman welcomed Grant and told him that despite the bad year on the gridiron, he knew that Grant would have better times in the future and that he was glad to have Grant and his assistant coach honor him by hunting on his property. However, he had one request. "See that old mule leaning against the barn? The vet was out here yesterday and wanted to put him to sleep, but I wouldn't allow it. Now I know I was wrong, and I don't have the heart to put him out of his misery myself. Grant, would you please shoot that mule for me?" Grant was shocked at this unusual request, but decided to have a little fun at the expense of his assistant. He walked back to the pickup shaking his head; sat behind the wheel and remarked, "I can't believe that old cuss! He said he didn't allow losers to hunt on his property! You know what I'm gonna do. I'm gonna teach that old man a lesson he won't forget! I'm gonna kill that mule over there!" Grant took the rifle from the rack behind him, took dead aim at the mule, and fired three times. As the mule fell and Grant was enjoying the joke he was playing on his assistant, he heard several more shots. His assistant coach yelled, "I got three of his cows! Come on, let's get the rest!"

Now that's what I call *love*!

The Capacity to Learn   Graduates, you are to be commended for your level of learning that has brought you to this commencement. But do not let the name of your degree deceive you. You can spend a lifetime in your chosen career without really *mastering* that vast sea of knowledge before you. Alexander Pope observed: "A little learning is a dangerous thing: Drink deep, or taste not the Pierian spring." I hope that your years at SWT have left you with more questions than answers— questions that you will spend the rest of your life attempting to answer. I hope that the example of your professors and the academic environment of graduate school have developed in you a capacity for inquiry—a healthy skepticism that causes you to question the answers at the same time that you answer the questions! After all, one generation's facts have a way of becoming the next generation's myths. Lord Kelvin, president of the Royal Society in 1895, remarked: "Heavier-than-air flying machines are impossible." Grover Cleveland, the twenty-second and twenty-fourth President of the U.S., observed in 1905: "Sensible women do not want to vote." Robert Millikan, Nobel prize winner in physics, emphatically stated in 1923: "Man can never tap the power of the atom."

For those of us planning to remain in education for the rest of our careers, the continuing search for knowledge is vital. As Kathryn Mohrman observed in the July 1988 issue of *Academic Leader*, "A person does not have enough intellectual capital coming out of graduate school to sustain a 35- to 40-year career; research is the basic source of intellectual capital." It is not a question of whether we will teach *or* be involved in research. As Mohrman reports, "Research enhances teaching. Faculty engaged in scholarly work in their laboratories and libraries are more exciting teachers in the classroom."

May Chaucer's famous line describing the Clerk of Oxenford apply to all of us: "And gladly wolde he lerne, and gladly teche."

The Capacity to Labor   In my opinion there are far too many "tricks of the trade" seminars and books promising shortcuts to quick success. It was a wise person, however, who observed that "the only place where success comes before work is the dictionary." Edison described genius as 1 percent inspiration and 99 percent perspiration. Our nation, our great industries, and our universities were built upon the foundation of hard work and a willingness to assume risks. Perhaps the best teachers that you will ever have will be named *trial* and *error*. Mike Markkula of Apple Computers says: "Success does not breed success. It breeds failure. It is failure which breeds success." Tom Peters in his recent *Thriving on Chaos* quotes Soichiro Honda: "Success represents the 1 percent of your work that results only from 99 percent that is called failure." We would all do well to remember that the home-run hero, Babe Ruth, struck out 1,330 times during his career of 714 home runs. At 8:01 P.M. on September 11, 1985, baseball star Pete Rose surpassed Ty Cobb's record when he hit his 4,192nd career hit. However, Rose holds another record, most outs (9,518). In the business world and in academe we are all too often paralyzed by the fear of failure. Instead of launching bold new initiatives, we worry about what the competition is doing or what the other universities in our mission class are doing. I like the sign that hangs on the wall in Renn Zaphiropoulos's office. The president of Versatec, Inc., keeps a framed quotation on his wall which reads: "Do not follow where the path may lead. Go instead where there is no path and leave a trail." Rather than appointing committees and hiring consultants, more managers need to exercise initiative and assume risks. In comparing the operations of EDS and General Motors, Ross Perot said: "When an EDSer sees a snake he kills it. At GM they form a committee on snakes; the committee brings in a consultant who knows a lot about snakes; then they talk about it for a year."

Take a look at recent publications. *The Creative Corporation* (by Karl Albrecht), *The Creative Edge* (by William Miller), *The Improvement Process* (by James Harrington), *The Future 500* (by Hickman and Silva), *The Energetic Manager* (by Fred Pryor), and *The Leadership Challenge* (by Kouzes and Posner) all stress the need for leaders who will exercise initiative and assume risks associated with creative solutions.

Perhaps Shakespeare was issuing a warning to those who would seek the security of the harbor when he said: "There is a tide in the affairs of men, which, taken at the flood, leads on to fortune; omitted, all the voyages of their life is bound in shallows and in miseries."

The Capacity to Laugh King Solomon, a man possessing encyclopedic knowledge, told us thousands of years ago that "a merry heart doeth good like a medicine." Rabelais said: "One inch of joy surmounts of grief a span, because to laugh is proper to the man." Finally, there is Ella Wheeler Wilcox's famous admonition: "Laugh and the world laughs with you, weep and you weep alone; for the sad old earth must borrow its mirth, but has trouble enough of its own."

We all know people who were born in crab-apple time and dipped in vinegar— people who by comparison make the face on an iodine bottle look like a happy face. These individuals need to develop the capacity to laugh—at themselves and with others. Recent studies in major universities have actually discovered digestive and circulatory benefits associated with a good belly laugh. We now know that all these years of humorous after-dinner speeches have had therapeutic value. Indeed, Solomon was right. Merry hearts do serve like a medicine!

The Capacity to Leave All of us at some point will come face to face with the reality of failed relationships, shattered dreams, and lost jobs. Grief at such times is natural, and to an extent healthy. However, there comes a time when we must face facts and cease our longing looks over our shoulders. Indeed, we will fail in the present and the future if we do not develop the capacity to leave the past. Someone wrote, "The lightning bug is brilliant, but it hasn't much of a mind, it blunders through existence with its headlight on behind." In "Hyperion," Longfellow admonished mankind: "Look not mournfully into the past. It comes not back again. Wisely improve the Present. It is thine. Go forth to meet the shadowy future, without fear, and with a manly heart."

The capacity to *love*, the capacity to *learn*, the capacity to *labor*, the capacity to *laugh*, and the capacity to *leave*. Development of these capacities will not necessarily add years to your life—but such development will add life to your years! Development of these capacities may not make you a captain of industry or the master of many—but such development can help you become the "captain of your soul and the master of your fate!" And finally, if you develop these capacities, you won't miss half your life!

August 23rd, 1984. The thirteen passengers on Wings West flight #628 were admiring the picture-postcard day. It was to be just a short commuter hop to San Francisco. A twenty-five-year-old air traffic controller, a new trainee, proceeded to give directions. Yet his directions were wrong, and the resulting head-on collision with another small aircraft killed all thirteen passengers aboard.

The scary thing is that this incident is not isolated. The risk in our skies is increasing, due to the lack of the quality and quantity of air traffic controllers today. Ever since the 1981 Professional Air Traffic Controllers Organization, or PATCO, strike, situations such as the one previously mentioned are becoming more common and the friendly skies are becoming less friendly.

So, to further illustrate the problem of air traffic controllers and convince you it needs amending today, I will deal with three areas: First, I will go into the history of the problem; secondly, the effects, and lastly, some probable solutions.

The one word to best describe an air traffic controller's job is *stress*, and a lot of it. This stress results in tangled nerves, high blood pressure and occasional alcoholism. PATCO had complained to the FAA for years that this stress just wasn't worth the 33,000 dollars a year average salary they were receiving. So, for years both PATCO and the FAA were at odds over this. As time progressed, PATCO grew more fanatical. This continued until 1981, when they finally exploded against the FAA and the new Reagan Administration.

Initial negotiations, according to the August 17, 1981, issue of *U.S. News and World Report*, went something like this: The FAA offered an 11.5% pay increase, including benefits, to PATCO workers. However, 95.3% of them voted "no," for they wanted more money and less hours to deal with their stress. They threatened to strike.

This made President Reagan furious, for three reasons: First, every federal worker knows that he or she has to sign an oath not to strike against the federal government before beginning his or her job. PATCO was threatening to break this oath. Secondly, President Reagan realized that the lack of thousands of PATCO workers would be detrimental to the safety in our skies. Lastly, they were just breaking the law. So, the President gave an ultimatum: "If you strike, you get fired." They did it anyway, as the first declared national strike against the federal government commenced, with 13,000 of 15,000 PATCO workers leaving their jobs. President Reagan held true to his word: he fired every single one of them.

Whether or not the PATCO issue was right or wrong wasn't the issue. The issue was this: with only a few thousand PATCO workers remaining you can imagine what kind of problems occurred. There were flight delays, a lot of them, some scary near misses and airline industries were losing millions a day because they could not get off the ground. Somehow the rag-tag group that remained after the strike managed to do their job.

The FAA has gradually built up that skeleton crew of about 5,000 controllers after the strike to about 15,000 today. Yet, there still remain some serious problems:

First, the *quality* of air traffic controllers is just not how it was before the strike. According to *The Nation*, June 1, 1985, only 7,779 air traffic controllers are fully qualified and over half of them will be eligible for retirement within just four years.

That was two years ago. Come June 1st of this year, they will be eligible for retirement within just two years. More significantly, according to the January 12, 1987, issue of *Time* magazine, only 62% of air traffic controllers today are fully qualified versus 80% before the strike. The remainder of the workforce consists of assistants and trainees.

THE FRIENDLY SKIES[2]

Erik S. Tavares

Anchorage Community College, Alaska, 1987

Sadly, this lack of quality is seen more often than we'd like. I refer you back to the beginning of my speech with the Wings West disaster. The controller was a 25-year-old, inexperienced trainee. He lacked experience, and people died.

Secondly, the *quantity* of air traffic controllers is not enough to deal with the increased amount of traffic in our skies. According to *The Nation*, air traffic controllers are now having to deal with traffic eight to ten times higher than the pre-strike level. According to the FAA, there were only six days in history, prior to 1984, where air traffic controllers had to deal with over 100,000 flights nationwide. There were 54 such days in 1984 alone.

Seventy-eight percent of controllers who were polled state that this increase in air traffic is detrimental to the safety in our skies.

The frantic controller at the Los Angeles Airport must have agreed to this, as he wearily said to those pilots he was guiding on that smog-filled day: "There are just too many flights for me to take care of at once. Please be careful out there."

Stress conditions today are believed to be worse than before the PATCO strike, doing exactly opposite of what they wanted in the first place.

Anthony Skirlick, Jr., a veteran controller, contends now that personnel shortage is due less to the PATCO firings and due more to the FAA itself in its efforts to cut costs. The FAA plans to cut 300 controller jobs by 1990, for they say that near and mid-air collisions have decreased with time. Yet the statistics say otherwise.

Near collisions have increased dramatically, from 312 in 1982 all the way up to over 816 just last year. In 1985 alone, over 525 people died in commercial aircraft disasters while over 1,200 people died in small aircraft disasters. This is just in one year and just in the United States.

Obviously, not all of these are due to air traffic controller error, but when will the FAA and the Reagan Administration realize that hundreds of men, women and children have died due to the risks in our skies? The lack of the quality and quantity of air traffic controllers does not help the problem one bit, and we have to start somewhere. Yet the FAA still plans to cut 300 jobs by 1990, and the idea doesn't make sense. Both myself and all of you that fly at all are not immune to these risks.

On March 31, 1986, at the Minneapolis/St. Paul Airport, a Northwest DC-10 was taxiing to the runway preparing for takeoff. Suddenly, another DC-10 shot out in front of it. The pilot, cool and collected said, "I see it." He jerked the nose up and lifted into the air, his wing missing the other aircraft by a mere 50 feet. This 50 feet saved a total of 501 persons from what could have been the second worse aircraft disaster in history.

What caused this near disaster on March 31st, a perfectly clear day? Two air traffic controllers, sitting right next to each other, had no idea what the other had done. We are not immune.

So, to solve this problem will take some time and some effort, and the solutions should be grouped into two areas:

First, *the fired PATCO workers should be rehired.* It's been six years since the strike, and the added boost would help lift the sagging quality and quantity of air traffic controllers today. Both Ralph Nader and Hank Duffy, the chairman of the Airline Pilots Association, have urged the Reagan Administration to lift their blacklist, saying in that rehiring those several thousand seasoned controllers would be the quickest and surest way of improving air safety.

Secondly, *a new union should be developed.* Already a sort of "pre-union" has been created, it is the American Air Traffic Controllers Council, or AATCC. It is the beginnings of a new union and is already being endorsed by such larger unions as the AFL-CIO and the Airline Pilots Association. Yet it is still in the process of submitting certification petitions and the government isn't helping one bit.

FAA chief Donald Eagan has stressed the opinion of the Reagan Administration more than once on both of these issues: "No way."

The January 12, 1987, issue of *Time* magazine stated that already 500 of the less militant PATCO workers have been quietly rehired back into the system. So far, it seems they've been able to adapt to the new technology. This added boost would help lift the sagging quality and quantity, boost morale and perhaps decrease the risk in our skies.

When thinking about a new union, the first question that obviously comes to mind is: aren't you going to be repeating history as with PATCO? The answer is no. The AATCC is vastly better than PATCO for two reasons. First, it is backed by a variety of larger unions, [which] PATCO never was. Secondly, it is better organized and managed so it can more effectively and efficiently deal with the FAA and its cost-cutting procedures, to give the controllers a voice, to show that perhaps cutting costs is necessary but cutting personnel isn't.

But what can we do? If you have any friends or family in any way connected with an air traffic controller, ask to see what they suggest. If not, go to the phone book in the government section to determine the nearest division of the FAA, to obtain phone numbers or addresses as to where to voice your opinion. We must urge the FAA to change their minds about these two solutions, that the risks in our skies are not decreasing and that we are not immune to these risks.

But until a solution can be implemented, the risks in our skies continue to increase. The threat exists, as I've shown in both the history and the effects, but there are solutions.

It is said that if people were meant to fly, they'd have wings. Yet, we have beaten the odds, but in doing so we have a responsibility to maintain safety on the ground as well as in the sky. Working together to avoid such tragedies such as the Wings West flight #628. Working together to making the unfriendly skies a little friendlier.

ADVICE TO YOUTH

Mark Twain

Saturday Morning Club, Boston, April 15, 1882

Being told I would be expected to talk here, I inquired what sort of a talk I ought to make. They said it should be something suitable to youth—something didactic, instructive; or something in the nature of good advice. Very well; I have a few things in my mind which I have often longed to say for the instruction of the young; for it is in one's tender early years that such things will best take root and be most enduring and most valuable. First, then, I will say to you, my young friends—and say it beseechingly, urgingly—.

Always obey your parents, when they are present. This is the best policy in the long run; because if you don't, they will make you. Most parents think they know better than you do; and you can generally make more by humoring that superstition than you can by acting on your own better judgment.

Be respectful of your superiors, if you have any; also to strangers, and sometimes to others. If a person offends you, and you are in doubt as to whether it was intentional or not, do not resort to extreme measures; simply watch your chance and hit him with a brick. That will be sufficient. If you shall find that he had not intended any offense, come out frankly and confess yourself in the wrong when you struck him; acknowledge it like a man, and say you didn't mean to. Yes, always avoid violence; in this age of charity and kindness, the time has gone by for such things. Leave dynamite to the low and unrefined.

Go to bed early, get up early—this is wise. Some authorities say get up with one thing, some with another. But a lark is really the best thing to get up with. It gives you a splendid reputation with everybody to know that you get up with the lark; and if you get the right kind of a lark, and work at him right, you can easily train him to get up at half-past nine, every time—it is no trick at all.

Now as to the matter of lying. You want to be very careful about lying; otherwise you are nearly sure to get caught. Once caught, you can never again be, in the eyes of the good and the pure, what you were before. Many a young person has injured himself permanently through a singly clumsy and ill-finished lie, the result of carelessness born of incomplete training. Some authorities hold that the young ought not to lie at all. That, of course, is putting it rather stronger than necessary; still, while I cannot go quite so far as that, I do maintain, and I believe I am right, that the young ought to be temperate in the use of this great art until practice and experience shall give them that confidence, elegance, and precision which alone can make the accomplishment graceful and profitable. Patience, diligence, painstaking attention to detail—these are the requirements; these, in time, will make the student perfect; upon these, and upon these only, may he rely as the sure foundation for future eminence. Think what tedious years of study, thought, practice, experience went to the equipment of that peerless old master who was able to impose upon the whole world the lofty and sounding maxim that, "Truth is mighty and will prevail"—the most majestic compound fracture of fact which any of woman born has yet achieved. For the history of our race, and each individual's experience, are sown thick with evidences that a truth is not hard to kill, and that a lie well told is immortal. There in Boston is a monument to the man who discovered anesthesia; many people are aware, in these latter days, that that man didn't discover it at all, but stole the discovery from another man. Is this truth mighty, and will it prevail? Ah, no, my hearers, the monument is made of hardy material, but the lie it tells will outlast it a million years. An awkward, feeble, leaky lie is a thing which you ought to make it your unceasing study to avoid; such a lie as that has no more real permanence than an average truth. Why, you might as well tell the truth at once and be done with it. A feeble, stupid, preposterous lie will not live two years—expect it be a slander upon somebody. It is indestructible, then, of course, but that is no merit of yours. A final word: begin your practice of this gracious and beautiful art early—begin now. If I had begun earlier, I could have learned how.

Never handle firearms carelessly. The sorrow and suffering that have been caused through the innocent but heedless handling of firearms by the young! Only four days ago, right in the next farmhouse to the one where I am spending the summer, a mother, old and gray and sweet, one of the loveliest spirits in the land, was sitting at her work, when her young son crept in and got down an old, battered, rusty gun which had not been touched for many years, and was supposed not to be loaded, and pointed it at her, laughing and threatening to shoot. In her fright she ran screaming and pleading toward the door on the other side of the room; but as she passed him he placed the gun almost against her very breast and pulled the trigger! He had supposed it was not loaded. And he was right: it wasn't. So there wasn't any harm done. It is the only case of the kind I ever heard of. Therefore, just the same, don't you meddle with old unloaded firearms; they are the most deadly and unerring things that have ever been created by man. You don't have to take any pains at all, with them; you don't have to have a rest, you don't have to have any sights on the gun, you don't have to take aim, even. No, you just pick out a relative and bang away, and you are sure to get him. A youth who can't hit a cathedral at thirty years with a Gatling gun in three-quarters of an hour, can take up an old empty musket and bang his mother every time, at a hundred. Think what Waterloo would have been if one of the armies had been boys armed with old rusty muskets supposed not to be loaded, and the other army had been composed of their female relations. The very thought of it makes me shudder.

There are many sorts of books; but good ones are the sort for the young to read. Remember that. They are a great, an inestimable, an unspeakable means of improvement. Therefore be careful in your selection, my young friends; be very careful; confine yourself exclusively to Roberson's *Sermons*, Baxter's *Saint's Rest*, *The Innocents Abroad*, and works of that kind.

But I have said enough. I hope you will treasure the instructions which I have given you, and make them a guide to your feet and a light to your understanding. Build your character thoughtfully and painstakingly upon these precepts; and by and by, when you have got it built, you will be surprised and gratified to see how nicely and sharply it resembles everybody else's.

Notes

Chapter 1

1. Ronald Reagan, address to the American Society of Newspaper Editors, Wednesday, April 13, 1988. Quoted in "Invented Quotes Upset President." *Austin American-Statesman*. April 14, 1988. A2.

Chapter 2

1. *Spectra*, 9 (December 1973): 4. Survey conducted by R. H. Bruskin and Associates.

2. Edward R. Robinson, "What Can the Teacher Do about Students' Stage Fright?" *Speech Teacher*, 8 (January 1959): 9–11.

3. J. Ayers and T. S. Hopf, "Visualization: A Means of Reducing Speech Anxiety," *Communication Education*, 34 (1985): 318–323.

Chapter 3

1. Douglas Ehninger, Bruce E. Gronbeck, Ray E. McKerrow, and Alan H. Monroe, *Principles and Types of Speech Communication* (Glenview, Ill.: Scott, Foresman, 1986), p. 43.

2. Paul Rankin, "Listening Ability: Its Importance, Measurement and Development," *Chicago Schools Journal*, 12 (January 1930): 177–79.

3. Study conducted by Paul Cameron, as cited in Ronald B. Adler and Neil Town, *Looking Out/Looking In: Interpersonal Communication* (New York: Holt, Rinehart and Winston, 1981), p. 218.

4. Ralph G. Nichols and Leonard A. Stevens, "Six Bad Listening Habits," in *Are You Listening*? (New York: McGraw-Hill, 1957).

5. Albert Mehrabian, *Nonverbal Communication* (Hawthorne, N.Y.: Aldine, 1972).

6. Nichols and Stevens, "Six Bad Listening Habits."

7. Ibid.

Chapter 4

1. Olaf E. Rankis, "The Effects of Message Structure, Sexual Gender, and Verbal Organizing Ability upon Learning Message Information," unpublished Ph.D. dissertation, Ohio University, 1981; Carl H. Weaver, *Human Listening: Processes and Behavior* (Indianapolis: Bobbs-Merrill, 1972).

2. John T. Masterson and Norman Watson, "The Effects of Culture on Preferred Speaking Style." Paper presented at the Speech Communication Association Conference, November, 1979.

3. John Wait Bowers and John Courtwright, *Research Methods in Communication* (Glenview, Illinois: Scott, Foresman and Company, 1982.)

4. Abraham H. Maslow and N. L. Mintz, "Effect of Esthetic Surroundings," *Journal of Psychology*, 41 (1956): 247–254.

Chapter 5

1. Alex F. Osborn, *Applied Imagination* (New York: Scribner, 1962).

2. Marilyn Hernandez, "The Work-Study Program," student speech, University of Miami, 1983.

3. Monique Russo, "The 'Starving Disease' or Anorexia Nervosa," student speech, University of Miami, 1984.

4. Linda Loehr, "Ignorance Kills," in *Winning Orations*, 1985 (Mankato, Minn.: Interstate Oratorical Association, 1985), p. 4.

5. Josh Willson, "Sudden Infant Death Syndrome," student speech, Southwest Texas State University, 1987.

Chapter 6

1. Eleanor L. Doan, ed., *The Speaker's Sourcebook* (Grand Rapids, Mich.: Zondervan, 1960), p. 229.

2. Cited in Bob Hood, "Speaking Personally," *Scouting*, January-February 1987, p. 50.

3. Marilyn Hernandez, "The March of Dimes," student speech, University of Miami, 1981.

4. Sandra D. Lindquist, "Diploma Mills vs. Responsible Training: Sending Degrees to the Dogs," in *Winning Orations*, 1985 (Mankato, Minn.: Interstate Oratorical Association, 1985), p. 53.

5. "Tiny Tick, Big Worry," *Newsweek*, May 22, 1989, p. 66. Courtesy *Newsweek*.

6. Brenda Dempsey, "Burn Education: Giving Our Children a Fighting Chance," in *Winning Orations*, 1987 (Mankato, Minn.: Interstate Oratorical Association, 1987), p. 57.

7. Professor Frazer White, University of Miami.

8. Kathy Deutsch, "Parrots as Pets," student speech, University of Miami, 1980.

9. Jo Leda Carpenter, "Sun Exposure and Cancer: A Cause and Effect," in *Winning Orations*, 1987, p. 17.

10. Patrick Osowski, "The Contras: Founders of the United States of Nicaragua," in *Winning Orations*, 1985, p. 63.

11. "Emotional Abuse," *Austin American-Statesman*, January 14, 1988, p. E2.

12. William Morris, ed., *The American Heritage Dictionary of the English Language* (Boston: American Heritage, 1969), p. 308.

13. Percy Bysshe Shelly, "Ode to the West Wind."

14. Osowski, "The Contras," p. 65.

15. Elizabeth Cady Stanton, address to the first women's rights convention (1848) in Houston Peterson, ed., *A Treasury of the World's Great Speeches* (New York: Simon & Schuster, 1965), pp. 388–392.

16. Attributed to Benjamin Disraeli in Mark Twain, *Autobiography*.

17. Richard D. Propes, "Alone in the Dark," in *Winning Orations*, 1985, p. 23.

18. Ibid.

19. Kathryn Kasdorf, untitled speech, in *Winning Orations*, 1985, p. 16.

20. Brenda Gerlach, "The Thickening Fog," in *Winning Orations*, *1985*, p. 73.

21. Joseph D. Stephens, "Corporate Sponsored Day Care," in *Winning Orations*, *1985*, p. 83.

22. John J. Isaza, "The Phone Muggers," in *Winning Orations*, *1985*, p. 11.

23. Sharyn Kolstad, "None of Your Business!" in *Winning Orations*, *1984* (Mankato, Minn.: Interstate Oratorical Association, 1984), p. 100.

24. Jay W. Brown, "The Burning Question of Our Nation's Books," in *Winning Orations*, *1984* (Mankato, Minn.: Interstate Oratorical Association, 1984), p. 43.

25. Cited in Joan Braaten, "It's English," in *Winning Orations*, *1984*, p. 64.

26. Lester L. Tobias, letter to the editor, *Newsweek*, February 22, 1988, p. 4. Courtesy *Newsweek*.

27. Deidre Wallace, "Utility Company Abuse of the American Consumer," in *Winning Orations*, *1984*, p. 17.

28. Chris Wallace, "The Big Mac Attack," in *Winning Orations*, *1984*, p. 59.

29. Robert Rager, "Amusement Park Safety," in *Winning Orations*, *1985*, p. 38.

30. Ibid., p. 39.

31. Ibid., p. 40.

32. Ibid., p. 41.

33. Joseph K. Ott, "America's Internal Cold War," in *Winning Orations*, *1985*, p. 45.

34. Ibid.

35. Beth Wolff, "The Technological Twilight Zone," in *Winning Orations*, *1985*, p. 76.

Chapter 8

1. Adapted from Craig Scott, "The American Farm Crisis," in *Winning Orations*, *1986* (Mankato, Minn.: Interstate Oratorical Association, 1986), pp. 15–18.

2. Adapted from Laurel Johnson, "Where There's a Will There's a Way," in *Winning Orations*, *1986*, pp. 59–62.

3. Adapted from Vonda Ramey, "Can You Read This?" in *Winning Orations*, *1985* (Mankato, Minn.: Interstate Oratorical Association, 1985), pp. 32–35.

4. Craig Scott, "AIDS: The Need for Education," in *Winning Orations*, *1987* (Mankato, Minn.: Interstate Oratorical Association, 1987), pp. 13–16.

5. Erik S. Tavares, "The Friendly Skies," in *Winning Orations*, *1987*, pp. 4–7.

6. Ibid., pp. 4–5.

7. Loren Schwarzwalter, "An Answer for America's Future," in *Winning Orations*, *1987*, pp. 86–87.

8. Irma Levy, "Transplantation: The Miracle of Life," in *Winning Orations*, *1984* (Mankato, Minn.: Interstate Oratorical Association, 1984), p. 80.

9. Vic Vieth, "Prisoners of Conscience," in *Winning Orations*, *1984*, p. 47.

10. Jo Leda Carpenter, "Sun Exposure and Cancer: A Cause and Effect," in *Winning Orations*, *1987*, p. 17.

11. Sharon Fong, "The Stigma of Epilepsy," in *Winning Orations*, *1987*, p. 80.

12. Heather Green, "Radon in Our Homes," in *Winning Orations*, *1986*, p. 4.

13. Kent Busek, "Farm Suicides," in *Winning Orations*, *1986*, p. 82.

14. Melody Hopkins, "Collegiate Athletes: A Contradiction in Terms," in *Winning Orations*, *1986*, p. 111.

15. Johnson, "Where There's a Will," p. 59.

16. Green, "Radon in Our Homes," p. 4.

17. Vonda K. Ramey, "Make My Day," in *Winning Orations*, *1986*, p. 45.

18. Neela Latey, "U.S. Customs Procedures: Danger to Americans' Health and Society," in *Winning Orations*, *1986*, p. 22.

19. Susan Stevens, "Teacher Shortage," in *Winning Orations*, *1986*, p. 27.

20. Green, "Radon in Our Homes," p. 5.

21. Terry O'Bryan Kiszka, "Your Last Gift to Life—Your Human Organs," in *Winning Orations*, *1986*, p. 35.

22. Lori Van Overbeke, "NutraSweet," in *Winning Orations*, *1986* (Mankato, Minn.: Interstate Oratorical Association), p. 58.

23. Adapted from Heath Honaker, "A New Brand of Homeless," in *Winning Orations*, *1986*, pp. 108–111.

Chapter 9

1. All sample outlines in this chapter are based on Mark Culkins, "A Tisket, a Tasket, a Tandem Truck Casket," in *Winning Orations*, *1986* (Mankato, Minn.: Interstate Oratorical Association, 1986), pp. 9–12.

Chapter 10

1. Kathryn Kasdorf, untitled speech, in *Winning Orations*, *1985* (Mankato, Minn.: Interstate Oratorical Association, 1985), p. 16.

2. Amy Gillespie, "Listen Up!" in *Winning Orations*, *1985*, p. 48.

3. Vic Vieth, "Prisoners of Conscience," in *Winning Orations*, *1984* (Mankato, Minn.: Interstate Oratorical Association, 1984), p. 46.

4. Mary Tatum, "Silver Dental Fillings: The Toxic Poison," in *Winning Orations*, *1987* (Mankato, Minn.: Interstate Oratorical Association, 1987), p. 1.

5. Lisa Shemwell, "In Pursuit of Liberty," in *Winning Orations*, *1987*, p. 46.

6. Loren Schwarzwalter, "An Answer for America's Future," in *Winning Orations*, *1987*, p. 85.

7. Jo Leda Carpenter, "Sun Exposure and Cancer: A Cause and Effect," in *Winning Orations*, *1987*, p. 17.

8. Patrick R. Riestenberg, "Diplomatic Immunity: Living above the Law," in *Winning Orations*, *1984*, p. 67.

9. Terry O'Bryan Kiszka, "Your Last Gift to Life—Your Human Organs," in *Winning Orations, 1986* (Mankato, Minn.: Interstate Oratorical Association, 1986), p. 32.

10. Mary Beth Zuerlein, "Mortui Vivos Docent," in *Winning Orations, 1986*, p. 72.

11. Abigail Baker, "The Backseat Villain," in *Winning Orations, 1987*, p. 49.

12. Kelly Siemers, student speech, University of Miami, 1983.

13. Kasdorf, untitled speech, p. 16.

14. Victoria M. Thompson, "Superbabies," in *Winning Orations, 1984*, p. 49.

15. Theresa Clinkenbeard, "The Loss of Childhood," in *Winning Orations, 1984*, p. 4.

16. Adapted from Eleanor L. Doan, ed., *The Speaker's Sourcebook* (Grand Rapids, Mich.: Zondervan, 1960), p. 128.

17. Heath Honaker, "Illegitimate Graduates," in *Winning Orations, 1985*, p. 85.

18. Lisa M. Kralik, "Geographical Illiteracy," in *Winning Orations, 1987*, p. 76.

19. Richard Propes, "Alone in the Dark," in *Winning Orations, 1985*, p. 22.

20. Beth Moberg, "Licensed to Kill," in *Winning Orations, 1985*, p. 89.

21. Jane M. Hatch, *The American Books of Days* (New York: Wilson, 1978).

22. Ruth W. Gregory, *Anniversaries and Holidays* (Chicago: American Library Association, 1975).

23. Illustration and quotation from Loren Reid, *Speaking Well* (New York: McGraw-Hill, 1982), p. 111.

24. Robert Rager, "Amusement Park Safety," in *Winning Orations, 1985*, p. 38.

25. L. David Ferrari, "Parental Kidnapping," in *Winning Orations, 1984*, p. 10.

26. Winston Churchill, address to the Congress of the United States (December 26, 1941), in Bower Aly and Lucille F. Aly, eds., *Speeches in English* (New York: Random House, 1968), p. 230.

27. Marcie Groover, "Learning to Communicate: The Importance of Speech Education in Public Schools," in *Winning Orations, 1984*, p. 7.

28. This speech as well as all succeeding speeches without reference numbers were written by the authors.

29. Student speech, University of Miami, 1981.

30. John Ryan, "Emissions Tampering: Get the Lead Out," in *Winning Orations, 1985*, p. 63.

31. Douglas MacArthur, "Old Soldiers Never Die" (April 19, 1951), in Aly and Aly, *Speeches in English*, p. 259.

32. John O'Connor, "Buy the People," in *Winning Orations, 1984*, p. 27.

33. Jay W. Brown, "The Burning Question of Our Nation's Books," in *Winning Orations, 1984*, p. 46.

34. Kristin Amondsen, "Outfoxing Mr. Badwrench," *Winning Orations, 1987*, p. 32.

35. Shelley Schnathorst, "When the Child Knows the Truth," *Winning Orations, 1987*, p. 42.

36. Kralik, "Geographical Illiteracy," p. 78.

37. Lori Spiczka, "Farming: It's a Matter of Life and Death," in *Winning Orations, 1987*, p. 106.

38. Robert Browning, "Rabbi Ben Ezra," *Dramatis Personae* (1864). Quoted by John R. Mietus, Jr., "The Best Is Yet to Be," in *Winning Orations, 1987*, p. 54.

39. Ibid., p. 57.

40. Benjamin P. Berlinger, "Health and the Hubris of Human Nature: The Tragic Myth of Antibiotics," in *Winning Orations, 1987*, p. 35.

41. Martin Luther King, Jr., "I Have a Dream" (August 28, 1963). Reprinted by permission of Joan Daves. Copyright © 1963 by Martin Luther King, Jr.

42. Ronald Reagan, address to the Republican National Convention (August 15, 1988), *Austin American-Statesman*, August 16, 1988, p. A7.

43. Erin Farrar, "The Dangers of Light Trucks," in *Winning Orations, 1987*, p. 90.

44. Mark Culkins, "Killer in the Grass," in *Winning Orations, 1987*, p. 10.

Chapter 11

1. Mark Twain, *Autobiography* (New York: P. F. Collier and Son) 1925, p. 246.

2. James W. Gibson, John A. Kline and Charles R. Gruner, "A Re-examination of the First Course in Speech at U.S. Colleges and Universities," *Speech Teacher*, 23 (September 1974): 206–214.

3. Allen H. Monroe, "Measurement and Analysis of Audience Reaction to Student Speakers' Studies in Attitude Changes," *Bulletin of Purdue University Studies in Higher Education*, 22 (1937).

4. Paul Heinberg, "Relationship of Content and Delivery to General Effectiveness," *Speech Monographs*, 30 (June 1963): 105–107.

5. Albert Mehrabian, *Nonverbal Communication* (Hawthrone, N.Y.: Aldine, 1972).

6. Paul Ekman, Wallace V. Friesen, and K. R. Schere, "Body Movement and Voice Pitch in Deception Interaction," *Semiotica* 16 (1976): 23–27; Mark Knapp, R. P. Hart, and H. S. Dennis, "An Exploration of Deception as a Communication Construct," *Human Communication Research* 1 (1974): 15–29.

7. Michael J. Beatty, "Some Effects of Posture on Speaker Credibility," library paper, Central Missouri State University, 1973.

8. Steven A. Beebe, "Eye Contact: A Nonverbal Determinant of Speaker Credibility," *Speech Teacher*, 23 (January 1974): 21–25; Steven A. Beebe, "Effects of Eye Contact, Posture and Vocal Inflection upon Credibility and Comprehension," *Australian Scan Journal of Nonverbal Communication*, 7–8 (1979–80): 57–70; Martin Cobin, "Response to Eye Contact," *Quarterly Journal of Speech*, 48 (1963): 415–419.

9. Beebe, "Eye Contact," 21–25.

10. Paul Ekman, Wallace V. Friesen, and S. S. Tomkins, "Facial Affect Scoring Technique: A First Validity Study," *Semiotica* 3 (1971).

11. Adapted from Lester Schilling, *Voice and Diction for the Speech Arts* (San Marcos: Southwest Texas State University, 1979).

12. Stephen Lucas, *The Art of Public Speaking* (New York: Random House, 1986), p. 231.

13. For a review of listening comprehension literature, see Ralph Nichols and L. Stevens, *Are You Listening?* (New York: McGraw-Hill, 1957); G. Goldhaber, "Listener Comprehension of Compressed Speech as a Function of the Academic Grade Level of the Subjects," *Journal of Communication* 20 (1970): 167–173; and Gerry Goldhaber and C. H. Weaver, "Listener Comprehension of Compressed Speech When the Difficulty, Rate of Presentation, and Sex of the Listener Are Varied," *Speech Monographs* 35 (1968): 20–25.

Chapter 13

1. Georges Gusdorf, *Speaking*, trans. Paul T. Brockelman (Chicago: Northwestern University Press, 1965), p. 9.

2. F. K. Heussenstann, "Bumper Stickers and Cops," *Transaction*, (1971): 32–33.

3. Paul Roberts, "How to Say Nothing in Five Hundred Words," in William H. Roberts and Gregoire Turgeson, eds., *About Language* (Boston: Houghton Mifflin, 1986), p. 28.

4. George Orwell, "Politics and the English Language." Reprinted in *About Language*, p. 282.

5. William Faulkner, "A Rose for Emily," Reprinted in Sylvan Barnet, et al., *Literature for Composition* (Glenview, Illinois: Scott, Foresman and Co., 1988), p. 340.

6. Ernest Hemingway, *The Sun Also Rises* (New York: Scribner, 1970), p. 20.

7. Ronald Reagan, "Address to the United Nations," *Vital Speeches of the Day*, October 15, 1984, p. 6.

8. Jimmy Carter, "Soviet Military Intervention in Afghanistan," *Vital Speeches of the Day*, June 15, 1980, p. 195.

9. We acknowledge the following source for several examples used in our discussion of language style: William Jordan, "Rhetorical Style," *Oral Communication Handbook*, Central Missouri State University, Warrensburg, Missouri (1971–72), p. 32–34.

10. John Milton, *Paradise Lost*, ll. 482, 498.

11. Theodore Parker, "Eulogy for Daniel Webster" (October 31, 1852), in Houston Peterson, ed., *A Treasury of the World's Great Speeches* (New York: Simon & Schuster, 1965), pp. 410–416.

12. John F. Kennedy, inaugural address (January 20, 1961), in Bower Aly and Lucille F. Aly, eds., *Speeches in English* (New York: Random House, 1968), p. 272.

13. Abraham Lincoln, farewell address, Springfield, Ill. (February 4, 1861), in Peterson, *Treasury*, pp. 508–509.

14. Ralph Waldo Emerson, "The American Scholar" (August 31, 1837), in Glenn R. Capp, ed., *Famous Speeches in American History* (Indianapolis: Bobbs-Merrill, 1963), p. 84.

15. Frederick Douglass, Declaration of Independence commemoration (1852), in Peterson, *Treasury*, pp. 477–481.

16. Franklin D. Roosevelt, first inaugural address (March 4, 1933), in Aly and Aly, *Speeches in English*, p. 213.

17. Kennedy, inaugural address, p. 275.

18. William Faulkner, acceptance of the Nobel prize for literature (December 10, 1950), in Peterson, *Treasury*, pp. 814–815.

19. Patrick Henry, "Liberty or Death" (March 23, 1775), in Capp, *Famous Speeches*, p. 22.

20. Franklin D. Roosevelt, first inaugural address, delivered March 4, 1933 as published in Glenn R. Capp (ed.), *Famous Speeches in American History*, New York: Bobbs-Merrill Company, Inc., 1963, p. 196.

21. Roosevelt, first inaugural address, p. 217.

22. Franklin D. Roosevelt, first fireside chat (March 12, 1933), in Peterson, *Treasury*, pp. 751–754.

23. Winston Churchill, "finest hour" address (June 18, 1940), in Peterson, *Treasury*, pp. 754–760.

24. Winston Churchill, address to the Congress of the United States (December 26, 1941), in Aly and Aly, *Speeches in English*, p. 233.

25. Jordan, "Rhetorical Style," p. 34.

26. Emerson, "The American Scholar," p. 84.

27. Elizabeth Cady Stanton, address to the first women's rights convention (1848), in Peterson, *Treasury*, pp. 388–392.

28. Douglas MacArthur, "Old Soldiers Never Die" (April 19, 1951), in Aly and Aly, *Speeches in English*, p. 258.

29. Parker, "Eulogy for Daniel Webster."

30. Roosevelt, first inaugural address, p. 213.

31. Activity developed in Loren Reid, *Speaking Well* (New York: McGraw-Hill, 1982), p. 96.

Chapter 14

1. Clarence Petersen, "If You Can Say the Words, Take the Quiz . . . ," *Austin American-Statesman*, March 21, 1987, p. E5.

2. William Jennings Bryan, "Cross of Gold" address to the Democratic National Convention in Chicago, Illinois (1896) in Glenn R. Capp, ed., *Famous Speeches in American History* (Indianapolis, Indiana: Bobbs-Merrill Company, Inc., 1963), p. 130.

3. "'Chocoholic'? Look It Up," *Newsweek*, September 14, 1987, p. 69.

4. Marcie Groover, "Learning to Communicate: The Importance of Speech Education in Public Schools," in *Winning Orations, 1984* (Mankato, Minn.: Interstate Oratorical Association, 1984), p. 7.

5. Garrison Keillor, "A Prairie Home Companion," National Public Radio, May 1987.

6. Tamara Paulsen, "The Sounds of Silence," in *Winning Orations, 1984*, pp. 29–30. All four excerpts illustrating narrative development are from this speech.

Chapter 15

1. Alvin Toffler, *Future Shock* (New York: Bantam Books, 1970), p. 3.

2. Leon Festinger, *A Theory of Cognitive Dissonance* (Evanston, Ill.: Row, Peterson, 1957).

3. Vonda Ramey, "Can You Read This?" in *Winning Orations, 1985* (Mankato, Minn.: Interstate Oratorical Association, 1985), p. 36.

4. For additional discussion, see Wayne C. Minnick, *The Art of Persuasion* (Boston: Houghton Mifflin, 1967).

5. Abraham H. Maslow, "A Theory of Human Motivation," in *Motivation and Personality* (New York: Harper & Row, 1954), chap. 5.

6. John Ryan, "Emissions Tampering: Get the Lead Out," in *Winning Orations, 1985*, p. 50.

7. For a discussion of fear appeal research, see Irving L. Janis and Seymour Feshback, "Effects of Fear Arousing Communications," *Journal of Abnormal and Social Psychology*, 48 (January 1953): 78–92; Frederick A. Powell and Gerald R. Miller, "Social Approval and Disapproval Cues in Anxiety-Arousing Situations," *Speech Monographs*, 34 (June 1967): 152–159; and Kenneth L. Higbee, "Fifteen Years of Fear Arousal: Research on Threat Appeals, 1953–68," *Psychological Bulletin*, 72 (December 1969): 426–444.

8. C. W. Sherif, M. Sherif, and R. E. Nebergall, *Attitudes and Attitude Change: The Social Judgment–Involvement Approach* (Philadelphia: Saunders, 1965).

Chapter 16

1. Albert Mehrabian and J. A. Russell, *An Approach to Environmental Psychology* (Cambridge, Mass.: MIT Press, 1974); T. Biggers and B. Pryor, "Attitude Change as a Function of Emotion Eliciting Qualities," *Personality and Social Psychology Bulletin*, 8 (1982): 94–99; Steven A. Beebe and T. Biggers, "Emotion-Eliciting Qualities of Speech Delivery and Their Effect on Credibility and Comprehension," paper presented at the annual meeting of the International Communication Association, New Orleans, May 1988.

2. Donald C. Bryant, "Rhetoric: Its Functions and Its Scope," *Quarterly Journal of Speech*, 39 (December 1953): 26.

3. Douglas Ehninger, Bruce E. Gronbeck, Ray E. McKerrow, and Alan H. Monroe, *Principles and Types of Speech Communication* (Glenview, Ill.: Scott, Foresman, 1986), p. 15.

4. Vic Vieth, "Prisoners of Conscience," in *Winning Orations, 1984* (Mankato, Minn.: Interstate Oratorical Association, 1984), p. 46.

5. Ibid., p. 47.

6. Ibid.

7. Ibid., p. 49.

8. Martin Luther King, Jr., "I Have a Dream" (August 28, 1963), in Houston Peterson, ed., *A Treasury of the World's Great Speeches* (New York: Simon & Schuster, 1965), pp. 835–839.

9. Vieth, "Prisoners of Conscience," p. 49.

Chapter 17

1. William Faulkner, acceptance of the Nobel prize for literature (December 10, 1950), in Houston Peterson, ed., *A Treasury of the World's Great Speeches* (New York: Simon & Schuster, 1965), p. 815.

2. Elie Wiesel, acceptance of the 1986 Nobel Peace Prize, *New York Times*, December 11, 1986, p. A8.

3. Faulkner, acceptance, p. 815.

4. Barbara Jordan, keynote address delivered to the Democratic National Convention in New York City, July 12, 1976.

5. Beverly Chiodo, "Choose Wisely: Establish a Good Name and Reputation," *Vital Speeches of the Day*, November 1, 1987, p. 40.

6. Art Buchwald, as quoted by Win Borden in "Recommendations for Graduates: How You Play the Game of Life," *Vital Speeches of the Day*, April 15, 1985, p. 400.

7. Mario M. Cuomo, "Your One Life Can Make a Difference: Go for It, Harvard," *Vital Speeches of the Day*, July 15, 1985, p. 582.

8. Daniel Webster, "Bunker Hill Monument Address" (June 17, 1825), in David J. Brewer, ed., *World's Best Orations* (St. Louis: Kaiser, 1901), vol. 10, pp. 3828–3846.

9. Adlai E. Stevenson, "Sir Winston Churchill," January 28, 1965.

10. Ibid.

11. Ibid.

Chapter 18

1. Group communication principles presented in this chapter are adapted from: Steven A. Beebe and John T. Masterson, *Communicating in Small Groups: Principles and Practices*, 3rd edition (Glenview, Illinois: Scott Foresman/Little Brown, 1990).

2. Roger K. Mosvick and Robert B. Nelson, *We've Got to Start Meeting Like This! A Guide to Successful Business Meeting Management* (Glenview, Illinois: Scott, Foresman and Company, 1987), p. 3.

3. Randy Y. Hirokawa and Roger Pace, "A Descriptive Investigation of the Possible Communication-Based Reasons for Effective and Ineffective Group Decision Making," *Communication Monographs*, 50 (December 1983): 363–379.

4. Randy Y. Hirokawa, "Group Communication and Problem-Solving Effectiveness: An Investigation of Group Phases," *Human Communication Research*, 9 (Summer 1983): 291–305.

5. Dennis S. Gouran, "Variables Related to Consensus in Group Discussion of Question of Policy," *Speech Monographs*, 36 (August 1969): 385–391.

6. Kenneth D. Benne and Paul Sheats, "Functional Roles of Groups Members," *Journal of Social Issues*, 4 (Spring 1948): 41–49.

7. Ibid.

Appendix B

1. We thank Professor Russell Wittrup, Southwest Texas State University, for sharing his speech topic ideas with us.

Appendix C

1. Reprinted by permission of Joan Daves. Copyright © 1963 by Martin Luther King, Jr.

2. From *Winning Orations, 1987* (Mankato, Minn.: Interstate Oratorical Association, 1987). Coached by Cathy Hanson.

Index